NUMBERS
OF THE
GODS

Unlocking the Secret
Science of the Druids

Sylvain Tristan

NUMBERS OF THE GODS

Unlocking the Secret Science of the Druids

Second Edition

Published by ProgressivePress.com,
Dec. 12, 2016. Revised July, 2017
3716-37th St., San Diego, Calif. 92105
info@progressivepress.com

ISBN 1-61577-367-3, EAN 978-1-61577-367-1
Ebook ISBN 1-61577-372-X
370 pages, 6.14 x 9.21 in., approx. 107,000 words with index
List Price: $19.95

Subject Classification: Nonfiction, History, Religion

Library of Congress classification: Druids and Druidism, BL910

BISAC Subject Area Codes

OCC031000 Body, Mind & Spirit / Ancient Mysteries & Controversial Knowledge
SCI004000 Science / Astronomy
REL072000 Religion / Antiquities & Archaeology
SOC038000 Social Science / Freemasonry
OCC036010 Body, Mind & Spirit / Spirituality / Celtic

Contents

Prologue: Druids and the Harmony of the Spheres

Initially, this book was supposed to be about Celtic Druids—white-robed bearded sages who lived some two millennia ago in the northwestern fringes and isles of the European continent—and their knowledge. It soon became obvious that it would be much more than that.

First, my research for this book soon led me to contemplate the possibility that Druidic knowledge was far older than orthodox historians usually think it is. Second, it soon became just as obvious that this Druidic knowledge had not disappeared with the Druids, but that it had probably—and secretly—lived on until this very day. That makes two bold assertions already.

Finally, there was little doubt that this knowledge was, and indeed still *is*, of extreme importance. Not only does it include advanced mathematics, geometry and astronomy, but it also happens to reveal a beautiful harmony in our world, i.e. a mathematical order which is highly reminiscent of the Harmony of the Spheres referred to by Pythagoras in Antiquity. Pythagoras believed there was a harmony in the cosmos, a beautiful order of things, and that the movements of the celestial spheres, such as the Sun, the Moon and the planets, produced an imperceptible music which made human life on Earth harmonious. He may have called this celestial hum the 'music of the heavens.' His followers, the Pythagoreans, thought the Earth and the other heavenly spheres were separated from one another by intervals corresponding to beautiful numerical proportions similar to the harmonic lengths of strings, and that the movements of these bodies gave rise to this mysterious music.

In this book, we'll see that this mathematical harmony of our world appears to exist, to an extent that was never clearly perceived until very recently—a true 'Music of the Spheres' played out in our tiny part of the universe with three numbers—namely 366, 40 and 10. I allegorically refer to them as the 'Numbers of the Gods' in my title, or as the 'Divine Triad' in this book, although these nicknames are more poetical and philosophical than religious. Just as important, these three numbers are encapsulated in an ingenious integrated geometry and astronomical knowledge that Druids and their descendants appear to have passed down across the generations.

So let us get back to the Druids as they are historically known.

Most of us have heard about them, but the usual stereotype owes more to the Romantic era or, more recently, to Hollywood than to reliable written sources. It is supposed that Druids were something like priests or magicians amongst the Celtic societies of northwestern Europe and Britain, in Julius Caesar's time. They were dressed in white and grew long white beards. Most important of all, they were famous for their wisdom and great oral knowledge they never committed to writing, which was transmitted from Druid to Druid down the generations. Eventually, in the first century AD, the Romans estimated these people were a threat, so they decided to wipe the members of their institution off the face of Gaul and Britain.

First of all, we'll try to set the picture straight about what sort of individuals Druids really were. To do that, we'll use both primary and secondary sources, and also exploit the latest archaeological evidence available. This should confirm that Druidic knowledge was indeed quite *extraordinary*, in the true etymological sense of the word.

But this book will try to go well beyond that by advancing a new theory. If recognised as true, this theory will do much to undermine the foundational tenets of world history, and will also overturn the prevailing worldview of our universe. No less than a *paradigm shift* will prove necessary, meaning that the existing paradigm will have to give way to a novel hypothesis, one that will account for the amazing discoveries collected in this book, which necessarily means that

(1) history as we know it has to be rewritten, and

(2) the world we live in has an underlying mathematical harmony that has far-reaching philosophical implications.

Here are some of the questions that are dealt with in this book. Is it possible that the Druids' great knowledge had to do both with astronomy and an incredibly clever geometry based on a 366-day calendar? Were the Druids among the world's first philosophers? And did they significantly contributed to the rise of some of the world's greatest civilisations?

Is it possible that the Druidic institution is much more ancient than conventional history thinks it is? Were there already any Druids several millennia before the Christian era, namely in Megalithic times, when people erected giant standing stones in Britain? And is there a chance that this knowledge is directly connected to the Great Pyramid of Giza?

So much for the deep past. What about more recent times? Is it possible that, after the Romans massacred the last Druids on the island of Mona in 61 AD, the Druidic institution continued to thrive, albeit in absolute secrecy? Is it possible that the Knights Templar were amongst these Druidic Initiates, i.e. Druids who didn't call themselves Druids any longer and who perpetuated Druidic knowledge? And is it possible that this age-old Druidic knowledge still exists today in the highest ranks of the well-known institution of Freemasonry in France, England and the United States?

More generally speaking, is it possible that the locations of the grand Megalithic temples of Stonehenge in England or Newgrange in Ireland owe nothing to chance, and that these monuments were founded there because Druids carefully selected these sites? Is it possible that one of the Celts' most sacred cities, Alesia, is also a location carefully selected by the Druids? More recently, is there a chance that the location of the French capital city of Paris, and also of major French cities such as Rouen, or Reims and Troyes in Champagne, follow similar Druidic planning? More recently still, is it possible that the Paris and Greenwich Prime Meridians are also Druidic lines? Last but not least, might two of the world's most beautiful modern capitals, Washington DC in the United States and Astana in Kazakhstan, be living evidence that Druidic knowledge has never died?

It is fully appreciated that at first glance all this might sound like far-fetched, pseudoscientific theories of the worst kind. And yet, I hope to demonstrate in this book how well these suggestions fit the events that unfolded in Western Europe, and more recently in the New World and elsewhere, in the last 5,000 years

It should be stressed from the start that what we call Druids for literary convenience do not refer to some diamond-like, immutable entity, but simply to different people through time perpetuating a *similar* secret tradition with a strong component of geometry and astronomy. It is obvious that something that lasts for so long should evolve. What is utterly remarkable though is, one, the quality and the significance of the knowledge itself; two, the fact that there seems to be an unbroken chain of transmission for that long; and three, the fact that no one outside the secret circle, apparently, has ever noticed anything.

To support the thesis, we'll use both scientific tools and historical primary sources. We'll also use secondary sources from mainstream historians or scholars, and sometimes from less conventional researchers if we judge they are scientifically credible enough. I would define myself as a sceptic with an open mind. Of course we all are, in varying degrees.

Some people are more gullible than others and are prone to believe in odd, irrational things, even in our hyperscientific age. Others, being better versed in science, are less credulous and need evidence to be convinced, which of course is a very good thing. And still others are so sceptical that they won't even look at evidence that will contradict what they *think* is the 'obvious truth.' Well, the obvious truth, as you might soon find out, is not necessarily the actual truth. I personally loathe pseudoscience and love reason, and the conclusion I draw from years of research—based on objective data—is that the world is much stranger than first meets the eye.

I view myself as a rationalist, and wish to impose no dogmas of any kind on people. That's why this book only sets out objective, undeniable facts and data—historical, geographical, architectural, mathematical and so on—that appear to show a cohesive pattern throughout history. As my friend and fellow writer Alan Butler puts it, we follow the 'golden thread through the tapestry of time'. I also make clear suggestions that might account for this state of affairs. But the final conclusion about these facts and data is left to my readers, whom I esteem too much not to let them make their own inferences about the book's main question: has the Druidic knowledge, though kept totally secret or nearly so, been alive and kicking for the past 5,000 years, until this very day?

This book is my first essay on the subject in English. It is the result of almost fourteen years of research, which began with the millennium in January 2001, and follows two previous nonfiction books that were published in French. The first one is *Les Lignes d'or (The Golden Lines)*, which came out in Paris and Monaco in 2005, and the second one is *Atlantide, premier empire européen (Atlantis, First European Empire)*, also published in Paris and Monaco, in 2007. They both deal with what has come to be known as 366-degree geometry, or 'Megalithic' geometry, which was discovered by Alan Butler in the 1990s.

In *The Golden Lines* I set out to expound what 366-degree geometry is, i.e. an integrated system that potentially reconciles time, distance, volumes and masses, based on a 366-day calendar, in many ways superior to our own modern units of measurement. In the book I also try to show that the capital cities of the world's first great civilisations are located along the meridians and parallels of this geometry, and that there is a common denominator to these apparently independent cultures—the link being the Megalithic civilisation and its presumed sages, which I dubbed the Megalithic Druids (or Megalithic Proto-Druids, MPDs).

In the sequel *Atlantis, First European Empire*, I deal with the legendary continent of Atlantis, as the story is told by Plato and a few other writers of Antiquity. The myth appears to derive from the remembrance of a real civilisation which might actually have lost a gigantic, low-lying island in the middle of the North Sea—that of the Megalithic people who a few centuries later erected Stonehenge and Avebury in Britain.

My novel *The Divine Number* came out in 2012. This was my first English-language book. It used material from the two previous books, along with new, astonishing findings made in the interval.

Similarly, *Numbers of the Gods* aims at summing up my past research and adding to it my numerous latest discoveries. We'll begin the book with an in-depth study of Celtic druids (Part I), and proceed with getting back in time (Part II) to see if there is evidence of Druid-like people living well before the Celtic era, most notably during Megalithic times. In Part III we'll reverse the arrow of time, getting back to the Roman period, and cover the last 2,000 years to see if we can dig up any proof that Druidic knowledge has been perpetuated until the twenty-first century. Finally, in Part IV, we'll see why the numbers used in Druidic geometry truly deserve the appellation of 'Numbers of the Gods.'

If you are among those who are already convinced that history as it has been told to us is full of gaps and unexplained events, you might easily be convinced that the book's main argument is valid. But I beg you *not* to believe me on faith alone: please make your own research, check the data and references given in this book, verify the mathematics, visit the places if you have the opportunity to do so, and so on. Most of the time, common reference books and a computer with an Internet connection alone should suffice to assess the data. And once you've got all the clues, just like Hercule Poirot, you might sit still in an armchair and start to calmly think about all that. Most people will undoubtedly soon begin to draw many logical, yet astounding conclusions.

If you happen to be on the other end of the spectrum, i.e. what I am calling a hypersceptical person, then welcome on board too, for I am a sceptic myself (which is slightly different from a hypersceptic). But I also beg you to leave your 'certainties' aside for a short while and be ready to learn about very odd aspects of our history, and indeed of our world, no matter how outrageous the claims—a mystery that spans millennia and which you probably never imagined could exist, even in your wildest dreams.

Hopefully, most of you, dear readers, will soon discover and grasp the sheer magnitude of this hidden harmony that defies reason itself—the Eternal Music of the Spheres.

Sylvain Tristan,
Chambéry, France

PART I

THE CELTIC DRUIDS

(c. 800 BC - c. 100 AD)

Chapter One:
Who were the Druids?

Only a handful of Greek or Roman classical authors mentioned the Druids, making the quest for their true identity not always an easy task, but nevertheless offering historians some very interesting detective work.

The meaning of the term *Druid* is a matter of debate, but it is generally admitted that the word stems from the Proto-Celtic root **dru-wid-s*, meaning either 'oak-seer' or 'oak-knower' (from the Proto-Indo-European roots **deru-*, 'oak' and **weid-*, 'see.')[1] An alternative meaning is 'the very knowledgeable.'[2]

Posidonius's meeting with Druids

One of the first books ever to mention Druids is a treatise on magic called the *Magikos*, probably written by Antisthenes of Rhodes,[3] a Greek historian and philosopher living around 200 BC. According to him the Druids, along with other wise men from the Orient, such as Persian magi, Chaldean seers and the Gymnosophists (the 'naked philosophers') in India, were the originators of philosophy. By philosophy, one should understand the exploration of all spheres of knowledge. They were also teachers and judges.

The Druids are also mentioned in the twenty-third book of *Succession of Philosophers* by Sotion of Alexandria (c. 200 BC–170 BC), who classified philosophers into different schools of influence.

Unfortunately, both of these books have been lost to us. We know about them though because they were quoted by biographer Diogenes Laërtius in the 3rd century AD. According to him, Druids (and

---

[1] *The American Heritage Dictionary of the English Language*, Fourth Edition, 2000

[2] *TLFi, Le Trésor de la langue française informatisé*, 1971-94, http://www.cnrtl.fr/definition/druide

[3] Not Aristotle as it has often been claimed, see James B. Rives, "Aristotle, Antisthenes of Rhodes, and the *Magikos*," http://www.rhm.uni-koeln.de/147/Rives.pdf and Arnaldo Momigliano, *Alien Wisdom: The Limits of Hellenization*, Cambridge University Press 1971, p. 59-60

Gymnosophists) invented philosophy, rather than the Greeks, and uttered short cryptic remarks relating to religion or urging people to be good:

> But they who say that philosophy had its rise among the barbarians, give also an account of the different systems prevailing among the various tribes. And they say that the Gymnosophists and the Druids philosophize, delivering their apophthegms in enigmatical language, bidding men worship the gods and do no evil, and practice manly virtue.[4]

Other classical authors from the 1st century BC have given a few details about Druids, such as Greek geographer Strabo, Greek historian Diodorus Siculus, and Julius Caesar in his *Commentaries on the Gallic War.* From these details, it is possible to paint a reasonably accurate portrait of this mysterious class of citizens of ancient Celtic society.

But it seems these authors probably never actually met any Druids in their lives, rather relying on the in-depth work of Posidonius of Apameia (c. 135 BC-51 BC), a Greek polymath and traveller versed in philosophy, history, geography and astronomy who wrote dozens of volumes. Posidonius probably encountered Druids in Gaul, where he was able to directly observe their practices and exchange with them. Although none of his work has survived, Posidonius has been heavily quoted by others.

Three classes of people

Thanks to Posidonius, we know that Celtic priesthood divided itself into three classes. The first one was that of the *vates*, which refers to prophets or seers. The second was that of the bards, who were poets. The last category, of course, was that of the Druids. Although Caesar remains silent about vates and bards, Strabo (using Posidonius's material) mentions them all:

> Among all the Gallic peoples, generally speaking, there are three sets of men who are held in exceptional honour; the Bards, the Vates and the Druids. The Bards are singers and poets; the Vates, diviners and natural philosophers; while the Druids, in addition to natural philosophy, study also moral philosophy.[5]

So does Diodorus Siculus (also using Posidonius's writings):

---

[4] Diogenes Laërtius (3rd c. AD), *The Lives and Opinions of Eminent Philosophers*, I, V: http://classicpersuasion.org/pw/diogenes/dlintro.htm

[5] Strabo, *Geography*, IV, 4, 4, http://penelope.uchicago.edu/Thayer/E/Roman/Texts/Strabo/4D*.html

> Among them [the Gauls] are also to be found lyric poets whom they call Bards. These men sing to the accompaniment of instruments which are like lyres, and their songs may be either of praise or of obloquy. Philosophers, as we may call them, and men learned in religious affairs are unusually honoured among them and are called by them Druids. The Gauls likewise make use of diviners, accounting them worthy of high approbation, and these men foretell the future by means of the flight or cries of birds and of the slaughter of sacred animals, and they have all the multitude subservient to them.[6]

Druids as judges

According to Dio Chrysostom (c. 40 AD-c. 120 AD), who was a Greek philosopher and historian, Druids held a supreme rank within Celtic society, being even superior to the kings themselves whose final decisions depended upon what the Druids deemed wise or not:

> … the Celts appointed those whom they call Druids, these also being devoted to the prophetic art and to wisdom in general. In all these cases the kings were not permitted to do or plan anything without the assistance of these wise men, so that in truth it was they who ruled, while the kings became their servants and the ministers of their will, though they sat on golden thrones, dwelt in great houses, and feasted sumptuously.[7]

Although the above text was written in the 1st century AD, archaeologists have reason to believe that the scenes described in it date back to the 5th century BC.[8] In the same vein, Roman geographer Pomponius Mela (1st century AD) describes Druids as 'masters of wisdom.'[9]

Druids also had a quite darker side if we judge them from a modern perspective where human rights are central. We know from Caesar's writings that Druids were not only judges but also went so far sometimes as to practice human sacrifice:

> Druids... are engaged in things sacred, conduct the public and the private sacrifices, and interpret all matters of religion. To these a large number of the young men resort for the purpose of

---

[6] Diodorus Siculus, *The Library of History*, V, 31, http://penelope.uchicago.edu/Thayer/E/Roman/Texts/Diodorus_Siculus/5B*.html

[7] Dio Chrysostom, *Discourses*, XLIX, 8, http://penelope.uchicago.edu/Thayer/E/Roman/Texts/Dio_Chrysostom/Discourses/49*.html

[8] Jean-Louis Brunaux, *Les Druides. Des Philosophes chez les barbares*, Paris: Seuil 2006, p. 138

[9] Pomponius Mela, *Description of the World*, III, 2

> instruction, and they [the Druids] are in great honor among them. For they determine respecting almost all controversies, public and private; and if any crime has been perpetrated, if murder has been committed, if there be any dispute about an inheritance, if any about boundaries, these same persons decide it; they decree rewards and punishments; if any one, either in a private or public capacity, has not submitted to their decision, they interdict him from the sacrifices. This among them is the most heavy punishment. Those who have been thus interdicted are esteemed in the number of the impious and the criminal: all shun them, and avoid their society and conversation, lest they receive some evil from their contact; nor is justice administered to them when seeking it, nor is any dignity bestowed on them.[10]

Strabo claims that the Druids' authority was such that they had the power to settle all matter of judiciary disputes, including during wartime, having the ability to freeze a battle for a moment if necessary:

> The Druids are considered the most just of men, and on this account they are entrusted with the decision, not only of the private disputes, but of the public disputes as well; so that, in former times, they even arbitrated cases of war and made the opponents stop when they were about to line up for battle, and the murder cases, in particular, had been turned over to them for decision. Further, when there is a big yield from these cases, there is forthcoming a big yield from the land too, as they think.[11]

The themes of Druids practicing human sacrifice and arbitrating war issues are also taken up by Diodorus Siculus:

> And it is a custom of theirs that no one should perform a sacrifice without a 'philosopher'; for thank-offerings should be rendered to the gods, they say, by the hands of men who are experienced in the nature of the divine, and who speak, as it were, the language of the gods, and it is also through the mediation of such men, they think, that blessings likewise should be sought. Nor is it only in the exigencies of peace, but in their wars as well, that they obey, before all others, these men and their chanting poets, and such obedience is observed not only by their friends but also by their enemies; many times, for instance, when two armies approach each other in battle with swords drawn and spears thrust forward, these men step forth between them and cause them to cease, as though having cast a spell over certain kinds of wild beasts. In this way, even among

---

[10] Julius Caesar, *Commentaries on the Gallic War*, VI, 13, http://classics.mit.edu/Caesar/gallic.6.6.html

[11] Strabo, *Geography*, IV, 4, 4, http://penelope.uchicago.edu/Thayer/E/Roman/Texts/Strabo/4D*.html

> the wildest barbarians, does passion give place before wisdom, and Ares stands in awe of the Muses.[12]

Let us come back for a while to human sacrifice which, it cannot be denied, played quite an important role within Celtic society. As we saw, those were performed by Druids, who 'used' criminals and thieves to satisfy their divinities. However, when there was no outlaw at hand, *innocent* men were set on fire as well. Again, from Caesar:

> The nation of all the Gauls is extremely devoted to superstitious rites; and on that account they who are troubled with unusually severe diseases, and they who are engaged in battles and dangers, either sacrifice men as victims, or vow that they will sacrifice them, and employ the Druids as the performers of those sacrifices; because they think that unless the life of a man be offered for the life of a man, the mind of the immortal gods can not be rendered propitious, and they have sacrifices of that kind ordained for national purposes. Others have figures of vast size, the limbs of which formed of osiers they fill with living men, which being set on fire, the men perish enveloped in the flames. They consider that the oblation of such as have been taken in theft, or in robbery, or any other offense, is more acceptable to the immortal gods; but when a supply of that class is wanting, they have recourse to the oblation of even the innocent.[13]

It is important to stress one more time that Caesar derives his information from Posidonius. Now, whatever Posidonius heard or saw in Gaul, it is interesting to put his testimony into perspective with archaeological evidence. We know from archaeological finds that the most commonly sacrificed were not humans but domestic animals. So, even if human sacrifice by Druids cannot be denied, it seems that since at least the 4th century BC the most common religious ceremony in Gaul was, by far, the sacrifice of a domestic animal.[14]

Memory and secrecy

One of the Druids' most characteristic traits is that they carefully protected their knowledge. One of their ground rules was secrecy. Just like Pythagoreans in Greece, they met in secluded places such as caves or

---

[12] Diodorus Siculus, *The Library of History*, V, 31, 4-5 http://penelope.uchicago.edu/Thayer/E/Roman/Texts/Diodorus_Siculus/5B*.html

[13] Julius Caesar, *Commentaries on the Gallic War*, VI, 16, http://classics.mit.edu/Caesar/gallic.6.6.html

[14] Jean-Louis Brunaux, *Les Druides. Des Philosophes chez les barbares*, Paris: Seuil 2006, p. 236

forests where no one else was allowed, a situation probably amplified under Roman occupation, as we will see in later chapters.

An interesting aspect is that Druids were trained for a period of twenty years. Their initiation was pedagogical, probably punctuated by rites of passage.[15]

Another means of protecting their knowledge was by keeping their philosophy an oral essence. Writing was prohibited, quite an exceptional feature in the history of humankind,[16] and Druidic knowledge was imparted from memory only. Experts at mnemonics, Druids learned verses by heart, so that everything was stored up in their heads and never committed in stone or on a scroll of any kind. This system had the double advantage of safeguarding the knowledge not only from their enemies, but also from non-Druids within the Celtic society. It also trained the future Druids' minds, as it is now known that using your brain extensively, for instance by memorising many things, creates new neurones and makes you more intelligent. When Druids wished to converse with one another in public they used coded language.[17]

Pomponius Mela writes: 'They teach the most noble of the nation many things privately, and for a long time, even for twenty years, in a cave, or in inaccessible woods.'[18]

We know from Caesar's writings that Druids were not subject to compulsory recruitment for military service, and that writing was permitted for non-Druidic matters:

> The Druids do not go to war, nor pay tribute together with the rest; they have an exemption from military service and a dispensation in all matters. Induced by such great advantages, many embrace this profession of their own accord, and [many] are sent to it by their parents and relations. They are said there to learn by heart a great number of verses; accordingly some remain in the course of training twenty years. Nor do they regard it lawful to commit these to writing, though in almost all other matters, in their public and private transactions, they use Greek characters. That practice they seem to me to have adopted for two reasons; because they neither desire their doctrines to be divulged among the mass of the people, nor those who learn, to devote themselves the less to the efforts of memory, relying on writing; since it generally occurs to most men,

---

[15] Ibid., p. 267

[16] Ibid., p. 264

[17] Ibid., p.186

[18] Pomponius Mela, *Description of the World*, III, 2

> that, in their dependence on writing, they relax their diligence in learning thoroughly, and their employment of the memory.[19]

Annual assemblies

We also know that Druids had yearly assemblies. These meetings were held in a particular place of central Gaul. From Caesar's writings:

> These assemble at a fixed period of the year in a consecrated place in the territories of the Carnutes, which is reckoned the central region of the whole of Gaul. Hither all, who have disputes, assemble from every part, and submit to their decrees and determinations.[20]

The chief fortified towns of the Carnutes—a Celtic people living in the heart of the continental Celtic territories comprising Celtica and Belgica—were Cenabum (modern Orleans) and Autricum (modern Chartres). It is uncertain whether the annual Druidic assembly took place in Cenabum or Autricum, but there is reason to believe it did in the latter place, as the name *Chartres* itself derives from *Carnutes.*

Druids had a supreme leader. He was appointed by the other Druids or elected if there were several candidates to the job. Sometimes though, according to Caesar, they had to resort to fighting:

> Over all these Druids one presides, who possesses supreme authority among them. Upon his death, if any individual among the rest is pre-eminent in dignity, he succeeds; but, if there are many equal, the election is made by the suffrages of the Druids; sometimes they even contend for the presidency with arms.[21]

The immortality of the soul

Life after death is another important aspect of the Druids' mores. Druids were clearly dualists, believing souls to be immortal. From Caesar's *Commentaries on the Gallic War*:

> They wish to inculcate this as one of their leading tenets, that souls do not become extinct, but pass after death from one body to another, and they think that men by this tenet are in a great degree excited to valor, the fear of death being disregarded.[22]

---

[19] Julius Caesar, *Commentaries on the Gallic War*, VI, 14, http://classics.mit.edu/Caesar/gallic.6.6.html

[20] Ibid., VI, 13

[21] Ibid.

[22] Ibid., VI, 14

From Strabo's *Geography*:

> However, not only the Druids, but others as well, say that men's souls, and also the universe, are indestructible, although both fire and water will at some time or other prevail over them.[23]

Pomponius Mela is even more explicit about the Druids' belief system:

> One of their precepts has become public, namely, that they should act bravely in war, that souls are immortal, and that there is another life after death. Therefore along with the dead, they burn and bury things which belonged to them while living. Their debtor and creditor accounts were transferred below. Some even went so far as to ascend the funeral pyres of their friends of their own accord, as though about to live with them.[24]

Main points

- **Celtic Druids were held in high regard by classical authors**
- **They were philosophers, 'masters of wisdom'**
- **They were all-powerful judges**
- **They never committed anything to writing and valued memory and secrecy**
- **They met every year in assemblies, probably in Chartres**
- **They appointed a supreme chief**
- **They believed souls never died**

---

[23] Strabo, *Geography*, IV, 4, 4, http://penelope.uchicago.edu/Thayer/E/Roman/Texts/Strabo/4D*.html

[24] Pomponius Mela, *Description of the World*, III, 2

Chapter Two: The Druidic Knowledge

Let us now see what the Celtic Druids' knowledge consisted in. It seems clear that the Druids were very eclectic and that they were proficient at all the 'sciences' of their time (although the term *sciences* is here used in a sense which is both more philosophical and literary than literal, their array of knowledge can be said to have paved the way for modern science). After all, they are described as philosophers, and their power and hierarchy was assured through the safeguarding of this eclectic knowledge.

Druids as botanists

First of all, it is obvious that Druids were botanists. They knew plants and used them for medicinal and religious purposes. We know from Roman naturalist Pliny the Elder (23 AD-79 AD) that they viewed the oak (*robur*) as the most sacred tree of all, and the mistletoe that grew on it as a heavenly-sent panacea which had the virtue of making fertile those animals which could not reproduce themselves. Druids would climb the oaks and cut the mistletoe with a golden sickle, and then sacrifice bulls. Pliny's description goes as follows:

> Upon this occasion we must not omit to mention the admiration that is lavished upon this plant by the Gauls. The Druids—for that is the name they give to their magicians—held nothing more sacred than the mistletoe and the tree that bears it, supposing always that tree to be the robur. Of itself the robur is selected by them to form whole groves, and they perform none of their religious rites without employing branches of it; so much so, that it is very probable that the priests themselves may have received their name from the Greek name for that tree. In fact, it is the notion with them that everything that grows on it has been sent immediately from heaven, and that the mistletoe upon it is a proof that the tree has been selected by God himself as an object of his especial favour.
>
> The mistletoe, however, is but rarely found upon the robur; and when found, is gathered with rites replete with religious awe.

> This is done more particularly on the sixth day of the moon, the day which is the beginning of their months and years, as also of their ages, which, with them, are but thirty years. This day they select because the moon, though not yet in the middle of her course, has already considerable power and influence; and they call her by a name which signifies, in their language, the all-healing. Having made all due preparation for the sacrifice and a banquet beneath the trees, they bring thither two white bulls, the horns of which are bound then for the first time. Clad in a white robe the priest ascends the tree, and cuts the mistletoe with a golden sickle, which is received by others in a white cloak. They then immolate the victims, offering up their prayers that God will render this gift of his propitious to those to whom he has so granted it. It is the belief with them that the mistletoe, taken in drink, will impart fecundity to all animals that are barren, and that it is an antidote for all poisons. Such are the religious feelings which we find entertained towards trifling objects among nearly all nations.[25]

But botany is merely one aspect of the Druidic knowledge.

Druids as *physiologoi*

As we saw, there is little doubt that Druids were the polymaths of their time and that they were interested in *all* fields of knowledge. Cicero (106 BC - 43 BC), the Roman philosopher and orator, confirms this fact here:

> Nor is the practice of divination disregarded even among uncivilized tribes, if indeed there are Druids in Gaul—and there are, for I knew one of them myself, Divitiacus, the Aeduan, your guest and eulogist. He claimed to have that knowledge of nature which the Greeks call 'physiologia,' and he used to make predictions, sometimes by means of augury and sometimes by means of conjecture.[26]

The Greek term *physiologia* should be understood here as botany, geology, chemistry, zoology, and perhaps physics as well.[27] Just like Pre-Socratic philosophers in Ancient Greece—the so-called *physiologoi* or physical/natural philosophers—Druids made hypotheses about what

[25] Pliny the Elder, *The Natural History*, XVI, 95, http://www.perseus.tufts.edu/hopper/text?doc=Perseus%3Atext%3A1999.02.0137%3Abook%3D16%3Achapter%3D95

[26] Cicero, *De Divinatione*, I, 41, 90, http://penelope.uchicago.edu/Thayer/E/Roman/Texts/Cicero/de_Divinatione/1*.html

[27] Jean-Louis Brunaux, *Les Druides. Des Philosophes chez les barbares*, Paris: Seuil 2006, p. 262

matter was composed of, imagining it as a dynamic mixture of primary elements, such as water, air and fire.[28]

Druids as astronomers

One crucial aspect in our study of the Druidic knowledge is the fact that Celtic Druids were first-rate astronomers. Their knowledge of stars and their motions perhaps arises from the Gauls' reverence of night itself. From Julius Caesar:

> All the Gauls assert that they are descended from the god Dis, and say that this tradition has been handed down by the Druids. For that reason they compute the divisions of every season, not by the number of days, but of nights; they keep birthdays and the beginnings of months and years in such an order that the day follows the night.[29]

Thanks to Posidonius's most precious testimony about Druids, we know that these white-dressed men had long observed the skies and understood the mechanics of the stars. Here's what Caesar (using Posidonius's book) writes about it:

> They [Druids] likewise discuss and impart to the youth many things respecting the stars and their motion, respecting the extent of the world and of our earth, respecting the nature of things, respecting the power and the majesty of the immortal gods.[30]

This is confirmed by Pomponius Mela, who as we saw wrote that Druids were 'masters of wisdom':

> These [Druids] profess to know the magnitude and form of the earth and the world, the motions of the heaven and the stars, and the will of the gods.[31]

This is incredibly important information. Not only were Druids able to understand the motion of stars and perhaps planets, they were also aware of 'the extent of the world and of our earth' (Caesar) or 'the magnitude and form of the earth and the world' (Pomponius Mela).

Did they know the Earth was a sphere? Had they managed to determine its dimensions? The ancient Greeks knew the Earth is round, and they also had a good idea how big around, so there is good reason to

---

[28] Ibid.
[29] Julius Caesar, *Commentaries on the Gallic War*, VI, 18, http://classics.mit.edu/Caesar/gallic.6.6.html
[30] Ibid., VI, 14
[31] Pomponius Mela, *Description of the World*, III, 2

believe Celtic Druids knew as well. But as the Druids never left any written records, it seems at first to be difficult to guess whether their estimation was more accurate than that of the Greeks. We'll see in due time that the Celtic Druids probably knew the Earth's polar circumference with astonishing accuracy.

Not that the Druids' astronomical skills are in any way doubted by mainstream archaeologists. In the words of Jean-Louis Brunaux, a French archaeologist and researcher at the National Center for Scientific Research who undertook an extensive study of Druids and wrote a hallmark book about them:

> Their [the Druids'] favourite subject—in any case that which goes back deeper in time—is astronomy, as well as all the ways it was used in daily life. All ancient authors claim quite explicitly it is the only science which was practiced by them, and indeed it was their primary preoccupation.[32]

The Coligny lunisolar calendar, which was found in France in 1897 and dates back to the late 2nd century AD, shows that Druids had carefully tracked stars and the movements of the Sun and Moon in the previous centuries. A similar calendar was discovered in the nearby village of Villards-d'Héria. Such clever calendars demonstrate beyond any doubt the astronomical skills of the Celtic Druids:

> Such calendars, conceived in a perpetual form, required long-term skywatching and implied knowledgeable computations, if only to make the lunar cycle – upon which the month was calculated – and the solar cycle, which allowed them to determine the year, coincide.[33]

Druids as architects

We know that Gauls constructed sacred groves, called *nemeton*, which were cult enclosures dedicated to their divinities. In the words of Diodorus Siculus:

> And a peculiar and striking practice is found among the upper [northern] Celts, in connection with the sacred precincts of the gods; as for in the temples and precincts made consecrate in their land, a great amount of gold has been deposited as a dedication to the gods, and not a native of the country ever touches it because

[32] Jean-Louis Brunaux, *Les Druides. Des Philosophes chez les barbares*, Paris: Seuil 2006, p. 260

[33] Ibid., p. 260-1

> of religious scruple, although the Celts are an exceedingly covetous people.[34]

These 'sacred precincts' generally were enclosures surrounded by a ditch. Greeks such as Posidonius called them *temene*, which is the plural of a *temenos*. They also included a wall whose outside part was ornately decorated with offerings of weapons, bucrania and human skulls. They were quadrangular with sides measuring up to a few dozen yards, and possessed a herculean porch. Inside, you could find an altar, a circular pit and the sacred tree or grove proper, which was the place where divinities were supposed to make their appearance. In these sacred places Celts sacrificed domestic animals to their gods or made offerings (food, weapons, and so on).[35]

Druids were also architects. This is the logical consequence of the Druids' knowledge of mathematics, geometry and astronomy. The architecture and technique in Celtic sacred groves built between the late 4th century BC and the late 2nd century BC unambiguously shows Druidic knowledge in their devising:

> But purely scientific reasons permit us to identify Druids as the architects of these sanctuaries. Indeed, these arrangements obey to geometric plans which were carried out on more or less uneven terrain, implying necessary calculations only an elite could perform. Last but not least, the astronomical requirements for orienting the enclosures meant being helped by those men all ancient authors concur in acknowledging an exclusive skill in this field.[36]

The sacred groves were generally aligned to the rising sun during the winter or summer solstice. Sometimes, each side was oriented to a cardinal point, while the altar and the entrance porch were aligned to the rising sun at the summer solstice. According to archaeologist Jean-Louis Brunaux, '[t]his layout of architectural elements in relation to heaven realities required many calculations and genuine abilities in geometry.'[37] To put it in a nutshell, Druids literally were 'masters of geometry,'[38] and used their knowledge for art, architecture and techniques extensively.

---

[34] Diodorus Siculus, *The Library of History*, V, 27

[35] Jean-Louis Brunaux, *Les Druides. Des Philosophes chez les barbares*, Paris: Seuil 2006, p. 246-7

[36] Ibid., p. 254

[37] Ibid., p. 261

[38] Ibid., p. 263

Main points

- Druids had an eclectic form of knowledge
- They were botanists who revered mistletoe
- They were polymaths interested in sciences of all kinds
- They were accomplished skywatchers and astronomers who knew 'the magnitude and form of the earth' and the 'motions of the heaven and the stars'
- They had elaborate calendars
- They were excellent architects who could build astronomically oriented 'sacred precincts'
- Archaeologists think they were 'masters of geometry'

Chapter Three: Alesia, the 'mother-city of all Celtica'

There seems to be no doubt that the Druids were Celts, and the Druidic institution seems inextricably linked to Celtic culture. And yet, Druids were found in Gaul and the British Isles, but not in Germany, Transalpine Gaul or Galatia (modern Turkey), which seems to indicate Druidism probably antedates the Celtic culture, and was already extant in the northwestern part of Europe a long time before that.

We'll come back to the origins of Druidism in the following chapter. What concerns us here is that in the centuries preceding the Roman conquest, Druidism was indeed central to the Celtic culture of northwestern Europe. One important feature of Celtic culture is the city of Alesia, which according to the Ancient Greeks had been founded by Heracles.

Alesia, Heracles, Bretannus, Celtine and Celtos

According to Diodorus Siculus, Alesia was no less than the 'mother-city of all Celtica.' Alesia ultimately fell in 52 BC when Julius Caesar conquered Gaul and defeated Vercingetorix, a great Gallic chieftain, on the hill of Alesia:

> Heracles, then, delivered over the kingdom of the Iberians to the noblest men among the natives and, on his part, took his army and passing into Celtica and traversing the length and breadth of it he put an end to the lawlessness and murdering of strangers to which the people had become addicted; and since a great multitude of men from every tribe flocked to his army of their own accord, he founded a great city which was named Alesia after the 'wandering' (*alê*) on his campaign. But he also mingled among the citizens of the city many natives, and since these surpassed the others in multitude, it came to pass that the inhabitants as a whole were barbarized. The Celts up to the present time hold this city in honour, looking upon it as the hearth and mother-city of all Celtica. And for the entire period from the days of Heracles this city remained free and was never sacked until our own time; but at last Gaius Caesar, who has been pronounced a god because of the

> magnitude of his deeds, took it by storm and made it and the other Celts subjects of the Romans.[39]

More details about Heracles' connection with Alesia and the Celts are given in the *History* of Diodorus Siculus. We learn that Heracles married Celtine, the exquisitely beautiful daughter of a famous king living there, and that she gave birth to a great warrior named Galates or Celtos, whose name was later transferred to the lands around which came to be called Gaul, Galatia or Celtica:

> Now Celtica was ruled in ancient times, so we are told, by a renowned man who had a daughter who was of unusual stature and far excelled in beauty all the other maidens. But she, because of her strength of body and marvellous comeliness, was so haughty that she kept refusing every man who wooed her in marriage, since she believed that no one of her wooers was worthy of her. Now in the course of his campaign against the Geryones, Heracles visited Celtica and founded there the city of Alesia, and the maiden, on seeing Heracles, wondered at his prowess and his bodily superiority and accepted his embraces with all eagerness, her parents having given their consent. From this union she bore to Heracles a son named Galates, who far surpassed all the youths of the tribe in quality of spirit and strength of body. And when he had attained to man's estate and had succeeded to the throne of his fathers, he subdued a large part of the neighbouring territory and accomplished great feats in war. Becoming renowned for his bravery, he called his subjects Galatae or Gauls after himself, and these in turn gave their name to all of Galatia or Gaul.[40]

This story is also mentioned by Parthenius of Nicaea, a Greek grammarian and poet who lived in the 1st century BC. Interestingly, Celtine's father, the unnamed 'renowned man' evanescently referred to by Diodorus Siculus, appears to have been called Bretannus, a name strangely reminiscent of Britannia, the ancient name of Britain. Could it mean that Celtine came from the isle of Britain? We'll come back to this crucial point in the next chapter.

Here's what Parthenius of Nicaea has to say about Hercules' visit in Gaul:

> Hercules, it is told, after he had taken the kine [i.e., cows] of Geryones from Erythea, was wandering through the country of the Celts and came to the house of Bretannus, who had a daughter

---

[39] Diodorus Siculus, *The Library of History*, IV, 19: http://penelope.uchicago.edu/Thayer/E/Roman/Texts/Diodorus_Siculus/4B*.html#17

[40] Ibid., V, 24

> called Celtine. Celtine fell in love with Hercules and hid away the kine, refusing to give them back to him unless he would first content her. Hercules was indeed very anxious to bring the kine safe home, but he was far more struck by the girl's exceeding beauty, and consented to her wishes; and then, when the time had come round, a son called Celtus was born to them, from whom the Celtic race derived their name.[41]

A similar story is to be found in the works of Timagenes, a Greek writer and historian from Alexandria who was captured and taken to Rome in 55 BC. The *Universal History* he wrote hasn't survived, but he was later quoted by Ammianus Marcellinus:

> The ancient writers, in doubt as to the earliest origin of the Gauls, have left an incomplete account of the matter, but later Timagenes, a true Greek in accuracy as well as language, collected out of various books these facts that had been long forgotten; which, following his authority, and avoiding any obscurity, I shall state clearly and plainly. Some asserted that the people first seen in these regions were Aborigines, called Celts from the name of a beloved king, and Galatae (for so the Greek language terms the Gauls) from the name of his mother. Others state that the Dorians, following the earlier Hercules, settled in the lands bordering on the Ocean... But the inhabitants of those countries affirm this beyond all else, and I have also read it inscribed upon their monuments, that Hercules, the son of Amphitryon, hastened to destroy the cruel tyrants Geryon and Tauriscus, of whom one oppressed Spain, the other, Gaul; and having overcome them both that he took to wife some high-born woman and begat numerous children, who called by their own names the districts which they ruled.[42]

So, if Greek historians are to be trusted, the city of Alesia was founded by a Greek hero with the help of 'a great multitude men from every [Gallic] tribe' who had joined his army. The reader will remember from Chapter One that 'the [Gallic] kings were not permitted to do or plan anything without the assistance of these wise men [Druids], so that in truth it was they [Druids] who ruled.' We can infer from this that the location of Alesia, the symbol of Heracles' wanderings across the northwestern territories of Europe, a city meant to unite the soon-to-be-called Celts, was probably not determined by Heracles alone, but with the help of these wise local men—Druids.

---

[41] Parthenius of Nicaea, *Love Stories*, XXX: http://www.theoi.com/Text/Parthenius2.html

[42] Ammianus Marcellinus, *The History*, XV, 9: 2, 3 and 6: http://penelope.uchicago.edu/Thayer/E/Roman/Texts/Ammian/15*.html

Of course, it can immediately be pointed out that Heracles is a purely mythological character, meaning that anything relating to him does not necessarily describe reality. There is simply no way of knowing whether any given myth is ultimately based on true events and real people, an allegory deriving from real-world facts, the personification of inanimate objects or forces, the inflated reminiscences of a long-forgotten ritual, or a merely fictitious story with obscure origins. That mythological figures are embellished stories of real kings or heroes who lived long ago was suggested as early as in the 4th century BC by the Greek mythographer Euhemerus. He believed that Greek heroic tales were the distorted stories of real, historical people of the distant past.

According to Herodotus, who lived in the 5th century BC and who already tended to have the same viewpoint as Euhemerus, Heracles truly lived about nine centuries before him, which would place Heracles' life in the late 14th century BC.[43] Or, still per Herodotus, about a century before the wars of Troy in the late 13th century BC.

Of course, at this point in our study we can't even be sure that Druids already existed back in 1300 BC, or that the details regarding the founding of Alesia are not mere legend or myth without any historical value. The only thing that matters at the moment is that Alesia did exist in the last centuries before the Christian era, that it must have been a highly significant city in the eyes of the Celts, and that its location may not be completely random. In other words, in the hypothesis that Alesia was indeed founded by Druids, its location might betray some astronomical or geometrical importance, which would be the hallmark of the Druids. Let's take a closer look at Alesia then, to see if this hypothesis holds true or not.

Xavier Guichard and his Salt Lines

In the course of my research for the book *The Golden Lines*, I came across the work of a Frenchman named Xavier Guichard (see Chapter Eight). A police inspector and amateur archaeologist, Guichard published a book entitled *Eleusis Alesia* in 1936. In it Guichard claimed to have discovered that an inordinate number of hamlets, villages or towns in Western Europe bore a name which seemed to derive from the root *Alesia* or the like. These Alesias didn't appear to be located in random places across the map, but were aligned in some way.

---

[43] Herodotus, *The Histories*, II, 145: http://www.sacred-texts.com/cla/hh/hh2140.htm

Guichard's huge book counts close to 550 maps. According to him, orthodox history has greatly underestimated the capacities of Bronze Age people in Western Europe. After more than twenty years of research, Guichard reached the conclusion that these people knew the Earth was a sphere, that they were expert astronomers and accomplished geometricians. They had also managed to approximate the Earth's circumference to within a high degree of accuracy.

One of his conclusions was that the town of Alaise in eastern France was the main Alesia, and that the other locations had been carefully created on some 24 lines radiating out from this central Alesia. Upon examination, this contention seemed quite far-fetched and unscientific, as the angles between the lines do not exhibit any regular pattern, and most of his sites occur not along the lines themselves but rather in their vicinity. However, another hypothesis of his was that these Alesia-like locations had also been placed on the parallels (or lines of latitude) and meridians (lines of longitude) of an early 360-degree Earth geometry, showing that Bronze Age people had invented the 360-degree circle. This contention, although given minor importance in Guichard's weighty volume, immediately caught my attention.

Three maps in the book are quite intriguing. One of them shows France and its neighbouring countries. North-south meridian-like lines have been drawn on it, and along them you can see village or town names such as Alais, Allay, Alet, Allais, Alusa, Alzieu, Laix and so on. The other two maps show northern and southern France respectively. On it east-west parallel-like lines have been drawn, and along them you can see more place names which are reminiscent of Alesia, such as Allet, Alaise, Alsen, Alex, Alassio, Lizy, and so on.[44] All these names bear a vague resemblance with 'Alesia,' evidence to Guichard that they derive from it, which can indeed be proved true in some cases. Guichard also pointed out that most Alesias are more or less surrounded with rivers: they stand on peninsulas[45] and all of them possess, or have possessed at some time, a mineral spring.[46]

---

[44] Xavier Guichard's book can be consulted online here (maps can be seen in Chapter XIV, 'Atlas'): http://transcommunication.eu/index.php/vieux-livres

[45] Ibid., p. 32

[46] Ibid., p. 33

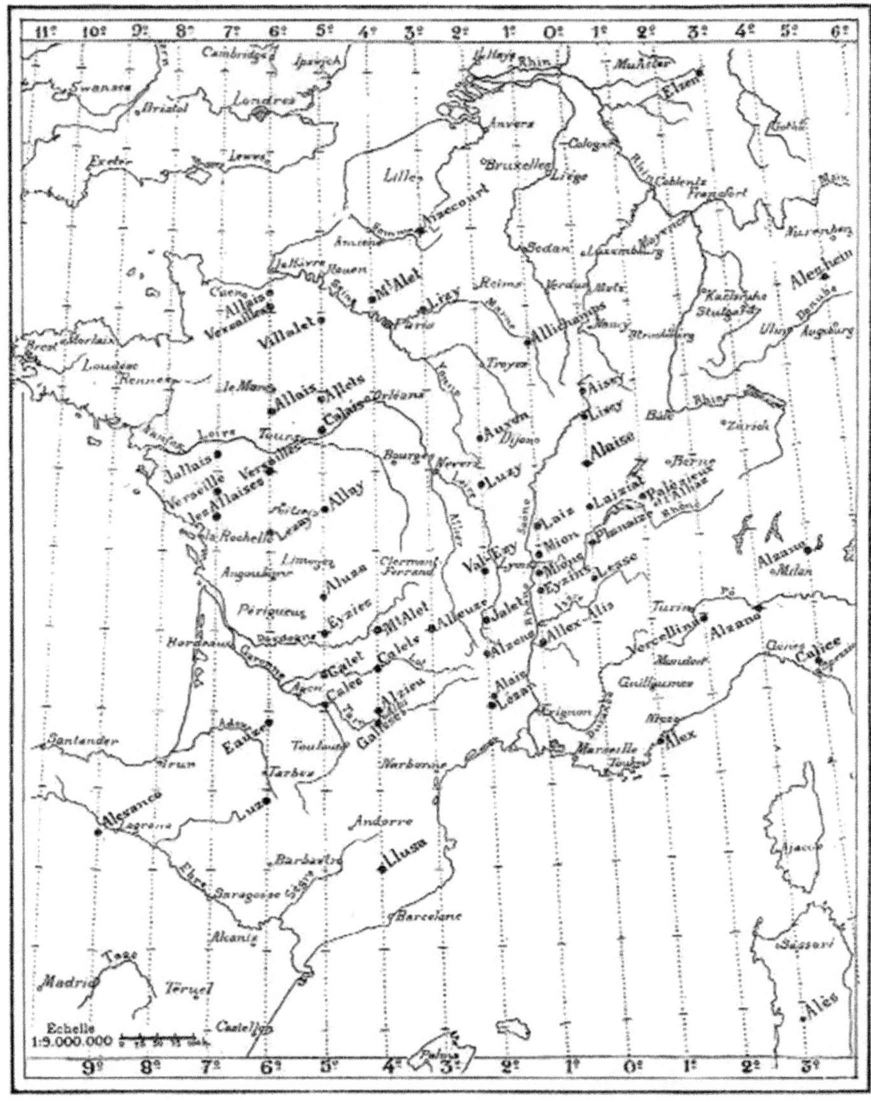

Fig. 1. Xavier Guichard's longitudinal 'Salt Lines,' or Salt Meridians in Western Europe.

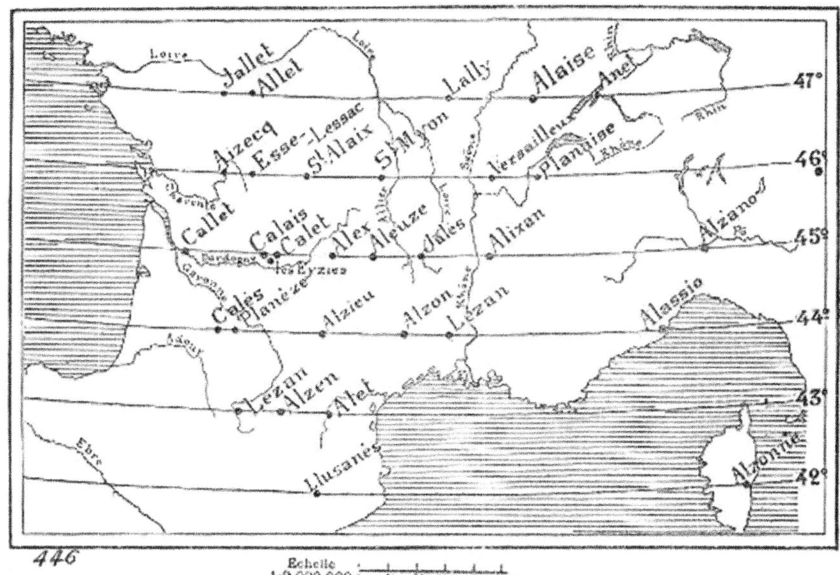

Carte 446. — Carte des régions du Sud-Ouest de l'Europe du 42e au 47e degré de latitude.

Fig. 2. Xavier Guichard's latitudinal Salt Lines, or Salt Parallels, in southern France.

According to him though, whoever had designed the system of longitudes in the first place had made a slight mistake:

> But if the Alesian lines of latitude are exactly established from degree to degree between the Equator and the Pole and the distribution of Alesias precisely indicate them where they run on modern maps designed from the antique division of the sphere in 360 degrees, an easy verification shows that the Alesian lines of longitude are slightly inaccurate: the intervals between those lines are equal, but they don't amount to an exact degree of 60 minutes on the great circle of the Earth; they measure only 58 minutes 1/2. This error of a minute and a half is easy to miss between two meridians, but it is a constant one and, adding up on itself each degree, in the end the differences are quite great; for fifteen degrees, this difference amounts to about 25 minutes, or close to half a degree. The error would have been spotted only if the primitive geographers had been able to expand their work to the entire Earth. In that case they would have noticed that the system counted 369 longitudes instead of 360.[47]

[47] Ibid., p. 158

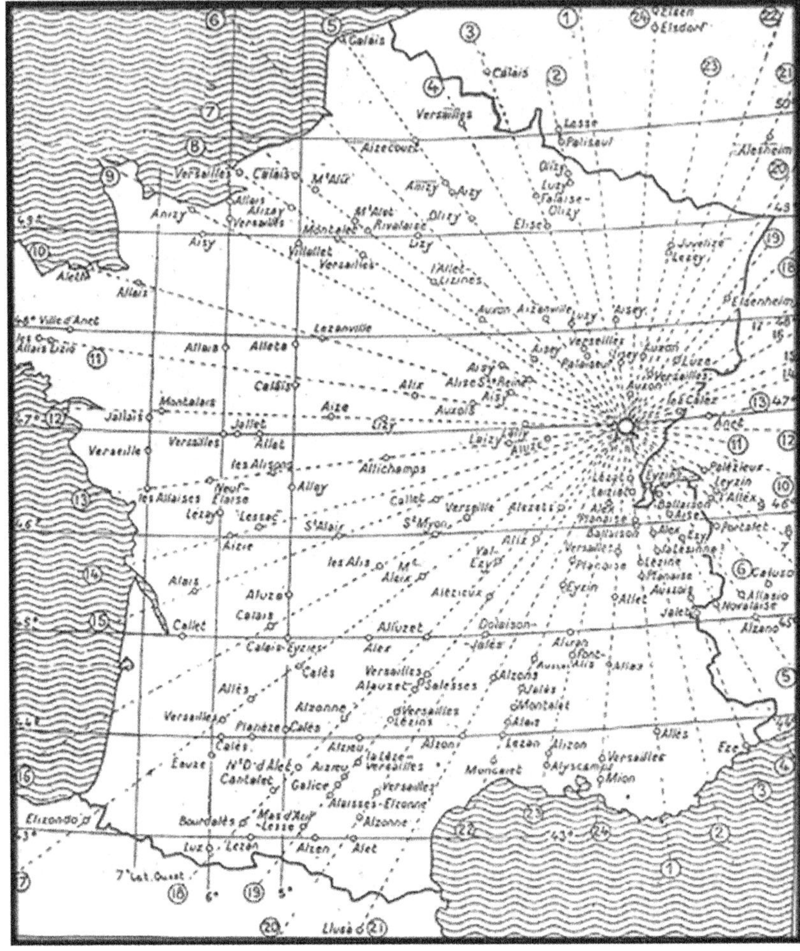

Fig. 3. Xavier Guichard's 'radiating lines,' which all have their starting point in the village of Alaise, France.

Curiously enough, it seems that Guichard's own assessment of the error was inaccurate as well. This was first pointed out to me by my friend and fellow researcher, the English writer Alan Butler. Working from Guichard's maps, he understood that whoever decided to build Alesia-like towns along meridians and parallels in Western Europe used a *366*-degree circle on the Earth, not a system of 360 or 369 degrees. We'll come back to this in a short while.

The name Guichard gave to these meridians and parallels was 'Salt Lines,' because he thought these axes were used to transport salt across ancient Europe. Furthermore, the Greek name for salt is *alati*, and police inspector Guichard thought the words *Alesia* and *alati* were cognates.

The name of the town of Eleusis in Greece, famous for its famous Eleusinian mysteries during Antiquity, was also cognate with Alesia in Guichard's view, hence the name of his book, *Eleusis Alésia.*

Probably because most of his book is more or less pseudoscientific, Guichard's work was never taken seriously, and has remained largely unknown to the public. Guichard's contention regarding the existence of meridians and parallels marked on the ground with a recurrent name in Bronze Age Europe, however, merits further examination, especially so as we have seen that the first Alesia is supposed to be the 'mother-city of all Celtica.'

The battle of Alesia

We've said that in 52 BC the city of Alesia fell to the Romans. According to Diodorus Siculus, this location and the Alesia supposedly founded by Heracles more than a millennium earlier were one and the same place. Of course, if Guichard was right, there were not just one but a raft of Alesias across Western Europe. It is outside the range of this book to decide whether all these places are truly derivations of the name Alesia or not, but let us discuss for a while the question of the location of the battle of Alesia.

If mainstream archaeology is to be believed, the battle of Alesia transpired in a place today known as Alise-Sainte-Reine, a toponym which of course bears an uncanny resemblance with Alesia, and could well be an alteration of it after two thousand years. Indeed, the place is known to have been called *Alisia* in the past, which seems close enough to the name *Alesia.*

The only problem is that the topography of the site does not correspond to Caesar's descriptions. Michel Reddé, director of studies at the Ecole Pratique des Hautes Etudes in France and himself a strong proponent of the idea that Alise-sainte-Reine is Alesia, recognises that the defensive system deployed by the Romans around it 'does not quite match Caesar's description.'[48] Although one of the aims of Caesar's book *The Gallic War* was to increase his popularity in Rome, meaning that the book can at times be slightly biased, the depictions in it are generally considered 'paradigms of pertinent information and stylistic clarity'.[49] So,

---

[48] Michel Reddé interviewed by Vincent Charpentier, editor, *Redécouverte des Gaulois*, Paris: Errance, 1995, p. 112

[49] Hans Herzfeld (1960): *Geschichte in Gestalten* (*History in figures*), vol. 1: *A-E.* Das Fischer Lexikon 37, Frankfurt, 1963, p. 214

if Caesar's information is trustworthy, how do we explain the paradox that the topography of Alise-Sainte-Reine and what remains of the defensive system supposedly deployed by Julius Caesar there do not match Caesar's graphic account?

The truth is that the location of the battle is still a matter of debate. Many claims have been made as to where the real Alesia is to be found. It was once asserted that the village of Alaise, Guichard's own favourite, was the place where Vercingetorix was defeated by Caesar, although no one seriously believes in this hypothesis any more.

One serious contender is the French *commune* of Chaux-des-Crotenay in Jura, whose geography very closely parallels Caesar's account of the siege of Alesia. Amongst the staunch defenders of the theory are the late French archaeologist André Berthier. Using topographical data from historical sources and maps to see what place best fitted the description, he was able to locate the site of the Jugurthine War between Rome and the North African kingdom of Numidia in the 2nd century BC. More recently, the French historian and radio anchorman Franck Ferrand has also been earnestly defending this thesis.

Another serious contender, albeit less known to the public except for a few history buffs, is a hill overhanging the village of Guillon in Burgundy. Located about twenty miles west of Alise-Sainte-Reine, the hill is actually a double one: the southern hill is called the Montfault (or 'Mount Fault'), and the northern mount, which is immediately adjacent to the first one, is called the Montagne de Verre (the 'Glass Mountain'). Most astonishingly, according to Bernard Fèvre—the discoverer of the site—in Guillon everything precisely matches Caesar's description.

Alesia in Guillon, Burgundy

I first visited the site of Guillon on my own on 31 October 2002, and then came back again on 24 May 2003, this time with Bernard Fèvre as a guide, who unfortunately passed away the following year.

Fèvre had discovered the site back in the early 1980s. At the time, he was enjoying retirement in the village of Guillon in the French *département* of Yonne, Burgundy. Having heard of 'ruins of an old castle' on the neighbouring hill by locals, he decided to take a walk there. What he found on the Montfault and the Montagne de Verre left him speechless: a six-kilometer-long wall, sometimes five meters wide and two meters and a half high, stood around the hills, halfway down its slopes, lost in small high grass fields and quiet woods. His estimation was that there were about 150,000 cubic meters of stone, or three times the outside volume of Notre Dame Cathedral in Paris.[50] In Fèvre's mind there was no doubt this place wasn't the mere remains of a castle, but rather a Gallic *oppidum*, or fortified town. It suddenly dawned on him that these hills could well be the remains of the Celtic city of Alesia. Caesar described Alesia as 'a town of the Mandubii,'[51] the Mandubians being a Gallic tribe no other author ever mentioned before Caesar. Mandubians were probably established in Burgundy, of which more later.

Fèvre's subsequent research showed that there was a network of twelve kilometers of fortified walls—much longer than anything found around Alise-Saine-Reine. Fèvre showed me many parts of the highly impressive walls on the northern part of the Montfault. One segment in particular—near where the hill joins the Montagne de Verre—is still 350 meters long, two meters tall and five meters wide. Strangely enough, this portion looks like typical Mycenaean walls in Greece: the style is similar and they have a 'slope' so that defenders could shoot arrows down on their assailants at the foot of the wall, who weren't protected by any blind spot a strictly vertical wall would provide. Fèvre was adamant that this was the most ancient wall of the site, dating back to the time of the mythical Heracles.

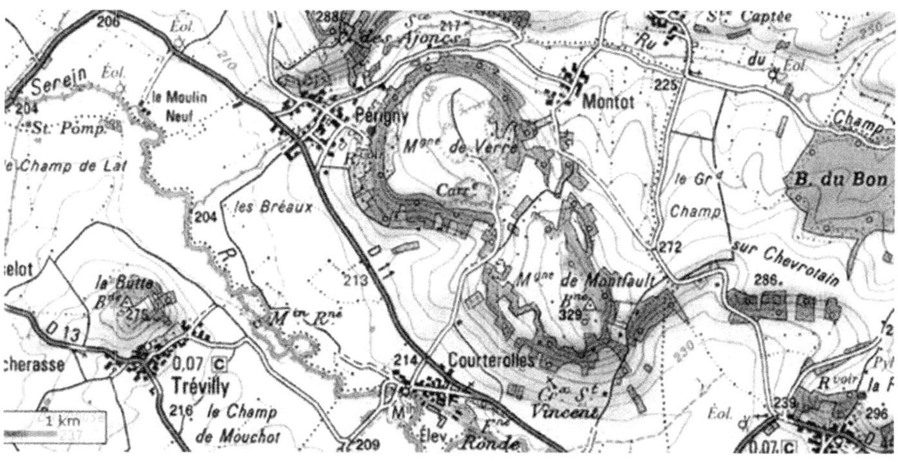

Fig. 4. The dual hill of Alesia in Guillon, France, with the Glass Mountain in the northwest and Mount Fault in the southeast.

[50] Fabien Gruhier, 'On se bat toujours pour Alésia,' *Le Nouvel Observateur*, 20 January 1984

[51] Julius Caesar, *Commentaries on the Gallic War*, VII, 68

Also of interest are these well-preserved portions of wall either in fields or in woods interspersed with numerous little gates or with half-crumbled huge watchtowers. These walls also include redans (arrow-shaped fortifications) which allowed the Gauls to defend themselves by shooting on the right side of their assailants, thus hitting the side unprotected by the attackers' shield, a technique also used in Mycenae. According to Fèvre these segments were more recent and had probably been built in the 5th century BC.

Fèvre set out to compare Caesar's text to the local topography, and found that the site of Guillon was a close match. Caesar's description of Alesia is as follows:

> The town itself was situated on the top of a hill, in a very lofty position, so that it did not appear likely to be taken, except by a regular siege. Two rivers, on two different sides, washed the foot of the hill. Before the town lay a plain of about three miles in length; on every other side hills at a moderate distance, and of an equal degree of height, surrounded the town.[52]

The Montfault isn't a very high hill, culminating at about 325 meters high. Today it overhangs the village of Guillon, which has an elevation of a bit more than 200 meters above sea level. Still, the Montfault cliff stands out as a 'lofty position.' There are indeed two rivers on two different sides, the Serein at the southwest, and the Ru du Champ Millet north. The rivers meet at the foot of the Montagne de Verre, in the west. There is indeed a plain about three Roman miles (4.45 km) long immediately to the southwest—the Terre Plaine. And there are indeed four other hills nearby, each about 300 meters high. By contrast, the Plaine des Laumes, at the foot of the Mont Auxois at Alise-Sainte-Reine, is only about two kilometers long, and in Chaux-des-Crotenay the hills are really high but there is hardly any plain around.

Fèvre then started to compare what could be found on the site and the description of the battle in the text. And again, text and terrain matched. For instance, the circumvallation—the line of fortifications constructed by the Romans around the besieged town—as described by Caesar could be found in Guillon, with the right length. Caesar also writes that '[t]he army of the Gauls had filled all the space under the wall, comprising a part of the hill which looked to the rising sun,'[53] a description that really fits the landscape near Guillon, as there is a sort of plateau about 270 meters high immediately east of the Montfault. But

---

[52] Ibid., VII, 69

[53] Ibid.

perhaps the most striking correspondence between Caesar's text and the geography of Guillon is what concerns the number of redoubts with guards Caesar had raised in his camp to keep watch around Alesia:

> The camp was pitched in a strong position, and twenty-three redoubts were raised in it, in which sentinels were placed by day, lest any sally should be made suddenly; and by night the same were occupied by watches and strong guards.[54]

Incredibly, twenty-three is the exact number of redoubts found by Fèvre onsite, neither one more nor one less, a staggering confirmation that Guillon is indeed the location of the siege of Alesia in 52 BC.

Another interesting piece of evidence is the presence, only 35 meters away from what is taken by Fèvre to be the contravallation (Caesar's second line of fortifications), of a buried stake with a sharpened top[55] so as to impale any approaching Gaul who would attack Romans. Caesar is very specific about them:

> These stakes being sunk into this trench, and fastened firmly at the bottom, to prevent the possibility of their being torn up, had their branches only projecting from the ground. There were five rows in connection with, and intersecting each other; and whoever entered within them were likely to impale themselves on very sharp stakes. The soldiers called these 'cippi.' Before these, which were arranged in oblique rows in the form of a quincunx, pits three feet deep were dug, which gradually diminished in depth to the bottom. In these pits tapering stakes, of the thickness of a man's thigh; sharpened at the top and hardened in the fire, were sunk in such a manner as to project from the ground not more than four inches; at the same time for the purpose of giving them strength and stability, they were each filled with trampled clay to the height of one foot from the bottom: the rest of the pit was covered over with osiers and twigs, to conceal the deceit.[56]

According to Fèvre, the presence of this trap or 'lily,' as it was nicknamed because it resembled the flower, is highly significant, as nothing of the sort has ever been found in Alise-Sainte-Reine so far.

---

[54] Ibid.

[55] Bernard Fèvre, *Complexe du siège d'Alésia en Terre-Plaine*, Guillon: SEGAMM/Association Alexandre Parat, document No 8, Dec. 1997, p. 62

[56] Julius Caesar, *Commentaries on the Gallic War*, VII, 73: http://www.perseus.tufts.edu/hopper/text?doc=Perseus%3Atext%3A1999.02.0001%3Abook%3D7%3Achapter%3D73

Toponymy around Guillon

Can toponymy or place names shed some light on the puzzle as well?

The Montfault is named after the natural extended break which cuts the rocky spur close to the top of the hill. A very interesting fact is that another local name for the Montfault is *La Roche Bretain*,[57] literally the 'Bretain Rock'—possibly translating as the 'Breton/British Rock.' In French, Brittany and Britain are both known as *Bretagne*, Brittany being *(Petite) Bretagne*, and Britain being *Grande-Bretagne*, literally 'Great Britain.' The name could also derive from the mythical Bretannus, Celtine's father according to Parthenius of Nicaea, a 'renowned man' in Diodorus Siculus' words, mentioned earlier in this chapter. La Roche Brétain would thus be Bretannus' Rock, a strong indication that the hills at Guillon indeed harboured the Alesia founded by Heracles according to Greek tradition, the mother city of the Celts.

Nobody really knows why the Montagne de Verre or 'Glass Mountain' bears this name, but in Fèvre's opinion it probably has nothing to do with glass, and instead represents the eroded form of the name 'Vercingetorix.'[58] The name Guillon, Fèvre adamantly asserted, comes from the Greek *guyow*, which means 'pass under the yoke,'[59] from the Roman practice of compelling defeated soldiers to stoop under a 'yoke' of spears while being jeered at by the victors.

The neighbouring village of L'Isle-sur-Serein, northwest of the hills, used to be called in remote times Insula in Mandubiis[60] or 'Island in Mandubiis', which demonstrates the region of Guillon was Mandubian territory, just as Caesar wrote. According to Strabo, the Mandubian tribe 'has a common boundary with the Arverni,'[61] which is consistent with the Mandubians being part of the Aedui (a better-known Gallic tribe) territory, which is adjacent to that of the Arverni, another Gallic tribe which thrived in what today is Auvergne.

---

[57] Bernard Fèvre, *Complexe du siège d'Alésia en Terre-Plaine*, Guillon: SEGAMM/Association Alexandre Parat, document No 8, Dec. 1997, p. 2-4

[58] Ibid., p. 59

[59] Ibid., p.61

[60] Information from the section *Histoire* ('History') on the official website of the village of L'Isle-sur-Serein: http://www.isle-sur-serein.com/plan-origine/

[61] Strabo, *Geography*, 4, 2, 3

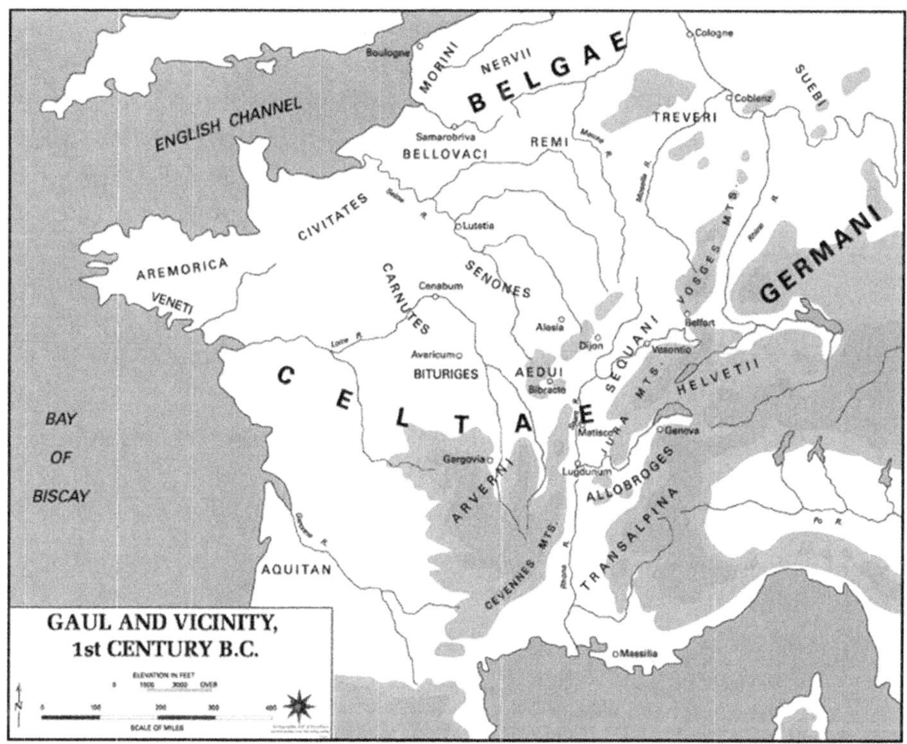

Fig. 5. Some of the Gallic tribes in Western Europe when Caesar conquered Gaul.

Another interesting toponym is the Combe d'Auvergne, a hollow or valley northeast of the hills. Fèvre thinks it was named so because a Gallic army marched there to head for the camp of Roman legions posted nearby. This army was led by an Arverni, Vercassivellaunos.[62]

Also, the name of Cisery, a village only 2.2 kilometers (or, interestingly, one Gallic league) from Guillon, bears an odd resemblance with 'Caesar.' According to Fèvre, the toponym could derive from *Caesarii*, meaning 'Caesars.'[63] And not far from Guillon—about ten miles west—stands the French city of Avallon, a Celtic toponym possibly deriving from 'apple' or 'apple-tree,' but which is also highly reminiscent of the island of Avalon, the legendary *Ynis Afallon* featured in Arthurian literature. We'll have more to say about Avalon.

[62] Bernard Fèvre, *Complexe du siège d'Alésia en Terre-Plaine*, Guillon: SEGAMM/Association Alexandre Parat, document No 8, Dec. 1997, p. 59 and 61
[63] Ibid., p. 52

Etymological considerations about Alesia

What about the name *Alesia* itself? As we've seen, Guichard thought the word was cognate with the Greek *alati* or 'salt', and Diodorus Siculus thought Alesia had been named after the *alê* ('wanderings') of Heracles.

Another serious 'Greek' hypothesis is a possible connection with the mythological Elysian Fields, also known as Elysium, the eternal home of the favoured of Zeus, or more generally of the souls of gods and heroes after their death. Interestingly, Homer located this paradise of the blessed on the western edge of the world by the stream of Oceanus, the World Ocean that was supposed to surround the Earth:

> but the gods will take you to the Elysian plain, which is at the ends of the world. There fair-haired Rhadamanthus reigns, and men lead an easier life than any where else in the world, for in Elysium there falls not rain, nor hail, nor snow, but Oceanus breathes ever with a West wind that sings softly from the sea, and gives fresh life to all men.[64]

The *Encyclopaedia Britannica* states that the myth was probably retained from Minoan religion.[65] Could this myth refer to Alesia in Western Europe? An alternate explanation is that the Elysian Fields are what the Greeks later called the Isles of the Blessed, probably the Canary Islands and their famed everlasting spring. The word may be cognate with the Greek verb *eleusô*, 'relieve' or 'release,' as from pain.[66] It may be significant that among the toponyms listed by Xavier Guichard in his book *Eleusis Alésia* are Alichamps, Allichamps and Les Alyscamps, all of which appear to be local derivations of the Latin *Elysii-Campi* or *Alysii-Campi*, literally 'Elysian Fields.'[67]

Still Greek-wise, an *alsos* was a sacred grove, the tree plantation which bordered the holiest area of a sanctuary. One famous *alsos* was the oak grove at Dodona, one of the most celebrated oracles in Ancient Greece (see Chapter Twelve). It is in a grove sacred to the divinity Ares that Jason and the Argonauts find the Golden Fleece. Some *alsos* were allegedly so sacred that their access was theoretically prohibited to mortals.

Interestingly, there is a Megalithic site in Sweden whose 59 (initially 60?) standing stones form the shape of a ship: it is named Ale's Stones

---

[64] Homer, *The Odyssey*, IV: http://classics.mit.edu/Homer/odyssey.4.iv.html
[65] *Encyclopaedia Britannica online*, entry 'Elysium': http://www.britannica.com/EBchecked/topic/185418/Elysium
[66] http://www.theoi.com/Kosmos/Elysion.html
[67] Xavier Guichard, *Eleusis Alésia*, p. 72

(*Ales stenar*) in Swedish, a name which seems to derive from a Germanic root *Ahls* meaning 'sanctuary'.[68]

And it was of course in Eleusis in Greece that the famous Eleusinian mysteries were held every year during antiquity. These initiation ceremonies honoured the goddesses Demeter and Persephone. The rites were kept totally secret—no details were ever written down—and the initiates hoped to be rewarded in the afterlife. It is speculated that participants at Eleusis used psychedelic substances.[69] Do these traditions derive from rites previously practiced by Druids in Alesia in Western Europe?

To put it in a nutshell, there is consistent evidence that the word *Alesia* or the like related to some highly sacred place or sanctuary where secrecy was the key word. And we do know how important the notion of secrecy was to Druids.

Other explanations have been suggested. According to the late Professor Albert Dauzat, who was recognised as an expert in the study of place names, the toponyms Alise-Sainte-Reine and Alaise come from the reconstructed Gallic word **alisa*, which means 'cliff.'[70] As there is also a cliff at the Montfault, the Roche Brétain, this hypothesis would also make sense for the presumed Alesia near Guillon.

Circumstantial evidence

Alesia is also mentioned in the writings of Pliny the Elder, along with some information which in Fèvre's opinion lends credence to the Guillon hypothesis:

> It was in the Gallic provinces that the method was discovered of coating articles of copper with white lead, so as to be scarcely distinguishable from silver: articles thus plated are known as 'incoctilia.' At a later period, the people of the town of Alesia began to use a similar process for plating articles with silver, more particularly ornaments for horses, beasts of burden, and yokes of oxen: the merit, however, of this invention belongs to the Bituriges.[71]

---

[68] http://www.zwoje-scrolls.com/as/aleseng.html

[69] See R Gordon Wasson, A Albert Hofmann and Carl A P Ruck, *The Road to Eleusis: Unveiling the Secret of the Mysteries*, Harcourt, Brace, Jovanovich, 1978

[70] Albert Dauzat and Charles Rostaing (1963), *Dictionnaire étymologique des noms de lieux en France*, Paris: Guénégaud, 1989, p. 8

[71] Pliny the Elder, *The Natural History*, XXXIV, 48

First of all, in this passage Pliny mentions Alesia without stating its location, which tends to confirm that Alesia was a major town at the time (Pliny was accustomed to list even large towns with their locations). Secondly, according to Fèvre, there is a white lead mine only 4 miles away from the Montfault, whereas there is none in the vicinity of Alise-Sainte-Reine.

The Aalst-Alesia-Alès line

When I studied Guichard's maps I realized what Alan Butler had told me about the ancient system of latitudes and longitudes, on which so many Alesias were to be found. It had to be based on a 366-degree circle around the Earth, and not a 360-degree one like we use today. We'll see in the next part of this book how we can account for the existence of what Alan Butler, Christopher Knight and I today refer to as 366-degree geometry or Megalithic geometry.

What also struck me was that most Alesias pointed out by Guichard were in villages or hamlets, not big towns or cities. One notable exception was Alès in southern France, which today is a town of 40,000 inhabitants. Alès, which was named *Alesto* in Merovingian times (c. 5th-8th centuries AD),[72] is a very old town which dates back to at least the 1st century BC.[73]

Strangely enough, on almost exactly the same longitude, but much further north, I found that another Alesia-like city exists, one that had been overlooked by Guichard: Aalst (French *Alost*) in Belgium, which today has a population of more than 80,000 people. The centers of the two cities[74] are only about one arc minute apart in longitude. It is known that Aalst was named *Alost* or *Alosta* in the 9th century AD.[75] It is not known when Aalst first came to be, but it already existed in the first millennium AD.

More intriguingly still, if Alise-Sainte-Reine did not appear to fall on Guichard's lines, the dual hill overlooking the village of Guillon stood on

---

[72] Albert Dauzat et Charles Rostaing, *Dictionnaire étymologique des noms de lieu en France*, Paris: Guénégaud, 1979, p. 10a

[73] J. Salles and M. Wienin, 'Alès, Ermitage, fouilles de sauvetage, campagne 1981,' in *Groupe Alésien de Recherches Archéologiques. Activités et Travaux Alès*, 1981, p. 3-15

[74] I used the centers of the main city churches as reference points

[75] Maurits Gysseling, *Toponymisch woordenboek van België, Nederland, Luxemburg, Noord-Frankrijk en West-Duitsland*, Belgisch interuniversitair centrum voor Neerlandistiek, 1960

the very same meridian (i.e. the same Salt Line). The longitude of Alès, in modern terms, is 04°04' E, whereas that of Aalst is 04°03' E. By comparison, the Montfault and the Montagne de Verre have a longitudinal coordinate of 04°05'E. It meant that what looked like the biggest remaining Alesias in France and Belgium had almost the same longitude as the presumed Alesia at Guillon. That in itself was startling enough of course, but that was far from being all—it was only the beginning of a very surprising series of oddities.

The Montfault appeared to stand roughly halfway between Aalst and Alès. I then precisely measured the distances, and to my amazement I realized that the site stood almost exactly halfway between Aalst and Alès. So what we had here was (if the Guillon hypothesis was true) three Alesias on the same meridian, with the presumed sacred Alesia (the 'mother-city of all Celtica') midway between two major Alesian cities. What if these two other towns had been built as 'markers' of the central one—the holiest one? What if these two cities had been built after the fall of the main Alesia as 'reminders' of what had for centuries been viewed as the hub of Celtica?

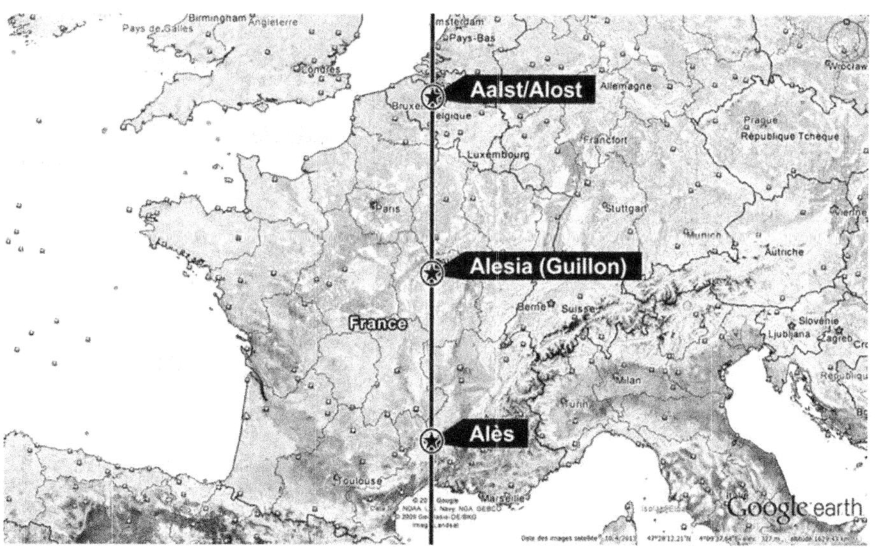

Fig. 6. The three Alesias: Aalst in Belgium, Alès in southern France, and the proposed Alesia site in Guillon, France (halfway between them).

The distance between St. Martin's Collegiate Church in Aalst and the center of the Montagne de Verre[76] is 377.8 km[77], and the distance

---

[76] As I best estimated it

between the center of the Montfault and the St. John the Baptist Cathedral in Alès is 379 km.[78] Taking into consideration that both towns are built along rivers (Alès being in the curve of one), this state of affairs is pretty amazing. But again, that was far from being all.

Converted into Gallic leagues (a Gallic league is usually considered to be 1.381 miles or 2.2225 km long), the distance of 377.8 km becomes a perfectly round number—170 Gallic leagues.

The implications of all this were quite phenomenal. Apart from being persuasive additional proof that the Montfault had once been the 'hearth and mother-city of all Celtica,' it meant that its location owed nothing to chance. The place had probably been carefully selected by people who were both great astronomers and talented geometers and mathematicians. They had used the Gallic league and had built three cities along the same meridian. Who else but the Druids would have been able to accomplish such precise work at that time?

According to archaeologists, Alès was built right after the fall of Alesia. As far as Aalst is concerned, the date it is more difficult to determine, but in any case—unless we are faced here with an incredible coincidence—this city was built so as to be symmetrically opposed to Alès, the Montfault and the Montagne de Verre being the central point. The conclusion seems irrefutable: the location of the presumed Alesia and Alès have been determined by Druids, and that of Aalst either by Druids or later on by people who had somehow inherited from that Druidic knowledge.

Impressive enough perhaps, but again, there was more. On the map of Guichard where he shows lines of longitudes, two major French cities also appear on what we'll now refer to as the Aalst-Alesia-Alès Meridian: Reims and Troyes, both located in the French region of Champagne. It is known that these cities already existed in some form before the Roman era. The Reims Cathédrale Notre Dame has a longitude of 04°02'E, and the Basilique Saint-Urbain in Troyes has a longitude of 04°04'E.

That two major French cities should appear on the same 'Salt Line' as the three large Alesias is in itself astonishing enough. These cities do not seem to have been placed at arbitrary points either. Reims is 187.3 km[79] (116.4 mi) from Aalst and 190.4 km[80] (118.3 mi) from the Alesian hills, putting Reims almost exactly halfway between these two Alesias.

---

[77] Google Earth data
[78] Google Earth data
[79] Google Earth data
[80] Google Earth data

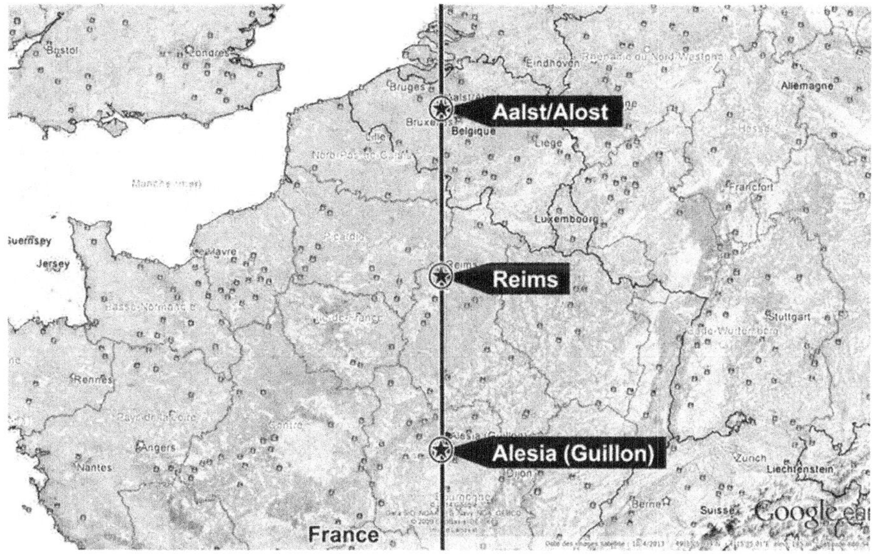

Fig. 7. The city of Reims stands halfway between Aalst and Alesia.

Troyes, on the other hand, is 293.6 km[81] (182.4 mi) from Aalst and 464 km[82] (288.3 mi) from Alès, meaning that Troyes stands at the golden section between the other two, to an accuracy of more than 99.6 per cent.[83] Is it conceivable that Druids might have known about Phi, the golden ratio or eye-pleasing 'Divine Proportion,' this 'magic' number found in nature and in Greek architecture? Of course these results might just be accidental, but we'll see in Part III that these cities have played a key part in the preservation of Druidic knowledge in more recent times.

All this is really astonishing enough. But here comes the icing on the cake. Still on the same Salt Line (at a longitude of 04°02'E) is Bibracte, which was a Gallic oppidum and no less than the capital of the Aedui, the Gallic tribe which included the Mandubians. Bibracte is thought to be located on Mont Beuvray, about forty miles south of Guillon. It is located a neat 140 Gallic leagues from **Alès**, a neat 200 Gallic leagues from Aalst, and hence a neat 30 Gallic leagues from the Alesian hills.[84]

---

[81] Google Earth data

[82] Google Earth data

[83] The results presented are obtained with straightforward calculations made with the numbers observed on Google Earth, using the Ruler instrument.

[84] Arbitrarily taking as a reference point the monumental 1st-century-BC fountain at Bibracte, the distance to the St. John the Baptist Cathedral in Alès is 140.2 Gallic leagues, which is 140 Gallic leagues to an accuracy of more than 99.8 per cent; there are 200.6 Gallic leagues to the Saint Martin's Collegiate Church in Aalst, which is 200 Gallic leagues to an accuracy of 99.7 per cent; and there are 30.17 Gallic leagues

Bibracte was abandoned in the very last decades before the Christian era in favour of Augustodunum, now called Autun, a city founded by the Romans about fifteen miles east of Bibracte. We'll have much more to say further on about Augustodunum, the *soror et aemula Romae* (the 'sister and emulator of Rome'), also known for the Couhard Pyramid that overlooks the city.

The origin of the Gallic league

It is generally thought that ancient units of measurement developed from small units such as the length of a foot or, in the case of the cubit in Egypt, the length of a forearm. It seems this logic has to be reversed: it is likely that most ancient units of measurement developed from subdividing very large distance units into smaller ones.

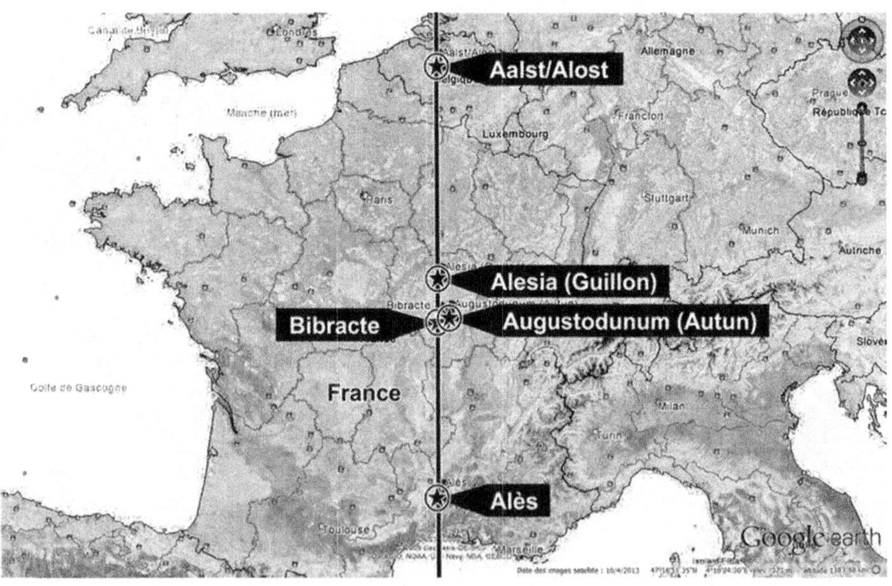

Fig. 8. The city of Troyes stands at the Golden Section of the line segment Aalst-Alès.

We've seen that, according to Caesar, the Druids taught their students about 'the stars and their motion,' and also that they knew 'the extent of the world and of our earth,' a notion which has been reprised by Pomponius Mela, who wrote that the Druids 'profess[ed] to know the

---

to the Montfault, which is 30 Gallic leagues to an accuracy of more than 99.4 per cent.

magnitude and form of the earth and the world, the motions of the heaven and the stars.'

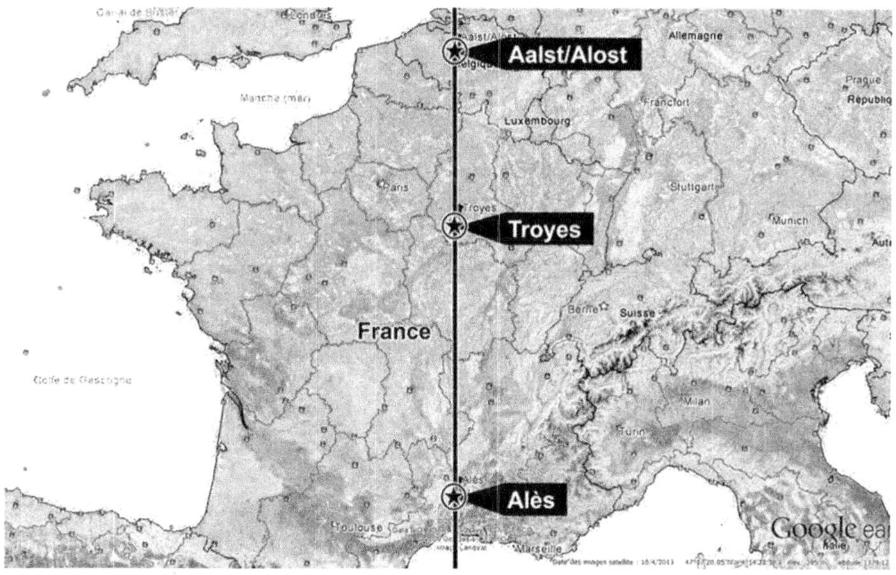

Fig. 9. The Gallic city of Bibracte, which was replaced by Augustodunum under Roman occupation.

These statements strongly suggest that the Druids knew the Earth was a sphere and that they knew about its dimensions. Does the length of the Gallic league give any clue that this hypothesis has some validity? The *leuga gallica* or Gallic league of 2,222.5 m is usually thought to be a Romanised league, as was argued by Jacques Dassié,[85] a specialist in aerial archaeology. Dassié believes that the Gauls also made use of another league of about 2,450 m, or 10% longer. As the Gallic league is also exactly 1½ times the Roman mile, which measured 1,481.5 m, one possibility is that in Roman times the Gauls adopted a new league which was easy to convert to the Roman mile. Why not after all?

One problem with this explanation is that both the Gallic league and the Roman mile are almost perfect subdivisions of the Earth's circumference. A Gallic league is 1/50th of a degree and a Roman mile is 1/75th of a degree: if you multiply the Gallic league by 50 then by 360 the circumference you get is 40,005 km, and if you multiply the Roman mile by 75 then by 360 the circumference you get is 40,000.5 km, both of

---

[85] Jacques Dassié, 'La Grande lieue gauloise. Approche méthodologique de la métrique des voies,' *Gallia*, 56, 1999, p. 285-311: http://www.persee.fr/web/revues/home/prescript/article/galia_0016-4119_1999_num_56_1_3011

which are extremely close approximations of the true polar circumference of the Earth, which is about 40,007.86 km.

The accuracy of the result in the case of the Roman mile is over 99.98 per cent, and in the case of the Gallic league over 99.99 per cent. So, using the lengths as they are usually given by scholars, the Gallic league appears to have been a more accurate unit than the Roman mile in terms of subdividing the Earth's circumference. This astounding accuracy for the Gallic league suggests that it was derived from our planet's circumference. Moreover, it is more natural to divide a degree into 50 parts than into 75. Thus once again it seems more likely that the Roman mile derives from the Gallic league, rather than the other way round. And who else but the Druids had the potential knowledge to accomplish such a feat of measurement?

I perfectly realize that at this stage such a connection between ancient units of measurements and the polar circumference of the Earth, in spite of mathematical accuracy, might appear like a coincidence and nothing more to the sceptical reader, even if these results are in keeping with what classical authors said about the Druids' abilities. But we'll soon see that these connections are too recurrent to be accidental. In fact, this is just the beginning.

Main points

- **Ancient Greeks thought that Alesia, a city in present-day France, had been founded by Heracles**
- **They wrote that Celts held Alesia in honour and that it was the 'mother-city of all Celtica'**
- **Xavier Guichard thought Bronze Age people in Western Europe had invented 360-degree geometry**
- **He identified 'Salt Lines,' often sprinkled with place names similar to Alesia, which he thought were markers of this Earth geometry**
- **Gallic chieftain Vercingetorix was defeated in Alesia by Caesar in 52 BC**
- **The Guillon area fits Caesar's description of Alesia**
- **There are three major 'Alesias' (Alès, Alesia and Aalst) at equidistant points on the same Salt Line (Salt Meridian)**
- **The Gallic cities of Bibracte, Troyes and Reims are also located at mathematically significant distances on this Salt Line**
- **The Gallic league seems to be a near-perfect subdivision of the Earth's circumference**

Chapter Four: The Origins of Druidism

We are now coming to the crucial question of the origin of Druidism. Where does the Druidic institution come from? Is it Celtic or pre-Celtic? Is it indigenous to northwestern Europe or was it imported there?

One striking thing about Druids is that, if they were clearly part of the Celtic culture at Caesar's time, they certainly weren't found in all Celtic territories. On the contrary, they appear to have been confined to the *northwestern part of Europe*. As Nora Chadwick—a respected scholar who wrote a reference book about the Druids—points out, 'we have no evidence for the institution of the druids among the Celts of Italy, or Spain, nor among the Galatians of Thrace or of Asia Minor, nor even among the Celts east of the Rhine. Caesar states categorically that the Teutonic peoples were entirely without them.'[86] It is then highly probable that the Druidic institution is *not* Celtic, but that it predates the Celts, who might have absorbed Druidism as they spread across northwestern Europe.

Now, if Druidism is indeed from northwestern Europe, is it rather British, Irish, or Gallic? Or was it imported there by some other people than the Celts? Is it possible, for instance, that Druidism comes from Greece?

Caesar's testimony

Julius Caesar quite clearly states that Druids originate from Britain:

> This institution is supposed to have been devised in Britain, and to have been brought over from it into Gaul; and now those who desire to gain a more accurate knowledge of that system generally proceed thither for the purpose of studying it.[87]

The use of the word 'supposed' suggests that Caesar's informant, probably Posidonius, wasn't totally sure of the fact, as if it seemed strange to Graeco-Romans that Druidism could have been born in a

---

[86] Nora K. Chadwick (1966), *The Druids*, Cardiff: University of Wales Press, 1997, p. 15

[87] Julius Caesar, *Commentaries on the Gallic War*, VI, 13, http://classics.mit.edu/Caesar/gallic.6.6.html

northern island such as Britain, so far from the 'enlightened' Mediterranean world. On the other hand, the second part of the sentence seems to validate the presumption, as a majority of Druids appeared to cross the Channel from Gaul to Britain, to study Druidism on the main British isle. What this clearly means is, one, there was some kind of Druidic school in Britain, and two, there are reasons to believe Druidism was born there, but the theory has yet to find confirmation. Let's now see if we can confirm this assumption.

A Greek origin?

Modern scholars, in general, doubt a British origin of Druidism and think that the Druids' knowledge and practices must be some degenerate form of Greek philosophy. Nora Chadwick, for example, who made an in-depth study of Druids through the eyes of Greek and Roman classical sources, has been criticised for her 'denial of druidic ideas and concepts having any great value in their own right.'[88] She writes:

> I would suggest that their 'discipline' represents a peripheral and remote survival of the brilliant speculative era which had achieved its highest expression in the great Ionian philosophers of the sixth century B.C. and which penetrated the more remote countries of the West, transformed by many and varied superimpositions at a later date.[89]

Calling for a foreign origin of Druidism, she also unhesitantly downgrades their knowledge, writing that 'their ideas could be no more than the outer ripple on the circumference from the great centers of thought elsewhere,' ideas which are nothing more than 'a share in the current views of the intelligentsia of the Western Mediterranean world, orally and therefore imperfectly transmitted, orally learnt and imperfectly apprehended.'[90]

This view that Druidism certainly did not arise in Britain is also shared by Jean-Louis Brunaux, who confidently writes: 'It is however now accepted by all historians that the doctrine of the Druids could not rise in Britain to be transmitted to Gaul, rather the contrary is true.'[91] Jan De Vries, a Dutch scholar who wrote about the Celts' religions, concurs with

---

[88] Foreword to the Second Edition by Anne Ross in Nora K. Chadwick (1966), *The Druids*, Cardiff: University of Wales Press, 1997, p. xi

[89] Nora K. Chadwick, *op. cit.*, p.101-2

[90] Ibid., p. 57

[91] Jean-Louis Brunaux, *Les Druides. Des Philosophes chez les barbares*, Paris: Seuil 2006, p. 350

Brunaux. According to him, Druidism came to Britain with the Belgae, possibly as early as the late 4th or early 3rd century BC.[92]

Are we to believe Brunaux and De Vries who think that Druidism penetrated Britain only late in time, coming from the continent? And is there any evidence that, as Chadwick contends, Druidism is only an imperfect form of the Greek intelligentsia's brilliant knowledge that somehow reached the westernmost coasts of Gaul and then Britain? The problem with assuming a more local origin of Druidism in Britain is that it is contrary to conventional history, according to which Britain was basically a barbaric land before Greek thinking lately contaminated this coldish, remote island.

True, it has often been noted that there are many similarities between Pythagorean philosophy and the metaphysical beliefs of Druidism. Pythagoras lived in the 6th century BC. Is there really a connection between Pythagoras' teaching and Druidism? If so, which thinking system influenced the other?

First of all, let's see what are the common points between the two.

Similarities between Druidism and Pythagoreanism

The connection between Druids and Pythagoreans have long been pointed out by classical authors. As Ammianus Marcellinus wrote, both systems included a belief in an immortal soul:

> The Druids, being loftier than the rest in intellect, and bound together in fraternal organisations, as the authority of Pythagoras determined, were elevated by their investigation of obscure and profound subjects, and scorning all things human, pronounced the soul immortal.[93]

Apart from this metaphysical belief, Pythagoras is known to have worn a white robe,[94] just like the Druids. Memory was very important in both systems. What was taught to members, like the mathematical discoveries of Pythagoras, including the famous theorem he was the first to demonstrate, had to be kept a complete secret,[95] which is highly

---

[92] Cited by Jean-Louis Brunaux, *Les Druides. Des Philosophes chez les barbares*, Paris: Seuil 2006, p. 350

[93] Ammianus Marcellinus, *The History*, XV, 9: 8: http://penelope.uchicago.edu/Thayer/E/Roman/Texts/Ammian/15*.html

[94] Daniel Saintillan in *Dictionnaire de la Grèce antique*, Paris: Encyclopaedia Universalis and Albin Michel, 2000, p. 1111

[95] Guy and M.-F. Rachet (1985), *Dictionnaire de la civilisation grecque*, Paris: Références Larousse, 1986, p. 221

reminiscent of the Druidic rule. Of course, one of the main interests of Pythagoras and his movement was mathematics—arithmetic and geometry—and we have good reason to believe geometry was also central to Druidism (see Part II). As Aristotle wrote, 'the so-called Pythagoreans, who were the first to take up mathematics, not only advanced this study, but also having been brought up in it they thought its principles were the principles of all things.'[96]

Let us now turn to the key question: which school of thought influenced the other? Interestingly, it appears that Alexandrian authors disagreed with each other on the direction of transmission. It stands to reason that if some of them were right, then the others must have been wrong. The goal of the next section is to determine who was right and who was wrong.

Druids learning from Pythagoreans?

According to Hippolytus, a Roman theologian living in the early 3rd century AD, the Druids had 'profoundly examined the Pythagorean philosophy' and consequently could 'foretell matters by the ciphers and numbers according to the Pythagorean skill.'[97]

Diogenes Laërtius, also living in the 3rd century AD, expressed the same opinion. In the very first line of his book, however, he mentions a traditional view that appears to have been shared by many authors at the time: 'Some say that the study of philosophy originated with the barbarians. In that among the Persians there existed the Magi, and among the Babylonians or Assyrians the Chaldaei, among the Indians the Gymnosophistae, and among the Celts and Gauls men who were called Druids and Semnothei ['Holy men']…'[98] A few lines later, he concludes that traditions must be wrong, that some people 'ignorantly impute to the barbarians the merits of the Greeks,'[99] as the word *philosophy* itself is Greek: 'And thus did philosophy arise among the Greeks, and its very name shows that it has no connection with the barbarians.'[100]

---

[96] Aristotle (c. 350 BC), *Metaphysics*, 1, 5: http://classics.mit.edu/Aristotle/metaphysics.1.i.html

[97] Hippolytus (3rd c. AD), *Philosophumena*, i. 22, cited by Nora K. Chadwick (1966), *The Druids*, Cardiff: University of Wales Press, 1997, p. 60

[98] Diogenes Laërtius (3rd c. AD), *The Lives and Opinions of Eminent Philosophers*, I, I: http://classicpersuasion.org/pw/diogenes/dlintro.htm

[99] Ibid., I, III

[100] Ibid., I, IV

Diogenes Laërtius thus draws his conclusions mainly because his own intuition (not to say chauvinism) tells him that Greek philosophy is too refined and prestigious to have been invented anywhere else than in Greece. And yet, he knows perfectly well that by asserting this *he goes against an extant tradition.* Because the word *philosophy* is Greek, does that necessarily make all philosophy Greek?

Pythagoreans learning from Barbarians?

By contrast, Clement of Alexandria (c. 150 AD - c. 215 AD), a Christian theologian who lived about a century before Hippolytus and Diogenes Laërtius, fully endorsed this tradition. He writes that 'the oldest wise men and philosophers among the Greeks' were mostly 'barbarians by extraction' who had been 'trained among barbarians.'[101] He adds that 'Plato does not deny that he procured all that is most excellent in philosophy from the barbarians.'[102]

Plato, a most famous philosopher and mathematician, lived in the late 5th and early 4th century BC—about six centuries and a half *before* Hippolytus and Diogenes Laërtius. Who must have known better than the others? The obvious answer is Plato.

Clement also makes it clear that Pythagoras himself derived most of his philosophy from non-Greek teachers:

> And it is well known that Plato is found perpetually celebrating the barbarians, remembering that both himself and Pythagoras learned the most and the noblest of their dogmas among the barbarians. Wherefore he also called the races of the barbarians, 'races of barbarian philosophers'[103]

More specifically, Clement states that Pythagoras was taught by the *Galatae*, or Gauls: 'Alexander [Polyhistor], in his book *On the Pythagorean Symbols*, relates that... Pythagoras was a hearer of the Galatæ and the Brahmins.'[104]

Clement's conclusion is then unambiguous. He clearly thinks the tradition related, yet not accepted as true by Diogenes Laërtius, is correct:

> Thus philosophy, a thing of the highest utility, flourished in antiquity among the barbarians, shedding its light over the nations. And afterwards it came to Greece. First in its ranks were the

---

[101] Clement of Alexandria (2nd-3rd c. AD), *The Stromata*, I, 15: http://www.newadvent.org/fathers/02101.htm

[102] Ibid.

[103] Ibid.

[104] Ibid.

> prophets of the Egyptians; and the Chaldeans among the Assyrians; and the Druids among the Gauls; and the Samanæans [shamans] among the Bactrians; and the philosophers of the Celts; and the Magi of the Persians ... The Indian gymnosophists are also in the number, and the other barbarian philosophers.[105]

It is interesting to note that one of the items in the list is redundant: 'the philosophers of the Celts' undoubtedly are one and the same thing as the 'Druids among the Gauls.' It is now well understood—and this is not a matter of debate any more—that the terms *Galatae* and *Keltae* (i.e. Celts) were interchangeably used by both Strabo[106] and Diodorus Siculus.[107]

We also know that this tradition was endorsed by Celsus, a Greek (or possibly Roman) philosopher. An opponent of early Christianity, he wrote a treatise called *The True Word* in Alexandria in the 2nd century AD, in which he set out to refute the validity of Christianity. His work is now lost but he was quoted by Origen, an Alexandrian scholar and theologian living in the 3rd century AD. Origen writes that Celsus classed 'the Odrysians, and Samothracians, and Eleusinians, and Hyperboreans among the most ancient and learned nations,' and styled 'the Galactophagi of Homer, and the Druids of the Gauls, and the Getae [Thracian tribes of the Lower Danube], most learned and ancient tribes.'[108] Interestingly, the Eleusinians are part of this list of 'ancient and learned nations.'

Cyril of Alexandria, the Patriarch of Alexandria in the 5th century AD, in his thesis *Contra Julianum*, also presents a list honouring the Druids of the 'Gauls' and the *Philosophati* of the Celts, and barbarians in general for their 'probity, justice and philosophy,' giving Alexander Polyhistor as his source.[109]

As British archaeologist Thomas Downing Kendrick commented: 'To have had even this much of reputation outside their own Keltic world in

---

[105] Ibid.

[106] Strabo, *Geography*, IV, 4, 2, and II, 5, 28; IV, 1, 1; IV, 1, 5; IV, 1, 14; IV, 4, 2: http://penelope.uchicago.edu/Thayer/E/Roman/Texts/Strabo/4D*.html

[107] Diodorus Siculus, *The Library of History*, V, 24; XVII, 113; XXV, 13: http://penelope.uchicago.edu/Thayer/E/Roman/Texts/Diodorus_Siculus/5B*.html

[108] Origen (3rd c. AD), *Contra Celsus*, I, 16

[109] cited in Nora K. Chadwick (1966), *The Druids*, Cardiff: University of Wales Press, 1997, p. 62

the second century before Christ the druids must have been already long established.'[110]

As a conclusion, it is fair to say that there was among the Ancient Greek and Roman authors—as early as Plato's time—a tradition which made philosophy a non-Greek invention, and which cited the Gallic Druids among those great philosophers who had taught their art and knowledge to Greeks. True, a few authors decided to run against the wind of tradition at some point, but this came only in the 3rd century AD. This tradition goes back several centuries before that, as even Nora Chadwick acknowledges:

> The tradition ... is given by Diogenes on the authority of two works of c. 200 B.C. ... and is probably considerably earlier than the period of 200 B.C. when it was evidently already in a written text ... we may in all probability go back to written sources of at least as early as the third century B.C.[111]

So I must disagree here with Hippolytus, Diogenes Laërtius and Nora Chadwick, and agree with Clement of Alexandria, Celsus, Cyril of Alexandria, Kendrick, and of course Plato. Denying a tradition only because it seems counter-intuitive doesn't explain why the tradition existed in the first place. Lacking any evidence to the contrary and applying Occam's razor or principle of parsimony, it seems logical to assume that this tradition was probably correct. If not, it is the onus of the one who denies this tradition to provide some explanation to its very existence. This being said, it is now left to the appreciation of the reader what conclusion to draw.

Pythagoras the Hyperborean Apollo

Many ancient authors, including Claudius Aelianus, a Roman author living in the early 3rd century AD, wrote that Pythagoras was a miracle worker with a golden leg, and that some of his contemporaries referred to him as the 'Hyperborean Apollo':

> Aristotle saith that Pythagoras was call'd by the Crotonians Hyperborean Apollo. The son of Nicomachus [Aristotle] farther saies, that he was at the same hour of the same day seen by many at Metapentium and at Croton, where he stood up at the Games. There also he shewed one of his Thighs, which was of Gold. The

---

[110] Thomas Downing Kendrick, *The Druids, A Study in Keltic Prehistory*, London, 1927, p. 75, cited by Nora K. Chadwick (1966, *The Druids*, Cardiff: University of Wales Press, 1997, p. 65

[111] Nora K. Chadwick, op. cit., p. 65

> same Author saies, that as he was passing over the River Nessus it called him, and that many heard the call.[112]

This is particularly interesting as we'll see in Part II that Hyperboreans referred to the people living in the North, and typically to Britain. We have seen before that Celsus classed the Hyperboreans 'among the most ancient and learned nations.'

Apollo was a major Greek deity. He was a God of Light and the Sun, a God of Truth and Prophecy, and a God of Music, among other attributes. Interestingly, Greeks thought that every winter Apollo rode the back of a swan and flew back to the land of the Hyperboreans, where he was said to originate, as sung by Callimachus—a Greek poet and scholar living in the 3rd century BC—in his 'Hymn to Apollo.'[113]

Milo of Croton, who according to tradition married Pythagoras' daughter Myia and was an associate of the philosopher, is also said to have been a Hyperborean Apollo.[114] Milo, a famed wrestler who won the Olympics six times, lived in Croton, a Greek colony in southern Italy, where Pythagoras founded his school.

Were Pythagoras and Milo taught by Druids coming from northwestern Europe? Was Milo himself a Celt?

Another similar figure, predating Pythagoras by a few decades, is Abaris the Hyperborean, a sage with the reputed ability to predict the future. He was also said to be a priest of Apollo, and was called 'the Hyperborean' because he was supposed to have learnt his knowledge in his homeland, Hyperborea, the far North. He was also said to travel the world flying on a golden arrow given to him by Apollo. As the Greek historian Herodotus, who lived in the 5th century BC, wrote:

> Let this suffice which has been said of the Hyperboreans; for the tale of Abaris, who is reported to have been a Hyperborean, I do not tell, namely how he carried the arrow about all over the earth, eating no food.[115]

Was Abaris a Druid? Could this arrow, given by the northern God of Light, on which he travelled around the world, allegorically refer to the Druidic abilities to know 'the extent of the world and of our earth' or

---

[112] Aelian (3rd c. AD), *Various History*, II, 26: http://penelope.uchicago.edu/aelian/varhist2.xhtml#chap26

[113] Callimachus, *Hymns*, 2, 5

[114] Aristotle, *fragment 191*

[115] Herodotus (5th century BC), *The Histories,* IV, 36: http://www.sacred-texts.com/cla/hh/hh4030.htm

'the magnitude and form of the earth and the world,' as Caesar and Pomponius Mela would have it?

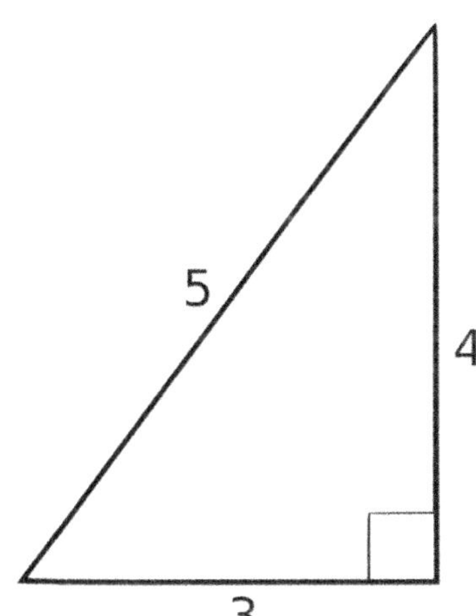

Coming back to Pythagoras, the theorem which bears his name to this day may not be his own discovery after all. True, Pythagoras is the first one to have ever demonstrated the theorem. But Pythagorean triangles—right-angled triangles whose sides are all integers, such as the well-known 3-4-5 triangle—were already known to the Megalithic people of Britain, as we'll see in Part II. Again, is it possible that Pythagoras was taught these mathematical facts by Druids?

Fig. 10. The first 'Pythagorean' triangle, a right-angled triangle with sides of respectively 3, 4 and 5 units.

We see that there is every reason to believe that the similarities between Druidism and Pythagoreanism are probably not accidental, and that the direction of transmission was from Druidism to Pythagoreanism, and not the other way round. This conclusion takes us back to the question of the origin of Druidism: if not from Greece, where did it come from?

The origin of the Druids in the British Isles?

Another argument that opposes a Greek origin of the Druids is that they did not seem to exist in southern Gaul, which is closer to Greece, and where Greek colonies existed, such as in Marseille, Nice, Agde, and so on. On the contrary, Druids were to be found in northern Gaul and in the British Isles. And if Druids were a Celtic institution, why weren't there any Druids in southern Gaul, in Germany or Galatia in Asia Minor, which was also conquered by Celts?

As Salomon Reinach, an early 20th-century French archaeologist points out:

> The Druids were the national clergy; they were found in the British Isles, and in Gaul, but not in Cisalpine Gaul, Germany or Galatia... According to Caesar, the Druids came from the island of Britain, and it is often held that they only penetrated into Gaul as

> missionaries some five hundred years before Christ. To this it may be objected that the megalithic monuments attest the power of a priesthood at an earlier period and that though the center of the Druidical association may have been Britain at the time of Caesar, it does not prove that the Druids came to Gaul from this island at a recent date. I am inclined to believe that Druidism first flourished in the neolithic period, especially in Ireland, that its influence soon spread to the continent, and that the Druids rejoined their Irish confreres after the Roman conquest, and came to an end where they had begun.[116]

Whether Druids originate in Ireland, Britain or northern Gaul, they weren't found anywhere else, so it is safe to think that whoever informed Caesar may have been right, which would mean that the Druidic institution is British. Alternatively, they could just as well have come from Ireland, as Reinach contends. Such was also the opinion of Sir John Rhŷs, a Welsh scholar and fellow of the British Academy in the late 19th century, who thought that there is no evidence of Druidism in southern Britain at the time of Caesar, with the exception of the island of Anglesey, which is very close to Ireland.[117]

In addition, a few ancient authors thought that Druids had influenced other cultures. According to Pliny the Elder in the 1st century AD, the magic art of the Druids was still alive in Britain in his time, even after the Druids had been repressed by the Romans, and his opinion was that their art had 'crossed the very Ocean.' Pliny also thought that the mages of Persia had probably learnt from the British Druids, rather than the other way round:

> The Gallic provinces, too, were pervaded by the magic art, and that even down to a period within memory; for it was the Emperor Tiberius that put down their Druids, and all that tribe of wizards and physicians. But why make further mention of these prohibitions, with reference to an art which has now crossed the very Ocean even, and has penetrated to the void recesses of Nature? At the present day, struck with fascination, Britannia still cultivates this art, and that, with ceremonials so august, that she might almost seem to have been the first to communicate them to the people of Persia. To such a degree are nations throughout the

---

[116] Salomon Reinach, *Orpheus: a General History of Religion*, London: W Heinemann, 120-1: http://www.ebooksread.com/authors-eng/salomon-reinach/orpheus-a-general-history-of-religions-ala/page-13-orpheus-a-general-history-of-religions-ala.shtml

[117] Proceedings of the British Academy (1903-4), i. 55, cited by Nora K. Chadwick (1966), *The Druids*, Cardiff: University of Wales Press, 1997, p. 41

whole world, totally different as they are and quite unknown to one another, in accord upon this one point![118]

The ultimate origin of the Druids in the North Sea?

Another possibility is that the Druids indeed came from the British Isles, but that some of them originated from other islands more to the north, perhaps in the North Sea or beyond. Their lands or islands would have been submerged by the rising sea level. This is precisely what Ammianus Marcellinus wrote:

> The Drysidae [Druids] say that a part of the people was in fact indigenous, but that others also poured in from the remote islands and the regions across the Rhine, driven from their homes by continual wars and by the inundation of the stormy sea. Some assert that after the destruction of Troy a few of those who fled from the Greeks and were scattered everywhere occupied those regions, which were then deserted.[119]

That part of the Celts came from regions across the Rhine is well attested by archaeology, as the Celtic culture is generally considered to be descended from the Iron Age Hallstatt culture (c. 800 BC-450 BC), located in southern Germany and Austria, east of the upper or southern Rhine.

But Ammiannus' statement clearly indicates these people mostly fled lands east of the *lower* Rhine in Northern Europe, coming from lands flooded by the 'stormy sea,' most probably the North Sea, and even 'remote islands,' which again were probably located in the North Sea.

The North Sea hasn't always been a sea: there used to be a vast plain, and then a large island, but it was finally swallowed up by the sea a few millennia ago, right after the last Ice Age. Today it is known as the Dogger Bank—an underwater 160-mile-long sandbank in a shallow area of the North Sea. It was part of a huge landmass, today referred to as Doggerland, which once connected Britain to northern France, Belgium, the Netherlands, Germany and Denmark. As geophysicist Dr Richard Bates puts it,

> Doggerland was the real heartland of Europe until sea levels rose to give us the UK coastline of today. . . . We have now been able to model its flora and fauna, build up a picture of the ancient

---

[118] Pliny the Elder, *The Natural History*, XXX, 4: http://www.perseus.tufts.edu/hopper/text?doc=Perseus%3Atext%3A1999.02.0137%3Abook%3D30%3Achapter%3D4

[119] Ammianus Marcellinus, *The History*, XV, 9: 4-5: http://penelope.uchicago.edu/Thayer/E/Roman/Texts/Ammian/15*.html

people that lived there and begin to understand some of the dramatic events that subsequently changed the land, including the sea rising and a devastating tsunami.[120]

Fig. 11. Doggerland in the North Sea once became an island before being completely submerged in later times.

Among these amazing discoveries are underwater rivers and hills, flint used by humans, human burial sites, intriguing standing stones, and a mass mammoth grave.[121] With the gradual rising sea level this hilly landscape turned into an archipelago of low islands, before disappearing

---

[120] 'Hidden Doggerland underworld uncovered in North Sea,' BBC News, 4 Jul. 2012: http://www.bbc.co.uk/news/uk-scotland-edinburgh-east-fife-18687504
[121] Ibid.

completely underwater. According to archaeologists, who used geophysical modelling of data from oil and gas companies, the submersion was a slow process over thousands of years, ending between 6500 BC and 5500 BC.[122] We now know that a five-meter-high tsunami hit Doggerland, probably wiping out the last people living there at the time.[123]

I have personally long defended the idea that the myth of Atlantis emerged from the memory of a lost civilization in the North Sea,[124] a view which is strongly vindicated by the recent discoveries in this undersea area. Coming back to Ammianus Marcellinus' statement, that part of the Celts came from Troy, in the eastern Mediterranean region, this would clearly contradict a Northern European origin. However, there is the controversial but nevertheless highly documented hypothesis by Iman Jacob Wilkens, a Dutch researcher. In his book *Where Troy Once Stood*, he makes a convincing case that Troy was actually located in the Gog Magog hills near Cambridge in England, and that the Trojan war took place in the Atlantic, the English Channel and the North Sea.[125]

We know about the Trojan War thanks to Homer's poem the *Iliad*, which dates back to the 8th century BC, or about four centuries after the war actually took place. The war is also mentioned in the *Odyssey*. It was indeed Strabo's opinion that part of Ulysses' journey in the *Odyssey* had taken place in the Atlantic rather than in the Mediterranean. He drives his point home here, disagreeing with Greek historian Polybius (2nd century BC):

> But when he [Polybius] demolishes the argument that places the wanderings of Odysseus on Oceanus, and when he reduces the nine days' voyage and the distances covered thereon to exact measurements, he reaches the height of inconsistency. For at one moment he quotes the words of the poet: 'Thence for nine whole days was I borne by baneful winds'; and at another moment he suppresses statements. For Homer says also: 'Now after the ship had left the river-stream of Oceanus'; and 'In the island of Ogygia, where is the navel of the sea,' going on to say that the daughter of Atlas lives there; and again, regarding the Phaeacians, 'Far apart we live in the wash of the waves, the farthermost of men, and no

---

[122] ' "Britain's Atlantis" found at bottom of North Sea—a huge undersea world swallowed by the sea in 6500 BC,' Mail online, 2 Jul. 2012: http://www.dailymail.co.uk/sciencetech/article-2167731/Britains-Atlantis-North-sea--huge-undersea-kingdom-swamped-tsunami-5-500-years-ago.html

[123] http://www.bbc.com/news/science-environment-27224243

[124] See Sylvain Tristan, *Atlantide, premier empire européen*, Paris: Alphée, 2007

[125] Iman Jacob Wilkens, *Where Troy Once Stood*, Rider & Co, 1990

other mortals are conversant with us.' Now all these incidents are clearly indicated as being placed in fancy in the Atlantic Ocean.[126]

Conclusion

When you examine the ancient sources with an unbiased eye, you find that there is overwhelming evidence that Druidism is probably a *northern* institution—meaning either the British Isles or islands in the North Sea, possibly the lost island of Doggerland—not something Gallic, and even less something Greek. It might sound surprising, or even improbable, but one should not deny evidence just because it contradicts intuition.

Of course, a northern origin of Druidism does not mean that it was not born somewhere else *before it spread to northern Europe.* We'll see in Chapter Eleven that there are reasons to believe Druidism might ultimately come from Egypt, before spreading to northern Europe, and later arriving in Gaul.

Main points

- **Celtic Druids don't seem to have existed outside of Gaul and the British Isles**
- **Caesar thought Druids ultimately came from Britain**
- **Druids and Pythagoreans share many traits**
- **Alexandrian authors traditionally held Druids in high esteem, and thought the ancient Greek philosophers like Pythagoras had been 'trained among barbarians'**
- **Plato believed 'the noblest ideas' that he and Pythagoras shared had originally come from the 'barbarian philosophers'**
- **Pliny thought Druids had influenced other cultures on the planet**
- **The Megalithic monuments attest to the former power of a 'priesthood' similar to that of the Druids**
- **The Druids' ancestors seem to have lost a vast area of land ('Doggerland') in the North Sea, which might have given rise to the myth of Atlantis**

---

[126] Strabo, *Geography*, I, 2, 18: http://penelope.uchicago.edu/Thayer/E/Roman/Texts/Strabo/1B1*.html

Chapter Five: The Druids' Fall?

Most scholars consider that at the time of Caesar, the Druids' prestige had already considerably lost its shine. This was clearly Salomon Reinach's opinion: 'But it seems perfectly evident that at the time of Caesar, the power of the Druids had already declined; Gaul was no longer a theocracy.'[127] More recently, Jean-Louis Brunaux expressed the same view, as the latest archaeological finds appear to validate this thesis: 'The rise of the Druids brutally stops between the late 2nd century BC and the Roman conquest... In our opinion and on the basis of renewed archaeological data, the Druids left the social and political scene much before the massive arrival of the Romans.'[128]

The situation, of course, could only get worse after the Romans' conquest of Gaul. Pomponius Mela's remark that the Druids 'teach the most noble of the nation many things privately... in a cave, or in inaccessible woods'[129] seems to apply to a time when the Roman occupation made it hard for the Druids to practice their function openly.

How much do we know about the Druids' fall? Did Druidism disappear with the last Druids, or is it possible that their knowledge lived on one way or another?

The Druid Diviciacus, an ally of the Romans

According to mainstream archaeology, the decline of the Gauls came earliest among the Aedui Druids, dating back to at least the late 2nd century BC.[130] The Aedui had long been allied to Rome, signing a first treaty with the Romans in the late 3rd century BC. At the time of Caesar and contrary to most other Gallic people, the Aedui had long abandoned

---

[127] Reinach, op. cit. *Orpheus: a General History of Religion*, London: W Heinemann, 122

[128] Jean-Louis Brunaux, *Les Druides. Des Philosophes chez les barbares*, Paris: Seuil 2006, p. 293

[129] Pomponius Mela, *Description of the World*, III, 2

[130] Brunaux, *op. cit.*, p. 318

monarchy in favour of a more democratic form of government. It is a fact that Caesar's conquest of Gaul would have probably been less successful without the help of some Gallic tribes, especially that of the Aedui, amongst whom Diviciacus played a key part.[131]

Although never referred to by Caesar as a Druid, we know from Cicero (106 BC-43 BC), the famed Roman orator, statesman and philosopher, that Diviciacus was indeed a Druid. Cicero had interests in the commerce of wine in Gaul, more particularly in Diviciacus' family, and when the Sequani and Arverni attacked the Aedui in 63 BC, Diviciacus travelled to Rome and expounded the situation to the Senate, refusing to sit and pleading his cause leaning on his shield.[132] It is known that he stayed in Rome for quite a while, where he was Cicero's guest. We have already seen that Cicero reports that Diviciacus, just like himself, practiced divination and that he 'claimed to have that knowledge of nature which the Greeks call "physiologia," and he used to make predictions, sometimes by means of augury and sometimes by means of conjecture.'[133]

It is undeniable that Diviciacus helped Caesar. According to the Roman conqueror, Diviciacus was a chief of the Aedui, a great politician and a diplomat. Caesar recognised his 'distinguished faithfulness, justice, and moderation,'[134] as well as his paramount 'influence at home [among the Aedui] and in the rest of Gaul'.[135] This is probably because of the highly positive vision Caesar had of Diviciacus that the conqueror of Gaul deliberately omitted to mention in his text that Diviciacus was a Druid. Because of his closeness to the Romans, Diviciacus may not be a typical Druid: maybe he was more 'a product of the Roman policy of "romanizing" the young Gallic nobility.'[136] On the other hand, considering the help he provided to Caesar, this influential Druid perfectly fits the description by Dio Chrysostom, who wrote that 'the kings were not permitted to do or plan anything without the assistance of

---

[131] Ibid., p. 312

[132] *Latin Panegyrics*, 8, 3, cited by ibid., p. 305

[133] Cicero, *De Divinatione*, I, 41, 90, http://penelope.uchicago.edu/Thayer/E/Roman/Texts/Cicero/de_Divinatione/1*.html

[134] Julius Caesar, *Commentaries on the Gallic War*, I, 19: http://www.perseus.tufts.edu/hopper/text?doc=Perseus%3Atext%3A1999.02.0001%3Abook%3D1%3Achapter%3D19

[135] Ibid., I, 20

[136] Nora K. Chadwick (1966), *The Druids*, Cardiff: University of Wales Press, 1997, p. 108

these wise men, so that in truth it was they who ruled, while the kings became their servants and the ministers of their will'.[137]

Diviciacus had a little brother, Dumnorix, who contrary to him was a staunch anti-Roman chieftain. Diviciacus once managed to obtain pardon for his brother from Caesar, who had him placed under close surveillance after that. But on another occasion Caesar wished to take Dumnorix with him on an expedition to Britain, and the devoted Gallic patriot proved reluctant to go. Dumnorix 'said he was prevented by divine admonitions,'[138] which could mean he was also a Druid. In the end, Dumnorix refused embarkation and resisted, shouting that 'he was free and the subject of a free state.'[139] Caesar finally had him slain, which enabled the Roman conqueror to regain the Aedui cavalry to his side.

So, although they were brothers and quite possibly both of them were Druids, Diviciacus clearly did everything to help the Romans, whereas Dumnorix opposed them. So there is no doubt that Diviciacus was a Druid, and that he came from a region which was very close to Alesia, and yet he was an ally to Caesar in the Romanisation of Gaul. How could that be?

It seems clear that Diviciacus belonged to those Druids who believed that the Romanisation of Gaul was a 'necessary evil,' perhaps because he was fond of certain aspects of Roman civilisation, which he saw as a form of progress and pleasant sophistication, or perhaps because he simply didn't want his people to be exterminated, hence viewing collaboration as a required way of surviving the otherwise 'inevitable' annihilation of the Gallic culture. Did it mean that he also viewed the predictable decline of Druidism that would necessarily follow as something inevitable too, or had he, and/or his fellow Druids, anticipated a form of secret safeguarding of the institution? We'll come back to this key point in due time.

---

[137] Dio Chrysostom, *Discourses*, XLIX, 8, http://penelope.uchicago.edu/Thayer/E/Roman/Texts/Dio_Chrysostom/Discourses/49*.html

[138] Julius Caesar, *Commentaries on the Gallic War*, V, 6: http://www.perseus.tufts.edu/hopper/text?doc=Perseus%3Atext%3A1999.02.0001%3Abook%3D5%3Achapter%3D6

[139] Ibid., V, 7

The gradual repression of Druidism

Around 12 BC[140] a prestigious Roman school of learning—a university, no less, to use a term frequently used to describe this school—opened in Augustodunum, the newly built Roman city which replaced Bibracte, the former capital of the Aedui. In this school the young Gallic nobles learnt the liberal arts, and of course this meant the Druids were no longer the sole ones to hold knowledge in Gaul.

Nora Chadwick perfectly epitomises the situation in this sentence: 'The bell which announced the opening of the first session of the Roman university of Augustodunum sounded the death-knell of the oral druidical schools of Bibracte, and drove their teachers [the Druids] to the backwoods.'[141] One can easily imagine the ravages the wider spread of writing must have caused on Druids, who must have suddenly appeared to many as obsolete. Druids had always been regarded as 'very knowledgeable' philosophers, people who were the intermediaries between humans and the divinities, and astronomers who knew the motions of stars and hence made calendars. With such Roman schools arriving in Gaul, the Druids would inevitably lose their supremacy.

Because they were under the pressure of heavy debts, in the reign of Roman emperor Tiberius in 21 AD many Gallic cities broke into revolt. They may also have been protesting against the suppression of Druids, and perhaps even encouraged by them to revolt, as Druids were probably 'the most formidable nationalist and anti-Roman force with which the Romans had to contend.'[142] According to the German historian Theodor Mommsen, the main goal of the revolt of the Aedui and the Treveri was to gain the control back of Augustodunum, because the Gallic youth were studying there.[143] Tacitus (56 AD-117 AD), the Roman senator and one of the greatest historians of this period, relates this event in his *Annals*:

> Among the Aedui trouble came in the graver form to be expected from the superior wealth of the community and the remoteness of the suppressing force. The tribal capital, Augustodunum, had been seized by armed cohorts of Sacrovir, whose intention was to enlist those cadets of the great Gallic families who were receiving a

---

[140] Nora K. Chadwick (1966), *The Druids*, Cardiff: University of Wales Press, 1997, p. 71

[141] Ibid., preface, xix

[142] Ibid., p. 72

[143] Theodor Mommsen, *The Provinces of the Roman Empire* (translated by W P Dickson), vol. i, London, 1909, p. 112

> liberal education at the city-schools, and to use them as pledges [hostages] for the adhesion of their parents and relatives[144]

Tacitus also reports that in 16 AD the Pythagoreans and magi were expelled from Italy, or quite simply killed:

> Other resolutions of the senate ordered the expulsion of the astrologers and magic-mongers from Italy. One of their number, Lucius Pituanius, was flung from the [Tarpeian] Rock; another—Publius Marcius—was executed by the consuls outside the Esquiline Gate according to ancient usage and at sound of trumpet.[145]

'Serpents' eggs' or a Druidic practice the Romans frowned upon

Roman naturalist Pliny the Elder (23 AD-79 AD) vehemently upheld the Roman policy of suppressing the Druids, whom he viewed as a tribe of magicians with 'monstrous rites,' such as performing human sacrifices:

> The Gallic provinces, too, were pervaded by the magic art, and that even down to a period within memory; for it was the Emperor Tiberius[146] that put down their Druids, and all that tribe of wizards and physicians... Such being the fact, then, we cannot too highly appreciate the obligation that is due to the Roman people, for having put an end to those monstrous rites, in accordance with which, to murder a man was to do an act of the greatest devoutness, and to eat his flesh was to secure the highest blessings of health.[147]

In another passage Pliny reports that Druids were using 'serpents' eggs' as charms to win lawsuits, supposedly made up with the gluey substance produced by the mouth of two entwining snakes. In reality, these 'eggs' were most probably sea-urchin shells, fossilised or not, or sometimes artificial rings of stone, glass or baked clay. This shows that in their way Druids were probably dexterous conjurors who used the credulity of

---

[144] Tacitus, *Annals*, III, 43:
http://penelope.uchicago.edu/Thayer/E/Roman/Texts/Tacitus/Annals/3C*.html

[145] Ibid., II, 32

[146] Tiberius was the second Roman emperor from 14 AD to 37 AD. But it is quite possible that Pliny made a mistake, and actually meant Claudius, who was the fourth Roman emperor from 41 AD to 54 AD, and whose first name was Tiberius (See Haarhoff, *Schools of Gaul*, Oxford, 1920, p. 15).

[147] Pliny the Elder, *The Natural History*, XXX, 4:
http://www.perseus.tufts.edu/hopper/text?doc=Perseus%3Atext%3A1999.02.0137%3Abook%3D30%3Achapter%3D4

their devotees to achieve their goals. Interestingly, these beliefs seem to have endured till very recent times in Cornwall and Wales.[148] Also of interest is the fact that Pliny attributes the symbol of snakes entwined around a caduceus to this alleged interlacement of snakes.

Pliny here cites the case of a Gallic chief who had been granted Roman knighthood and who was eventually sentenced to death for possessing such a serpents' egg, which shows that anything connected to Druidic rites and superstitions was considered a crime at some point in Rome. The passage is reported here in full, as the story is quite entertaining. It is also an enlightening account, both with regard to this singular Druidic practice and to the way Druidism or superstitions even remotely connected to it came to be seen in Rome in the course of the 1st century AD:

> In addition to the above, there is another kind of egg, held in high renown by the people of the Gallic provinces, but totally omitted by the Greek writers. In summer time, numberless snakes become artificially entwined together, and form rings around their bodies with the viscous slime which exudes from their mouths, and with the foam secreted by them: the name given to this substance is 'anguinum.' The Druids tell us, that the serpents eject these eggs into the air by their hissing, and that a person must be ready to catch them in a cloak, so as not to let them touch the ground; they say also that he must instantly take to flight on horseback, as the serpents will be sure to pursue him, until some intervening river has placed a barrier between them. The test of its genuineness, they say, is its floating against the current of a stream, even though it be set in gold. But, as it is the way with magicians to be dexterous and cunning in casting a veil about their frauds, they pretend that these eggs can only be taken on a certain day of the moon; as though, forsooth, it depended entirely upon the human will to make the moon and the serpents accord as to the moment of this operation.
>
> I myself, however, have seen one of these eggs: it was round, and about as large as an apple of moderate size; the shell of it was formed of a cartilaginous substance, and it was surrounded with numerous cupules, as it were, resembling those upon the arms of the polypus: it is held in high estimation among the Druids. The possession of it is marvellously vaunted as ensuring success in law-

---

148 Ibid., XXIX, 12, note 1 (John Bostock, M.D., F.R.S. H.T. Riley, Esq., B.A. London. Taylor and Francis, Red Lion Court, Fleet Street, 1855): http://www.perseus.tufts.edu/hopper/text?doc=Perseus%3Atext%3A1999.02.0137%3Abook%3D29%3Achapter%3D12

suits, and a favourable reception with princes; a notion which has been so far belied, that a Roman of equestrian rank, a native of the territory of the Vocontii, who, during a trial, had one of these eggs in his bosom, was slain by the late Emperor Tiberius, and for no other reason, that I know of, but because he was in possession of it. It is this entwining of serpents with one another, and the fruitful results of this unison, that seem to me to have given rise to the usage among foreign nations, of surrounding the caduceus with representations of serpents, as so many symbols of peace - it must be remembered, too, that on the caduceus, serpents are never represented as having crests.[149]

Claudius' repression of the Druids

According to the Roman historian Suetonius (c. 69 AD-c. 122 AD), author of *The Twelve Caesars*, a 'classic' set of biographies of Julius Caesar and the first eleven emperors of Rome, Claudius severely repressed the Druids from 54 AD on, probably because they were seen as a dissident and insubordinate political element. 'He [Claudius] utterly abolished the cruel and inhuman religion of the Druids among the Gauls, which under Augustus had merely been prohibited to Roman citizens'.[150]

In one famous passage Tacitus describes how the Druids, who had drawn back to the island of Mona—modern Anglesey in northwestern Wales—let themselves be massacred by the Roman troops in 60 AD:

> He [Suetonius Paulinus] prepared accordingly to attack the island of Mona, which had a considerable population of its own, while serving as a haven for refugees; and, in view of the shallow and variable channel, constructed a flotilla of boats with flat bottoms. By this method the infantry crossed; the cavalry, who followed, did so by fording or, in deeper water, by swimming at the side of their horses.
>
> On the beach stood the adverse array, a serried mass of arms and men, with women flitting between the ranks. In the style of Furies, in robes of deathly black and with dishevelled hair, they brandished their torches; while a circle of Druids, lifting their hands to heaven and showering imprecations, struck the troops with such an awe at the extraordinary spectacle that, as though their limbs were paralysed, they exposed their bodies to wounds

---

[149] Ibid., XXIX, 12

[150] Suetonius, *The Lives of the Caesars*, 'The Life of Claudius,' 25, 5: http://penelope.uchicago.edu/Thayer/E/Roman/Texts/Suetonius/12Caesars/Claudius*.html

> without an attempt at movement. Then, reassured by their general, and inciting each other never to flinch before a band of females and fanatics, they charged behind the standards, cut down all who met them, and enveloped the enemy in his own flames. The next step was to install a garrison among the conquered population, and to demolish the groves consecrated to their savage cults: for they considered it a duty to consult their deities by means of human entrails.[151]

We also know from Tacitus that in 70 AD the Druids, by then probably teaching in sequestered places—such as the caves or inaccessible glades referred to by Pomponius Mela—for their own safety, were nonetheless still prestigious and influential, and still wishing to free Gaul, resorting to prophecies according to which a power shift from Rome to Gaul was about to be witnessed. This happened right after the death of Vitellius, a Roman emperor for eight months only, who himself had succeeded to two other emperors who had risen and fallen very quickly, within the context of a civil war which had started after the suicide of Nero (this period is known as the Year of the Four Emperors):

> 'Once long ago Rome was captured by the Gauls, but since Jove's home was unharmed, the Roman power stood firm: now this fatal conflagration has given a proof from heaven of the divine wrath and presages the passage of the sovereignty of the world to the peoples beyond the Alps.' Such were the vain and superstitious prophecies of the Druids. Moreover, the report had gone abroad that the Gallic chiefs, when sent by Otho to oppose Vitellius, had pledged themselves before their departure not to fail the cause of freedom in case an unbroken series of civil wars and internal troubles destroyed the power of the Roman people.[152]

This passage is significant because it shows that the Romans' imperial efforts had not been able to suppress the Druidic institution. Even Nora Chadwick concedes this fact, and goes on to say that Druidism probably survived for quite a long time: 'After this we hear no more of the druids as an organized body, but it is unlikely that they would completely disappear quickly.'[153]

She adds that:

---

[151] Tacitus, *Annals*, XIV, 29-30: http://penelope.uchicago.edu/Thayer/E/Roman/Texts/Tacitus/Annals/14B*.html

[152] Tacitus, *The Histories*, IV, 54: http://penelope.uchicago.edu/Thayer/E/Roman/Texts/Tacitus/Histories/4C*.html

[153] Nora K. Chadwick (1966), *The Druids*, Cardiff: University of Wales Press, 1997, p. 74

> We cannot doubt that, like the Gallic anti-Roman Aeduan king Dumnorix, the druids had ample scope in Gaul for underground activities in the interest of militant conservative Gallic nationalism, and that they continued to exert their influence on the Gallic youths sent to them for their education. As time went on the scope of the druids would inevitably weaken, especially with the development of the romanizing educational policy of Augustodunum and other Roman schools in Gaul, and the more direct proscription of druidism which we can trace briefly from Augustus to Claudius... What, after all, does our evidence for the actual 'suppression' amount to? Very little indeed![154]

What if these 'underground activities' had not completely disappeared? Chadwick states that the repression was quite 'brief' in historical terms. What's more, we know that the Roman descriptions of Druidic practices and the repression of Druids by them are very likely to be tinged with political bias. So, if the Romans hadn't been able to fully eradicate the institution, why should we think that Druidism would die off for good? What if Druidism—or more precisely Druidic knowledge—had survived more than is usually recognised by historians, albeit through 'underground' channels? We'll come back to this topic in detail in Part III.

Main points

- **Druids used to be even more powerful than kings, and were their advisors**
- **Diviciacus, a Druid from Aedui, helped the Romans conquer Gaul**
- **The Roman city of Augustodunum replaced Bibracte as the Aedui Capital**
- **Under Roman occupation Druidism was briefly repressed**
- **Druids had no choice but to meet in backwoods or caves**
- **Druidic practices, such as possessing a 'serpents' egg,' became a crime in Rome**
- **Under Emperor Claudius, Druids were massacred in Anglesey**
- **Nora Chadwick thinks Druids have long continued their activities 'underground'**

---

[154] Ibid., p. 76

PART II

REWIND: PROTO-DRUIDS IN MEGALITHIC TIMES AND BEFORE

(5000 BC - 800 BC)

Chapter Six:
The Megalithic People

We have seen in Part I that the Druidic institution is very likely to have existed in northwestern Europe before the Celts settled the area. Is there any evidence that a particular people might have had their own Proto-Druids? According to Salomon Reinach, 'the megalithic monuments attest the power of a priesthood at an earlier period'. What proof is there that the Megalithic people may have had their own Proto-Druids, who would have been the ancestors of the Celtic Druids?

Although archaeologists generally do not regard the Megalithic monuments as the work of a unique, cohesive civilisation, there is no denying that a 'Megalithic idea' swept along the coasts of northwestern Europe, as well as on its numerous islands, from about 5000 BC on.

The word *megalith* derives from the Ancient Greek and literally means 'great stone.' Thousands of these huge pieces of rock were erected during nearly four millennia! That is roughly between 5000 BC and 1200 BC.

The Megalithic monuments assume different forms. There are portal tombs called dolmens, which are chambers made from upright stones on the sides and usually a huge flat capstone at the top. Passage graves consisted of long passageways leading to a chamber, the whole structure being covered with earth. Another common type of megalith is the standing stone, or menhir, which could be either on its own or arranged with others, forming stone circles or stone alignments.

A Megalithic timeline

Scholars initially believed that megaliths in Western and Northern Europe represented the degenerate variations of the magnificent cultures of the eastern part of the Mediterranean, such as the ziggurats of Mesopotamia, the pyramids of Egypt or the palaces of Minoan Crete. A plausible theory, but radiocarbon dating altered this simplistic vision, as the most ancient megaliths are older than many of the stone structures erected by these civilisations.

If radiocarbon dating suggests that the first megaliths were erected in Turkey and Egypt, they may or may not be connected to the Megalithic wave that started in Western Europe around 5000 BC, seven millennia ago, that quickly rolled over the coasts of both northwestern Europe and the British Isles, and those of the Mediterranean.

The most ancient Megalithic structures in Europe seem to have been created in Portugal and Spain around 5000 BC. After that, megaliths were erected in France, especially in Brittany, around 4800 BC. The Great Broken Menhir at Locmariaquer was erected c. 4800 BC, and the Barnénez cairn or stone mound—the first European pyramid—c. 4700 BC. There are also some Megalithic temples on the Mediterranean island of Malta, which date back to c. 4400 BC. The oldest Megalithic structures in Britain (England and Wales) and in Corsica seem to have been constructed around 4000 BC, and c. 3700 BC they had started to appear in Ireland as well.

Circa 3500 BC, megaliths began to make their appearance in Germany and Belgium, and also on the Mediterranean islands of Sardinia and Sicily. In the following century the 'Megalithic idea' had reached Scandinavia, with megaliths in Sweden and Denmark, and also in the Netherlands. Circa 3200 BC, numerous dolmens and stone circles were erected in the Caucasus, east of the Black Sea, and in the following century—c. 3100 BC—in the Middle East. The date of 3100 BC also corresponds to the first phase of Stonehenge in Britain.

Circa 3000 BC the Megalithic wave hit Orkney in northern Scotland. By 2500 BC megaliths started flourishing in the Arabian peninsula, for instance in Yemen. Megalithic monuments, smaller in size but in great numbers, also spread over northern Africa, in what is today known as the Mahgreb, especially on the Mediterranean coast. Although they are difficult to date, they seem to have appeared in the 2nd millennium BC.[155] And by c. 1500 BC the Megalithic phenomenon appeared in India, Nepal and Tibet.

Circa 1200 BC the Megalithic culture quite abruptly came to an end. The reasons for its collapse remain unclear. But it is interesting to note that it roughly corresponds to the date Heracles is supposed to have founded Alesia (see Chapter Three).

-[155] Jean Guilaine (1994), *La Mer partagée. La Méditerranée avant l'écriture, 7000-2000 avant Jésus-Christ,* Paris: Hachette Littératures, 2005, p. 492-5

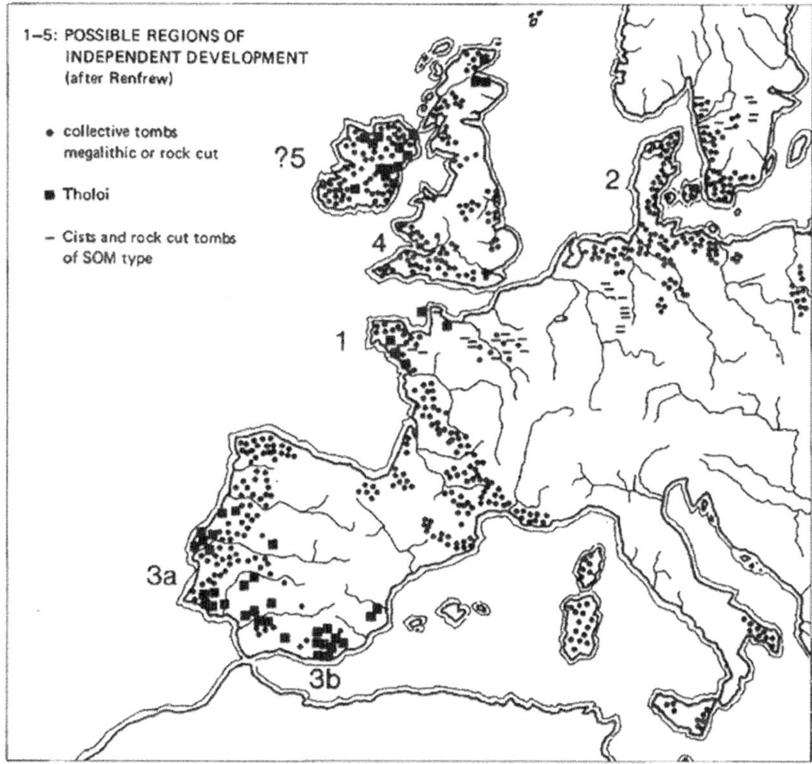

Fig. 12. Megaliths in Western Europe.

There are also some megaliths in Korea and Japan (1st millennium BC), and even in the New World (Colombia), but these structures are much more recent (c. 600 BC) and do not seem to be connected to those of the Old World. Another independent Megalithic culture also flourished in comparatively recent times (18th century AD) in Madagascar.

Sea people

Most megaliths are concentrated on the coastal areas and the islands of northwestern Europe and the Mediterranean. This seems to indicate that most, if not all, Megalithic people were experienced navigators. The lack of megaliths near the North Sea might be explained by the fact that the North Sea coastline has greatly receded with time, and that many megaliths are now below sea level, as has been confirmed by recent findings in the Dogger Bank area (see Chapter Four).

There is no doubt the Megalithic idea is associated with sea people. French historian Fernand Niel is positive:

> Whatever way the 'dolmenic idea' spread, it is certain this idea was propagated by sea people. No dolmenic grouping far from the seashore, or radically cut off from the clusters along the coast, exists. What's more, the insular quality of the Megalithic expansion proves it. The examples of Ireland, the Isles of Scilly, the Channel Islands or Corsica show that the custom of raising portal tombs and standing stones was brought in these islands by navigators. It is certain that the sea was the route used by the 'dolmenic idea.' Where did these navigators come from? We don't really know and the mystery remains total.[156]

It is highly unlikely that the Megalithic idea spread overland, as the main continental routes, such as the Danube, the Rhone or the Garonne are mostly empty of Megalithic sites. In any case, at the time the Megalithic monuments were made, Britain, Ireland, Orkney, Malta, the Balearic islands, Corsica and Sardinia were already islands, which is sufficient proof that the Megalithic people—even if they belonged to 'different' peoples—were skilful seafarers, able to navigate in high sea, including the Mediterranean and also the Atlantic Ocean, and probably the North Sea as well. Coincidental developments are, by way of consequence, highly unlikely.

An enigma

Oddly enough, the oldest megaliths are sometimes the most impressive, as if the culture had somehow degenerated with the millennia rather than getting more sophisticated with time.

In the village of Locmariaquer in Brittany, the Great Broken Menhir of Er Grah, the tallest standing stone ever erected in Europe—now broken into four enormous pieces—was erected c. 4800-4700 BC. Only in the 4th century AD (or five *millennia* after it) was a taller standing stone erected in Ethiopia. The fallen giant is located on an isthmus in a megalith-rich land, not very far from the famous Carnac alignments, which stand about 10 km (6 mi) to the west.

I won't ever forget that day of April 2002 when I first caught a glimpse of these huge pieces of stone in the pouring rain, sitting in my car on the small road curving only a few yards away from the broken piece of rock. I slowed the speed of the vehicle to a deliberate crawl so as to enjoy the view. I was both breathless and fascinated. I parked the automobile in a nearby car park and, ignoring the violent rain, I rushed

---

[156] Fernand Niel, *Dolmens et menhirs*, Paris: Que sais-je ? Presses universitaires de France, 1957, p. 70

outside to take another look at the age-old giant. Thousands of years of rain had only partially worn this 300-ton, 21-meter-long piece of gneiss which is thought to have been felled—unless it accidentally fell on its own, but this hypothesis isn't favoured by archaeologists—as early as half a millennium after its erection. This huge piece of rock appears to have been extracted about 15 km (10 miles) from its current location, in the isthmus of Rhuys or Arradon, requiring the cooperation of countless individuals and oxen, as well as the power of tides.

According to Jean L'Helgouac'h, a French prehistorian and archaeologist, such a project—the transport as much as the erection of the stone—could only be carried out by ingenious brains and exceptional means and organisation, a surprising feat as agriculture had by then just reached Armorica (Brittany): 'It seems obvious that a lot of people were involved—first and foremost, excellent engineers, skilful technicians who had precise knowledge about manoeuvring forces, supports, levers, reduction of friction.'[157]

Originally, the standing stone had been polished and thus was scintillating in the sunlight, like a glaring beacon visible from the sea. Once towering at 17 meters—the remaining four meters being underground—the Great Menhir is thought to have been the first in a stone alignment of nineteen menhirs, each successive stone being smaller than the previous one.[158]

A few days later, I visited the cairn of Barnenez, a one-of-a-kind Megalithic site lost on a peninsula on the indented northern coast of Finistère. The cairn, which is the prototype of a step pyramid, is almost as ancient as the Great Broken Menhir. Older than the Egyptian pyramids,[159] this 72-meter-long cairn was built in two distinct phases, around 4850 BC for the greenish dolerite base and 4450 BC for the light-coloured granite addition, and counts eleven passage graves inside. It is thought[160] that several such cairns once existed on the Atlantic coastline, but most of them have been destroyed by unscrupulous farmers. Some still exist elsewhere in Brittany and on the island of Jersey. It is then fortunate that this formidable structure hasn't been destroyed too. Although its top part has crumbled with the passing of time, and part of one side was bulldozed away in 1955 to reuse the stones for modern buildings, most of the cairn is still standing as another prominent

---

[157] Jean L'Helgouac'h, *Locmariaquer*, France: Jean-Paul Gisserot, 1994, p. 13

[158] information from the onsite tour guide

[159] i.e., *most* Egyptian pyramids, as the Giza pyramids might be much older than what Egyptologists generally think (see Chapter Eleven)

[160] information from the onsite tour guide

example of the advanced technical expertise of the early Megalithic people.

Interestingly, as our blond-haired, gruff, but knowledgeable guide explained, this cairn contains an early example of *tholos*, or beehive tomb—a domed burial structure. Beehive tombs are a common feature in Oman (c. 3500 BC), in some Megalithic sites of southern Spain and Portugal around 3000 BC, and much later in Crete and Greece (c. 1500 BC).

Although not exactly a pyramid, in many ways the Barnenez cairn prefigures the later pyramidal structures that grace many countries in the world today: Egypt, Mesoamerica, South America, Tenerife and China, to cite only the oldest examples.

What is quite odd is that the Megalithic phenomenon appeared quite *suddenly*, without any apparent transitional phases. French author Christine Louboutin, in a very enlightening book about the very first farmers in the Neolithic era, writes: 'Passage graves in southern Portugal and the westernmost part of France—Barnénez, in Finistère, or Bougon, in the Deux-Sèvres—are the most ancient known megaliths. Nothing precedes or foreshadows the technical expertise and the massive scale of these constructions.'[161]

How come the tallest standing stone ever recorded in Europe was erected at the *very beginning* of the Megalithic wave? How was this civilisation able to raise pyramid-like cairns *so early in time*? Was Atlantic Europe the cradle of an unknown civilisation which might have initiated construction techniques that were subsequently developed and perfected in other parts of the world, or were they imported there? This is perhaps one of the greatest mysteries attached to the Megalithic civilisation, and this enigma will have to be tackled further on.

More examples of Megalithic marvels

In the centuries and millennia that followed, the Megalithic monuments spread all over Western Europe and the western part of the Mediterranean.

Among the Megalithic marvels are the Megalithic temples of Malta, the oldest of which were made c. 3600 BC, perhaps even earlier; the richly ornate Gavrinis passage grave in Brittany, which was built c. 3500

---

[161] Christine Louboutin, *Au Néolithique. Les Premiers paysans du monde*, Paris: Découvertes Gallimard, 1990, p. 81

BC; still in Brittany, Carnac and its three impressive sets of alignments that count more than 3,000 stones in all, which date back to at least 3300 BC; Newgrange, a huge circular mound in Ireland with a stone chambered passage made around 3200 BC; Stonehenge in England, a temple-like structure comprising a circle of 30 stones topped with another ring of 30 lintel stones, and five giant trilithons inside, originally a simple circular bank with a ditch enclosure made c. 3100 BC; the Callanish Stones in the outer Hebrides of Scotland, whose arrangement is reminiscent of the shape of a Celtic cross, and which were made between 2900 and 2600 BC; in England again, Avebury, the largest stone circle ever built in Europe, which is dated c. 2600 BC; the nearby Silbury Hill, which is the tallest human-made mound (or pyramid) in Europe, built around 2400 BC; and the Ring of Brodgar in Orkney, a magnificent stone circle which originally counted 60 stones, made between 3000 and 2000 BC. These are just a few significant examples amongst many. The interested reader will find that there are literally tens of thousands of Megalithic monuments in Europe alone.

We'll have reasons to discuss many of these impressive, awe-inspiring monuments further on.

Astronomical alignments

Many Megalithic sites appear to have been oriented astronomically. According to French archaeologist Jean-Pierre Mohen, who received his doctorate in prehistory at the Sorbonne in Paris and who is a specialist of megaliths, there is absolutely no doubt that many Megalithic monuments served astronomical purposes:

> Orientation toward the sun, particularly in relation to sunrise, is common in megalithic structures, especially along the axis of the grave passage (at Gavrinis and Newgrange, for example). Lunar observation is attested to by circles of raised stones in Scotland, where the purpose of the stone altar, or recumbent stone, southwest of the monument was to observe the course of the moon.[162]

Standing stones or stone circles also appear to have had astronomical aims. Basing his conclusions on extensive studies made by Scottish engineer Alexander Thom, the rediscoverer of the Megalithic yard, as we'll see in Chapter Seven, Mohen thinks the large menhir of the Manio

---

[162] Jean-Pierre Mohen (1998), *Standing Stones. Stonehenge, Carnac and the World of Megaliths*, London: New Horizons (Thames and Hudson, 1999), p. 126

tumulus in Brittany, for instance, was a reference point for solar and lunar observations.[163] To British archaeologist Aubrey Burl, who was generally quite conservative in his conclusions with regard to the astronomical claims of Megalithic monuments made by some, the Ring of Brodgar in Orkney served a dual function: 'it had a funerary purpose, and it was also an observatory for the stars'.[164]

Among the Megalithic monuments usually associated with astronomy are the Callanish stones in Scotland and, of course, Stonehenge in Wiltshire, England. To Mohen, these two monuments 'exemplify how a megalithic observatory of the sun's course functioned.'[165] According to Jean-Pierre Pautreau, who directs research at the French National Center for Scientific Research, the Stonehenge 'link with astronomy is obvious. Its exact function (the prediction of eclipses?) has given birth to many theories.'[166]

Interestingly, astronomy at Stonehenge seems to have been a very ancient concern, as three post holes, dated c. 8000 BC for the first, c. 7000 BC for the second, have been recovered.[167] It is also quite well-known that at every summer solstice, an observer standing within the central part of the monument will see the Sun rise right above the Heelstone, a large block of sandstone known as sarsen stone, standing outside the main entrance to Stonehenge.

In 1965 English astronomer Gerald Hawkins, in his controversial *Stonehenge Decoded*, reached conclusions even he himself didn't expect: 'I was prepared for *some* Stonehenge-sun correlation. I was not prepared for total sun correlation—and I had not at all suspected that there might be almost total moon correlation as well.'[168] According to Mohen, Hawkins

> showed that the monuments [at Stonehenge] functioned as an instrument able to chart solar and lunar movements. The solar and lunar cycles would intersect, and eclipses in particular could be predicted. The later improvements at Stonehenge . . . are more spectacular in that they include the central crown of three trilithons within the sarsen 'horseshoe' as well as the circle of

---

[163] Ibid., p. 122

[164] Ibid., p.123

[165] Ibid., p. 124

[166] Denis Vialou et al, *La Préhistoire. Histoire et dictionnaire*, Paris: Robert Laffont, 2004, p. 1264

[167] Ibid.

[168] Quoted by Jean-Pierre Mohen (1998), *Standing Stones. Stonehenge, Carnac and the World of Megaliths*, London: New Horizons (Thames and Hudson, 1999), p. 149

bluestones. The sole aim of these improvements ... was to realize the initial astronomical purpose.[169]

According to British astronomer and archaeologist Clive Ruggles, also Emeritus Professor of archaeoastronomy at the University of Leicester, 'a solsticial alignment' was incorporated at Stonehenge around the time of the arrival of the bluestones in c. 2550 BC.[170] More generally speaking, Ruggles thinks 'it is quite clear that orientation was of great symbolic importance even in the Early Neolithic.' Giving the example of earthen long barrows in Northern Europe, he adds that 'such consistency over wide areas could only have been achieved by reference to the daily motions of the heavenly bodies.'[171] He holds a similar view about Megalithic monuments and henges (circular banks with internal ditches that are found only in the British Isles). In his words, 'astronomical alignments found repeatedly among henges and stone and timber rings give numerous hints that astronomy was very much part of ceremonial tradition and practice in the Late Neolithic, at least in certain places at certain times.'[172]

These views represent only a tiny sampling of what mainstream archaeologists think of the subject, and yet they clearly show how impossible it is for them to deny that many Megalithic structures are unambiguously linked to astronomical bodies. In a nutshell, even conventional archaeologists happily recognize that there is ample evidence that many Megalithic structures served astronomical purposes.

To conclude, we see that there must have existed a caste of learned individuals within the Megalithic people who were very much interested in astronomy. In addition, these sages had constructions made that clearly reflected that concern. To be sure, these people seem to have been very much like the Celtic Druids of later times.

The Megalithic Proto-Druids

The Megalithic people were able to cut, transport and erect huge pieces of stone—sometimes astronomically oriented—and regularly navigate in

---

[169] Ibid., p. 125-6

[170] Clive Ruggles, 'Ritual Astronomy in the Neolithic and Bronze Age British Isles: patterns of continuity and change,' in *Prehistoric Ritual and Religion. Essays in Honour of Aubrey Burl*, ed. by Alex Gibson and Derek Simpson, Phoenix Mill: Sutton Publishing Limited, 1998, p. 205

[171] Ibid.

[172] Ibid., p. 205-6

the high sea, which in turn also implies knowing about stars to get their bearings. From that we have to infer that there were amongst them some sages who had both the technical and astronomical knowledge for this, as well as the political or spiritual power to have thousands of people collaborate for a common purpose. These people ought to have mastered a considerable amount of knowledge that they had to pass down the generations, and clearly ought to have played a key role within the Megalithic civilisation.

Seeing the distribution of Megalithic monuments on a map, Italian geneticist Luigi Luca Cavalli-Sforza hypothesised the existence of astronomer-priests among the Megalithic people; in his view, astronomy and religion were probably linked in these ancient times. In other words, a caste of people who not only had the knowledge and expertise but also the psychological power necessary for the achievement of these architectural feats. He initially thought these people must have left a distinctive genetic imprint on the European shores and islands, as they were settling new areas. The study of European genetics, however, did not confirm his premise, as no particular gene was found in areas that would correlate the distribution of megaliths on the map. But as there was no denying that the Megalithic distribution was somehow associated with the ocean and the sea, Cavalli-Sforza came to the conclusion that the Megalithic people had probably never been very numerous, and rather than genes, had left some *memes* on the local populations they had encountered:

> Rather than settlers, it is possible that these megalith men might have been a caste of priests, a small prehistoric aristocracy who had good ships and also perhaps good weaponry, not even mentioning astronomical and architectural knowledge much more advanced than those of their contemporaries. They would impose their superiority on the people they met, but were probably not very numerous as compared to the farmers who had by then settled the Mediterranean coasts and reached a substantial density of population. That's why the genetic input of the Megalithic people remained low, not high enough to alter the genetic picture of the peoples with whom they interacted, although culturally speaking, they left behind them very noticeable footprints.[173]

These knowledgeable people, who must have had great expertise in astronomy and architecture, who were also powerful and persuasive, and

---

173 Luca and Francesco Cavalli-Sforza, *Qui sommes-nous ?*, translated from Italian to French by Françoise Brun, Paris: Flammarion, 1997, p. 185

who are called astronomers-priests by Cavalli-Sforza, bear an uncanny resemblance to the sages that existed in Caesar's time, i.e. Druids, in places that once had been Megalithic lands. Although the Celtic Druids weren't raising megaliths anymore, we see that chances are pretty high that the origin of Celtic Druids is to be found within these putative Megalithic astronomers-priests.

Although the link is still unproven but appears to be a likely possibility, we'll call these presumed Megalithic sages *Megalithic Proto-Druids* or *MPDs*, as they clearly fit the portrait of 'very knowledgeable people' living a few millennia before the Celtic Druids in the same lands. We'll soon come to the question of proving our point that there is an observable continuum between MPDs and Celtic Druids, meaning the latter ones certainly inherited from much of the MPDs' knowledge.

Main points

- **Megalithic monuments have been erected by the tens of thousands in Northern and Western Europe, and in the Mediterranean, for at least four millennia**
- **The Megalithic people were sea people**
- **The highest standing stone is also one of the oldest, and the pyramidal cairn of Barnenez is one of the most ancient Megalithic structures of Western Europe**
- **It is a fact that many Megalithic monuments are astronomically oriented**
- **Geneticist Cavalli-Sforza thinks there must have existed highly influential Megalithic 'astronomers-priests' who sailed along the European coasts**
- **Druids may have been preceded in time by Megalithic Proto-Druids**

Chapter Seven: Megalithic Geometry

The point of this chapter is to show that there is compelling evidence that MPDs, thought to have preceded Celtic Druids, used an Earth geometry with a *366*-degree circle, rather than a 360-degree circle. This division of the circle appears to be based on a calendar.

This presumed 366-degree geometry was rediscovered by English author and researcher Alan Butler in the 1990s, and its principles explained in his book *The Bronze Age Computer Disc*, which was first published in 1999.[174] The goal of the book was to offer a decryption of the Phaistos Disc, which I will briefly talk about in a moment. I first read this book in 2001, contacted its author afterwards (who became a valuable friend), and have been working on 366-degree geometry and its numerous implications ever since.

For those who have never heard of 366-degree geometry, what you are about to read is nothing short of extraordinary. This might at first look like an astonishing, glorious cascade of coincidences, added to Alan Butler's and, to a lesser extent, my own imagination, but it should soon appear to most rational people like an inescapable historical reality. Once more, the reader will be shown a body of evidence, and can make their own conclusions. If recognised as true, this hypothesis might overturn the reader's view of history. If the existence of this geometry is one day admitted by academic science, it will prove that the Megalithic people were expert geometricians who knew the Earth was a sphere and who were aware of its exact dimensions. In other words, it would mean that their capabilities have been greatly underestimated by mainstream prehistorians, which in itself is a revolution.

In addition, if this geometry proves *not* to be a figment of our imagination, it will also be seen as an incredibly harmonious mathematical ensemble which can potentially reconcile time, angular and linear distances, and perhaps even mass in one integrated system. Better than that, the nature of the system works on whole numbers that

[174] Alan Butler, *The Bronze Age Computer Disc*, Cippenham, Slough, Berkshire: Quantum (1999)

naturally describe the physical characteristics of our planet, the Moon and the Sun, water, and even some biological characteristics of the human body. If recognised as true, these considerations will certainly upturn the reader's view of the very universe we live in.

The existence of this geometry, and its manifest use by Proto-Druids in Megalithic times, inevitably begs two questions:

One, 'How was it initially discovered by MPDs?'—rather than 'Who created it?'—as it seems to be intrinsically embedded in the physics of the universe, or at least our solar system. Two, 'How is it possible that such an integrated geometry exists in the first place?'

The Phaistos Disc

Alan Butler first heard about the Phaistos Disc during a stay in Greece in the 1990s. The Phaistos Disc is an artefact made of fired reddish clay discovered in 1908 by Italian archaeologist Luigi Pernier in the Minoan palace of Phaistos in Crete. The Minoans belonged to a beautiful civilisation that flourished in Crete in the 3rd and 2nd millennia BC. The disc is about 15 cm in diameter and is thought to have been manufactured roughly some time between 1850 and 1400 BC. On both sides of the disc are spirals with stamped hieroglyphic symbols in it, the meaning of which has long remained a total mystery. Many researchers have attempted to decrypt the enigmatic symbols. The object is kept on display at the archaeological museum of Heraklion in Crete. The fact that the symbols have been stamped like seals suggests that this object is not one of a kind, but if several such objects were ever made, they have yet to be found.

Alan thought this disc might have been a 366-day calendar. His main conclusions, along with mine, are summed up in Appendix 1. The problem with the Phaistos Disc is that, because of its uniqueness, no firm conclusion can be made as to what it was exactly. Although this is pure guesswork, there are many intuitive reasons to think it might have been a calendar, either a 365-day or a 366-day calendar. In any case, it was this ancient object that first steered Alan Butler toward 366-degree geometry.

A 366-degree circle

Alan Butler's reasoning was that if Minoans did split the year in 12 more or less equal parts or months, then maybe they also split the day in 12 equal parts. One day is the microcosm of a year, with each of the 12 zodiac signs going past an observer's eyes in one day or Earth rotation, just as these signs shift places to an observer's eyes watching the sky in one particular direction every day for a year, as the Earth revolves around the Sun.

We know that Sumerians in Mesopotamia—who are credited with the invention of 360-degree geometry—did have 12 hours in their day, before the 24-hour day was invented. These hours, which were equivalent to two modern hours, were named *danna*.[175] It is interesting to note that the Chinese also divided the full day in only 12 hours: they had 12 'double hours' called *shih*.[176] The fact that today we use 24 hours suggests that the system was altered at some point, entailing that day divisions (hours) do not match year divisions (months) any longer.

The fact that the Minoans probably used an elaborate calendar has many implications. That's why Alan also hypothesised that Minoans might have used some kind of circle geometry already. The possible existence of a 366-day calendar made it possible, at least theoretically, for the Minoans to have used a 366-degree circle. Sticking to the idea that a day is the microcosm of a year, Alan wondered if ancient Cretans might have first thought of dividing a day, and then a circle, into 366 parts. It takes one day for the Earth to circle around its axis and face the Sun again in almost the same way. In a year, it describes a circle around the Sun once and around itself 366 times, so why not also divide the day into 366 parts?

Today, we divide a circle into 360 parts, probably because 360 is a very convenient number with many divisors. It is generally believed that a circle is traditionally divided into 360 parts because it is a round number approximating the number of days in a year, and because Babylonians used a 360-day calendar with 12 months of 30 days each.[177]

There are some good reasons to think that a 366-day calendar would have naturally induced a 366-degree circle.

Still studying this macrocosm-microcosm relationship, it is also interesting to note that we use the same words for the division of circles

---

[175] Georges Ifrah, *Histoire universelle des chiffres. L'intelligence des hommes racontée par les nombres et le calcul, Vol. 1* (1981), Paris: Robert Laffont, 1994, p. 222

[176] Joseph Needham, Ling Wang, and Derek John de Solla Price, *Heavenly Clockwork: The Great Astronomical Clocks of Medieval China*, Cambridge: Cambridge University Press, 1986, p. 199: http://books.google.fr/books?id=bCA9AAAAIAAJ&pg=PA199&redir_esc=y#v=onepage&q&f=false

[177] http://mathworld.wolfram.com/Degree.html

(angles) and hours (time). In a circle, an arc degree divides in arc minutes, which then subdivide into arc seconds. An hour divides in minutes of time, which then subdivide into seconds of time. If in both cases the number used is the same—there are 60 arc minutes to the degree, and 60 arc seconds to the arc minute, and there are 60 minutes of time to the hour, and 60 seconds of time to the minute—the two systems do not coincide, as the arc degree does not correspond to the hour. Consequently, arc minutes and arc seconds do not relate to the minutes and seconds of time either—it takes only one minute of time[178] for the Earth to turn 15 arc minutes on its axis.

Was it possible that the same words were still used in geometry and time reckoning because they were once linked in one integrated system reconciling angular measurement and time measurement? Perhaps there had been a time when both systems were synchronized, so that when the Earth turned one arc minute on its axis, one minute of time also passed? This would only work if minutes of time were very short, only one 60th of one 360th or 366th of a day, rather than of one 24th of a day.

The only problem with this theory is that there is no proof that any people ever did that. There is simply no shred of evidence that the Minoans ever measured such tiny durations of time. But is there any evidence that they ever used the 366-degree circle? As it turns out, there *is*.

But what would the Minoans divide a circle for in the first place? Alan sums up his Eureka moment in this sentence: 'Then suddenly it came to me: it was neither time nor angles that the Minoans sought to measure, it was distance. This was an astonishing discovery and I realized that it could revolutionise the way in which we view the capabilities of Bronze Age cultures.'[179]

Alan thought that the Minoans may have divided the Earth's circumference into 366 degrees, and then subdivided this degree into smaller units to measure distances on the ground. In such a geometry (using the polar circumference of the Earth) the length of the degree on the Earth's surface would have been

$$40{,}007.86/366=109.31 \text{ km}$$

[178] In reality, it takes even a bit less than a minute of time, as there is a slight discrepancy between a sidereal minute and a solar minute.
[179] Alan Butler, *The Stone Age Computer Disc*, Cippenham, Slough, Berkshire: Quantum (1999), p. 100

If this hypothetical Minoan degree was divided into 60 arc minutes—just like the modern degree is divided into 60 arc minutes—the length of the Minoan minute would have been

109.31/60=1.8218 km

And the Minoan arc second would have been

1.8218/60=.030364 km or 30.364 m

Was the result in any way connected to units of length in the Minoan culture? As it turned out, it was. The length of this theoretical Minoan arc second was exactly 100 times the length of the Minoan foot, 30.364 cm, which was the basic unit of length the Minoans used in the construction of their palaces!

The Minoan foot

In the 1960s, Canadian architect J. Walter Graham had carefully measured the Minoan palaces at Knossos, Phaistos and Malia. Following this work, he had made comparisons and had eventually come to the conclusion that the Minoans had used a standard unit of measurement: 'I found that there were two reliable types of evidence: *round* numbers of feet in *long* dimensions—the city-blocks measured 300 by 120 feet; and *whole* foot-lengths in *short* dimensions recurring in a series—the three-foot intervals between the vertical incised lines on carefully decorated stuccoed walls.'[180] He dubbed this unit the Minoan foot, as it is just a bit shorter than the 30.48 cm length of the Imperial foot.[181] He estimated it to be 30.364 cm long. The round numbers also showed that Minoans used base 10.

As no measuring rod was found, however, it was still possible that Graham could have been wrong. But when a previously unknown palace was discovered at Zakro on the eastern coast of Crete, its linear dimensions confirmed beyond any doubt that it had been built with the Minoan foot as well, and nobody today denies its existence any more. In the words of Paul Faure, a French archaeologist and a professor of Greek language and civilisation who graduated from the Ecole Normale supérieure, and who eventually became Doctor Honoris Causa at the University of Athens:

---

[180] 'The Minoan Unit of Length and Minoan Palace Planning,' J. Walter Graham, *American Journal of Archaeology*, Vol. 64, No. 4 (Oct. 1960), p. 335-41: http://www.jstor.org/discover/10.2307/501332?uid=3738016&uid=2&uid=4&sid=21102145760793

[181] Ibid.

> There is no doubt at all, after the precise measurements by J. Walter Graham, that the plans of the four great sanctuaries of Phaistos, Knossos, Malia and Zakro—not even mentioning Hagia Triada—were predetermined and that these great architectural bodies follow both horizontally and vertically designed proportions, based upon a sacred foot of 30.36 cm.[182]

One last confirmation of the validity of the Minoan foot comes from Dr John Cherry from the University of Michigan.[183] He was one of the first to use the trigonometric function defined and tested in 1974 by D G Kendall, a statistician of the University of Cambridge. We shall briefly deal again with this trigonometric function when we talk about the Megalithic yard in the next segments of this chapter.

So, once again—and quite astoundingly—the Minoan foot is precisely one hundredth of the theoretical Minoan arc second suggested by Alan Butler. A perfect subdivision that uses base 10.

I later found that the round numbers of Minoan feet referred to by Graham are in no way random. For example, the central courtyard at Knossos is 180 feet by 90, numbers which are redolent with Babylonian and modern 360-degree circle geometry, half of such a circle being of course 180 degrees, and one quarter being 90 degrees. More importantly, the ancient architects seem to have had a penchant for the number 60 in the dimensions of their palaces. In Paul Faure's words: 'We are surprised to note... how much number 60 appealed to the architects' minds.'[184] This actually comes as no big surprise if the Minoan foot derived from the Minoan arc second, which was 1/60th of the Minoan arc minute, just like the Minoan minute was 1/60th of the Minoan degree. To be sure, 60 is a key number in both 360-degree geometry and the 366-degree geometry proposed here. Were the Minoans conversant with both geometries?

Thanks to the Minoan foot, Alan's hypothetical Minoan geometry was vindicated. But he did not stop there. The Cretan palaces, just like the Phaistos Disc, are no more than 4,000 years old. By contrast, we saw that the Megalithic culture predated the Minoan civilisation by at least three millennia.

Was there any evidence that the Megalithic people had used a similar form of geometry *before* the Minoan foot was invented, perhaps even teaching them their own geometry? In other words, can we find

---

[182] Paul Faure, *La Vie quotidienne en Crète au temps de Minos*, Paris: Hachette, 1973, p. 421

[183] *Antiquity*, vol. 57, 1983, p. 52-6

[184] Paul Faure, *La Vie quotidienne en Crète au temps de Minos*, Paris: Hachette, 1973, p. 421

incontrovertible evidence that MPDs (the Megalithic astronomer-priests of Cavalli-Sforza) used units of measurement derived from a 366-degree Earth circle?

Again, as it turned out, there was.

The Megalithic yard

Beginning in the early 1930s and ending in the late 1970s, Scottish engineer Professor Alexander Thom spent more than four decades surveying the major Megalithic stone circles, alignments and isolated standing stones in England, Wales, Scotland and Brittany, France. He and his son Archie carefully measured about 600 Megalithic sites.

Thom's work revealed the existence of a common unit of linear measurement which he christened the Megalithic yard. Astonishingly, the precision of the Megalithic arrangements was particularly high: 'They [the Megalithic people] were intensely interested in measurements and attained a proficiency which... is only equalled today by a trained surveyor.'[185] This discovery indicated that the Megalithic people had advanced mathematical and geometrical knowledge, as well as astronomical knowledge, as we will soon see.

Thom carefully measured the diameters and circumferences of the surviving stone circles in Britain, or what remained of them. Of course, many stone circles haven't survived the ravages of time, an inevitable fate after several millennia. Some of them have been damaged by local people over time, more particularly in recent centuries. However, from the stone circles that remained more or less intact, Professor Thom managed to establish that the Megalithic people had created geometrical figures. What was special about these figures is that they 'had as many dimensions as possible arranged to be integral multiples of their units of length.'[186] As Thom puts it, '[the Megalithic people] abhorred "incommensurable" lengths.'[187] What it means is that what we call stone 'circles' today never were circles in a true sense but were actually flattened circles, egg-shaped rings or ellipses.

Why didn't they make circles? Perhaps because they did not want to deal with irrational numbers. The circumference of a circle is equal to the diameter of the circle multiplied by π, an irrational number whose value

[185] Alexander Thom, *Megalithic Sites in Britain*, Oxford: Oxford University Press, 1967, p. 27
[186] Ibid.
[187] Ibid.

is about 3.1415927. It is easy to understand that if an integral number of units is used in a diameter, there won't be another integral number of this same unit in a true circle, or vice versa. That's why they seem to have created geometrical figures that removed the need to deal with irrational numbers, by having the longest diameter, as well as the circumference, integral multiples of their basic unit of length. Sometimes, Thom writes, 'a small adjustment [was] made by the erectors to the diameter, to bring the circumference nearer to an integer.'[188]

That they chose to do so rather than not is fortunate as it made Thom's task much easier: once he had determined their unit of measurement, he could often unravel designs that would otherwise be much trickier to comprehend. Because this unit of length was not too far from one modern yard of 3 feet or 91.44 cm, he christened this ancient unit the Megalithic yard. Its length in England was, according to him:

1 MY (Megalithic yard)=2.722 ft±0.003[189] (82.967 cm)

In Scotland Thom found that the Megalithic yard was a tiny bit shorter, with a length estimated at 2.720 ft or 82.906 cm.

Thom's results were published in the *Journal of the Royal Statistical Society* in 1955, and then in numerous other articles after his retirement. His book *Megalithic Sites in Britain* came out in 1967. In it he summed up his main findings with numerous diagrams to illustrate them. He also bolstered his work with complex statistical data showing that his findings were not fanciful numerical patterns resulting from the wishful thinking of the engineer, but trustworthy results derived from empirical reality.[190]

Another surprising conclusion from Professor Thom's study was that a nearly identical unit of length (the Megalithic yard) had been used from northern Scotland to as far south as Brittany, entailing cultural uniformity all across Britain, as well as on part of the continent. Thom surmised that there must have existed some place in Britain or elsewhere where a standard Megalithic yard was used to copy their measuring rods from, but at the same time wondered how the Megalithic people could get it so right, as the differences between the Scottish and English values of the unit were extremely small:

---

188 Ibid., p. 44

189 Alexander Thom, 'Megalithic geometry in standing stones,' *New Scientist*, 12 Mar. 1964, p. 690: http://books.google.fr/books?id=c2iCzjpnd4EC&pg=PA690&redir_esc=y#v=onepage&q&f=false

190 Alexander Thom, *Megalithic Sites in Britain*, Oxford: Oxford University Press, 1967, Chapter 2: Statistical Ideas, p. 6-13

> There must have been a headquarters from which standard rods were sent out but whether this was in these islands or on the Continent the present investigation cannot determine. The length of the rods in Scotland cannot have differed from that in England by more than 0.03 in or the difference would have shown up ... If each small community had obtained the length by copying the rod of its neighbour to the south the accumulated error would have been much greater than this.[191]

We'll see in a further section of this chapter that there was probably another way to determine the Megalithic yard with the use of a pendulum. In any case, the level of accuracy attained by the Megalithic people is quite simply mind-boggling: 'There is ample evidence that, when they wanted, these people could measure with an accuracy better than 1 in 500, so it is certain that they knew what they were doing'.[192]

Along with the Megalithic yard, Thom determined that a subunit of ½ MY was also used, more particularly visible in alignments and ellipses.[193] Ever so often, 'it was more important to have the perimeter a multiple of 2½ than to have it an integer.'[194]

Pythagorean triangles

Another notable discovery of Professor Thom is that the Megalithic stone circles exhibit the knowledge of Pythagorean triangles... well before Pythagoras was even born! In Thom's words:

> It is remarkable that 1000 years before the earliest mathematicians of classical Greece, people in these islands not only had a practical knowledge of geometry and were capable of setting out elaborate geometrical designs but could also set out ellipses based on Pythagorean triangles.[195]

As we now know by radiocarbon dating, British stone circles are sometimes as old as 3000 BC, so we can easily double Thom's estimate and safely say that the Pythagorean triangles were known to the Megalithic people in northwestern Europe about *2,000 years before the*

---

[191] Ibid., p. 435

[192] Ibid., p. 47

[193] Ibid., p. 41

[194] Ibid., p. 47. Note that 2.5 also derives from our "numbers of the Gods," as it equals 10 x 10 / 40. And 25 is the square of the hypotenuse in the Pythagorean 3-4-5 triangle (editor's note).

[195] Ibid, p. 3

Greek philosopher and mathematician demonstrated the theorem that today bears his name.

The Pythagorean Theorem shows that in any right-angled triangle, the area of the square whose side is the hypotenuse is equal to the sum of the areas of the squares of the other two sides (those which form the right angle). Pythagoras, who lived in the 6th century BC, is the first person in history known to have demonstrated this theorem. But again, there are reasons to believe Pythagoras himself might have inherited much from the Druids' knowledge.

If the two sides forming the right angle of the triangle happen to be integers of a given unit, the length of the hypotenuse rarely is an integer too. The exceptions to this rule are the triangles which are termed Pythagorean triangles: these right-angled triangles have their three sides with integral numbers. The first Pythagorean triangle is the 3-4-5 triangle, as $3^2+4^2=5^2$, meaning that any right-angled triangle with its perpendicular sides being respectively 3 and 4 units (any unit) long will have its hypotenuse 5 units long. According to Thom, the Megalithic people knew this triangle well. It was even the one they used the most in their geometrical figures, for instance in the geometry of their egg-shaped rings. They seem to have known and exploited at least three Pythagorean triangles, among which a much bigger (12-35-37) one.[196]

When Professor Thom continued his study in Brittany, he saw that what had been true in Scotland and England was also true on the continent. The Megalithic yard of Brittany in northwestern France was the same as in Britain, and the two semicircular rings at the tip of the Carnac alignments, for example, are the same type of Megalithic 'eggs' as there are in Britain.

In his later book *Megalithic Remains in Britain and Brittany*,[197] published in 1978, Thom explained that he had also come to the conclusion that the Megalithic yard was sometimes divided into 40 equal parts he dubbed the Megalithic inch:

1 MY=40 Megalithic inches (MI) of about 2.02 cm (.817 inches)

He also identified a 'Megalithic rod' of 2½ MY:[198]

1 Megalithic Rod (MR) = 2½ MY = 100 MI

---

[196] Ibid., p. 27

[197] Alexander Thom et A.S. Thom, *Megalithic Remains in Britain and Brittany*, Oxford: Clarendon Press 1978, p. 49

[198] Ibid.

Thom also thought that the Megalithic people were accomplished astronomers who oriented their monuments to the stars, the Moon or the Sun. His own statistical examinations showed, in his opinion, 'a high degree of probability that many of the sites contained lines with an astronomical meaning.' [199] But he also admitted that, whilst his conclusions regarding the Megalithic yard were watertight, his astronomical considerations necessitated further research:

> The conclusions in previous chapters regarding Megalithic metrology rest on sound statistical basis: the probability levels are such as to leave no doubt about the reality of the units. But it is much more difficult to deal with astronomical hypotheses in the same rigid manner.[200]

True, some of Thom's archaeoastronomic conjectures do not really hold up to scrutiny. But we already saw in the previous chapter that there was ample evidence to show that MPDs were accomplished astronomers. Do we get more evidence from Megalithic monuments that MPDs were first-rate astronomers?

The Crucuno Rectangle in Brittany might just be the piece of evidence we are looking for.

The Crucuno Rectangle

Not very far from Carnac in Brittany, in the picturesque hamlet of Crucuno in the *commune* of Plouharnel, the visitor can see a magnificent, if quite unusual, portal tomb amongst the cluster of old houses. The dolmen is adjacent to a long stone house and is thought to be the remaining part of a huge passage grave. But even more interesting in Crucuno is the arrangement of standing stones that were erected just outside the hamlet. They form a rectangle... but not just *any* rectangle.

The Crucuno Rectangle consists of 22 standing stones from one to 2½ meters high. As it is neither an alignment nor a circular figure—as is usually the case—the stone rectangle is a pretty much unique kind of geometrical figure in Megalithic architecture. Is there a purpose to such a singular arrangement?

When the Breton stone rectangle was restored in 1882, just like many other Megalithic monuments, only nine stones out of the 22 were still standing. Although this restoration has been criticised, with some people thinking some of the stones had not been placed at their original

---

[199] Alexander Thom, *Megalithic Sites in Britain*, Oxford: Oxford University Press, 1967, p.92

[200] Ibid.

positions so as to make up a fantastic geometrical figure that had never existed in the first place, the plan produced by Revd W C Lukis and Sir Henry Dryden in 1867 clearly shows that Gaillard, who later restored the site, made a point of respecting the initial positions of the stones.[201] It is precisely *because* the shape of the monument is particularly unusual that some people theorised that the restoration had been inadequate.

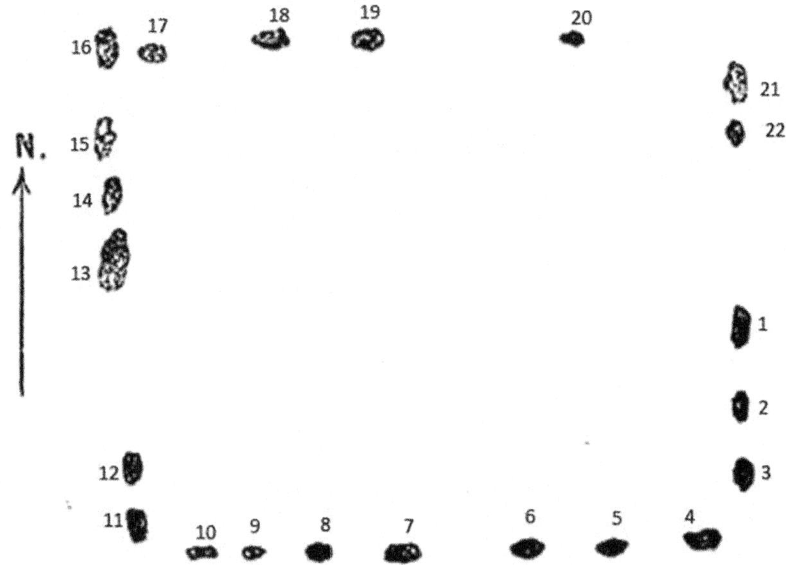

Fig. 13. The Crucuno Rectangle in Brittany, France.

Professor Thom's own surveying made in 1970 shows that the Crucuno Rectangle perfectly fits in two Pythagorean 3-4-5 rectangles, the first one being 24.9 m x 33.2 m—or exactly 30 x 40 MY, the second one being 27.4 m x 36.5 m, or 33 x 44 MY. The diagonals are, of course, 50 MY long in the inner rectangle and 55 MY long in the outer rectangle. As Gaillard is unlikely to have known the Megalithic yard when he restored the site in 1882 (the Megalithic yard was only rediscovered by Thom in the 1930s), it certainly looks like the restorations were done by the book.

French prehistorian Roger Joussaume, who leads studies at the CNRS, the National Center for Scientific Research, thinks the Crucuno Rectangle has 'perplexing metric and astronomic characteristics.'[202] He

---

[201] Aubrey Burl, *Guide des dolmens et menhirs bretons. Le mégalithisme en Bretagne.* translation of *Megalithic Brittany: A Guide* (1985), by Bruno Blasselle, Paris: Errance, 1987, p.135

[202] Denis Vialou et al, *La Préhistoire. Histoire et dictionnaire*, Paris: Robert Laffont, 2004, p. 504

adds that the monument is 'a rectangle of standing stones whose sides are oriented to the cardinal points and diagonals to the sunrise at the summer and winter solstices'[203] (at the time of construction). This last point is highly important as it implies that the location of the Crucuno Rectangle owes nothing to chance. The angles in a 3-4-5 rectangle are fixed by geometry: the angle between the longer side of the rectangle (4 units) and the diagonal (5 units) is *always* 36.87 degrees. At the latitude where the Crucuno Rectangle was placed, the Sun rises at midsummer and midwinter at an angle of 36.87° north or south of the east-west axis, so that it beams exactly along one or the other diagonal of this rectangle. This is the only line of latitude in the northern hemisphere where the angle of the rising Sun at the solstice could coincide with the diagonal, and this is precisely the latitude that was chosen by the builders. Crucuno is only an hour's walk from the sea. Tens of thousands of megaliths have been erected on the Atlantic coast of Europe, but there was *only one latitude* on this coast (i.e. the Crucuno region) where the angles would coincide, and this is precisely where they chose to construct this 3-4-5 Pythagorean rectangle, which makes it hard to think it is just a coincidence. The most likely explanation, again, is that the MPDs who designed this architectural project were excellent geometricians and astronomers.

Let's sum things up. The Crucuno Rectangle can be said to be a combination of highly interesting mathematical and astronomical facts, because:

1- It is a 3-4-5 Pythagorean rectangle of the type Professor Alexander Thom noticed in the geometry of British stone circles → The monument appears to confirm that Pythagorean triangles were known to MPDs

2- The sides of the rectangle are integral multiples of the Megalithic yard → The Megalithic yard is not a figment of Thom's imagination

3- The lengths of the sides of the inner rectangle are exact multiples of 10 in Megalithic Yards → The monument confirms that the Megalithic people used base 10, which is also the number of fingers on two human hands, and the presence of this round number makes it unlikely for these results to be arbitrary

[203] Ibid.

4- The rectangle is perfectly oriented to the four points of the compass → The monument is astronomically oriented, so the Megalithic people were probably good astronomers

5- The Crucuno area is the only maritime region in Europe where the angles formed by the diagonals of this type of rectangle coincide with the solstice sunrises → There are very good reasons to believe that the MPDs who designed the monument were skilful geometricians and astronomers

This combination of these five astonishing facts shows that the Crucuno Rectangle is not a mere quadrilateral of standing stones, but strong evidence of the high abilities of MPDs.

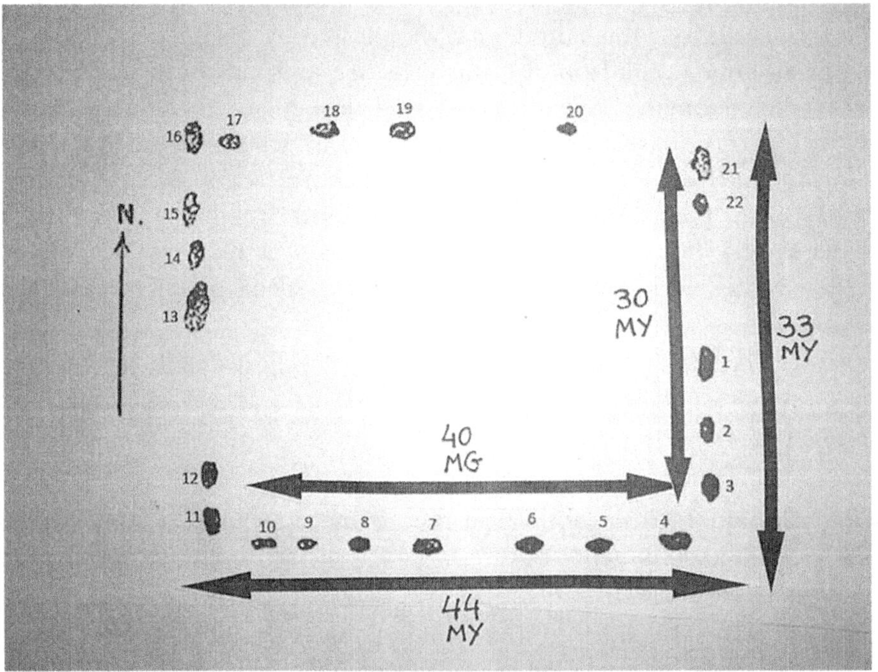

Fig. 14. The Crucuno Rectangle coincides with two 3-4-5 Pythagorean rectangles (each consisting of two Pythagorean triangles joined along the hypotenuse) of 30-40-50 MY and 33-44-55 MY.

Even if Gaillard, when he restored the stone arrangement, had wished to 'fake' the monument and fabricated a Pythagorean rectangle, how is it possible that the monument happens to be located at the precise latitude where the positions of the solstice sunrises match the angles of the diagonals in a 3-4-5 rectangle? Even more baffling, how could he manage to make the dimensions of the rectangle conform to the Megalithic yard, decades *before* the Megalithic yard was even rediscovered by Alexander Thom? The only satisfying answer to the problem is that the Crucuno

Rectangle was designed and made by MPDs, who may have regarded this particular latitude as sacred.

More generally speaking, was the whole Megalith-rich Carnac region elected because it was situated at this sacred latitude?

Confirmations of the Megalithic yard

Professor Thom's work was examined by two statisticians, S R Broadbent and D G Kendall in 1974, who sought to see if his claims had any scientific validity. Astronomer Douglas C Heggie also made an extensive survey of the statistical methods used to scrutinise Thom's measurements. Here is one of his comments about Kendall's 'quantum' analysis:

> Omitting sites already discussed in 1955, or those with diameters noted as being particularly uncertain, we obtain a probability level far below 0.1 %. This is a highly significant result, for it implies that such good agreement with Thom's unit would occur only once in many thousands of samples of random data.[204]

In other words, there were 99.9 chances in 100 that the Megalithic yard was a true unit of measurement, not an invention of Thom's. Heggie, however, remained circumspect in his conclusions. As stated by Jay Kappraff, an American professor of mathematics at the New Jersey Institute of Technology:

> Heggie feels that as striking as these results are, there are several reasons why they may not be as decisive as they seem. One of these is the suspicion that the choice of the geometry open to Thom allowed the operation of a quite unintentional bias in favour of the Megalithic yard.[205]

In Heggie's eyes, new independent measurements were necessary to see if Thom's results could be confirmed by others. Kendall, on the other hand, considered that there was sufficient evidence for a uniform Megalithic yard, at least in the Scottish Megalithic stone circles.[206] Kendall's conclusions regarding the validity of the Megalithic yard in Scottish stone circles were confirmed by P. R. Freeman of University College London in 1975, even if in his view two other values 'fit the data

---

[204] Quoted by Jay Kappraff, *Beyond Measure. A Guided Tour Through Nature, Myth and Number*, Singapore: World Scientific Publishing Co Pte Ltd, 2002, p. 239

[205] Ibid.

[206] D. G. Kendall, 'Hunting quanta,' *Philosophical Transactions of the Royal Society of London. Series A, Mathematical and Physical Sciences (276),* 1974, p. 231-66

almost as well as the yard.'[207] It can be objected, however, that in measurements, 'almost as well' isn't the same as 'as well,' so Thom's theory isn't that easy to dismiss: in other words, the Megalithic yard remained the best way to explain Thom's data.

Following Kendall and Freeman's papers, Alexander Thom provided more evidence for the Megalithic yard by making 'an entirely new survey of the site [of Avebury] using methods of greater accuracy' and then 'a mathematical analysis of the data obtained,'[208] as in his eyes the geometry of Avebury is well-known and the huge dimensions of the stone circles there—one very big and two smaller ones inside—made it an ideal place to undertake such work.

More recently, according to Karl M. Petruso of the University of Texas at Arlington, who has studied historical metrology, or the study of measurement systems of past cultures, for over 25 years, D. G. Kendall 'determined with a high degree of probability—and in the process put the venerable Megalithic yard controversy to rest—that there was indeed a Megalithic yard in Britain.'[209]

More confirmation of the existence of the Megalithic yard appears to have been found very far from Britain or Brittany, under the blue Mediterranean skies of the Maltese Megalithic temples. The man who claims this discovery is Chris Micaleff, the nephew of Paul Micaleff, an archaeoastronomer who had come to the conclusion that the Megalithic temple complex of Mnajdra in Malta was an astronomical observation site and a solar calendar in stone whose major axis is illuminated by the Sun at the equinoxes. Chris Micaleff asserts that the perimeter of the Mnajdra complex 'comes out to whole numbers in Megalithic yards.'[210] Mnajdra is thought to have been constructed c. 3600 BC. If Micaleff is correct, it would not only vindicate Professor Thom's unit of measurement, but also mean that the Megalithic yard wasn't only used in northwestern Europe, but also in the Mediterranean in early times.

---

[207] P. R. Freeman, 'A Bayesian Analysis of the Megalithic yard,' *Journal of the Royal Statistical Society A, 139, Part 1*, 1976, p. 20: http://www.jstor.org/discover/10.2307/2344382

[208] Alexander Thom and A.S. Thom, *Megalithic Remains in Britain and Brittany*, Oxford: Clarendon Press 1978, p. 30

[209] Karl M. Petruso, *Systems of Weight in the Bronze Age Aegean, Part 2*: http://www.uta.edu/honors/faculty/petruso/metrology.2.html

[210] From a conversation with Graham Hancock, quoted in Graham Hancock, *Underworld. Flooded Kingdoms of the Ice Age*, London: Michael Joseph, 2002, p. 433

As Thom himself noted, the old Spanish unit of length called the *vara* might be a modern survival of the Megalithic yard. Its value in Castile was 83.59 cm (2.742 ft), just a 0.75 per cent longer than the MY. Variants of the *vara* have also been used in many parts of Latin America.

Megalithic geometry

Let us now come back to our main point. Is the Megalithic yard a subdivision of the Earth, just like the Minoan foot was exactly 1/100th of an arc second in 366-degree geometry?

Once again, Alan Butler divided the polar circumference of the Earth into 366 degrees, and then subdivided the result into 60 arc minutes, and then into 60 arc seconds. As we've seen before, one Minoan arc second on the Earth's surface would have had a length of 30.364 m. The division of this hypothetical arc second on Earth, divided by the value of the Megalithic yard, yielded a most startling result:

30.364 m/.8296 m=36.6 MY

What an astonishing result! Could this be a coincidence? This was a decimal number, but what a number! The length of the Minoan arc second was exactly one-tenth of 366 MY.

There was only one slight problem of course—the presence of a decimal number. What if the Megalithic people did not know about decimals? If the *Megalithic* arc second was defined as one 6th (rather than one 60th) of the Minoan arc minute, it meant that there were exactly 366 MY to the Megalithic arc second! A perfectly logical number indeed in 366-degree geometry.

To sum things up:

40,007.86 km/366=109.31 km=1 Meg. degree (1°M)

109.31 km/60=1.8218 km=1 Meg. arc minute (1'M)

1.8218 km/6=303.64 m=1 Meg. arc second (1"M)

303.64 m/366=1 Meg. yard (1 MY)

The Minoans seem to have used a very similar system. Using the same number of degrees and the same number of arc minutes, the final subdivisions of the Earth circle would have been:

1.8218 km/60=30.364 m=1 Minoan degree

30.364 m/100=1 Minoan foot

There is of course the likely possibility that the Minoans inherited their geometry from the Megalithic system, kept the Megalithic arc second, and simply divided it into *1,000* parts:

1.8218 km/6=303.64 m = 1 Meg. arc second (1"M)
= 1 Minoan arc second
303.64 m/1,000 = 1 Minoan foot

This would make sense, as the Minoans often subdivided their foot into 6 equal parts,[211] which would echo the 6-part division of the Minoan minute. Whatever the truth regarding the nature of the arc minute in the Megalithic and Minoan systems, and whichever people inherited it from the other (or from yet another people), it has to be admitted that the intrinsic beauty and neatness of these results makes it extremely difficult for them to be accidental by-products. The most reasonable conclusion then is to admit that both Minoan and Megalithic units of measurements are probably subdivisions of the Earth's polar circumference using a 366-degree circle.

366, 40 and 10

But that is not all.

We saw earlier in this chapter that Professor Thom had reached the conclusion that the Megalithic people divided their MY into 40 Megalithic inches (MI). The immediate consequence is that there would have been 366 x 40=14,640 MI to the Megalithic arc second.

This number, of course, immediately calls to mind the number obtained when multiplying the number of symbols on each side of the Phaistos Disc together, which is 14,637, only three units short of the above number (see again Appendix 1). We also saw that 40 was a key number in the presumed Minoan calendar as a 366-day calendar gets one month late after a period of precisely 40 years, or 14,640 days.

Again, it seems highly unlikely that this numerical correlation is the result of chance. Why would we get lucky so easily? Applying as always Occam's razor, the easiest solution that comes to mind is that number 40 was deliberately introduced into the presumed geometric system, as it appears to be part of the time system (i.e. the Minoan calendar). If Alan Butler is right to think that the Megalithic yard is indeed 1/366th of the Megalithic arc second, then it would have been logical for MPDs to

[211] Paul Faure, *La Vie quotidienne en Crète au temps de Minos*, Paris: Hachette, 1973, p. 437

define the subdivision of the Megalithic yard as 1/40th of its length, as it reflected a significant number of days in the calendar.

In fact, there is no need at all to assume that the Megalithic people used the same calendar as the one thought to have been used by the Minoans. I spent years pondering this question, until one day, it struck me that in a year there are almost exactly 366¼ (i.e. 366 10/40) Earth rotations.

In astronomical terms, these two numbers, 366 and 40 (along with 10, the number of our fingers and the base of our number system), are absolutely fundamental, as they describe the number of times the Earth spins on itself in one year, which is the time it takes our planet to make one full revolution around the Sun (more on this in Part IV).

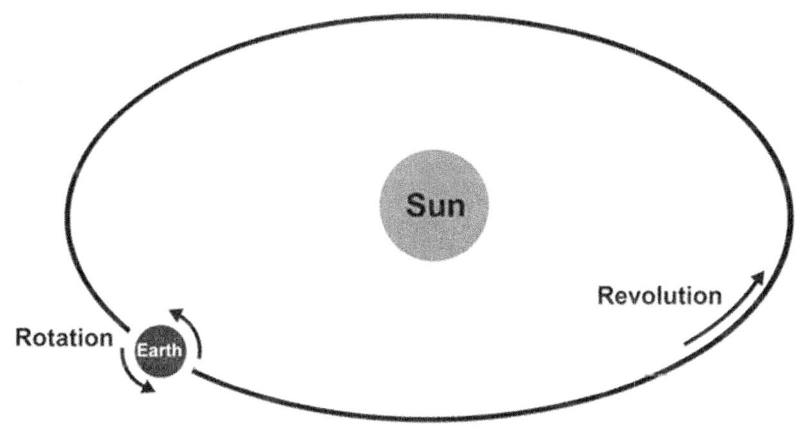

Fig. 15. The Earth makes 366¼ spins on itself (or rotations) in a year.

Is it possible that whoever created this geometry decided to use these numbers (366, 40 and base 10) as much as possible because they directly echo one fundamental physical characteristic of our planet, i.e. the fact that the Earth makes 366 10/40 spins on itself as it makes one full revolution round the Sun?

Of course, a seasonal year lasts 365¼ days, not 366¼, because there's a slight difference between a tropical or solar day, and a sidereal or star day.

Each time the earth rotates, the stars appear to return to the same position. This makes a sidereal day, or night if you will, which is slightly shorter than a solar day. Careful and perceptive observers of the night sky in ancient times could thus reckon that the earth rotates 366 times in a year. In fact, the Druids measured time by nights.[212]

Time and distance reconciled

Let us hypothesise a reasonable argument: Could the system have been created so has to be harmonious? Is it possible that, for ancient people, the use of the very same numbers in different systems was seen as beautiful and logical, something akin to the natural 'Music of the Spheres' suggested by Pythagoras? We already saw that setting the number of hours in a day equal to the number of months in a year was done both in Mesopotamia and China, with the microscopic level mirroring the macroscopic level. Is it that far-fetched to suggest that MPDs (or whoever designed the system) would have created a similarly harmonious system?

Actually, considering the clues that are starting to pile up, this suggestion doesn't seem far-fetched at all. On the contrary, it would make a lot of sense, as the pieces of the puzzle seem to fit perfectly into one another. These numbers, after all, neatly subdivide the Earth's circumference in a logical way.

We also have to assume, from this data, that MPDs knew the Earth was a sphere and had somehow calculated its exact dimensions, for the degree of accuracy observed in the subdivisions of our planet's polar circumference is on the order of the millimeter, incredible though this may seem! If the Megalithic yard were a mere half millimeter longer (83.017 cm instead of 82.967 cm), then the resulting circumference of the Earth would be more than 20 km (12.5 miles) too long! That a people who lived so far in the past, long before the Minoans in Crete, for example, attained such accuracy is truly mind-boggling. Is that just the result of luck? Or did they inherit their scientific knowledge from someone else? In any case, it certainly looks like our hypothetical MPDs, just like the Celtic Druids, knew the magnitude and shape of the world, as Caesar and Pomponius Mela explicitly wrote.

Did MPDs make precise geodetic measurements thousands of years ago? Did they manage to perfectly estimate the Earth's circumference by observing the angles of the stars above the horizon at different latitudes? Did they manage to get to such accuracy just because they wanted to

[212] Their holidays extended from one evening to the next. We also have, for instance, New Year's Eve, and we count the date from midnight to midnight (editor's note).

define small units of lengths in the first place? Or did they inherit all this knowledge from the bright minds of another unidentified people?

As the Megalithic people were obviously great seafarers, the possibility that they made all these discoveries themselves, given a sufficient amount of time of course, is plausible. On the other hand, they might have met, in the course of their travels, more advanced people who taught them this knowledge. What is really astonishing, once again, in the high degree of accuracy attained, which doesn't seem to fit either hypothesis.

But the most astonishing part of the system is that, at least theoretically, *the concepts of time and distance were reconciled within a common geometry*. It is as though we used today some degenerate form of it, as though we have forgotten the integrated system that might have existed in the past, and almost certainly did. Had there been a time when the concepts of time and distance were just *one*?

Let us provide the reader with a specific example. If this theory is correct, in the Megalithic system a second of time and an arc second would have had a very direct link: it was both the *distance* measured at the equator of one terrestrial arc as the Earth rotated one arc second, and the *time* it took for the Earth to accomplish that. Actually, a Megalithic yard obtained by dividing the Earth's equatorial circumference is slightly longer than the one derived from the polar circumference, as the Earth's diameter is slightly larger at its equator than from pole to pole. However, as a sidereal day is slightly shorter than a solar day, the two 'problems' cancel each other out. What a superb coincidence again! The apparent distance covered by the Earth's equator relative to the Sun in 1"M is almost exactly 366 MY.[213]

With today's systems, one second of time corresponds to 15 arc seconds on Earth. Our modern time and distance systems just don't fit with each other quite as neatly.

The Megalithic system is arguably more harmonious and elegant than the one we use today. True, a 360-degree circle is simpler and easier to divide which makes it very practical too. Yet a 366-degree circle is so closely in tune with our planet's physics that one might wonder why we don't use this integrated system any longer.

---

[213] The length of an 'equatorial' MY (as opposed to a 'polar' MY of 82.967 cm) is 83.102 cm, but as a sidereal day is about .9973 mean solar days, the distance covered by the Earth relative to the Sun in 1/366th of 1"M is only 82.878 cm at the equator, which is 99.9 per cent of a polar MY.

The Megalithic Pendulum

We have seen that no measuring rod one MY long has so far surfaced. How did MPDs manage to achieve such consistency, using a MY that was apparently always the same length across vast areas and during centuries, or perhaps millennia? As this seems to defy common sense, there must be a rational explanation. In other words, there must have existed a 'universal' way for MPDs to work out the exact length of their standard unit whenever they needed to.

Although the idea is speculative, there is a distinct chance the Megalithic people used a pendulum. The idea was first suggested in the book *Uriel's Machine* by Christopher Knight and Robert Lomas in 1999,[214] and in many of Alan Butler's subsequent books.

Working together with Alan Butler on this problem, Knight and Lomas found out that the best way for an ancient people to measure time without any watch or modern clock was by swinging a pendulum. A pendulum is a bob or weight suspended from a piece of string that can be made to oscillate back and forth. No matter the mass of the bob, a pendulum produces regular swings that mainly depend on two things, the gravity of Earth (*g*) and the length of the piece of string: the longer it is, the shorter the period of the pendulum, which means a smaller pendulum will produce faster swings.

If MPDs indeed used a 366-degree geometry, it might have occurred to them to divide the horizon into 366 parts. Let's assume they decided to time the movement of stars. Stars are fixed points so they don't really move—at least, not until very long periods—but the rotation of our planet gives them an apparent movement in the heavens. They might have wished to time a star moving about one Megalithic degree over the horizon, or 1/366th of a sidereal day. In order to do that, they might have positioned two poles with a gap of 1/366th of the horizon apart, and then swung a pendulum as one star moved from one pole to the other.

Incredibly, the length of a string (between fulcrum and gravity center of the weight) that swings 366 times (183 periods) in one 366th of a solar day[215] (that's 236.06 modern seconds or about four minutes less four

[214] Christopher Knight and Robert Lomas, *Uriel's Machine*, London: Arrow Books, 1999, p. 300-1

[215] Logic tells us that we should use 1/366th of a sidereal day or 235.42 seconds, but again a much better approximation of the Megalithic yard is obtained by dividing a solar day rather than a sidereal day.

seconds)—is almost exactly ½ MY! Thus it is also the radius of a circle that is almost exactly one MY in diameter. Thom himself claimed the unit of ½ MY was often used as well, and there was also, of course, the so-called Megalithic rod which was 2½ MY long or 5 times this unit of ½ MY. This result might seem almost magical, but it is true. When I checked the results later on, and examined the problem under different angles, I could never spot any flaw in their reasoning.

Fig. 16. A Megalithic pendulum with a length of ½ MY swings 366 times in one 366th of a solar day.

Of course, because our planet is not a perfect sphere, the gravity of the Earth is not constant and slightly varies from the equator to the poles (g is about 9.780 m/s^2 at the equator, and 9.833 at the North Pole). Interestingly, as gravity is higher in Scotland than in England or Brittany, the length of our pendulum string is very slightly longer in Scotland, and closer to Thom's approximation of the Megalithic yard. For example, at the latitude of 60°N, corresponding to the Shetland Islands, many Megalithic monuments are to be found. Here g is 9.819 m/s^2, and the length of string obtained via this method is 41.36 cm, which doubled is 82.78 cm, or 99.85 per cent of the Megalithic yard as observed by Thom himself for Scotland. The difference is only one part in 645, which is within the 1 in 500 variation Thom claimed to observe from site to site. This result is also perfectly in tune with the Megalithic yard observed by Thom at the Ring of Brodgar in Orkney, at a similar latitude of 59°01'N.

At the latitude of Stonehenge, England, the results are not quite as good as they are in Scotland, yet still quite impressive. The length obtained is 41.36 cm, which doubled gives an 82.72-cm-long MY, which is 99.71 per cent of the Megalithic yard as observed by Thom in English sites (different to Thom's MY in one part in 345). Subsequent research though showed me something even stranger, almost 'miraculous,' but then again perfectly true. Mathematically speaking (that is, using the mathematical formula of pendulums), if you are to use the 365.2422th part of a sidereal day, the pendulum that will beat 365.2422 times at the latitude of Stonehenge will be *exactly* ½ MY! (365.2422 days is the length of a tropical year). This result is purely mathematical, and I leave it to the reader to conjecture why this might be, as it is beyond the scope of my research to account for it.

In their book *Civilization One*[216] and *Before the Pyramids*,[217] Alan Butler and Christopher Knight suggested that when planet Venus is an 'evening star,' or apparently moving *against* the direction followed by the backdrop of stars in the night sky, it can (as seen from the Earth) move faster than ever in its cycle. At its fastest in this retrograde movement, it completes one Megalithic degree (or moves across 1/366th of the horizon, say, from one side of an adequate braced wooden frame to the other) in about 236.25 seconds, which is about 0.19 modern seconds more than the 366th part of a solar day. The length of string that will swing 366 times in this duration is, at a 60°N latitude, 41.45 cm, which doubled is 82.9 cm, again almost exactly the Megalithic yard as observed by Thom in Scotland! Again, this sounds almost miraculous, but it means that if MPDs would actually do that when Venus travelled across the sky at its fastest speed, it would result in an exactly ½-MY-long piece of string.

All this of course is speculative, and might be purely coincidental, but the fact that it actually works, against all odds, is really intriguing. Once again, even if we can't know for sure, the simplest solution is that the Megalithic people indeed used a pendulum while observing the stars and/or Venus to find the Megalithic yard whenever they needed to, as it provided a very accurate means to do it. If this truly did happen, it would explain why Professor Thom observed the Megalithic yard with such consistency.

Now if MPDs indeed used this pendulum, are we to presume they noticed it worked *after* they had estimated the circumference of the Earth? Or are we to presume that they calculated it afterwards? It is even to be wondered whether they *did* calculate it at all. In other words, did they even notice that, by some remarkable coincidence of nature, the Megalithic yard was *both* a perfect subdivision of the Earth's polar circumference in 366-degree geometry *and* twice the length of a pendulum string that swings 366 times when the Earth rotates on itself by one Megalithic degree? How is that even possible? Or did they simply inherit this knowledge from another even more advanced civilisation? As we said before, the degree of precision of all this is just staggering.

Is there any material evidence that pendulums have been used in the deep past? For obvious reasons, pieces of twine or string don't seem to have made it through the millennia, but a few bobs might have survived.

---

[216] Alan Butler and Christopher Knight, *Civilization One*, London: Watkins, 2004, p. 220-5

[217] Alan Butler and Christopher Knight, *Before the Pyramids: Cracking Archaeology's Greatest Mystery*, London: Watkins, 2009, p. 222-5

Bronze Age drilled pebbles which are cylindrical, triangular and even pyramidal in shape have been found in Britain, for instance at Runnymede, Surrey, and Aldermaston Wharf, Berkshire. They are usually interpreted as loom-weights for the weaving of cloth or fabric, but some of them could just as well have been weights for pendulums. Fragments of perforated artefacts made out of baked clay have also been unearthed at the Megalithic site of Knowth (very close to the Megalithic circular mound of Newgrange), Ireland.[218] Were they pendulum bobs?

Main points

- **The Phaistos Disc is likely to have been a calendar, perhaps a 366-day calendar**
- **The Minoans in Crete and the Megalithic people before them may have used a 366-degree geometry**
- **The Minoan foot and the Megalithic yard are perfect subdivisions of the Earth's circumference**
- **The Megalithic people used Pythagorean triangles two millennia before Pythagoras**
- **The Crucuno Rectangle in Brittany perfectly exemplifies the Megalithic yard**
- **366 and 40, along with base 10, lie at the heart of the Megalithic system, and these numbers are in tune with our planet's physics**
- **Time and distance were potentially reconciled in an integrated, harmonious geometry**
- **A pendulum that beats 366 times in one 366th of a day describes a circle 1 Megalithic yard in diameter**

---

[218] http://irisharchaeology.ie/2011/05/mystery-artefact-sheds-new-light-on-irish-bronze-age-weaving/

Chapter Eight: The Druidic Lines

Back in 2001, I found it hard to believe that the knowledge and expertise that had been put to good use by the Megalithic people in erecting mammoth stones, or in navigating along the shores of the European continent and beyond, had completely disappeared with time. Similarly, I found it extremely difficult to believe that the extensive astronomical knowledge of the Celtic Druids as described by classical authors had also faded into oblivion without having been passed down to anyone.

I felt that people who had been able to raise such huge pieces of rock, arranged in such complex structures, built such magnificent cairns, made such beautiful engravings, and used such an advanced form of geometry, couldn't possibly have failed to leave any geometrical, astronomical, architectural, or artistic memes to their descendants. In other words, these ancient sages must have left some cultural imprint that influenced further generations of Europeans. I stress that my feeling wasn't born out of European pride: I didn't care whether this knowledge ultimately came from somewhere else on the globe or not. What interested me was the thought that knowledge in general, especially extraordinary knowledge of that kind, probably never completely dies off. It somehow contributes, even if indirectly, to the life of future generations, or even future peoples who eventually settle an area.

It was nothing more than an intuition, of course, but as I wrote that to Alan Butler in my second email to him, I felt that at least some of this former knowledge had probably lived on under some form or another till more modern times, and had partially contributed to the eventual rise to power of the continent during the Renaissance. At the time of course, I was far from imagining how true this intuition would prove to be. I was equally far from being conscious of the sheer magnitude of this past knowledge.

In his reply, Alan revealed something that was to focus my attention for years to come. Not only did he drop the name of Xavier Guichard (see Chapter Three), a man I had never heard of back then. He also told me that the system of latitudinal and longitudinal Salt Lines (parallels and meridians), which Guichard thought were invented by the Bronze Age people of Western Europe, actually appear to have existed long *before* the Celts.

As we have seen before, Guichard himself thought that whoever had designed this geometry had made a slight mistake, for the 'Alesian lines of longitude' were too close to one another and measured 58 minutes ½ on the great circle of the Earth, instead of 60 modern minutes. Guichard thought this inaccuracy had gone unnoticed by these early geographers, but that anyone who would have expanded their work to the entire planet 'would have noticed that the system counted 369 longitudes instead of 360.' In Alan Butler's view, there had never been any mistake, and each degree was actually closer to 59 modern arc minutes (59.016 precisely) than 58 minutes ½, which could mean only one thing: a 366-degree great circle of the Earth had been used.

In addition, according to Alan, the system appeared to be older than Guichard had assumed, as key Megalithic sites such as Stonehenge and Avebury in England seemed to be Salt Line locations as well. Stranger still, the Valley of the Kings in Egypt was also a Salt Line location, just like the River Jordan in Palestine. Were these observations merely arbitrary results? Last but not least, Alan told me I was right in thinking that this ancient knowledge had never died, and had apparently lived on until very recent times. There seemed to be a golden thread through the tapestry of time, an unbroken chain of knowledge that had been secretly passed down hundreds of generations from the Megalithic times to the modern period (see Part III).

At this point I started to wonder if Alan was serious or not, because the whole thing was going way too far and was becoming quite absurd to the eyes of a novice as myself in the field of ancient geometry. That a prehistoric people had been able to deploy an Earth geometry on such a scale and marked it on the ground with gigantic monuments sounded ludicrous to me, and I figured the results had to be coincidental. More incredible still was the idea that this knowledge had been transmitted in secret until more modern times. This could be good material for an Umberto Eco novel, but in my humble opinion there was no way it could be real (a Dan Brown novel would be a more appropriate description, but that was two years before *The DaVinci Code* was published, and I hadn't yet heard of the now-famous novelist).

Intrigued though, I set out to verify these claims, mostly in the hope of disproving them, or at least shrugging them off. As it turned out, I couldn't have been more wrong.

Checking the existence of Salt Lines

The first thing to do was to establish the system of Salt Lines on Earth. If MPDs or others after them had indeed decided to build huge monuments on the planet along these lines, it shouldn't be too difficult to spot them.

Alan provided me with a Salt Lines World List he had established. The parallels on the list had been relatively easy to determine, as they are derived from the equator. The meridians, on the other hand, run from pole to pole and you normally have to know the prime meridian, or at least one line for sure, in order to determine the others. Alan had used Guichard's maps to see which towns and cities the meridians crossed, and extrapolated the others from those. We'll see shortly that in my estimation his meridians were about two arc minutes too far to the west.

Using Alan's list, the first thing I did was to check whether Alesia-like place names were located on this system of parallels and meridians, or not. Of course, it is not always easy to know what particular village or town name actually derives from *Alesia*, or if any does at all. As most locations cited by Guichard are hamlets or very small villages, the etymology of such toponyms is not always given in specialised books. Sometimes the etymology of a place name is given but debated by linguists; sometimes it is obscure, or even totally unknown. In any case, so as not to be influenced in any way, I decided to ignore what was said about their origin, and selected the place names that Guichard had himself selected in his book, adding to the list those that were identical or similar but that he had—deliberately or not—overlooked.

This casual analysis showed me two things: first, many Alesia-like place names were indeed Salt Line locations, or were quite close to Salt Lines; second, many other *Alesias* which were not Salt Line locations were situated in river curves, as Guichard had claimed.

Alan had also told me that, according to him, an inordinate number of middling and large cities in northern France were Salt Line locations. A casual study of the main cities of France, but also of Spain, Portugal, Italy, Switzerland, Germany, Belgium, the Netherlands, Luxemburg, Britain and even Denmark showed me that the number of cities that were on or near Salt Lines was indeed out of proportion in northern France, although this was not particularly so anywhere else. A few other cities such as Canterbury and Birmingham in England, or Cologne in Germany, were also Salt Line locations, but their relatively small number didn't seem to go beyond what was to be statistically expected from chance.

A few probabilities

I then decided to compare the actual number of average or big cities in northern France that were also Salt Line locations to the number expected by probabilities. One of the goals of this book being to keep as many numbers out as possible—a daunting task in a book about ancient mathematics and geometry—the reader who is interested in the details of this study should refer to my first book.[219]

Suffice it to say here that the probabilities were double-checked by two mathematicians.[220] In all, three different mathematicians checked all the numbers, calculations and probabilities presented in my first book. In taking the distance relative to the Salt Line into account, the reference point in cities was defined as the biggest church or cathedral, and a city was considered to be a Salt Line location if the site stood on or immediately adjacent to a parallel or meridian of the Salt Line system.

So that the reader can appreciate what is the distance between two Salt Lines, or one Megalithic degree, let us say that it is a nearly constant 109.3 km (or 67.9 mi) or so between parallels (with only very slight variations as the Earth is not a perfect sphere), and from 109.3 km at the equator to 0 km at the poles between meridians, depending on the latitude. For example, the interval between two Salt meridians is 109.3 km (68 mi) at the equator, but only 54.6 km (33.9 mi) at 60° North, the latitude of the Shetland Islands or the southern coast of Alaska.

The geographic coordinates of the locations studied were rounded off to the nearest arc minute, which is about 1.85 km along a meridian, that is, between parallels. It proved pointless to work with an accuracy to the arc second, which is only about 30 yards or less.

Because a line has by definition no breadth, I actually worked on *bands* one Megalithic arc minute wide. As there are about 59'M (i.e. Megalithic arc minutes) to the modern degree, there are about 59 such bands between two modern degrees, and the probabilities were calculated from that definition. Of course, one particular reference point can be intersected by a parallel or a meridian, or by both. To cut a long story short, the probability for any particular reference point to fall arbitrarily on either a Salt Parallel or a Salt Meridian was about $1/59 + 1/59 - 1/59^2$ or one chance in 29.75, meaning that, statistically speaking, there

---

[219] Sylvain Tristan, *Les Lignes d'or*, Paris: Alphée, 2005, p. 206-28

[220] My heartfelt thanks to my friends and ex-colleagues Yannick Leclerc and Alain Pennetier in Bourges, France. Any remaining error in the maths is mine and mine alone.

was a 96.6 per cent chance (on average) for any chosen location *not* to stand on a Salt Line. At least in theory. Using probability laws it was also easy to determine the statistical chance for any particular reference point to stand on a Salt Line one, two, or even three arc minutes away from a Salt Line—for instance, there is statistically one chance in 4.48 for a reference point to be located three arc minutes or less away from either a Salt Parallel or Salt Meridian.

The first result of this study was quite odd. Out of 29 large towns or cities which were in direct proximity of Salt Meridians, 28 were about *two arc minutes east* of a line. This strange fact strongly suggested that the Salt Lines World List I had was slightly erroneous. In other words, it looked as though Salt meridians had to be moved two arc minutes *east.* Similarly, for Stonehenge to be a Salt Meridian location, as Alan suggested, again the meridians had to be displaced two arc minutes eastwards. Two conclusions had to be drawn. First of all, it really looked like the system was not a dream: Salt Lines appeared to exist, and many northern French cities or large towns appeared to be located along Salt Meridians in particular. Secondly, the system required a minor adjustment to work optimally.

If this first observation was merely accidental, why weren't there approximately as many reference points too much to the east as there were too much to the west? Why did there seem to be a consistent two-arc minute error *in one direction only*, with a massive number of city centers about two minutes east of the presumed meridians? The most reasonable explanation was that the Salt Meridians had to be positioned about two arc minutes[221] east of where Alan initially estimated them to be.

Alesias located on Salt Lines

Before we deal with these large cities in northern France, let us come back for a while to Alesias. Table 1 shows some examples of Alesia-like place names in Western Europe that are also Salt Line locations. It uses as a reference system the new Salt Line list I have established, with each Salt Meridian two minutes east of those as defined by Alan Butler (the full Salt Lines World List can be found in Appendix 2).

As can be seen, the village of Alaise, which was the cornerstone of Guichard's theory, is too far from the nearest Salt Line (4 arc minutes

[221] In my previous book *Les Lignes d'or*, I had wrongly assumed the Salt Meridians to be three arcminutes east of Alan Butler's system, but much better results are obtained on average with displacing them only two arcminutes east.

away) for us to make any sound conclusion as to its location. The fact remains that Alaise stands on a hill in a river curve. Was the village originally founded there because the hill was in a river curve *and* because it rose tolerably close to a Salt Line? We shall probably never know.

The other Alesia-like place names presented in the table, by contrast, are *all* Salt Line locations, in the sense that they are either spot on the course of a Salt Line, or three arc minutes or less away from one. It should be stressed that perhaps some of these places which happen to bear a name that looks like a plausible derivation of Alesia and that are also Salt Line locations might just be lucky happenstances. Nor is it claimed that all of these 36 examples truly represent eroded forms of ancient Alesias; some of them just *might* be. As I said, this list was established by intuition, looking at both Guichard's maps and modern maps, without even caring to see what etymologists thought of the place names so as not to bias the results. That's why no probability study accompanies the table.

Alesia-like name places	***Modern latitude***	***Modern longitude***	***Distance in arc minutes from the nearest Salt Lines, parallels (left) and meridians (right)***	
Alaise, France	*47°01' N*	*05°58' E*	*-12*	*-04*
Presumed Alesia near Guillon, France	*47°32' N*	*04°05' E*	*+19*	***+01***
Alès, France	*44°08' N*	*04°05' E*	*-08*	***+01***
Aalst, Belgium	*50°56' N*	*04°03' E*	*-13*	***-01***
Alleuze, France	*44°58' N*	*03°05' E*	*-19*	***00***
Allos, France	*44°15' N*	*06°38' E*	***-01***	*-23*
Alós d'Ensil, Spain	*42°42' N*	*01°05' E*	*+24*	***-02***
Olost, Spain	*41°59' N*	*02°06' E*	*-19*	***00***
Allouis, France	*47°10' N*	*02°14' E*	***-03***	*+08*
Alluyes, France	*48°14' N*	*01°22' E*	***+02***	*+15*
Aylesbury, England	*51°50' N*	*00°50' W*	*-18*	***+01***
Alborg, Denmark	*57°03' N*	*09°56' E*	***00***	***-02***
Alloa, Scotland	*56°07' N*	*03°49' W*	***+03***	***+01***
Laz, France	*48°08' N*	*03°50' W*	*-04*	***+02***
Laiz, France	*46°15' N*	*04°54' E*	***+01***	*-09*
Lézat-sur-Lèze,	*43°17' N*	*01°21' E*	***00***	*+14*

France				
Lessay, France	*49°13' N*	*01°32' W*	***+02***	*-18*
Lèz, France	*44°13' N*	*04°43' E*	***-03***	*-20*
Lezay, France	*46°16' N*	*00°01' E*	***+02***	*-07*
Lez-Fontaine, France	*50°11' N*	*04°04' E*	***+01***	***00***
Lézan, France	*44°01' N*	*04°03' E*	*-15*	***-01***
Losse, France	*44°07' N*	*00°06' E*	*-09*	***-02***
Lixing-lès-Rouhling, France	*49°09' N*	*07°00' E*	***-02***	***-01***
Alexain, France	*48°13' N*	*00°46' W*	***+01***	*-05*
Als Island, Denmark	*54°59' N*	*09°55' E*	*-06*	***-03***
Alstätte, Germany	*52°08' N*	*06°55' E*	***00***	*-06*
Alster, Germany	*53°36' N*	*09°59' E*	*+29*	***+01***
Alstern, Sweden	*59°40' N*	*13°55' E*	*-21*	***+01***
Olizy, France	*49°09' N*	*03°45' E*	***-02***	*-19*
Olley, France	*49°10' N*	*05°46' E*	***-01***	*-15*
Ors, France	*50°06' N*	*03°38' E*	*-04*	*-26*
Oost, Island of Texel, Netherlands	*53°06' N*	*04°53' E*	***-01***	*-10*
Alsting, France	*49°11' N*	*07°00' E*	***00***	***-01***
Alseno, Italy	*44°54' N*	*09°59' E*	*-21*	***+01***
Alzonne, France	*43°15' N*	*02°11' E*	***-02***	*+05*
Vaals, Netherlands	*50°47' N*	*06°01' E*	*-22*	***-01***

Table 1. Alesia-like place names in Europe that are also (with the exception of Alaise) Salt Line locations, i.e. that are no further than 3 arc minutes away from either a Salt Parallel or a Salt Meridian

The *A-r-s* and *A-r-z* place names

I then decided to somewhat broaden my search, by studying place names which looked liked *Aresia* or *Ars*. The letters *l* and *r* are both liquid consonants, with a similar sound, produced in a similar way, and tending to be interchangeable over time. For example, the Spanish word *playa* ('beach') corresponds to the word *praia* in Portuguese. Similarly, Japanese speakers do not differentiate easily between these two sounds, as they have only one intermediate such sound. In the case of old French, the letter *r* was traditionally rolled, and thus not that distant phonetically to an *l*, as can still be heard in some parts of the French countryside, or in Quebec. It is also known that speakers of Latin, the mother tongue of French, rolled their *r*'s.

In France, a constellation of villages or small towns bear such names like Ars, Arz, Aroz, Arrosès, Aressy, and so on, and a very high number of these places are also Salt Line locations. I could find 30 place names in France (29 villages and one island) that bore a name of the type *Ars-* or *Arz-*. These place names are reported in Table 2. Again, I didn't wish to see what etymologists had to say about these place names, as I didn't want to be influenced in my study. I was amazed to see how many of these were also Salt Line locations.

Place name	**Modern latitude**	**Modern longitude**	**Distance in arc minutes from the nearest Salt Lines, parallels (left) and meridians (right)**	
PLACES NAMED EITHER ARS OR ARZ				
Arz Island (56)	47°35' N	02°48' W	+22	**-01**
Ars-en-Ré (17)	46°13' N	01°31' W	**-01**	-19
Ars (16)	45°39' N	00°23' E	+24	+15
Ars (23)	46°00' N	02°05' E	-14	**-01**
Ars-Laquenexy (57)	49°06' N	06°16' E	-05	+14
Ars-les-Favets (63)	46°12' N	02°45' E	**-02**	-21
Ars-sur-Moselle (57)	49°05' N	06 05' E	-06	**+03**
Ars-sur-Formans (01)	46°00' N	04°49' E°	-14	-14
PLACE NAMES BEGINNING IN A-R-S/Z				
Arsy (60))	49°24' N	02°41' E	+13	-24
Arras (62)	50°17' N	02°47' E	+07	-18
Aroz (70)	47°38' N	06°00' E	+25	**-02**
Auros (33)	44°30' N	00°09' E	+14	**+01**
Ayros-Arbouix (65)	43°00' N	00°04' E	-17	-04
Arrosès (64)	43°33' N	00°07' E	+16	**-01**
Arrest (80)	50°08' N	01°37' E	**-02**	-29
Arès (33)	44°49' N	01°02' W	-26	+11
Aressy (64)	43°17' N	00°19' E	**00**	+11
Les Aires (34)	43°35' N	03°06' E	+18	**+01**
Arsy (60)	49°24' N	02°41' E	+13	-24

Arcy (71)	*46°20' N*	*04°01' E*	*+06*	***-03***
Arzay (38)	*45°26' N*	*05°10' E*	*+11*	*+07*
Arcis-sur-Aube (10)	*48°32' N*	*04°08' E*	*+20*	*+04*
Arces (17)	*45°33' N*	*00°52' W*	*+18*	***+01***
Arcizans-Dessus (65)	*42°59' N*	*00°10' E*	*-18*	***+02***
Arcizans-Avant (65)	*42°59' N*	*00°06' E*	*-18*	***-02***
Arzens (11)	*43°12' N*	*02°12' E*	*-05*	*+06*
Arzacq-Arraziguet (64)	*43°32' N*	*00°25' E*	*+15*	*+17*
Arzano (29)	*47°54' N*	*03°26' W*	*-18*	*-22*
Arsac (33)	*45°00' N*	*00°42' E*	*-15*	*-25*
Arzal (56)	*47°31' N*	*02°23' W*	*+18*	*-26*

Table 2. Place names in France beginning in a-r-s *or* a-r-z *(or* a-r-c*, if the* c *is pronounced like an* s*). The numbers in brackets correspond to the administrative numbers of French departments.*

Xavier Guichard had not looked into these *Ars-* and *Arz-* place names. In his book he mentions only one such name (Aresia in Corsica) as being on one of his 24 radiating lines springing from Alaise, but he dismisses it, doubting the place is an actual Alesian site. It seems he missed the phonetic proximity of the sounds *l* and rolled *r*, making him miss in turn what I think was a crucial clue in his investigation.

According to basic probability laws, we can expect about one place name[222] among these 30 to be a perfect Salt Line location, either a Salt Parallel or a Salt Meridian. The number observed is in fact one, Aressy, which is neatly intersected by a Salt Parallel. We can also expect about three place names[223] to be located one arc minute or less from a Salt Line. The number observed is... eight (Arz Island, Ars-en-Ré, Ars 23, Auros, Arrosès, Aressy, Les Aires and Arces), or close to three times the expected number! We can expect about 5 place names[224] to be located two arc minutes away maximum from a Salt Line. The number observed is... 13 (adding Ars-les-Favets, Aroz, Arrest, Arcizans-Dessus and Arcizans-Avant to the previous list), or nearly three times the expected number! And we can expect about 6 or 7 place names[225] to be located three arc minutes away maximum from a Salt Line. The number

[222] 30/29.75=1.01
[223] 30/10.09=2.97
[224] 30/6.16=4.87
[225] 30/4.48=6.70

observed is... 15 (adding Ars-sur-Moselle and Arcy to the list), or more than twice the number expected according to probability. Isn't that odd?

Again, these results might be purely accidental, but it seems coincidence already has a lot on its back to bear! Although by no means in themselves a definitive proof of Guichard's thesis, these findings definitely support the theory that these types of place names are linked to our hypothetical Salt Lines. It really looks like most of these place names are not distributed in a random manner, but rather in a meaningful one. And again, outside of 366-degree geometry, this distribution would be meaningless.

Let us now come back to the link between Salt Lines and the major cities of northern France.

Salt Line cities ('Druidic Cities') of northern France

The following table (Table 3) shows large towns and cities which are also Salt Line locations in northern France (i.e., north of the city of Bourges, which lies very near the heart of the country). As anyone familiar with the geography of France can see, many famous cities happen to be Salt Line locations: among them, Beauvais (famous for its huge cathedral), Dijon (famous for its mustard, it also has a cathedral), Le Havre (the second busiest port in France after Marseille, its name means harbor), Lille (the capital of Flanders), Metz (the capital city of Lorraine), Nantes (the capital of the ancient duchy of Brittany), Reims (famous for its cathedral, where French kings used to be crowned), Rouen (the historic capital city of Normandy and the place where Joan of Arc was burnt at the stake), Sens (famous for its cathedral), Troyes (which long remained the capital of the Province of Champagne, and the place where the Order of the Knights Templar was recognised in 1129), Vannes (from the Veneti, a seafaring Celtic people mentioned by Caesar), and Versailles (famous for Louis XIV's immense Palace). As big cities are more likely to be renamed in the course of history than smaller towns or villages (for example by new conquerors), we often don't know for sure what they were called originally. Were some of these places once called *Alesia* too? Unfortunately, we will probably never know.

Two cities (Besançon and Vierzon) happen to be both Salt Parallel locations and Salt Meridian locations (meaning these two particular cities are intersected by *two* Salt Lines). The other ones are either Salt Parallel locations *or* Salt Meridian locations.

Interestingly, the majority of all these cities are Salt *Meridian* locations. It is to be remembered that meridians are (at least in theory) the most difficult lines to establish for an ancient people who did not have any GPS in their rucksacks.

City name	***Modern latitude***	***Modern longitude***	***Distance in arc minutes from the nearest Salt Lines, parallels (left) and meridians (right)***	
Beauvais	*49°26' N*	*02°05' E*	*+15*	***-01***
Besançon	*47°14' N*	*06°02'E*	***+01***	***00***
Caen	*49°11' N*	*00°22' W*	***00***	*-29*
Cambrai	*50°10' N*	*03°14' E*	***00***	*+09*
Dieppe	*49°56' N*	*01°05' E*	*-14*	***-02***
Dijon	*47°19' N*	*05°02' E*	*+06*	***-01***
Douai	*50°22' N*	*03°05' E*	*+12*	***00***
Epinal	*48°11' N*	*06°27' E*	***-01***	*+25*
Evreux	*49°01' N*	*01°09' E*	*-10*	***+02***
Le Havre	*49°30' N*	*00°07' E*	*+19*	***-01***
Lille	*50°38' N*	*03°04' E*	*+28*	***-01***
Lisieux	*49°09' N*	*00°14' E*	***-02***	*+06*
Nantes	*47°13' N*	*01°33' W*	***00***	*-17*
Reims	*49°15' N*	*04°02' E*	*+04*	***-02***
Rouen	*49°27' N*	*01°06' E*	*+16*	***-01***
Saint-Nazaire	*47°16'N*	*02°12'W*	***+03***	*+22*
Sens	*48°12' N*	*03°17' E*	***00***	*+12*
Troyes	*48°18' N*	*04°05' E*	*+06*	***+01***
Vannes	*47°39' N*	*02°46' W*	*+24*	***-03***
Versailles	*48°48' N*	*02°07' E*	*-23*	***+01***
Vierzon	*47°14' N*	*02°04' E*	***+01***	***-02***

Table 3. Cities and large towns in the northern half of France that are also Salt Line locations

The number of cities in northern France that are also Salt Line locations makes it hard to believe it is just a random event. The obvious city missing from that list, of course, is Paris, by far the largest of them all and the capital city of France. We'll see why it is absent in Part III. Let us say for the time being that it is only *apparently* missing.

Now for some probabilities. I took the 30 largest cities in the northern half of France (excluding for obvious reasons Parisian suburbs that have only grown large recently.) I then ticked those which are located 3 arc minutes or less from the nearest Salt Line, and compared the number of them to the number expected by probability. Using 1990 data in my first book, I already obtained quite impressive results,[226] but checking the data again for this book using 2010 data and more accurate geographic coordinates, the results are even more impressive. In a nutshell, there are three times more cities which are located one arc minute or less from a Salt Line than there should be according to probability, and three times more cities which are exact Salt Line locations than there should be (see Table 4). Once again, these remarkable results strongly suggest that the distribution of northern France cities is not random, and that many of these cities have been deliberately positioned there to begin with because they lie at the intersection of a major river and a Salt Line.

I realized that these results were quite simply startling, and I became more confident that Salt Lines were most probably a reality.

Since there is no evidence that these lines are in any way connected to salt, with Alan's consent I decided to rename these axes *Golden Lines* when I wrote my first book. Not to confuse them with the golden ratio, however, I shall refer to them as *Druidic Lines,* or *Druidic Meridians* and *Druidic Parallels* in this book. The cities that are located on these lines or immediately adjacent to them will be referred to as *Druidic cities.*

Table 4. The 30 largest cities in the northern half of France in 2010. 33.3% of them are located 2 arc minutes away or less from a Druidic Line (Salt Line), which is more than twice the number expected by chance. Impressively, 30% of them are located 1 arc minute away or less from a Druidic Line, which is more than three times than the number expected by chance. Finally, three cities or 10% of them are located right on a Druidic Line, which again is almost three times more than expected by chance.

[226] See Sylvain Tristan, *Les Lignes d'or,* Paris: Alphée, 2005, p. 220

Largest cities in France (excluding Paris suburbs)		**Salt Line cities**
1	*Paris*	
2	*Nantes*	●
3	*Strasbourg*	
4	*Lille*	●
5	*Rennes*	
6	*Reims*	●
7	*Le Havre*	●
8	*Dijon*	●
9	*Angers*	
10	*Le Mans*	
11	*Brest*	
12	*Tours*	
13	*Amiens*	
14	*Metz*	
15	*Besançon*	●
16	*Orléans*	
17	*Rouen*	●
18	*Mulhouse*	
19	*Caen*	●
20	*Nancy*	
21	*Roubaix*	
22	*Dunkerque*	
23	*Tourcoing*	
24	*Versailles*	●
25	*Calais*	
26	*Colmar*	
27	*Saint-Nazaire*	●
28	*Quimper*	
29	*Villeneuve-d'Ascq*	
30	*Troyes*	●
Proportion of Druidic cities / total number of cities **3 arcminutes away*	*(theoretical)* *100/4.48=22.3 %*	*(observed)* *36.7 %*
** 2 arcminutes away*	*100/6.16=16.2 %*	*33.3 %*
** 1 arcminute away*	*100/10.09=9.9 %*	*30 %*
** 0 arcminutes away*	*100/29.75=3.4 %*	*10 %*

There is of course no way to tell which cities were deliberately founded on Druidic Lines and which are fortuitously situated there. Only the fact that a high proportion of them are Salt Line locations is important, for it clearly seems to show intention.

Interestingly, among these cities is Besançon, which is intersected by two Druidic Lines, a parallel *and* a meridian. It is only 1'M away from the nearest Druidic Parallel, and stands exactly along a Druidic Meridian. Such a combination happens by chance only once in 300.[227]

Are we being extremely lucky, or do these results clearly suggest that whoever founded these cities did so with 366-degree geometry in mind? Doesn't it look like it was the intention of the ancients to reify 366-degree geometry on the territory, in other words to make it concrete, with stone on the ground—by building villages, towns or cities? Perhaps selected locations were held sacred because they lay on these earth lines, and were granted immortality by constructing long-lasting stone markers there.[228]

Main points

• Xavier Guichard's Salt Lines appear to be derived from a 366-degree great circle of the Earth

• Many Alesia-like place names (mainly in France but more generally in Western Europe) are located on Salt Lines

• There are about 3 times more place names starting in Ars- or Arz- that are located on, or immediately along, Salt Lines than the number expected by chance

• There are about 3 times more major cities in northern France located on, or immediately along, Salt Lines (renamed Druidic Lines) than the number expected by chance

• There are good reasons to believe that these villages, towns or cities are stone markers of these Druidic Lines

---

227 10.09 x 29.75 = 300.18

228 Or the original purpose could have been as an aid to navigation, so that travellers could find their way to these places, by reckoning by the stars, and following rivers. In addition to navigation, it was always useful to settle by a river for drinking water, fishing, irrigation and sanitation (editor's note).

Chapter Nine: Druidic Megalithic Sites of Britain

We have already seen that Stonehenge, in this slightly rectified Salt Lines system working with a 366-degree circle was precisely located on a longitudinal Druidic Line, i.e. a Druidic Meridian. (I find the beauty of it is more readily apparent when dubbed a 'Druidic' Lines system). Quite interestingly, it is also a Druidic Parallel location, as the ancient stone monument stands only two arc minutes north of the 52nd Druidic Parallel that runs at 51°09'N.

Stonehenge is of course a major Megalithic site, probably the most important Megalithic site of Britain—or tying for first place with Avebury, as we'll soon see—and arguably one of the most important Megalithic sites of Europe taken as a whole. Is Stonehenge isolated in being a Druidic Line location, or are there any other key Megalithic sites in Britain or beyond which fulfil this criterion? How much evidence do we have that MPDs erected giant stones as markers on Earth of 366-degree geometry, at much earlier times than Guichard himself would have thought possible?

Stonehenge

Stonehenge is a Megalithic marvel, and lies at the heart of a Megalithic-rich landscape in Wiltshire, southern England. It was built in three phases: around 3100 BC, a circular bank and a ditch enclosure were made, along with a circle of 56 pits known as the Aubrey holes. Then about a century later a timber structure was raised within the enclosure. Finally, the stone structures were raised in a third phase which started c. 2600 BC, using bluestones from the remote Preseli Mountains in Wales, and sarsen stones (sandstone blocks) from a quarry in the more local Marlborough Downs.

While no archaeologist today denies that Stonehenge is directly linked to astronomy, its precise function is still a subject of debate. Some see in it a healing center, a sort of pilgrimage site such as Lourdes in France today. Others contend it was a monument to unify the ancient peoples of Britain. Still others say it was an astronomical observatory designed to predict eclipses.

Once more, Diodorus Siculus might be able to help us understand what Stonehenge truly was. In a passage devoted to Hyperboreans, the Greek historian describes a northern island at least as big as Sicily. On this island—which might well be Britain—the people showed an absolute reverence for Apollo, one of the greatest Greek divinities, often equated to the Sun:

> Of those who have written about the ancient myths, Hecataeus and certain others say that in the regions beyond the land of the Celts there lies in the ocean an island no smaller than Sicily. This island, the account continues, is situated in the north and is inhabited by the Hyperboreans, who are called by that name because their home is beyond the point whence the north wind (Boreas) blows; and the island is both fertile and productive of every crop, and since it has an unusually temperate climate it produces two harvests each year. Moreover, the following legend is told concerning it: Leto was born on this island, and for that reason Apollo is honoured among them above all other gods; and the inhabitants are looked upon as priests of Apollo, after a manner, since daily they praise this god continuously in song and honour him exceedingly. And there is also on the island both a magnificent sacred precinct of Apollo and a notable temple which is adorned with many votive offerings and is spherical in shape. Furthermore, a city is there which is sacred to this god, and the majority of its inhabitants are players on the cithara; and these continually play on this instrument in the temple and sing hymns of praise to the god, glorifying his deeds.[229]

Although we may never be certain, there is a distinct probability that the 'notable temple' which was 'spherical in shape' was Stonehenge. If so, Stonehenge would have been a temple dedicated to the Sun god, where people sang and lyrically played the cithara or some similar instrument. Diodorus got the story from Hecataeus of Abdera, a Greek historian and philosopher living in the 4th century BC, hence about a millennium after Stonehenge was abandoned.

Whatever Stonehenge truly was, it is clear that it was a major Megalithic site for about 1,500 years. In spite of its name, though, it is *not* a henge. Henges are Bronze Age earthworks combining a circular bank and an inner ditch. This type of structure is very common in the British

---

[229] Diodorus Siculus, *The Library of History*, II, 47: http://penelope.uchicago.edu/Thayer/E/Roman/Texts/Diodorus_Siculus/2B*.html

Isles, but they are virtually absent on the continent. They may have first arisen in Orkney, and their purpose is still debated, although many believe they were used for rituals and/or skywatching. In the case of Stonehenge, the ditch has been dug *outside* the ring bank, rather than inside.

Interestingly, Alan Butler carefully measured Stonehenge and found that its original circular bank had a circumference of 366 MY.[230] In Alan's own words: 'Of course it is impossible to be absolutely specific about where the middle of the top of the bank originally was because in the case of Stonehenge the bank has virtually disappeared. However, we took an estimation on lots of different parts of the circle and we also checked our results against drawings of Stonehenge, both 18th century ones and more modern ones.'[231]

Let us now come back to the location of Stonehenge. The probability for Stonehenge to be a perfect Druidic Line location, which it is, according to our definition, is about 1 in 29.75 only. And let's not forget that the Megalithic site stands *both* on a Druidic Meridian and along a Druidic Parallel, which of course has an even smaller chance to occur (about 1 in 183[232]).

As we'll soon see, these results are made even more impressive when you consider that the truly exceptional Megalithic sites of Avebury and Silbury, about twenty miles north of Stonehenge, along with other major contemporary Megalithic sites, are also Druidic Line locations.

One last speculative thought: Stonehenge is located along the 52nd Druidic Parallel north of the equator. Is it just a coincidence that there are also 52 weeks in a year?

Avebury

If Stonehenge is undoubtedly one of the most famous Megalithic sites of all, Avebury is one of the most beautiful Megalithic monuments of Britain, and the largest stone circle ever erected—not only in Britain but in the whole world! Contrary to Stonehenge, Avebury is a henge in the true sense of the term, having a huge circular earthen bank and a deep inner ditch surrounding the stone circle. Alan Butler and Christopher Knight think that British henges were once filled with water, which could have reflected the stars, while the outer bank might have been used as a

[230] Alan Butler, *City of the Goddess*, London: Watkins, 2011, p. 103
[231] Private communication
[232] 29.75 x 6.16=183.26

perfectly level artificial horizon for star observation.[233] What it means is that Avebury might have been the greatest star observatory ever used in Megalithic times.

Inside the henge, no less than 98 sarsen stones used to stand (only 27 survive to this day) in a gigantic circle, some of them weighing over 40 tons. Two smaller circles within the main circle used to grace the center of the monument, but most of them, unfortunately, have also disappeared. Built c. 2600 BC, the monument is contemporaneous to the third stage of Stonehenge.

On my first visit there in 2005 with Alan Butler on my way to Stonehenge, I was awed by the sheer scale of this age-old Megalithic structure. Enormous stones, huge ditches, which had been twice as deep in their prime, still massive banks enclosing the gaunt megaliths, today share the space with grazing sheep and the much more recent, yet very picturesque village of Avebury. For those who love ancient history, Avebury provides a tremendously strong medley of emotions, as it is at the same time very pretty, imposing and mysterious. Just imagine the painstaking efforts the builders had to make to dig a 60-feet deep ditch almost a mile long, using as tools mere deer antlers. The compelling impression of past grandeur that pervades the whole site places Avebury in the author's personal top-ten list of the most poignant historical places in Europe, outranking even Stonehenge and Carnac.

According to the English antiquarian William Stukeley, a Freemason who lived in the 18th century, Avebury was part a much bigger complex which formed the shape of a winding serpent, the Avebury circle being a bulge in the middle of it. Today most of what Stukeley drew has been destroyed, although part of the serpent remains in the West Kennet Avenue, which is a set of two parallel lines of standing stones. Stukeley thought that the head of the serpent was marked out by what is today known as the Sanctuary, a now-destroyed set of six concentric rings of timber, of which 162 postholes remain (more about these in Chapter Fourteen).

Avebury is likely to be what Diodorus Siculus styled 'a magnificent sacred precinct of Apollo' (see above). If this is true, what a superb location for the 'priests of Apollo' to 'praise this god continuously in song and honour him exceedingly'! We know from Greek mythology that

---

[233] Alan Butler and Christopher Knight, *Before the Pyramids. Cracking Archaeology's Gretatest Mystery*, London: Watkins, 2009, p. 44

Apollo was 'the symbol of the Sun and the civilising light.'[234] Was Avebury some brand of solar temple? One can only imagine the ceremonies these priests (our presumed MPDs) would perform, perhaps in the music of the citharas as described by Diodorus.

Was the serpent Python, another figure of Greek mythology, who was conquered by Apollo and buried under the Omphalos ('Navel'), the sacred stone lying at the mid-point of the Earth? If this interpretation is correct, the henge of Avebury at the center of the winding serpent would represent the Omphalos or Navel of the World, and the purpose of the stone circle in the middle of the henge would indeed be to glorify Apollo.

The Avebury stone circle, according to Alexander Thom, was a complex geometric figure based upon a Pythagorean 3-4-5 triangle whose sides are multiples of 25 MY, with each side being respectively 75, 100 and 125 MY.[235] As many of the stones in Avebury are missing, archaeologists had to excavate the site in order to re-establish the positions of the once-standing stones. This was done by Scottish archaeologist Alexander Keiller in the 1930s, who managed to perfectly establish the diameter and position of the two inner circles inside the main ring, or that of many of the menhirs in the main ring. Thom and his assistant later surveyed the site, and if they felt 'perfectly certain of the geometry,' they could be certain of the geometry in only half of the ring (the half that had been excavated). Nevertheless, the presence of the Megalithic yard in Avebury is, according to Thom, perfectly established, and the engineer could ascertain that its length there was a precise 2.720 ft: 'Had, say, 2.730 ft been used, the ring would have been too large by some 5 ft and would have passed outside the stones, a striking proof of the value of the yard and of the precision with which the builders set out the ring.'[236]

Another aspect of Thom's discoveries at Avebury is that in all the arcs that he could ascertain in the geometry of the ring, there are multiples of 2½ MY, a rule which is 'almost universal for perimeters'[237] in British stone circles. What's more, each inner ring at Avebury was almost a perfect circle, with a diameter of 125 MY, or five MY cubed. This is

---

[234] Félix Guirand and Joël Schmidt, *Mythes et mythologies. Histoire et dictionnaire,* Paris: Larousse-Bordas, 1996, p. 616

[235] Alexander Thom, *Megalithic Sites in Britain,* Oxford: Oxford University Press, 1967, p.89

[236] Ibid., p. 90

[237] Ibid.

quite uncommon, as most stone circles were actually egg-shaped or elliptical.

We see that it is almost inescapable that the Megalithic yard was used in Avebury. Is there any other evidence that Megalithic geometry was used there? Yes, there is. Just like Stonehenge, Avebury is a Druidic Meridian location, as the Druidic Meridian running at 1°50'W—the one that perfectly intersects Stonehenge—also skirts the giant stone circle, being only one arc minute away.

Silbury Hill

Less than a mile away from the Avebury henge and stone circles lies one of the most enigmatic Megalithic structures ever made, Silbury Hill. Made up of local chalk and clay, this artificial hill that looks like a giant coconut macaroon culminates at 40 meters (131 feet). Its first phase dates back to c. 2750 BC,[238] but it was remodelled in the following centuries. In fact, it is known that the first mound was smaller, and that it was transformed into a larger one later on.

Just like Avebury or Stonehenge, Silbury is one of the Megalithic jewels of southern England. It is the tallest man-made mound in Europe during prehistory. Its proximity to Avebury leaves no doubt that it is closely associated to the Avebury complex. Interestingly, Silbury Hill was made in steps, in a way that is reminiscent of step pyramids in Egypt, except that it is roughly circular in shape; actually it is a polyhedron with various numbers of straight sides depending on the height. Recent survey work, though, suggests that there was a spiraling path all the way from the base to the summit, which would have made a very convenient processional route to the top of the mound.[239]

Frustratingly, when I first visited the site in 2005, it had already been closed to the public for three years, following the collapse (after some heavy rain) of an excavation shaft made in 1776. But the initial frustration was partially counterbalanced by the impressive height of the artificial hill rising behind a line of hawthorn trees, like a dormant volcano ready to awake. When seen at its foot, the feeling you get is not unlike the thrill you get at the base of an Egyptian pyramid, for that is really an imposing piece of work.

---

[238] Aubrey Burl, *Prehistoric Avebury*, Yale University Press, 1979, p. 129
[239] David Field, 'Great Sites: Silbury Hill' in *British Archaeology*, Issue 70, May 2003: http://www.archaeologyuk.org/ba/ba70/feat2.shtml

Legend has it that this huge step pyramid, today blanketed in grass, is the tomb of King Sil, who lies underneath with his golden horse. No ruler of this name, however, is known to have ever existed. The actual purpose of the mound remains unknown, and many suggestions have been made as to what Silbury Hill was in Megalithic times. Some think it was a sacrificial platform, some others an astronomical observatory or a temple to Mercury, still others a place for assemblies and lawmaking.[240] And just like Avebury, Silbury is encircled with a ditch, meaning Silbury is a very unusual form of henge as well. Was the henge once filled with water?

That Silbury Hill's ditch was once water-filled is by no means a view restricted to independent researchers such as Alan Butler, for example. David Field, a field archaeologist with English Heritage who was responsible for a recent landscape survey of Silbury Hill, writes in *British Archaeology* that '[i]t seems likely... that Silbury Hill's ditches were intentionally filled with water.'[241] His opinion is based upon the discovery in 2001 of what appears to have been a wide human-made channel running toward the ditch, apparently to collect water from local springs, and perhaps from the close-by River Kennet as well. This would explain why Silbury Hill is situated in a valley, rather than on a hilltop: apparently, it *had* to be surrounded with water, so that gravity had the last word, and a huge mound was erected in the middle in order to compensate the resulting lack of height.

So, if their ditches were truly water-filled, Avebury and Silbury once were artificial islands. Perhaps the rings of water were a way to emphasise the sacredness of the sites. The fact that these two sites may have been artificial islands is an important point on which I will come back shortly.

Just like Avebury, Silbury Hill stands about one arc minute away from the Druidic Meridian that runs at 01°50'W and that intersects Stonehenge. If this other major British Megalithic monument is again accidentally associated with Druidic Lines, then we are being very lucky.

Was this Druidic Meridian, in the eyes of MPDs, the *axis mundi*—the center of their world, the *omphalos* or navel of the world, the axis connecting Earth to Heaven? Was it the Greenwich of their time, the prime meridian of the 366 Druidic Lines that follow the Earth's axis of rotation all around the globe?

---

[240] Ibid.
[241] Ibid.

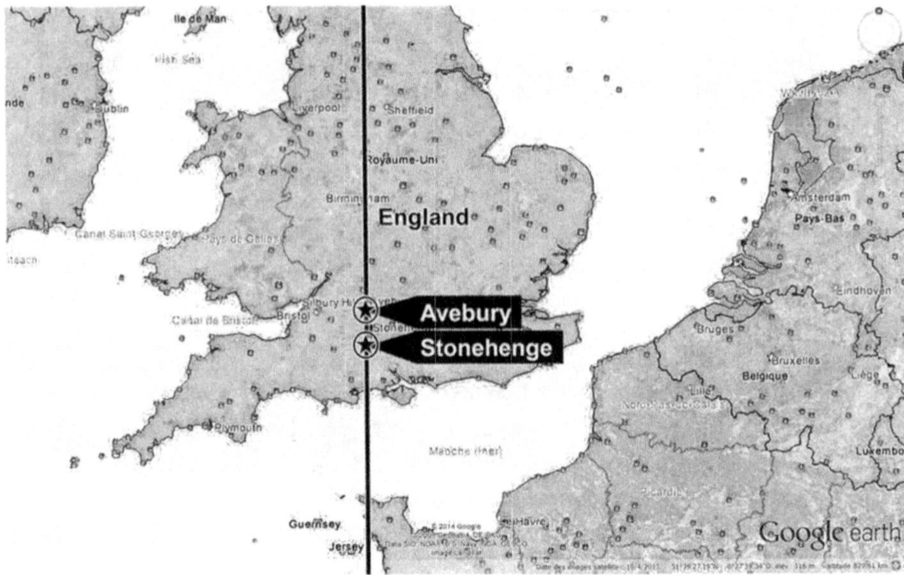

Fig. 17. The Druidic Meridian of Stonehenge and Avebury.

Is Avebury the famed Avalon?

I would like to make the case that the site of Avebury might have been the legendary Avalon of Celtic mythology. In Arthurian literature, Avalon is where King Arthur's magical sword Excalibur was forged, and where the king enjoyed an eternal blissful life after being wounded at the battle of Camlann.

The word *Avalon* is thought to derive from Middle Welsh *Aval Ynis*, 'the Isle of Apples.' In Old Welsh, the term for 'apple' was *abal*. But is the orthodox explanation the only one that holds true?

The name Avebury is the combination of the root *Ave* and the suffix *bury*. The suffix is Saxon (i.e. more recent than the root) and, just like the suffixes *-borough* or *-burgh*, indicates a fortified place. So Avebury is actually 'the Fortress of Ave,' whatever the ancient root *Ave* means.

Now, what if the root derives from *Aval Ynis*? We already saw that Avebury is a henge, meaning it was encircled by a deep ditch, making it an artificial island. Was Avebury the place that gave inspiration to the myth of Aval Ynis? Taking into account that Avebury once was probably a highly sacred place, this would not be surprising at all. But are we to believe that its original name was connected to apples?

The Welsh word for Sun is *haul*, which is phonetically quite close to either *abal* or *aval*. Is it possible that linguists got confused and missed the original meaning of Avalon, which, rather than being the 'Isle of Apples,' was the 'Isle of the Sun'? This hypothesis certainly gives credence to Avebury being the 'magnificent sacred precinct of Apollo' where the 'priests of Apollo' continuously honoured their Sun-God.

Now for the bombshell. The origin of the Greek divinity's name, Apollo, is uncertain and has long been the subject of a heated debate among linguists. We have seen that, according to Greek mythology, Apollo the Sun-God rode the back of a swan and flew back to his native land of the Hyperboreans, in the North of the world, during the cold season. Apollo was nicknamed either 'the Bright,' 'the Blond' or 'The One with the Golden Hair.'[242] What if his native place was Avebury, the 'Isle of the (Bright) Sun', possibly worked by blond-haired MPDs? Apollo the Sun-God of the Greeks would be the mythified remembrance of a *place*—Avalon, the 'Isle of the Sun' in Hyperborea, i.e. Britain. Don't the words *Avalon* and *Apollo* look cognate with each other? In Homeric Greek, Apollo was named *Apollōn*. The names *Avalon* and *Appollōn* are certainly very close phonetically.

Is there any circumstantial evidence to back up this theory? There certainly is. As we said, the origin of the name *Silbury* is unknown, except for the suffix *-bury* which comes from the Saxon. Silbury then was the 'Fortress of Sil.' We also saw that Silbury was most probably surrounded with water, meaning it was an artificial island as well. What if Silbury once was *Sil Ynis*, the 'Isle of Sil'? If Avebury was a Sun temple, it is by no means too big a stretch of imagination to think that Silbury was once connected to the Moon. Do the Greeks have anything in their mythology that would be a remembrance of this putative Moon temple that might at some point have been called *Sil Ynis*? They do. As many readers will have probably guessed by now, the Greek Goddess of the Moon was called *Selene*. Interestingly enough, the etymology of Selene is just as uncertain as that of Apollo.

As ever, there is always the possibility this is yet another uncanny coincidence. Or is it not? All the pieces of the puzzle appear to fall into place perfectly. It definitely looks like the Greeks and the Megalithic people were connected in the past one way or another, perhaps via the Minoans, who preceded and greatly influenced the Mycenaean culture that was to flourish later in Greece.

One side note about Arthurian legends. Tintagel Castle in Cornwall, England, is closely associated to Arthurian mythology, as King Arthur is said to have been conceived there. Oddly enough, the site is a Druidic

---

[242] Guirand and Schmidt, *op. cit.*, p. 144

Meridian location as well, as it is located right along the Druidic Meridian running at 04°47'W. Of course, the castle is much more recent than Avebury and Silbury. Is it a mere happenstance then? At the moment, it is safe to say that this result is probably coincidental, but we will see in Part III that the knowledge of Druidic Lines has probably been secretly kept by Druids well after the Megalithic period, meaning that perhaps it is not a coincidence after all.

Let us come back to the Avebury-Avalon-Aval Ynis-Apollo and Silbury-Sil Ynis-Selene correlations. Another final piece of evidence was required, one that would tie all the loose ends and leave no more room for doubt. It then occurred to me that the final proof might come from Stonehenge itself.

The Stonehenge confirmation via Diodorus' 'Alanteans'

In any scientific model you should be able to make predictions. If Apollo and Selene were indeed the Greek deifications of ancient British sacred places once named Aval Ynis and Sil Ynis, or the 'Isle and the Sun' and 'Isle of the Moon' respectively, then Stonehenge should also be remembered through Greek mythology as another major divinity.

The first problem we face in verifying this conjecture is that the name Stonehenge is purely Saxon. The word 'stone' is clear enough; as for 'henge,' it might refer to a classical henge (even though it is not one in the strict sense), but also to a hinge or to the verb 'hang,' as the stone lintels are 'hanging' upon standing stones, or yet relate to the German *Hang* meaning a slope or hillside, or even to a hedge in an old meaning of a barrier mound topped with stones, turf or bushes. Yet there is apparently no way of knowing how Stonehenge was called in pre-Saxon times. Or is there?

If Avebury was a Sun temple and Silbury a Moon temple, the complexity of Stonehenge suggests that the monument was dedicated to the heavenly bodies in general—the Sun, Moon, and perhaps the stars and planets as well. We saw in Chapter Six that many archaeologists themselves have suggested that Stonehenge was, *inter alia*, an instrument able to chart solar and lunar movements—an ingenious machine able to predict eclipses, a monument aligned to the solstices, and a host of other extravagant things that would require dozens of pages to describe.

One final conjecture. Stonehenge is positioned along the 52nd Druidic Parallel, which could be connected to the number of weeks in a year, further implying that it might have been a kind of calendar in stone.

So let us posit that Stonehenge was a monument dedicated to the heavens—a sky observatory. As Stonehenge was encircled by a ditch or moat, it might well have been called something like 'Isle of the Heavens' or 'Isle of the Sky,' in keeping with the 'Isle of the Sun' and 'Isle of the Moon' that lie twenty miles north on the same Druidic Meridian.

Now who was the God of the Sky in ancient Greece? It was Uranus (in Greek *Ouranos*). If today this name is associated with the 7th planet of the Solar System, it has only been so since the 18th century, when the planet was discovered. Unlike the other planets which bear Roman names, it was decided to name the planet after the Greek Sky God.

Plato is not the only one to have written about the myth of Atlantis. According to Diodorus Siculus, Atlanteans were a peaceful, humane people living in the northwestern part of the world, and their first king was Uranus, who taught them law and how to grow fruits:

> But since we have made mention of the Atlantians, we believe that it will not be inappropriate in this place to recount what their myths relate about the genesis of the gods, in view of the fact that it does not differ greatly from the myths of the Greeks. Now the Atlantians, dwelling as they do in the regions on the edge of the ocean and inhabiting a fertile territory, are reputed far to excel their neighbours in reverence towards the gods and the humanity they showed in their dealings with strangers, and the gods, they say, were born among them. And their account, they maintain, is in agreement with that of the most renowned of the Greek poets when he represents Hera as saying:
>
> > For I go to see the ends of the bountiful earth,
> > Oceanus source of the gods and Tethys divine
> > Their mother.
>
> This is the account given in their myth: Their first king was Uranus, and he gathered the human beings, who dwelt in scattered habitations, within the shelter of a walled city and caused his subjects to cease from their lawless ways and their bestial manner of living, discovering for them the uses of cultivated fruits, how to store them up, and not a few other things which are of benefit to man; and he also subdued the larger part of the inhabited earth, in particular the regions to the west and the north.[243]

It seems very likely that the Atlanteans and the Hyperboreans depicted by Diodorus in two different sections of his *Library of History* refer to one and the same people, and that the Greek historian didn't realize the material he was using from two different sources were two not so dissimilar descriptions of one particular civilisation: Hyperboreans live 'in

---

[243] Diodorus Siculus, *The Library of History*, III, 56, 1-3

the regions beyond the land of the Celts,' 'in the ocean,' on 'an island' which is 'in the north,' whereas Atlanteans live 'in the regions on the edge of the ocean' and have subdued most of the inhabited Earth, more specifically 'the regions to the west and the north.' What's more, Hyperboreans live on an island which 'is both fertile and productive of every crop,' just as Atlanteans inhabit 'a fertile territory.'

We have already seen that the term 'Hyperboreans' most probably referred to the Megalithic people, whose civilisation had already come to an end a millennium before Diodorus' time. Consequently, Diodorus' 'Atlanteans' might also be Megalithic people who once thrived along the Atlantic coast in northwestern Europe.

Very interestingly, Diodorus goes on to say that Uranus was a talented skywatcher who also taught his people astronomy and gave them a calendar. Uranus was able to understand the movements of the Sun, the Moon and the stars, and to make predictions about them:

> And since he was a careful observer of the stars he foretold many things which would take place throughout the world; and for the common people he introduced the year on the basis of the movement of the sun and the months on that of the moon, and instructed them in the seasons which recur year after year. Consequently the masses of the people, being ignorant of the eternal arrangement of the stars and marvelling at the events which were taking place as he had predicted, conceived that the man who taught such things partook of the nature of the gods, and after he had passed from among men they accorded him immortal honours, both because of his benefactions and because of his knowledge of the stars and then they transferred his name to the firmament of heaven, both because they thought that he had been so intimately acquainted with the risings and the settings of the stars and with whatever else took place in the firmament, and because they would surpass his benefactions by the magnitude of the honours which they would show him, in that for all subsequent time they proclaimed him to be the king of the universe.[244]

According to Diodorus' myth, Uranus' exceptional, even God-like skills earned him the title of 'king of the universe.' Now, what if this myth was once again based not on one individual, but on a particular *place* in Britain where the movements of the Sun, Moon and stars had been carefully tracked for centuries by our hypothetical MPDs? What if this place was Stonehenge, which for obvious reasons is the perfect fit of this star observatory of yore?

---

[244] Ibid., III, 56, 4-5

The name *Uranus* (from the Greek *Ouranos*) turns out to be a perfectly plausible alteration of a Celtic name such as *Ur Ynis*, the 'Isle of Ur,' which according to our hypothesis would have meant the 'Isle of the Heavens.' While linguists disagree upon the origin of the name *Uranus*, it is interesting to note the Welsh word for 'sky:' it is *awyr*, which is pronounced /ˈauːir/, phonetically very close to *Ur*. I stress that the names reconstructed for Avebury, Silbury and Stonehenge are Celtic. There is just no way to go back further in time and know what they were called in Megalithic times, but of course these Celtic names might at least describe the *function* of the monuments, not forgotten at the time.

So could Ouranos, the Greek name for the god of the sky, derive from the ancient Celtic name of an even more ancient Megalithic monument (i.e. Stonehenge), once called by the Celts something like Awyr Ynis, just like those of Apollo and Selene seem to do? Were Avebury, Silbury and Stonehenge, in Celtic times, once called the Isle of the Sun, the Isle of the Moon and the Isle of Heavens respectively? I'd say the evidence here is very convincing, and our prediction has been confirmed by both Greek mythology and the Welsh language. Readers can judge by themselves and make their own conclusions.

Woodhenge

Another important ancient site close to Stonehenge is Woodhenge. Named so because the monument is made not with stones but with timber, there is no doubt it was devised and made (c. 2500 BC) by the same people who built Stonehenge. The ditch is thought to have been dug out during the five following centuries. Although not unique, the site is quite unusual as it consists of six concentric oval rings of wood posts, plus one in the middle, 163 posts in all, surrounded by a circular bank and ditch. Today the wooden posts have disappeared but their positions are marked by concrete posts (more about the number of wood posts in Chapter Fourteen). It is known that there also used to be at least five standing stones onsite.[245] The size of Woodhenge is similar to that of Stonehenge, with an overall diameter of 360 feet.

The site was discovered through aerial photography in 1925, the dark spots of the former timber posts revealing themselves amidst what appeared to be a simple circular barrow in a wheat field. The monument might have been a sacrificial place, and it is likely that the timber posts

---

[245] http://www.english-heritage.org.uk/daysout/properties/stonehenge/world-heritage-site/map/woodhenge/

were free-standing, rather than supporting a roof.[246] The exact function of the monument, however, remains unknown.

Perhaps more here than anywhere else, evidence of the presence of the Megalithic yard is overwhelming. Professor Alexander Thom determined that the perimeters of the rings were intended to be multiples of 20 MY: from the smallest to the biggest, the values are 40, 60, 80, 100, 140 and 160 MY.[247] Why the value of 120 MY was skipped remains unclear.

It is interesting to note that the number of posts of the outer ring is 60, a number which plays an important part in our presumed Megalithic geometry, as there were probably 60 arc minutes to the Megalithic degree. The inner ring is made up of 12 posts, a number that calls to mind the 12 months of the year. Incidentally, these two numbers also play a key role in the Megalithic sites of Orkney, as the reader shall soon discover.

The oval rings all exhibit one smaller end and one larger. The arcs at the smaller end have a common center, and the arcs at the larger end have another common center. What's important is that the distance between these two centers is exactly 6 MY. As the reader will recall, 6 is another important Megalithic number, as there were probably 6 arc seconds to the Megalithic arc minute. In addition, this 6-MY-long segment is the smaller side of a 12-35-37 Pythagorean triangle expressed in units of ½ MY (incidentally the assumed length of the Megalithic pendulum). According to the professor, 'everyone must be impressed by the laborious, painstaking work which preceded the discovery of the sixth member of the list of perfect Pythagorean triangles and the construction of a set of rings based on this triangle with perimeters exact multiples of 20 yds.'[248]

Like Stonehenge, Avebury and Silbury, Woodhenge stands in direct proximity to the 01°50'W Druidic Meridian (showing once again that this particular Salt Line was of paramount importance in Britain), another confirmation of the link between this ancient site and Megalithic geometry. It is also two arc minutes away from the nearest Druidic Parallel (the 52nd Druidic Parallel north of the equator, and the one that skirts Stonehenge). We can thus safely say that Alexander Thom's

---

246 Ibid.

247 Alexander Thom, *Megalithic Sites in Britain*, Oxford: Oxford University Press, 1967, p. 73

248 Ibid., p. 77

findings on this site were probably not the product of a deluded man's imagination.

Durrington Walls

Immediately north of Woodhenge is another major henge enclosure known as Durrington Walls. It was made around 2600 BC. The ditch and bank have been considerably eroded by ploughing and the construction of roads in the 1960s, but with a diameter of about 500 meters it is Britain's largest henge,[249] making it the largest henge *in the world* known to this day.

According to Professor Mike Parker Pearson of Sheffield University, the leader of the Stonehenge Riverside Project, Durrington Walls were 'basically a wooden version of Stonehenge'.[250] He thinks the two monuments were complementary, as both had an imposing stone-paved roadway leading to the River Avon. Durrington Walls once had a set of five concentric timber rings made of extremely large wooden posts, aligned with the midwinter solstice sunrise.[251]

A Neolithic village was also uncovered there recently. Parker Pearson considers it to be the 'largest Neolithic settlement in the whole of northern Europe,'[252] with about 1,000 homes thought to have housed the builders of Stonehenge. Is this ancient settlement the one mentioned in Diodorus Siculus' writings ('a city is there which is sacred to this god [Apollo], and the majority of its inhabitants are players on the cithara'), as mentioned in an earlier section? The floor plans of these houses are very similar to some found in the Orkneys (see next sections). The professor thinks Durrington Walls might have been the land of the living, while Stonehenge and its surrounding would have been the land of the dead, of the ancestors.[253]

Again, the monument is located only three arc minutes away from both Druidic Lines (a Meridian and a Parallel) that also intersect, or skirt, Stonehenge and Woodhenge. According to our definition thus, these

---

[249] http://www.salisburyguidedtours.com/durrington-walls.htm

[250] John Noble Wilford, 'Traces of Ancient Village Found Near Stonehenge,' *The New York Times*, 30 Jan. 2007: http://www.nytimes.com/2007/01/30/science/30cnd-stonehenge.html

[251] Ibid.

[252] 'Stonehenge builders travelled from far, say researchers,' BBC News, 9 Mar. 2013: http://www.bbc.co.uk/news/uk-21724084

[253] http://www.salisburyguidedtours.com/durrington-walls.htm

three connected sites are double Druidic Line locations, as both their longitude and latitude are Golden.

West Kennet Long Barrow

To this already long list of major Megalithic monuments located along the 01°50'W Salt Line in Wiltshire, there is one more that should be added for good measure: West Kennet Long Barrow.

This is one of Britain's largest and most impressive chambered tombs, with a length of about 100 meters in an east-west orientation. Close to fifty people were once interred in the barrow, whose entrance is sealed with large slabs of sarsen stone.

It is located a mere half mile south of Avebury, right along the Druidic Meridian that is associated with the exceptional Megalithic sites we have already mentioned in this chapter. It is considerably older than Stonehenge and Avebury: it was commenced c. 3650 BC[254] and was used till 2500 BC.

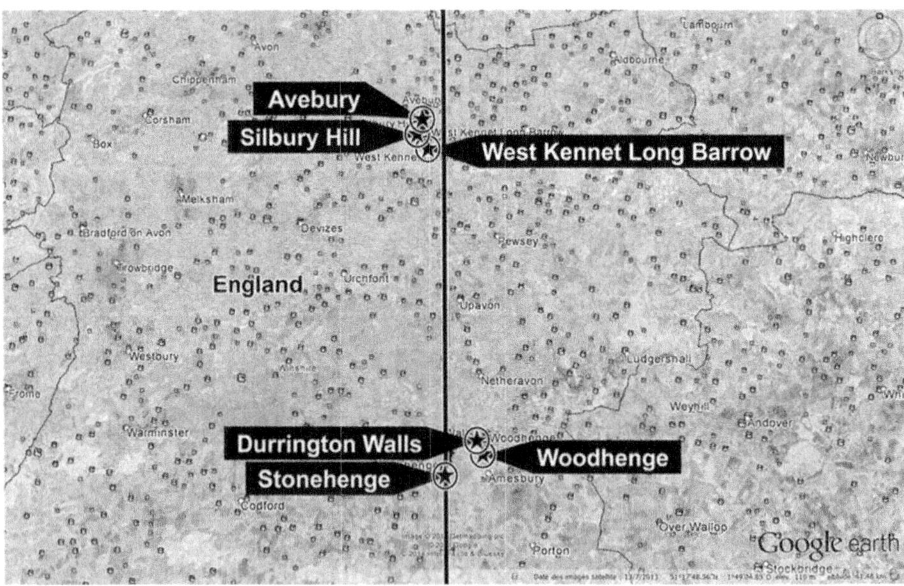

Fig. 18. Close-up on the Stonehenge Druidic Meridian, along which also stand Durrington Walls, Woodhenge, West Kennet Long Barrow, Silbury Hill and Avebury.

[254] http://www.english-heritage.org.uk/daysout/properties/west-kennet-long-barrow/

Because these Wiltshire Megalithic sites are exceptional in many regards, they were all inscribed as UNESCO World Heritage Sites in 1986.

The Ring of Brodgar in Orkney

The second highest concentration of major Megalithic sites in Britain (the first in Scotland) occurs in the remote islands of Orkney, an archipelago situated off the northeastern part of mainland Scotland. The islands, which enjoy a temperate climate thanks to the Gulf Stream, are nevertheless quite wet and almost constantly swept by a biting wind or a merciless gale that makes it hard for vegetation to grow, and are often enshrouded in a stinging damp fog.

In this desolate, northern atmosphere the Ring of Brodgar, the most famous Megalithic site of Orkney, still rises today in a stunning natural amphitheatre of hills and two lochs, one filled with sea water, the other with fresh water. Only 27 standing stones survive, but the stone ring once consisted of 60 stones surrounded by a deep ditch. The site dates back to c. 2500 BC, making it contemporaneous with the most beautiful sites of Wiltshire much further south. This stone circle, which is the third largest in Britain and the largest in Scotland, is locally nicknamed the Temple of the Sun, whereas the nearby Stones of Stenness (see next section) are known as the Temple of the Moon. Of course, there is no way to know whether these names are recent or hark back to very ancient astronomical functions. In any case, it is clear that the Ring of Brodgar, which is incidentally the same size as Avebury's inner rings, was a major Megalithic location.

The Ring of Brodgar is part of a larger complex of outstanding Megalithic monuments comprising also the Stones of Stenness, Maeshowe and Skara Brae (see next section), all of which are older than Brodgar. That such a civilisation flourished on this remote northern island so long ago is quite astonishing on its own. Here's what Historic Scotland writes on the official government website: 'The architectural achievements of the people living there speak for a level of architectural sophistication which matches that of the centers in Mesopotamia and North Africa. There is a piquant contrast between the small absolute size of the Orkney community 5000 years ago and its exceptional cultural vigour.'[255]

---

[255] http://www.historic-scotland.gov.uk/propertyresults/propertydetail.htm?PropID=PL_233

If the function of the huge stone ring remains unknown, there is little doubt it was somehow linked to astronomy. Professor Alexander Thom, who was Scottish, took a particular interest in the Ring of Brodgar. Just like they did in Wiltshire, the builders of the monument most probably used the Megalithic yard in its conception: the ring has a diameter of 125 MY.

The Ring of Brodgar is particularly interesting as it combines five singular facts closely associated with 366-degree geometry:

1- As we said, the Ring of Brodgar has been built with the Megalithic yard as a basic unit of length.

2- The Ring is almost a perfect Salt Line location. It is skirting a Druidic Parallel (the one that runs at 59°01'N), being about one arc minute away from the line, which according to our definition has approximately a 1 in 20 chance of occurring.

3- This Druidic Parallel is not *any* parallel, it is the 60th Druidic Parallel north of the equator, i.e. what we call a *round* number in the decimal number system.

4- Number 60 is not any round number, it is also a key number in Megalithic geometry, as it is presumed that there were 60 arc minutes to the Megalithic degree.

5- When the Ring of Brodgar was complete, there were 60 standing stones, which echoes the fact that the monument is located right along the 60th Druidic Parallel.

This combination of five simple facts leaves only two reasonable interpretations. The first one is that, once again, we are being fantastically lucky and that these findings are fortuitous. The second is that these results betray an obvious intention of the builders: in other words, MPDs using 366-degre geometry created this magnificent stone circle four millennia and a half ago.

The Standing Stones of Stenness, Maeshowe and Skara Brae

Three other major Megalithic sites lie in the immediate vicinity of the Ring of Brodgar: the Standing Stones of Stenness; Maeshowe, a superb chambered cairn and passage grave; and Skara Brae, an exceptionally well-preserved Neolithic village which has been nicknamed the 'Scottish Pompeii.' Let us briefly review them too.

The Stones of Stenness are a group of four surviving sixteen-foot-high standing stones, but originally the site comprised 12 stones in all. Many of these stones, which had survived several millennia, were destroyed as late as in the 19th century by a misguided and rather foolish farmer. Sometimes referred to locally as the 'Temple of the Moon,' this beautiful Megalithic achievement lies only three quarters of a mile away from the Ring of Brodgar. The stone circle had a large hearth inside, and once stood inside a henge, meaning it was encircled with a water-filled ditch, impressively cut into the rock,[256] and an earthen bank. It is thought to be considerably older than the Ring of Brodgar, and may date back to 3400 BC,[257] making it one of the earliest henges ever built in the British Isles.

The number of stones, 12, might have been linked to the 12 months of the year or the 12 hours of the day in Megalithic time-keeping.

Just like Brodgar, the Stones of Stenness are located only one arc minute away from the 59°01'N Druidic Parallel.

Very close to these two first-rate stone circles of Brodgar and Stenness rises another major Megalithic monument called Maeshowe. *Howe* most certainly derives from the word *haugr*, which meant 'hill' or 'mound' in Old Norse. It is a large grassy mound with a stone-built chamber lying inside at the end of a ten-meter-long passage. The site is yet another Megalithic wonder, especially the chamber which was capped with a corbelled roof. According to Historic Scotland, '[t]he monumental chambered tomb of Maeshowe is simply the finest Neolithic building in NW Europe. Built around 5,000 years ago, it is a masterpiece of Neolithic design and stonework construction, not least for its use of massive individual stones.'[258]

One remarkable feature of Maeshowe is that every winter solstice—more precisely for three weeks before and after the shortest day of the year—the reddish rays of the setting sun align with the passage and hit the back of the central chamber, illuminating the room. A very similar phenomenon is also observed at Newgrange in Ireland (see Chapter Eleven).

Maeshowe is also located only one arc minute away from the 59°01'N Druidic Parallel.

---

[256] http://www.orkneyjar.com/history/standingstones/stenstone2.htm
[257] http://www.historic-scotland.gov.uk/index/places/propertyresults/propertydetail.htm?PropID=PL_280
[258] http://www.historic-scotland.gov.uk/index/places/propertyresults/propertyabout.htmhttp:/www.historic-scotland.gov.uk/propertyresults/propertyabout.htm?PropID=PL_205&PropName=Maeshowe%20Chambered%20Cairn

This exceptional Megalithic Orcadian complex also includes the Neolithic settlement of Skara Brae. Revealed under sand dunes after a severe winter storm in 1850, this exceptionally preserved Neolithic village includes eight prehistoric houses with an astonishingly standardised form of furnishing: each dwelling was fitted with beds, dressers, cupboards with shelves, and seats, all of them in stone—almost modern comfort in the remote, windy islands of northern Scotland, three millennia before the splendour of Rome, or close to five millennia before the birth of New York City! The village is thought to have been inhabited between 3180 and 2500 BC,[259] making it contemporaneous to the Standing Stones of Stenness and Maeshowe.

Interestingly, the village also included a sophisticated drainage system, with each house having a private toilet. The people living there (MPDs?) also imported pre-cut venison from deer imported from mainland Scotland,[260] implying a highly organised society. There is no doubt that these people were surprisingly refined and sophisticated for their time.

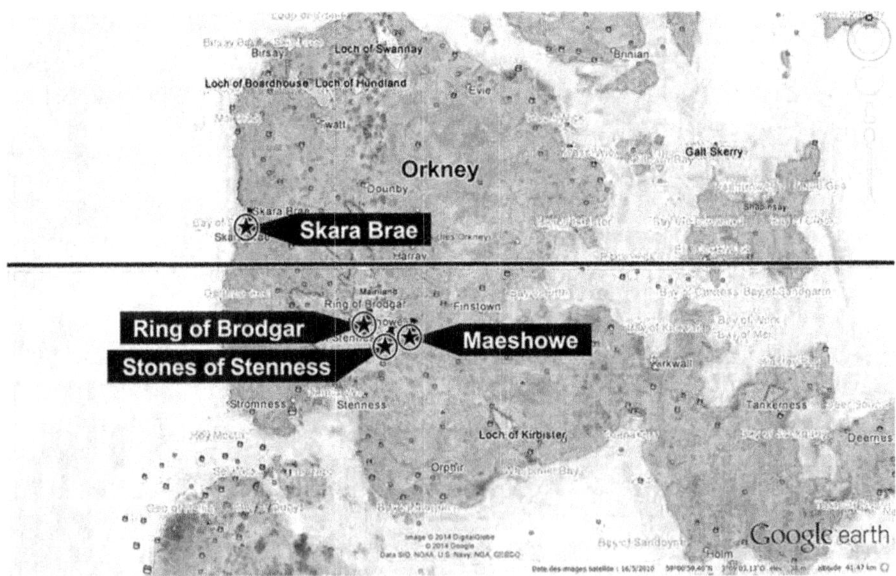

Fig. 19. The 60th Druidic Parallel in Orkney, Scotland, is close to major Megalithic sites: the Ring of Brodgar, the Stones of Stenness, Maeshowe and Skara Brae.

The site is only two arc minutes north of the Druidic Parallel running at 59°01'N, making it yet another Druidic site. And because these four

---

[259] http://www.bbc.co.uk/scotland/history/articles/skara_brae/

[260] Ibid.

Orcadian Megalithic sites are outstanding in many regards, they were also all inscribed as UNESCO World Heritage Sites in 1999.

What we have here in Orkney, which happens to be the second most important Megalithic complex of Britain, is closely associated to a particular Salt Line. While the Wiltshire sites were all to be found along a particular Druidic Meridian, the Orcadian sites are located along a particular Druidic Parallel. And just like in southern Britain, Megalithic geometry expresses itself both at the *microscopic* level (presence of the Megalithic yard) and the *macroscopic* level (location along a Druidic Line).

To believe all this to be purely accidental requires pushing luck to nearly miraculous levels. Still, more examples of Druidic Meridian locations were necessary to prove these axes existed in the first place. Back in the months when I first started to check what other sites of interest did happen to be located along these presumed sacred lines, I was far from imagining I would find a skyful of them, like bounties of nature on a paradise island.

Main points

- **Stonehenge fits well Hecateus of Abdera's description of a spherical temple on the island of the 'Hyperboreans' where the 'priests of Apollo' praised their God**
- **Stonehenge's circular bank had a circumference of 366 MY**
- **Stonehenge lies at the intersection of a Druidic Meridian and the 52nd Druidic Parallel North**
- **Avebury (the largest stone circle in the world) and Silbury (the largest pyramidal structure in Europe) are located on the same Druidic Meridian, which could have been the Megalithic Proto-Druids' axis mundi or prime meridian**
- **There are good reasons to believe Avebury is the Avalon of Celtic mythology**
- **Strong evidence suggests that Stonehenge was an 'Isle of Heavens,' Avebury an 'Isle of the Sun,' and Silbury an 'Isle of the Moon,' and that the Greek divinities Ouranos, Apollo and Selene are reminiscences of these sacred places**
- **Woodhenge (the largest woodpost-filled henge in the world), Durrington Walls (the largest henge in the world) and West Kennet Long Barrow (one of the largest chambered tombs in Britain) are all Druidic Line locations (sometimes doubly so), and are located on the same presumed axis mundi**

- **The Ring of Brodgar (the largest stone circle in Scotland) in Orkney had 60 standing stones, and is located right along the 60th Druidic Parallel north of the equator**
- **The Standing Stones of Stenness, Maeshowe and Skara Brae (all of which are outstanding Megalithic sites) are all located on the 60th Druidic Parallel too**

Chapter Ten: Druidic Cities of Mesopotamia

Curiously enough, most of the world's first great civilisations share a common trait: like the vast majority of Megalithic sites, they arose in areas that are never very far from a sea or an ocean. Is it possible that sea people somehow influenced the development of these civilisations?

History begins at Sumer

The Sumerian civilisation, according to mythology, owes much to seven civilising Sages called the Abgal or Apkallu. They are said to have come from the sea twice, the first time before the Flood, and the second time after it.[261]

Third-century BC Babylonian writer and astronomer Berossus described Oannes, a mythical half-man half-fish divinity who came from the Persian Gulf and taught early Mesopotamian people writing, sciences, temple construction and, interestingly enough, *geometry.* [262] Were Sumerians influenced in some way by MPDs? This would be a long shot if it would require the Megalithic people to circumnavigate Africa. They might have reached the Tigris or—more realistically—the Euphrates from the northwest, as both rivers rise not very far from the Black Sea. In addition, the course of the Euphrates (incidentally the longest river of Western Asia) at some point is only about 100 miles from the Mediterranean, rendering a trip from there not that difficult, even in early times. It is also less than 100 miles overland between the Nile Delta on the Mediterranean and Suez on the Red Sea, whence one could sail around the Arab peninsula to the Gulf.

Prehistory ended and history began in Sumer, as writing was invented there in the form of cuneiform (wedge-shaped) script some 5000 years

[261]Francis Joannes et al., *Dictionnaire de la civilisation mésopotamienne*, Paris: Robert Laffont, 2001, 746-7

[262]Yves Bonnefoy et al., *Dictionnaire des mythologies*, Paris: Flammarion, 1981, p. 719

ago, perhaps as early as 3400 BC.[263] Although another form of writing, though apparently limited in space and time, is recorded about two millennia before that in Romania (the Tartaria tablets, thought to be the first occurrence of writing in Europe),[264] it is in Sumer that writing really became commonplace, before spreading to Egypt and the Indus Valley, and then progressively to the rest of the world.

When I took up the task of checking whether major ancient cities of Mesopotamia were Druidic Line locations or not, I didn't expect to get so lucky again. Even my friend Alan Butler hadn't studied the area in terms of Druidic Lines. I was amazed to find out that the greatest Mesopotamian cities were Druidic Lines locations (see further on). This discovery was indeed another shock, as it seemed to mean that Mesopotamia had probably been greatly influenced by people using this early form of geometry known to have been used in Britain. Another distinct possibility was that Mesopotamia had been the birthplace of 366-degree geometry. Whatever the answer, the main cities of ancient Mesopotamia had probably not risen at random but in accord with this astonishing world geometry. Had the Megalithic people and Sumerians worked together and developed the 366-degree circle there?

In any case, the fact that 366-degree geometry was not confined to the northwestern fringe of Europe offered fascinating possibilities. Could mathematics prove beyond any reasonable doubt that the Mesopotamian myths contained a grain of truth when they mentioned sages coming from the sea, or when they spoke of a geometrician God?

Mesopotamia, as its Greek name indicates, is the Land Between Rivers—the Tigris and the Euphrates. Most of the territory is today's Iraq. The Sumerians are quite a mysterious people. In the words of renowned French historian and Assyriologist Jean Bottéro, who did extensive research in Mesopotamia, 'Who were they? Where did they come from? To which ethnic and linguistic family can they be linked? No one can answer such questions.'[265] Indeed, Sumerian is a language isolate.

The mystery, however, is only partial, as many convincing theories shed some light on the origins of Sumerians, who are generally thought

---

[263] Lesley Adkins, *Empires of the Plain: Henry Rawlinson and the Lost Languages of Babylon*, New York: St. Martin's Press, 2003, p. 47

[264] André Leroi-Gourhan, *Dictionnaire de la préhistoire*, Paris: Presses Universitaires de France, 1988, p. 1026; see also Marija Gimbutas, *The Language of the Goddess: Sacred Images and Symbols of Old Europe,* London: Harper and Row, 1989

[265] Jean Bottéro, *Babylone. A l'Aube de notre culture*. Paris: Découvertes Gallimard, 1994, p. 19

to be the descendants of Ubaidians, who in turn may have evolved from the Samarra culture of northern Mesopotamia.[266] During the third millennium BC Sumerian speakers met the Semitic Akkadian speakers and the two cultures greatly influenced one another, creating one of the world's first great civilisations.

The area had been occupied for millennia already, and it is in its northern part, which is graced with a milder climate, that agriculture was introduced. Geophysicists William Ryan and Walter Pitman found evidence that the legends of a great flood—such as Noah's Flood in the Bible or the epic of Gilgamesh in Mesopotamia—are based on a genuine catastrophic deluge of huge proportions which occurred in the Black Sea (indeed, *creating* the Black Sea) c. 5600 BC. According to them, Proto-Sumerians might have been some of the people who fled the shores of the lake which became the Black Sea in the aftermath of the Flood.[267] The Flood would have created a diaspora of people fleeing in many directions, some of them ending up in northwestern Europe (the Linear Pottery Farmers),[268] who might be the ancestors of the Megalithic people, others in modern-day Romania (the ancestors of the people who would later make the Tartaria tablets), and yet some others in Egypt (the ancestors of dynastic Egypt).[269]

Let us now come back to our main point. Is there any evidence that Sumerians and MPDs met at some juncture? We know that around 3200 BC, dolmens and stone circles made their appearance in the Caucasus, and soon after that in the Jordan Valley in the Middle East (see Chapter Six). Although there is no way to be sure whether these monuments are local innovations or the result of some other people's influence, there are grounds to think they represent the continued expansion of the Megalithic people, or at least the Megalithic idea, which by then had spread across the Mediterranean. Both the Caucasus and the Jordan Valley are quite close to Mesopotamia, and we have seen that cuneiform script is thought to have been invented at this time, possibly only two centuries before (c. 3400 BC).

In addition, we have seen that the Megalithic people don't seem be familiar with 366-degree geometry before 3400 BC, which is the probable age of the Standing Stones of Stenness in Orkney (see previous chapter).

---

[266] See Joan Oates's research in *Grandes civilisations du passé: Sumer*. Amsterdam: Time-Life, 1993, p. 66

[267] William Ryan and Walter Pitman, *Noah's Flood: The New Scientific Discoveries About the Event That Changed History*, New York: Simon & Schuster, 1998, p. 194

[268] Ibid., p. 189

[269] Ibid., p. 194

Was 366-degree geometry invented in Mesopotamia, or perhaps in the Middle East, when MPDs met local populations who were already highly developed?

The Golden Prime Meridian

If 366-degree geometry was used in the form of Druidic Lines in northern Scotland c. 3400 BC, and later in Stonehenge c. 3100 BC, the Megalithic people must have had a Prime Meridian from which to derive the Druidic Meridians, just like today Greenwich is the Prime Meridian of 360-degree geometry around the globe. Was this Prime Meridian the Druidic Line that runs through Stonehenge and Avebury? Or is there another location on Earth that might have played this role?

The most ancient Sumerian cities also date from the mid-4th millennium BC. Is the Golden Prime Meridian to be found in the land of Sumer in Mesopotamia? If many Megalithic sites of Portugal and Spain date back to as early as c. 5000 BC, or in Brittany as early as c. 4800 BC, nothing proves that at these early times the Megalithic people knew anything about the 366-degree circle. At this point in our research, there are good reasons to believe the Megalithic system was developed, or learnt, in the middle of the 4th millennium BC (c. 3500 or 3400 BC), not before that date.

Is there a natural feature somewhere in the region or its vicinity which could have been used as a Prime Meridian for 366-degree geometry longitudes? The first thing that comes to mind of course is a series of natural summits forming a north-south line which could be used for triangulation. Another possibility is that they used a fairly straight river happening to flow in a north-south direction. As it turns out, the Jordan Valley, between Lake Tiberias (also known as the Sea of Galilee) and the Dead Sea, is a rather straight line stretching in a north-south direction. In a beeline, this section of the River Jordan is about 105 km (65 mi) long. But the best part is that this particular north-south line is also a Salt Line—a Druidic Meridian! It is exactly 38 Megalithic degrees east of the Stonehenge Druidic Meridian.

We know that megaliths started to flourish in the Jordan Valley at about the same time as Sumerians and Egyptians built their first cities and Megalithic people in Orkney erected the Standing Stones of Stenness. What is particularly interesting is that the Jordan Valley is about halfway between the territories of two major civilisations that emerged about the same time, Sumer and Egypt.

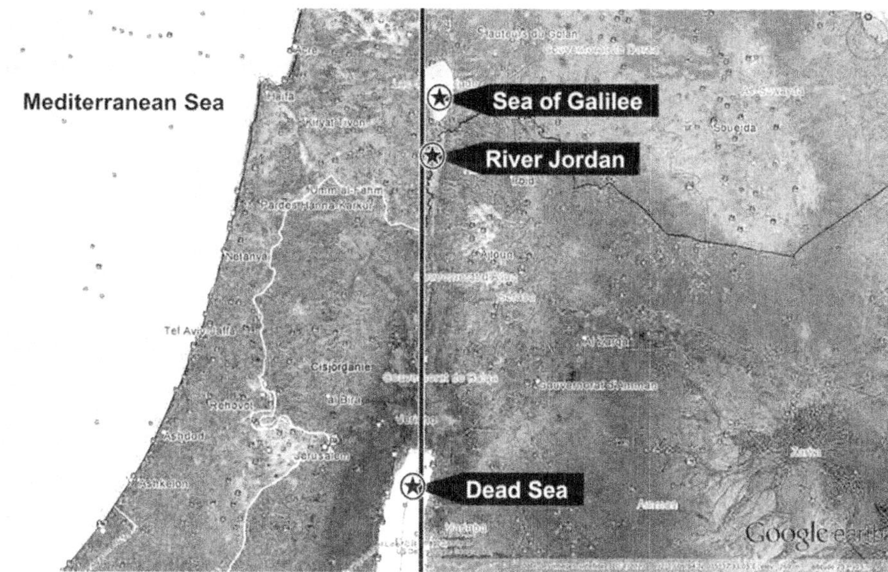

Fig. 20. The River Jordan in the Holy Land follows a Druidic Meridian exactly 38°M east of Stonehenge.

Even more interesting, this part of the world, which lies approximately at the geographical center of the Earth's land surface, is a key location for the three Abrahamic religions today, Judaism, Christianity and Islam. There is now good reason to think that what is often referred to as the Holy Land—the area between the Jordan Valley and the Mediterranean—has been a sacred place for a very long time—from a period that predates Islam, Christianity, and even the oldest religion of the three, i.e. Judaism.

Was the River Jordan, because it is a natural meridian, elected the Golden Prime Meridian by Proto-Druids and/or local people living there in the middle of the 4th millennium BC? It is interesting to note that the Hebrew Calendar starts from 3761 BC. Is this date the indirect reminiscence of the creation of 366-degree geometry, or perhaps the election of the River Jordan as the Golden Prime Meridian? Admittedly, the consideration is purely conjectural, but it might be worth investigating this line of research one day.

We know that the River Jordan is of prime importance in scriptures. In the Bible, River Jordan is held sacred and Jesus is baptised in its holy waters. Is it possible that when the Bible was written, the reason why River Jordan was sacred had been long forgotten?

According to Alan Butler, the course of the River Jordan ran *very close to* a Salt Line. Using my own, slightly different list of Druidic Parallels and Druidic Meridians, I found out that the River Jordan is *exactly* on the course of a Druidic Meridian, making it quite unlikely for the result to be fortuitous. There are thus many reasons to think that this river was the Golden Prime Meridian I was looking for.

The Jordan Valley is replete with dolmens, burial mounds and also stone circles, for instance in the Al Safat area where you can find passage graves surrounded with standing stones.[270] Unfortunately, no research regarding the Megalithic yard there has been made so far.

Here's a plausible scenario. Megalithic geometry required a Prime Meridian so it could be used on a large scale. During their travels in the eastern Mediterranean the Megalithic people discovered the Jordan Valley, a natural watery straight line between two inner seas which happened to run north-south, which means it followed the direction of the Earth's rotation axis. Incidentally, the length of this valley is 105 km, which is very close to the length of a Megalithic degree—between two Druidic Parallels, a Megalithic degree is always about 109 km. They viewed this river as a divine sign, declared River Jordan a holy place and decided to use it as their Prime Meridian. As this river came to be sacred, the land adjacent to it naturally came to be revered as well.

Is that why the place was still remembered as a divine land two millennia later? Is the 'Promised Land' of the Jews—from the desert to the Euphrates river[271]—a holy land because local populations had passed down this tradition across the generations, while forgetting its initial geometrical purpose? Has this sacredness been passed down until today through scripture, making the Middle East the most coveted land in the world, a place where countless believing people have died across the centuries and still die today because they claim this land as theirs, especially members of the three Abrahamic religions, Jews, Christians and Muslims? In other words, aren't all these people fighting for a land that was once held sacred by MPDs and/or local people living there more than five millennia ago because River Jordan was the divine river *par excellence*, the Prime Meridian of 366-degree geometry on Earth, even though this basic fact has long ago been erased from human memory?

Another scenario is that MPDs, upon discovering the River Jordan, devised 366-degree geometry there—perhaps with the help of local people who might have been more advanced than they were in terms of geometry—establishing its principles from the macroscopic (Druidic

---

[270] Jean Guilaine in *Le Grand Atlas de l'Archéologie*, Paris: Encyclopaedia Universalis, 1985, p. 46

[271] Exodus 23:31

Lines) to the microscopic (Megalithic yard), rather than the other way around. A third scenario is that the Megalithic people were taught about 366-degree geometry from scratch in the Jordan Valley, by a highly advanced culture which has yet to be identified.

As we know that the Megalithic People were keen astronomers[272] probably even before they can be traced to have known about 366-degree geometry, the first and second scenarios appear to be the most likely ones, but the third scenario remains a plausible, if intriguing, possibility. The truth is that we just don't know. More hypotheses will be formulated later in this book.

Whatever the answer, it seems clear that once a Golden Prime Meridian was defined, MPDs set out to determine other Druidic Meridians in different parts of the world, and to mark them for posterity in some key points by having major architecture built at these places, as we will soon see. If the question 'How did they determine the Druidic Meridians and Parallels with such high precision?' has several possible answers, it is clear that they perfectly succeeded in doing so.

It is well-known that Mesopotamians were first-rate astronomers as well, so chances that MPDs and Sumerians exchanged some astronomical knowledge are high. Living in a sun-drenched area with only rare clouds to veil the stars, Sumerians could predict Moon and Sun eclipses with a high degree of accuracy, as is well attested by archaeology.

Druidic cities of Mesopotamia

First of all, it is worth saying that amongst all of the first cities (or city-states) of Sumer, which appeared in southeastern Mesopotamia in the second half of the 4th millennium BC, none of them but one is a Salt Line location: famous cities like Ur, Uruk or Eridu have *not* been built along a Druidic Line, which implies that 366-degree geometry was apparently unknown to its builders at the time. The only exception is the city of Lagash, which rose only one arc minute away from a Druidic Meridian, but the fact that it is alone in this 'privileged' position strongly suggests that the result is purely coincidental.

Such is not the case with later cities emerging in *northwestern* Mesopotamia, which of course reinforces our thesis: MPDs coming from the Mediterranean or the Middle East met Mesopotamians at some point

[272] Evidence of alignment with the solstice is found in very ancient Megalithic sites.

in northwestern Mesopotamia and 366-degree geometry was either invented or transmitted in this part of the world from then on.

Babylon and its mythical Hanging Gardens

The first city that comes to mind when you think of Mesopotamia is Babylon, whose celebrated hanging gardens were one of the Seven Wonders of the Ancient World, just like the Great Pyramid of Giza, the Colossus of Rhodes or the Lighthouse of Alexandria. When I checked the geographic coordinates of the ancient city, I saw to my amazement that Babylon was a Druidic Meridian location. The ancient city was located only one arc minute away from a Druidic Meridian running exactly 9 degrees east of the River Jordan. The city was built along the Euphrates, meaning that it stood at the intersection of this major river and a Druidic Line.

If the existence of the Hanging Gardens of Babylon is a matter of debate among historians and archaeologists, that Babylon was a city of prime importance is an undisputed fact. The ziggurat Etemenanki (Sumerian for 'Temple of the Foundation of Heaven and Earth'), which was dedicated to the God Marduk, is often cited by scholars as being the monument which influenced the story of the Tower of Babel in the Bible. [273] Ziggurats, much like Egyptian pyramids or the cairn of Barnenez, symbolically linked the Earth to Heaven.

Interestingly, Babylon means 'Gateway of the God,' and the city was a major religious center. What made Babylon such a sacred place? Ancient sources generally date the foundation of Babylon to the late 3rd millennium BC, but the site has been occupied since the mid-4th millennium BC.[274] Is that evidence that the site was selected by MPDs at this early time because it was a Druidic Meridian location?

In any case, Babylon remained a prominent city for at least 3000 years. In 1894 BC Babylon became the capital of the Semitic nation state of Babylonia. After a period of bilingualism, Akkaddian (a Semitic language) gradually replaced Sumerian (a language isolate), but the Sumerian language was retained for religious use, much like Latin in many Western European countries in much more recent times.

---

[273]Stephen L Harris, *Understanding the Bible*, New York: McGraw-Hill, 2002, p. 50-1

[274] Francis Joannès et al., *Dictionnaire de la civilisation mésopotamienne*, Paris: Robert Laffont, 2001, p. 111

Assur and Nineveh

The Assyrian empire was a major Semitic kingdom located immediately to the north of Babylonia. It flourished for about two millennia, from the mid-3rd millennium BC to the mid-1st millennium BC.

It original capital was Assur, which was founded shortly after 3000 BC.[275] It is known that the place was already sacred by this time.[276] The ancient city was classified by UNESCO as a World Heritage site in 2003.

Another major Assyrian city was Nineveh, which by 3000 BC was already a religious center for worship of the Assyrian goddess Ishtar. It was also one of the greatest cities in antiquity, and archaeologists often cite Nineveh as 'one of the most prestigious capitals of the antique world'.[277] A twenty-meter-high trapezoidal wall enclosed the city, which also had its hanging gardens with an ingenious system of irrigation works.[278] Most spectacular of all, tens of thousands of astronomical tablets (or tablet fragments) with zodiacs and eclipse predictions have been found in Nineveh in the library of Ashurbanipal, a 7th-century-BC Assyrian king.[279]

When I checked their geographic coordinates, I was stunned to see that both cities had been built at the intersection of the Tigris River and Druidic Parallels running north of the equator: Assur stood along the 36th Druidic Parallel, while Nineveh rose along the 37th Druidic Parallel.

Most major sites we have studied so far have been built along Druidic Meridians, except the Orkney Megalithic sites, which follow the 60th Druidic Parallel, which appears to make sense as 60 is a 'Megalithic' number. Do the latitudes used in Assyria also convey a meaning of some sort? Well, it looks like it does, as the 36th and 37th Druidic Parallels are of course both immediately adjacent to a theoretical line running in-between at 36.6 Megalithic degrees north of the equator!

Why was Assur such a sacred place, and why was Nineveh such a major astronomical center? Is it because the location of these two Assyrian cities is not random, i.e. because they are both situated on sacred Druidic Parallels of 366-degree geometry?

---

275 Ibid., p. 100

276 Jean Bottéro and Marie-Joseph Stève, *Il était une fois la Mésopotamie*, Paris: Découvertes Gallimard, 1993, p. 104

277 Ibid., p. 65

278 Francis Joannès et al., *Dictionnaire de la civilisation mésopotamienne*, Paris: Robert Laffont, 2001, p. 575-6

279 Jean Bottéro and Marie-Joseph Stève, *Il était une fois la Mésopotamie*, Paris: Découvertes Gallimard, 1993, p. 76

The invention of 360-degree geometry

We've seen in Chapter Seven that modern 360-degree geometry, as we know and use it today, is thought to have been devised in Mesopotamia by Sumerians. Indeed, all the available evidence suggests that it is the case. But how was it invented exactly? Is it possible that the 360-degree circle was created as a simplification of a more ancient 366-degree circle based on a calendar?

As we have seen in Chapter Seven, it seems more logical for a civilisation to have invented a 366-degree circle from a 365-day or 366-day calendar, rather than starting off with a 360-degree circle for no particular reason. It looks like the 360-degree circle was an evolution of the 366-degree circle, as 360 is a more convenient number than 366 for splitting a circle into equal parts.

The location of such major Mesopotamian cities such as Babylon, Assur and Nineveh on three Druidic Lines makes the hypothesis of an ancient knowledge of the 366-degree circle plausible to say the least, while at the same time it may have sown the seeds of a later, simplified version of this geometry - the 360-degree circle. Then it would have been possible for Mesopotamians and other Mediterranean nations to devise a 360-day calendar, usually using 12 months of 30 days, plus five extra days.

That 360-degree geometry might have given rise to a later geometry of 366 degrees—which happens to be the number of earth rotations in a year—doesn't make sense. Although there is no absolute proof, the location of major Mesopotamian cities on 366-degree Druidic Lines also lead us to believe that 366-degree geometry must have preceded 360-degree geometry.

Baghdad

The more recent city of Baghdad, founded c. 762 AD, the city where many of the *One Thousand and One Nights* tales are set, is located on the same Druidic Meridian as Babylon, which might be purely coincidental... or not: it is *right* on the Druidic Line, an event which has only about one chance in 59 to occur. Was the knowledge of 366-degree geometry passed down until the time of its foundation?

It is also interesting to note that Baghdad is not only a perfect Salt Line location, it is also situated (like Assur and Nineveh) along the Tigris River.

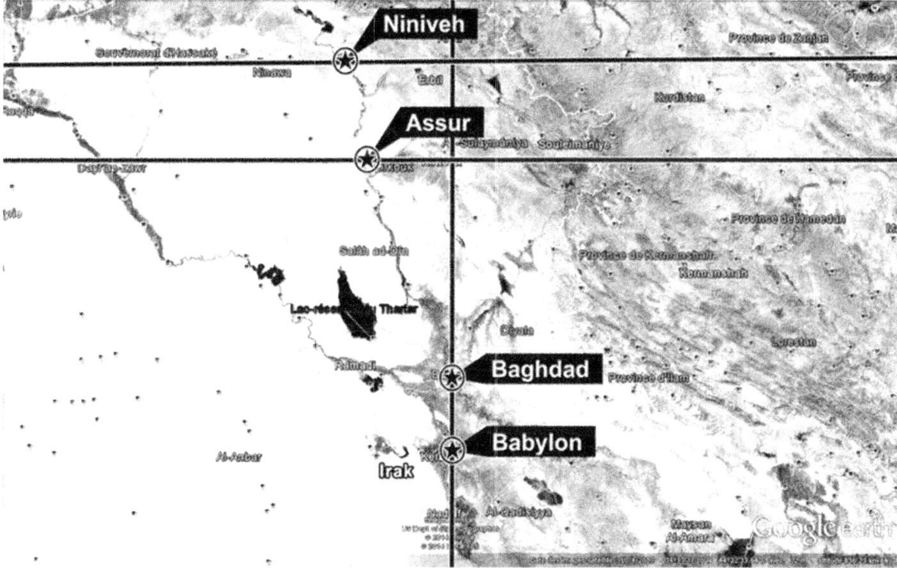

Fig. 21. Druidic sites of Mesopotamia: Babylon, Baghdad, Assur and Nineveh. Assur and Nineveh are located along the 36th and 37th Druidic Parallels.

Finally, Baghdad was founded as a 'round city': it was a perfect circle built by the Abbassid Caliph Al-Mansur, and the official name of the city was the City of Peace. Is it just a coincidence, or is this round city a tribute to 366-degree geometry?

Main points

- **Sumerian myths mention civilising sages coming from the sea, who were also experts in geometry**
- **The Jordan Valley in the Middle East is replete with megaliths**
- **The River Jordan is a natural north-south line which also happens to follow a Druidic Meridian, making it a plausible Prime Meridian for Druidic Lines**
- **The city of Babylon, the 'Gateway of the God,' is a Druidic Meridian location**
- **Two major Mesopotamian cities, Assur (a sacred place) and Nineveh (a major astronomical center), are Salt Line locations, as they are located on the 36th and 37th Druidic Parallels respectively**
- **360-degree geometry may have been invented in Babylon as a simplification of 366-degree geometry**
- **Baghdad, which was founded much later as a circular city, is also a Druidic Meridian location**

Chapter Eleven: Druidic Cities and Temples of Egypt

The great civilisation of Egypt, which left us exceptionally beautiful temples, sarcophagi, paintings and of course great pyramids which still stand today, rose to prominence at approximately the same time as Mesopotamia. And like the Sumerians, the origins of the Egyptians remain quite mysterious. The quick rise to magnificence of the Egyptian civilisation, and the degree of perfection it rapidly achieved in terms of architecture and sculpture, fills tourists and archaeologists alike with awe and admiration, and raises myriad questions which are far from being answered.

How can we account for the 'extraordinary acceleration'[280] observed in Egypt during the 4th millennium BC? Is the answer to be found in Egyptian myths, which tell us about civilising gods very similar to those of Sumerian mythology? Egypt is known to have been unified by the semi-legendary King Menes, usually identified as Pharaoh Narmer, who according to the Greeks was a civilising demiurge.[281] Is it possible that MPDs played some role, whatever it might have been, in the rise of Egypt? Or were MPDs instructed by ancient Egyptians?

According to myths, the civilising God Thoth was a magician with an expertise in mathematics, astronomy and... *geometry*![282] Was Thoth a MPD? It is also said that Osiris, God of Death and Resurrection, was born in Thebes, the capital of Upper Egypt, and then proceeded to civilise Egypt and the rest of the world.[283] Was Osiris a MPD, or conversely a teacher to MPDs?

---

[280] Béatrix Midant-Reynes, *Préhistoire de l'Egypte: des premiers hommes aux premiers pharaons*, Paris: Armand Colin, 1992, p. 235. The author is a doctor in Egyptology and engineer at the French National Center for Scientific Research,

[281] Pierre Gazio, *Petit dictionnaire des pharaons*, Cadeilhan: Zulma, 2002, p. 74

[282] Guirand and Schmidt, *op. cit.*, p., p. 42

[283] Ibid., p. 32

First of all, let's look for clues that MPDs did set foot in Egypt in the remote past.

Nabta Playa

Very old megalithic structures and stone circles in Nabta Playa in the Nubian desert, about 500 miles south of Cairo, suggest that MPDs visited southern Egypt between 5000 and 4700 BC,[284] or perhaps a bit later, c. 4500-4000 BC.[285] Not only is it interesting to note that these five Megalithic alignments are believed to be astronomical structures, but the fact that they are contemporaneous with the earliest Megalithic monuments known in Western Europe makes it more difficult for us to believe it is an independent development. The alignments of standing stones extend for up to a mile, and a ten-foot stone circle displays four 'windows.' Two of these openings were oriented due north and south, and the other two formed a line of sight corresponding to the summer solstice sunrise at the time.[286] Two other alignments stem out from a particular standing stone, involving about a dozen stones, leading both northeast and southeast.[287] Although it is difficult to prove, it looks very much like early Megalithic sailors observed the heavens in different locations of the globe, from Western Europe to the Mediterranean and then even further south, sailing down the Nile to Nabta, a latitude where the sun can reach the zenith.

More recently, work done by a team of archaeoastronomers and archaeologists at the University of Colorado, using both ground and satellite measurements, confirmed that the Megalithic structures in Nabta Playa showed possible alignments with several major stars, including Sirius, Arcturus, Alpha Centauri and Orion's Belt.[288]

---

[284] 'Neolithic Skywatchers,' by Andrew L Slayman, *The Archaeological Institute of America*, 27 May 1998: http://archive.archaeology.org/online/news/nubia.html

[285] 'Oldest Astronomical Megalith Alignment Discovered in Southern Egypt By Science Team,' 31 March 1998: http://www.colorado.edu/news/releases/1998/03/31/oldest-astronomical-megalith-alignment-discovered-southern-egypt-science

[286] 'Neolithic Skywatchers,' by Andrew L Slayman, The Archaeological Institute of America, 27 May 1998,: http://archive.archaeology.org/online/news/nubia.html

[287] 'Oldest Astronomical Megalith Alignment Discovered in Southern Egypt By Science Team,' 31 March 1998: http://www.colorado.edu/news/releases/1998/03/31/oldest-astronomical-megalith-alignment-discovered-southern-egypt-science

[288] J Mc Kim Malville, R. Schild, F. Wendorf and R. Brenner, 'Astronomy of Nabta Playa,' *African Sky*, 11 (2), 2007

Did the Nabta megaliths builders and astronomers somehow influence early Egyptians? Or, conversely, were these early skywatchers, who might very well have been the MPDs we are tracking down through time, influenced by the Egyptian people they met there at the time? Whatever the answer, it seems likely that MPDs and early Egyptians met at a very early period and that one culture influenced the other.

Egyptians venerated the star Sirius, whose appearance marked the beginning of their year and announced the flooding of the Nile, and the constellation Orion, which was closely linked to Osiris, the God of Rebirth and the Afterlife. Egyptians also revered Ra, the Sun God, who according to myth travelled on two solar boats across the heavens, the *Mandjet* (or Morning Boat) and the *Mesektet* (or Evening Boat).

Scholars usually believe Egyptian astronomy mainly had religious purposes,[289] and that it didn't match the quality and thoroughness of its Mesopotamian counterpart. It is known, however, that early Egyptians observed the sky, more particularly lunar phases, constellations (Ursa Major, Cygnus and Orion), and tracked stars, despite the fact that the skies were probably not as clear as in Mesopotamia. They also used the zodiac signs. Thoth was considered as the inventor of both the Egyptian calendar and writing. This could be the subject of another book, but whoever has studied the Great Pyramid can easily understand early Egyptians were first-rate astronomers.

Thebes and the Valley of the Kings

When one thinks of ancient Egypt, two places usually come to mind: the Giza pyramids and Thebes. Although the Great Pyramid and its neighbouring pyramids are not a Salt Line location, Thebes is, just like Assur, Nineveh and Babylon. We'll come back to the Great Pyramid shortly.

Thebes was the great capital of the New Kingdom of Egypt and the main Egyptian necropolis. Ancient Thebes and its necropolis were added to the UNESCO World Heritage list in 1979.

More specifically, a Druidic Meridian intersects the famous Valley of the Kings, with its beautifully painted tombs dug into the limestone mountains, located close to the gigantic Karnak temples, which are also part of the Thebes complex. The Valley of the Kings is situated on the Western bank of the Nile in Upper Egypt. There, hundreds of pharaohs

---

[289] Emile Biémont, *Rythmes du temps. Astronomie et calendriers*, Paris: De Boeck, 2000, p 169-86

and noblemen were interred during the 2nd millennium BC. But the site is even more ancient: when the royal family established the first dynasty in Thebes in 2134 BC[290] the place had already been a necropolis for a very long time.[291]

Even when Thebes lost its status of capital of the empire, the Valley of the Kings remained the prestigious place-to-be-buried: 'With the 19th and 20th dynasties, that of the Setis and the Ramses, the gravity center settled into the oriental delta. But *Thebes remained the City par excellence and pharaohs continued to be inhumated in the Valley of the Kings.*'[292] Until the end of Egyptian civilisation, Thebes always remained the holiest place in Egypt.[293]

According to Jean Leclant, professor at the Collège de France, Thebes is a 'majestic'[294] location, but he can't think of any rational, geographical explication for the choice of this far-off location as a primary burial site for kings and queens. In his opinion, it is thus an enigma: 'And yet no notable characteristic seemed to promise this site for such a glorious destiny: established about 700 kilometers south of the delta tip, it does not command the outlet of an important road. Nor does the fertility of the valley exceed that of the neighbouring regions.'[295] Was the place elected because it is a Druidic Line location? It looks like the fact that this place lay at the intersection of the Nile and a Druidic Meridian determined its importance and sacredness in the first place.

As Alan Butler pointed me out right at the beginning of my research, the Valley of the Kings (West Thebes) is a perfect Druidic Meridian location. As explained earlier, the probability for any given site to be a perfect Druidic Meridian location is about 1 in 59 only. And again, Druidic Meridians are the more difficult Druidic Lines to determine. The Salt Line runs exactly 3 Megalithic degrees west of the River Jordan, and exactly 35 Megalithic degrees east of Stonehenge and Avebury. Unless of course this result is purely coincidental, such accuracy is absolutely astounding. Once again, it looks like whoever decided to create a major burial place for pharaohs in Thebes was deeply involved in 366-degree geometry. And who else but MPDs knew about this geometry? Unless of course MPDs inherited from this knowledge in Egypt.

---

290 www.infoplease.com/ce6/history/A0848373.html

291 www.civilization.ca/civil/egypt/egca07f.html

292 Jean Leclant, 'Un sanctuaire dynastique: Karnak,' in *Le Grand Atlas de l'Archéologie*, Paris: Encyclopaedia Universalis, 1985, p. 202

293 Ibid.

294 Ibid.

295 Ibid.

Oddly enough, a pyramid-shaped hill named Al-Qurn (Arabic for 'The Horn') overhangs the Valley of the Kings. It is located right on the Druidic Meridian which intersects the Valley of the Kings. Culminating at nearly 1380 ft (420 m), it is also the highest point in the Theban Hills.

When you think of it, in a way the site had three reasons to become sacred: first, it is located along the Nile; second, it is a Druidic Meridian location; and third, there is a natural pyramid right above it, as to connect it to heaven. If we are not mistaken, Jean Leclant's enigma can now be explained by the presence of these three particular geographical and topographical features. MPDs seemed to be intent on finding the best places on Earth to display the 366-degree system.

Luxor Temple

Adjacent to the Valley of the Kings is the world-famous Luxor Temple, which was founded around 1400 BC. It comprises four temples located on the west bank of the Nile, and two on the east bank, where the modern city of Luxor stands.

On the left bank, the most magnificent temple is the Ramesseum, the Mortuary Temple of pharaoh Ramses III, which is commonly referred to as Medinet Habu, from the name of the local archaeological site which also includes the Temple of Amun, and the Temple of Ay and Horemheb. The Ramesseum is a huge temple, exceptional for the size of its architecture. It is famous for its inscribed reliefs depicting the invasion of the Sea Peoples, which were defeated by Egyptians during the reign of the pharaoh. The question of who the Sea Peoples were is a complex matter and was discussed in one of my previous books.[296] The details are largely outside the scope of the present book, but suffice it to say that persuasive evidence suggests that many of these people might have come from the shores and islands of the western part of the Mediterranean, the Atlantic Ocean and perhaps even the North Sea, not only from the eastern part of the Mediterranean as is generally assumed.

Located about two miles south of the Valley of the Kings, Medinet Habu is also a perfect Salt Line location, as it is situated right on the Druidic Meridian which runs 3 Megalithic degrees west of the River Jordan. Once again, chances for this major sacred place to be located right on a Druidic Meridian were only 1 in 59.

---

[296] Sylvain Tristan, *Atlantide, premier empire européen*, Paris: Alphée, 2007

The Karnak-Carnac arc

Opposite the Valley of the Kings and Medinet Habu, on the eastern bank of the Nile, immediately north of the modern city of Luxor, is the Karnak Temple Complex, standing right in the middle of an area called by the Ancient Egyptians *Ipet-isut*, meaning 'The Most Selected of Places.' It is located only three arc minutes east of the Druidic Meridian, making the place a Druidic site as well according to our definition (in any case, all these places are part of ancient Thebes). The most famous part of Karnak is the Hypostyle Hall in the Precinct of Amun-Re, which boasts no less than 134 enormous columns arranged in 16 rows, up to 21 meters tall (which was incidentally also the total height of the Great Broken Menhir at Locmariaquer in Brittany.)

Is it only a coincidence if the Breton name of Carnac in France and the name of Karnak in Egypt sound the same? Carnac boasts thousands of aligned standing stones, and Karnak has more than a hundred massive standing columns. What's more, Carnac is thought to date back to c. 3300 BC, whereas Karnak is thought to have been founded only about a century later, around c. 3200 BC. Is it possible that Karnak took its inspiration from Carnac, even though the two sites are located thousands of miles away from each other?

Tracing a line—it is such a long line on Earth that it is more accurate to refer to it as an *arc*—on Google Earth between the westernmost tip of the Carnac alignments and the easternmost tip of the Karnak Temple yields a length of 3,956.523 km, which is strangely one-tenth of the Earth's polar circumference to within 98.9 per cent. Is it just a meaningless coincidence, or was it an early attempt to materialize an Earth arc of one tenth of the polar circumference? We'll see later in this chapter that another such arc (this time much more accurate) exists, also linking the Megalithic world of Western Europe and Ancient Egypt, a truly astonishing fact which strongly suggests that the Karnak-Carnac arc is probably not just an accident, but an earlier attempt indeed.

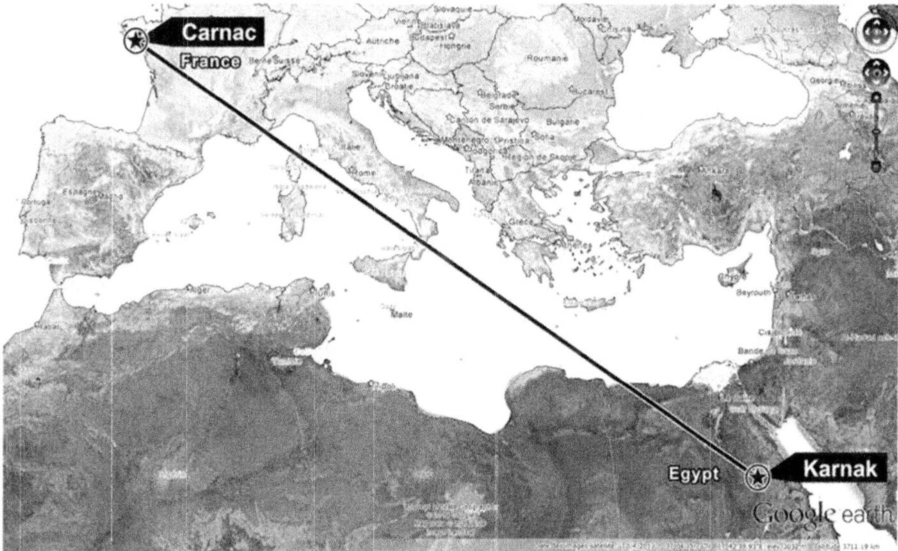

Fig. 22. The Karnak-Carnac Arc, which is almost exactly 1/10th of the Earth's polar circumference.

Abu Simbel

The Abu Simbel temples are situated in Nubia in southern Egypt, about 400 km south of Luxor. They also became World Heritage sites in 1979. They were carved out in the mountainside along the Nile during the rule of Pharaoh Ramses II (renowned as Ramses the Great) between 1264 and 1244 BC. The site of these superb rock temples is particularly isolated. It was allegedly chosen because the pharaoh wanted to show his all-powerfulness and divine nature to invaders from the south.

But was the site elected only because it is located in the south, or was it chosen because it is also a Salt Line location? The temples are located less than one arc minute east of the Druidic Line running at 31°37'E, or exactly 4 degrees west of the River Jordan. In the 1960s the temples had to be relocated on an artificial hill 200 meters away from their initial position and 65 meters higher because the creation of Lake Nasser would ultimately submerge the area.

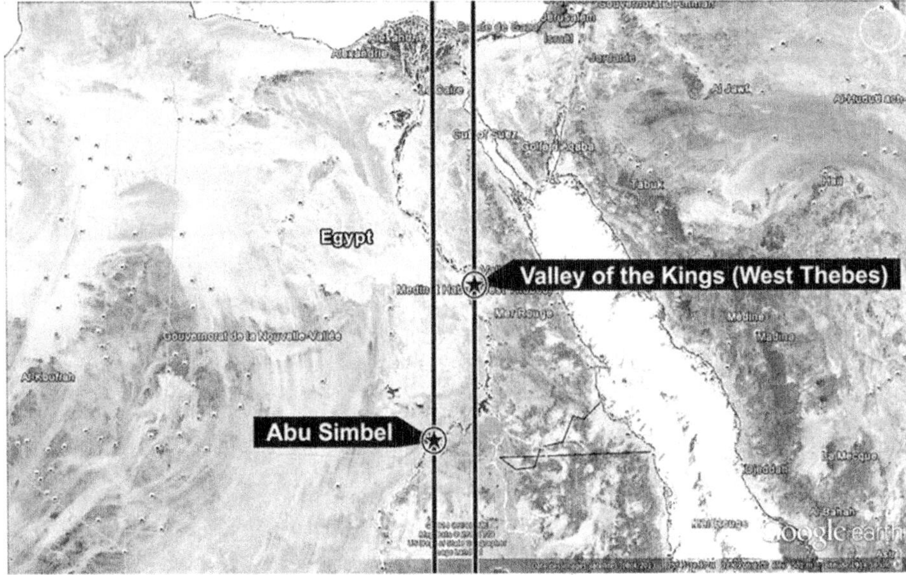

Fig. 23. The Druidic sites of Egypt: The Valley of the Kings and Medinet Habu in West Thebes, and Abu Simbel.

One of the most interesting aspects of the greater temple of Abu Simbel is that it has been conceived as a Sun temple. Twice a year, on February 22 and October 22, the morning sun's rays illuminate the sculptures on the back wall[297] (Amun, Ra-Horakhty and the deified Ramses), while the fourth sculpture, that of Ptah (a god of Architects) remains in the dark, showing all the ingenuity of the architect who designed the temple. The dates apparently correspond to the pharaoh's birthday and coronation day.

This solar phenomenon is evidently reminiscent of those observed in many Megalithic sites, which are oriented either to the winter or summer solstice sunrise (such as Stonehenge or Durrington Walls in England, Maeshowe in Scotland, Crucuno in Brittany, Newgrange in Ireland), or to the equinoxes (such as the Mnajdra temple in Malta), where the builders clearly included a 'Sun play' within the design of the temple. Later Celtic sacred groves, as we have already pointed out, were often oriented to the solstice sunrises as well. The fact that Abu Simbel also includes a similar peculiarity, combined to its Druidic Meridian credentials, is food for thought indeed: was the construction of the temple influenced (in an either direct or indirect way) by MPDs? The date of its construction

---

[297] Jean Leclant, 'Un sanctuaire dynastique: Karnak,' in *Le Grand Atlas de l'Archéologie*, Paris: Encyclopaedia Universalis, 1985, p. 202

roughly corresponds to the end of the Megalithic culture in Europe, and occurred about half a century before the attack of the Sea People.

Once again, the temples of Abu Simbel were designed at the intersection of a Druidic Meridian and the River Nile, just like Thebes up north, and just like the great Mesopotamian cities sprang at the intersection of Druidic Lines and major rivers.

With his amazing 66-year reign, Ramses II remains one of the most celebrated and prestigious monarchs of Ancient Egypt. The pharaoh, who was a very charismatic figure, had an outstanding personality and exceptional physical traits, and was more than 90 years old when he died. One particular aspect of this extraordinary pharaoh is that he was particularly tall and that his hair was red.

Studies of his mummified skeleton show that he was rather tall and robust, and that his hair was either red, auburn or blondish:

> Now what came as a surprise concerns Ramesses' hair colour. Thirteen specialists from the Identité Judiciaire in the L'Oréal laboratories . . . think that Ramesses' hair was either red or auburn. Of course, the mummy displayed white and depigmented hair (or most probably dyed with henna) but also genuine, still pigmented red hair.[298]

Red hair would seem more typical of northwestern Europe than of Ancient Egypt, and one wonders if Ramses II might have had Megalithic blood.

In Ancient Egypt, red hair was associated with Set, the Egyptian God of the Desert and Storms, who was also red haired. Red and auburn hair was ominous in Ancient Egypt and, according to mythology, Set was 'violent and wild,' and 'he had white skin and red hair, which Egyptians abhorred'.[299] Red-hair people were dubbed 'Set's followers'[300] in Ancient Egypt, and the fact that a pharaoh with auburn hair managed to become one of the most prestigious rulers of Egypt is as odd as it is remarkable, and is evidence to the man's stupendous personality. To be sure, Ramses II succeeded in overcoming a disadvantage and turning it into a quality. Interestingly, the name of Ramses II's father, Seti I, precisely means 'Set's follower.' Was Ramses II a MPD, or did he have MPDs either around him or in his ancestry? These questions cannot remain unasked.

---

[298] Rose-Marie Jouret et al., *Thèbes, 1250 av. J.-C. Ramsès II et le rêve du pouvoir absolu*, Paris: Editions Autrement – Séries Mémoires No2, 1990, p. 55
[299] Guirand and Schmidt, *op. cit.*, p. 35
[300] Jouret et al., *op. cit.*, p. 55

The Giza Pyramids

The Great Pyramid on the Giza Plateau near Cairo (attributed by historians and archaeologists to Pharaoh Khufu), along with its two sister pyramids (attributed to Pharaohs Khafre and Menkaure), are probably the most famous and impressive architectural achievements of the ancient world.

Right from the beginning of my research, I was surprised to learn that the Great Pyramid is *not* a Druidic Line location. Perhaps the reader, who may by now have grown accustomed to the fact that the most impressive sites and cities of the antique world (both the major Megalithic sites of Britain, and the major cities or temples of Mesopotamia and Egypt) are Salt Line locations, will share my surprise and, in a way, my initial disappointment. Why hasn't such a hallmark of the ancient world (a prestigious member of the list of the Seven Wonders of the World) been built on a Druidic Meridian or Druidic Parallel? Worse, does this absence somehow undermine our theory?

I must confess I have ruminated on this problem for years, and it now seems to me that the Giza Pyramids and the Sphinx that lies next to them do not have the age that mainstream historians and archaeologists usually think they have: they are either older or more recent. The Giza question is a huge one and is outside the scope of the present book. Let us briefly sum up the main astonishing facts about the Giza pyramids though. There are a great many amazing facts about these pyramids and the Sphinx. Here is a short selection of those:

1. The four sides of the Great Pyramid are almost perfectly oriented to the cardinal compass points (within three arc minutes).

2. No mummy has ever been found in any of the Giza Pyramids, meaning there is no hard evidence the pyramids were actual tombs.

3. The ground plan of the three Giza Pyramids seems to closely reproduce Orion's Belt in the constellation of Orion, which was revered by Ancient Egyptians, while the Nile seems to match the nearby Milky Way.[301]

4. The age of the site is difficult to determine. The Sphinx might be older than is usually thought (i.e. c. 2550 BC), as it seems to have been eroded by prolonged and extensive rainfall that can't be accounted for in the last five millennia, according to Boston University professor of

---

[301] See Robert Bauval and Adrian Gilbert, *The Orion Mystery*, London: Arrow, 1994

natural sciences Robert M Schoch.[302] On the other hand, the three Giza Pyramids might be more recent than is usually thought, which would explain why they are so sophisticated.

5. The dimensions of the Great Pyramid strongly suggest that those who designed it were familiar with the mathematical constants π (3.14159...) and φ (the golden ratio or 1.618...), and most surprisingly, the meter![303]

6. The Great Pyramid doesn't have four sides but eight, which made its construction incredibly more difficult.[304]

7. The Giza Pyramids are located immediately south of the Nile delta, which makes it a naturally interesting location (see further).

8. By a curious coincidence, the Giza area is approximately the geographical center of Earth's land surfaces[305] (see Chapter Twelve as well.)

9. By another mind-boggling coincidence, the modern latitude of the center of the Great Pyramid is 29.979°N, while the speed of light is 299,792,458 m/s (same sequence of digits).

10. The unit of length used in the Great Pyramid, the Royal Cubit (RC), which is usually quoted as 52.36 cm, is also $\pi/6$ in meters, and also π-φ^2 in meters.[306]

11. The Great Pyramid is almost exactly 30 modern degrees north of the equator, or 60 degrees south of the North Pole. Assuming the Earth's polar circumference to be Pi in meters, the arc from the North Pole to the Great Pyramid would measure 52.36 cm, the length of the Royal Cubit. Just an amazing coincidence?

Let's stop here, as the reader will easily understand that with the Giza pyramids, we enter the realm of the sublime.

Now, if indeed the astounding facts enumerated above are not trivial coincidences, and if indeed the Giza pyramids and the Sphinx either predate or postdate the Druidic sites and cities we have studied so far, and if indeed the Giza complex holds such a special status within the

---

[302] See Robert M Schoch's many books and articles

[303] Discoveries made by François Dupuy-Pacherand, expounded in Patrice Pooyard's film *The Revelation of the Pyramids*, freely available on the Internet at the time of writing

[304] Ibid.

[305] Charles Piazzi Smyth, *Our Inheritance in the Great Pyramid*, London: W. Isbister &Co., 1864

[306] Discoveries made by Dr. Charles Funck-Hellet expounded in *The Revelation of the Pyramids*

wonders of the ancient world, then it might explain why the Great Pyramid is *not* a Salt Line location, while sites such as Thebes or Abu Simbel are. In any case the Giza plateau seems to be an unequalled repository of knowledge.

The Megalithic yard at Giza?

Is there any trace of the Megalithic yard in Giza? Well, there is. The Great Pyramid today lacks its pyramidion or capstone, but is thought to have had an initial height of 146.6 m or 280 RC. The four sides of the base are about 230.36 m[307] or 440 RC, but with the missing casing stones that once made the Great Pyramid a smooth, light-reflecting structure, it might have been just a tad more.

Now for a new revelation. The intriguing thing is that 230.36 m is also 280 MY to an accuracy of 99.2 per cent. If the Megalithic yard was derived from the Megalithic pendulum, the result gets even more intriguing. The way the pendulum beats depends on gravity, and because *g* is smaller at the latitude of Giza[308] than in northwestern Europe, the Megalithic yard derived from the pendulum is slightly smaller at Giza than in Britain. At the 30 degree latitude of Giza, the Megalithic yard thus derived is .82558 m. Let's christen this particular length the Giza Megalithic yard (GMY). This time, 230.36 m is also 280 GMY to an accuracy of 99.7 per cent. Considering that the casing stones might have made the base side lengths a bit longer, it really looks like the intended length of the Great Pyramid base sides was 280 GMY! Is just another incredible coincidence, or was the number 280 somehow encapsulated into the design of the whole thing?

Now why would the Great Pyramid builders want the sides of the structure to be 280 GMY and its height 280 RC? Amusingly, 280 days correspond to exactly 40 weeks, the number of weeks of amenorrhoea for a pregnant woman. Is the Great Pyramid partly paying tribute to the human gestation period? Incidentally, we notice here that the number 40, which we saw in Chapter Seven plays a key role in Megalithic geometry, is also somehow encapsulated by nature in human biology (more about this in Part IV).

---

[307] Average number (the base sides are respectively 230.454 m, 230.253 m, 230.357 m and 230.394 m, an impressively small variation of 20 cm at most).

[308] The gravitational constant (g) is 9.79338 at a latitude of 30°N, while it is 9.80629 at a 45°N latitude (Bordeaux, France), and 9.81924 at a 60°N latitude (Orkney).

In addition, because twice the original height of the pyramid multiplied by π gives the perimeter of the Great Pyramid base (just as twice the radius of a circle multiplied by π gives the circumference of the same circle), it is at least possible to contemplate the possibility that a wheel was used to build the most famous pyramid in the world! Just imagine a wheel with a diameter of half a RC: it will necessarily have a circumference of 1 GMY! The base sides of the pyramid are thus obtained by turning the wheel 280 times, while the height of the pyramid is obtained by measuring twice 280 times the diameter of the wheel—simply amazing, and very clever! The only problem, of course, is that ancient Egyptians are not supposed to have known the wheel. Or have Egyptologists missed something?

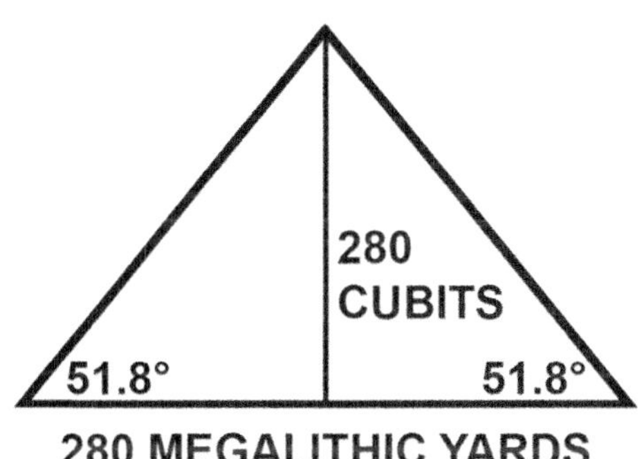

Fig. 24. The height of the Great Pyramid of Giza is 280 Royal Cubits, and the length of each of its sides is 280 'Giza' Megalithic yards.

Of course, all this might be another coincidence, but just think—what were the chances that the same number 280 would crop up by using the Megalithic yard to divide the pyramid sides and the Royal Cubit to divide its height?

Is there any more evidence of the use of the Megalithic yard at Giza? Maybe so. About 5 miles to the northwest of the Great Pyramid lie the remains of the so-called Pyramid of Djedefre, who was Khufu's first son. Although the pyramid was not as big as the Great Pyramid, its position on an elevated hill made the structure possibly even more visible from a great distance than the Giza pyramids. Interestingly, the axis Great Pyramid-Djedefre Pyramid is perpendicular (90 degrees) to the axis Great Pyramid-Khafre Pyramid, indicating that the pyramid was not built just anywhere but according to a precise geometric plan.

Incredibly, the distance between the center of the Great Pyramid and the pyramid of Djedefre is a neat 10,000 GMY, to an accuracy of 99.3 per cent. Even stranger, multiply this distance by 366, continuing in the same northwestern direction, and this Earth arc will get you... in Alesia, right on the double hill overhanging Guillon in France, with an astounding accuracy of 99.97 per cent! There is of course no way to tell whether this result is yet another lucky strike or not; but the combined facts that the unit used is the Megalithic yard, that the direction given by the Djedefre pyramid is the right one, and that the number used is an even 366, make it very hard for us to believe that this is unintentional. As an additional nugget, this arc flies right over the port of Alexandria.

Fig. 25. There are almost exactly 10,000 'Giza' MY from the Great Pyramid to the Djedefre Pyramid.

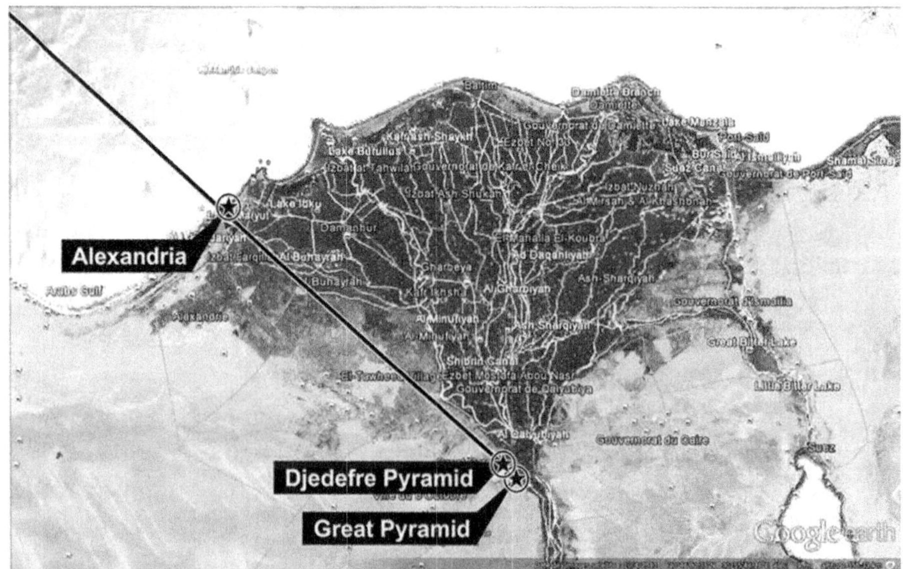

Fig. 26. The Great Pyramid-Djedefre Pyramid Line, if prolonged, flies over Alexandria.

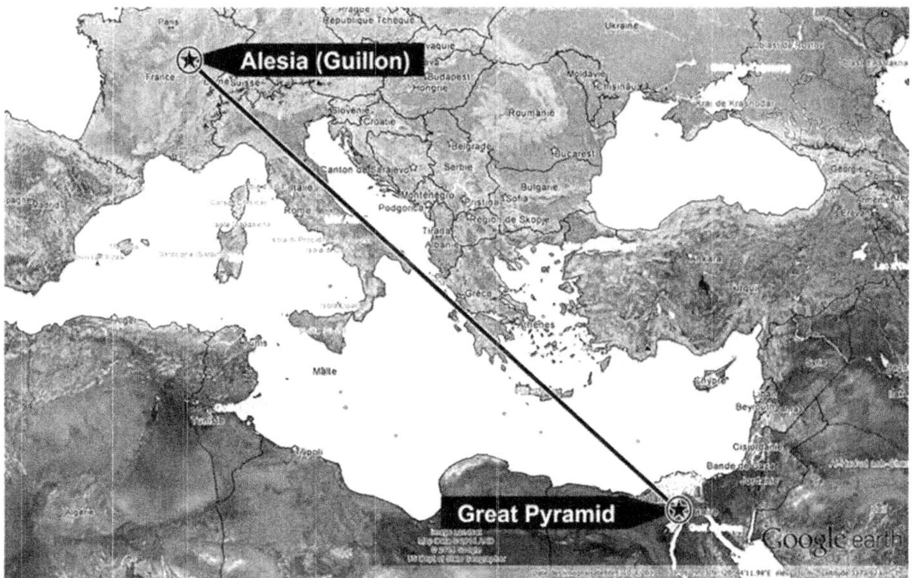

Fig. 27. The Great Pyramid-Djedefre Pyramid Line, if prolonged, leads right to Alesia, and the arc is precisely 366 times the distance between the two pyramids.

As the reader can now plainly see, the site of Giza might not be a Salt Line location, but it is both a highly intriguing place in terms of astronomy and mathematics, and it seems to be intimately connected to the Megalithic yard. Better still, Giza reveals a link between the Megalithic yard and the Royal Cubit used in Giza.

If all this is not a mere (mind-boggling) coincidence, it means that Giza, just like Thebes and Abu Simbel, is strongly linked to the geometric knowledge associated with our MPDs. We also see that, with Egypt, the question of who taught whom becomes more elusive.

The Great Pyramid-Newgrange Arc

I'd like to (nearly) finish this chapter with what is, in my humble view, one of the most incredible nuggets in the collection of links between Egypt and the Megalithic world.

There appears to be a link between Newgrange (unquestionably the most impressive Megalithic site of Ireland) and the Great Pyramid of Giza (unquestionably the most impressive architectural achievement of Egypt). We already pointed out earlier the Karnak-Carnac arc, which was close to being one-tenth of the Earth's polar circumference, but not exactly so.

Newgrange is a Megalithic stone passageway with chambers, covered by a large circular mound, located near the River Boyne in Ireland. It is one of the largest Megalithic monuments ever built in Europe and, in the words of well-known archaeologist Colin Renfrew, Newgrange is 'unhesitatingly regarded by the prehistorian as the great national monument of Ireland'.[309]

Every year at dawn at the winter solstice, the first sunrays in the morning flood across the long passage and hit the inner chamber, illuminating the triskele on the wall, making Newgrange somewhat similar to Maeshowe in Orkney and, in a certain way, to the great temple of Abu Simbel in Egypt.

Trace a line (i.e. an Earth arc) on Google Earth from the center of the Great Pyramid to the center of the Megalithic mound of Newgrange. The length you will come up with is 4,007.458 km. This is exactly one-tenth of the Earth's equatorial circumference (40,075.017 km, to an almost unbelievable accuracy of 99.999 per cent! In circle geometry, that's a neat 36 arc degrees out of the 360 degrees to go round the Earth (or 36.6 Meg. degrees out of the 366 Meg. degrees of the Earth).

Fig. 28. The Great Pyramid-Newgrange Arc is exactly one-tenth of the Earth's equatorial circumference.

309 Colin Renfrew in Michael J O'Kelly, *Newgrange: Archaeology, Art and Legend*, London: Thames and Hudson, 1982, p. 7

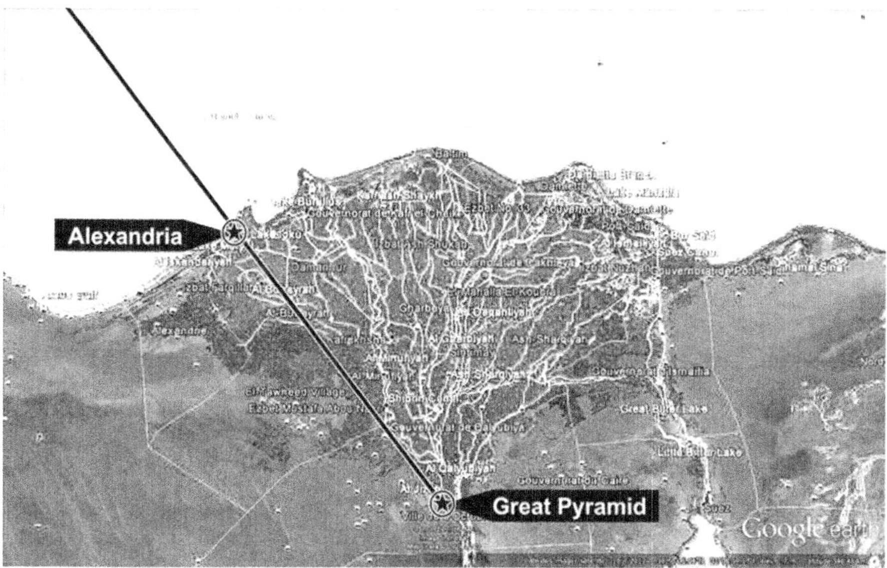

Fig. 29. The Great Pyramid-Newgrange Arc crosses the coastline at Alexandria, a precise 180 km away from the Great Pyramid.

One curious additional fact is that the line thus traced around the globe follows the western side of the Nile delta, and that it intersects the coast (with a right angle!) exactly 180 km from the Great Pyramid. Number 180, of course, is closely associated to modern circle geometry, as there are 180 degrees in a half-circle. This is especially interesting in light of the fact that the coastline above the Nile delta closely evokes a circle arc.

What about the unit used, the kilometer? The reader will certainly remember that the meter was probably known to the Great Pyramid's builders, astounding though this may seem, as we saw earlier. It should not be too surprising then to see the number 180 expressed here in kilometers.

Coincidence aside, the figures are so precise and accurate that it leaves little doubt that the Great Pyramid was placed where it is so that the number 180 shows up in the equation, as well as being located at the vertex of the Nile Delta. Likewise the Newgrange site was chosen at a distance of exactly one-tenth of the Earth's equatorial circumference from the Great Pyramid.

Newgrange is supposed to have been built in 3200 BC, whereas according to mainstream Egyptology the Great Pyramid was built only much later, c. 2550 BC. So, was the Great Pyramid constructed by taking into account its distance from Newgrange? Or was the Great Pyramid erected on the site of a predecessor monument, which antedated Newgrange as well? (see Chapter 19).

Newgrange, like Giza, is *not* a Salt Line location. This bothered me for years, until I realized that perhaps the purpose of these two huge stone monuments was entirely different: Newgrange and the Great Pyramid stand at their respective locations *in order to materialise on the ground a perfect one-tenth segment of the Earth's equatorial circumference.* Interestingly, the constructions of Carnac (c. 3300 BC), Karnak (c. 3200 BC) and Newgrange (c. 3200 BC) are contemporaneous, and correspond to the time when Megalithic geometry appears to have first been used. Carnac and Karnak both display great raised stones (be they megaliths or columns), while Newgrange and the Great Pyramid both are geometric elevated monuments (a circular mound and a pyramid).

Did MPDs learn from Egyptian sages at the time, then 'trace' the arcs around the globe, materialising them with the stone avenues of Carnac and the mound of Newgrange, and then proceed to use the Megalithic yard and the Druidic Lines derived from 366-degree geometry in different places around the world, materialising them with what I term Druidic sites or Druidic cities? Or was the Great Pyramid built after these three monuments, by people who still had the knowledge of 366-degree geometry, and who had also acquired much more mathematical knowledge, including the meter, allowing them to attain the astounding level of accuracy we now observe?

To finish on more speculative notes, is it just a coincidence if the Great Pyramid-Newgrange Arc intersects Alexandria in Egypt and the island of Crete, and skirts Delphi (which, according to Greek mythology, was the Omphalos, i.e. the 'navel' or center of the world) and Anglesey in Wales? As we saw in Chapter Five, Anglesey (formerly known as Mona) was an island sacred to the Druids, and the site where they had taken refuge in 60 AD before they were mercilessly slaughtered by Roman troops. On the westernmost part of the island, also skirting the Great Pyramid-Newgrange Arc, is another, smaller island called Holyhead Island (because of its rich Megalithic architecture). Have Mona and Holyhead Island been holy places from the time of MPDs to the time of Celtic Druids because both of these people knew they were located right along the Earth arc we have just spotted?

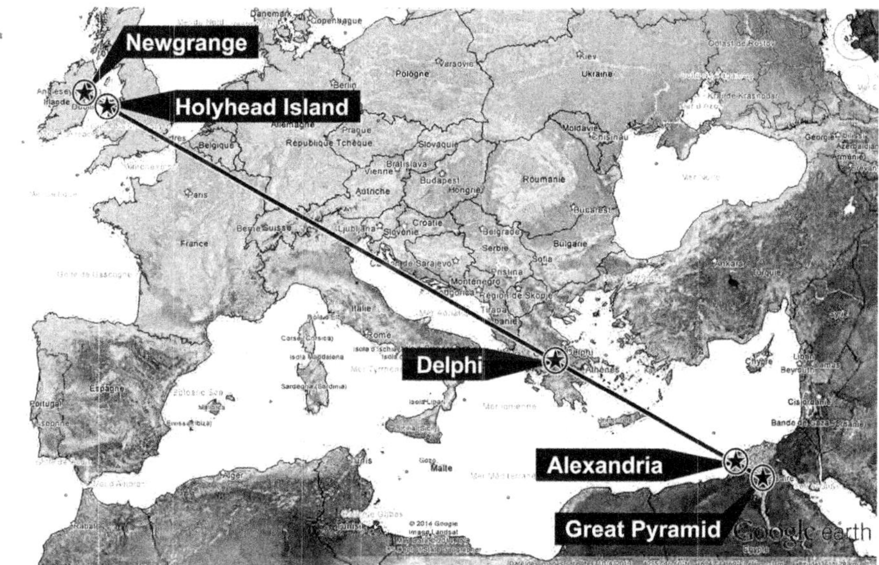

Fig. 30. The Great Pyramid-Newgrange Arc flies over Alexandria, along Delphi (the 'navel' of the Old World) and along Holyhead Island (west of Anglesey).

The Veneti, a sea people

Is it just a coincidence if the Great Pyramid-Newgrange Arc also flies over Venetia (the Italian region of Venice, which owes its name to the Veneti, a people of sailors in Roman times)? That it skirts Lake Constance, shared between Switzerland, Germany and Austria, which was named *Lacus Venetus* in Roman times? And that it neatly intersects the local government area of Gwynedd (*Venedotia* in Latin) in Wales, which was the Kingdom of Gwynedd for centuries after the fall of Rome? Don't the names *Veneti*, *Venetus* and *Venedotia* look strangely similar to each other? According to linguists, the term *Venedotia* could be etymologically linked to the name *Féni*, meaning 'Irish people'[310]... coming from the Newgrange area?

Interestingly, there was in Brittany another Celtic tribe called the Veneti. They lived precisely in the Carnac and Locmariaquer area and were great sailors. Caesar, who defeated them in a sea battle in 56 BC, described them as very powerful and influential seafarers:

> The influence of this state is by far the most considerable of any of the countries on the whole sea coast, because the Veneti both have

[310] Eric P Hamp, 'Goidil, Feni, Gwynedd,' Proc. Harvard Celtic Colloquium 12, 1995, p. 43-50

> a very great number of ships, with which they have been accustomed to sail to Britain, and [thus] excel the rest in their knowledge and experience of nautical affairs; and as only a few ports lie scattered along that stormy and open sea, of which they are in possession, they hold as tributaries almost all those who are accustomed to traffic in that sea.[311]

The Veneti gave their name to the Breton city of Vannes (*Gwened* in Breton), which, as we saw earlier, is a Druidic Meridian location.

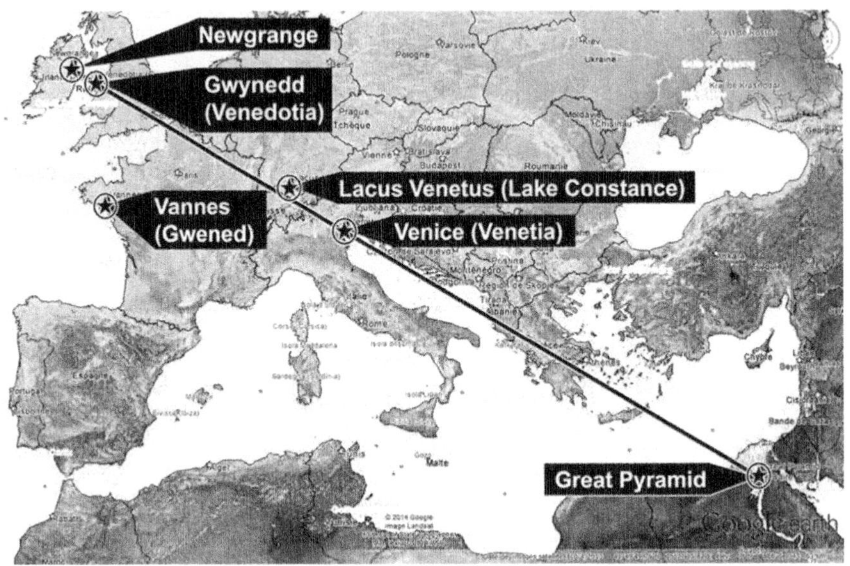

Fig. 31. The Great Pyramid-Newgrange Arc flies over Venice in Veneto, along Lacus Venetus (Lake Constance) and Venedotia (the former Kingdom of Gwynedd).

It is also interesting to note that Caesar gave us a precise description of their ships, whose 'prows were raised very high'.[312] Is it just a coincidence if gondolas, the traditional rowing-boats of Venice, also have a characteristic high prow? Isn't the word *gondola* strangely reminiscent of the words *Gwynedd* or *Gwened*, with the same sequence of sounds *g-o/w-n-d*?

Is it not also quite odd that the expression 'Venetian blond' refers to the reddish blond hair colour which, strangely enough, is quite common in this part of Italy? Is it just a coincidence if Ireland is the place in the world where red hair is most common? Or is there a genetic connection between ancient Irish people, Gwynedd people, people from Vannes in

---

[311] Julius Caesar, *Commentaries on the Gallic War*, III, 8: http://classics.mit.edu/Caesar/gallic.3.3.html

[312] *Ibid.*, III, 13

Brittany or Venice in Italy, and Ramses II in Egypt? Isn't the connection best explained in terms of Druidic geometrical knowledge secretly kept first by MPDs and then by Celtic Druids, who might well have once sailed along this arc from Alexandria to Venice to the Irish shores? Nobody can ever be sure, but it is certainly attention-grabbing food for thought.

Main points

- **Egyptian myths speak of Thot, a civilising God who was an expert both in astronomy and geometry, who then proceeded to civilise the rest of the world**
- **The Nabta Playa megaliths of southern Egypt, contemporaneous with the first European megaliths, are astronomically aligned**
- **Thebes, the great capital of Ancient Egypt, comprising the Valley of the Kings, Luxor and Karnak, is a Druidic Meridian location**
- **The solar temples of Abu Simbel are also a Druidic Meridian location**
- **Red-haired pharaoh Ramesses II may be of Megalithic descent**
- **The Giza pyramids appear to be a mind-boggling mathematical and astronomical reservoir**
- **The Megalithic yard appears to have been used in Giza and relates to the Royal Cubit through circle geometry**
- **The distance between the Great Pyramid and Newgrange is a stunningly perfect one-tenth segment of the Earth's equatorial circumference**

Chapter Twelve: Druidic Cities of the Indus Valley, Turkey and Greece

As I was soon to learn, many other major Old World cities of antiquity are also Druidic Line locations, most notably in the Indus Valley, Anatolia (modern Turkey) and Greece.

The Indus Valley Civilisation

About the same time as the Sumerian and Egyptian civilisations began to flourish in the most stunning manner, a third civilisation emerged further east, in the Indus Valley, in what is now Afghanistan, Pakistan and northwestern India. It is also known as the Harappan civilisation, after the city of Harappa, a major fortified city of the civilisation.

Although Harappan civilisation was born c. 3300 BC, the mature Indus Valley civilisation is usually dated to c. 2600 BC. This highly developed civilisation had ingenious, advanced sewerage and drainage systems, with houses sometimes equipped with a shower room.[313] Such systems, of course, remind us of those which were used at approximately the same time in Skara Brae in Orkney, Scotland. In the Indus Valley city of Mohenjo-daro, public hygiene was so important that the whole city was equipped with such a sewerage system.

What is particularly strange about this civilisation is that it seems to have appeared extremely rapidly. In the words of an archaeologist who specialised in the Indus Valley civilisation:

> What we know of the phases preceding the appearance of the Sindh [Indus Valley] gives its origins a mysterious character. The sudden blooming of a completely formed civilisation with its

---

[313] Arthur L Basham, *La civilisation de l'Inde ancienne,* Paris: Arthaud, 1976, p. 37

> writing system, its techniques, its conception of urbanisation and comfort . . . truly looks like a miracle.[314]

Another Asian civilisations specialist writes that the city of Mohenjo-daro 'appears suddenly with all its characteristics around 2500 BC' and that the Indus Valley civilisations in general 'were created by an unknown people of merchants who traded with Mesopotamia by sea, possibly by land'.[315] Interestingly, amongst the humans unearthed in the Indus Valley are Mediterranean and Alpine people.[316] According to the late historian and indologist Arthur L. Basham, Harappans were Mediterranean people, similar in type to people in the Middle East and Egypt, of a genetic type that is still present within the modern Indian population.[317]

The Druidic city of Harappa

When I started to study the Indus Valley civilisation, I made a little prediction. After all, I had been so lucky with Britain, Mesopotamia and Egypt that I felt pretty sure some of the major cities of such a brilliant civilisation must have its Salt Line cities as well. I went even so far as to bet with myself that, once more, there would be at least a Druidic Meridian site, as I had seen that these axes, theoretically more difficult to determine than Druidic Parallels, were very often marked by major Megalithic sites, temples or cities.

My first try was with Mohenjo-daro. Unfortunately, it wasn't a Druidic Line location.

Harappa, on the other hand, the city which gives the ancient Indus Valley Civilisation its modern name, is a Druidic Meridian city all right. The error relative to the Druidic Line is only three arc minutes, but the most curious aspect is that it is located 38 Megalithic degrees east of the River Jordan, while Stonehenge and Avebury are located 38 degrees *west* of the Jordan. That the city is located on a Druidic Meridian is impressive enough, though once again, it might be a pure coincidence; but to see such symmetry strongly suggests that our hypothesis that the River Jordan is the initial Golden Prime Meridian is valid, and that a common denominator (presumably our MPDs) exists between the creators of Stonehenge in Britain and the founders of Harappa in the Indus Valley.

---

314 Jean-Marie Casal, *La civilisation de l'Indus et ses énigmes,* Paris: Fayard, 1969, p. 98

315 Louis Frédéric, *Dictionnaire de la civilisation indienne,* Paris: Robert Laffont, 1987, p. 526

316 Casal, *op. cit.*, p. 211

317 Arthur L. Basham, *La civilisation de l'Inde ancienne,* Paris: Arthaud, 1976, p. 56

In other words, it looks like some sages who were well acquainted with 366-degree geometry, Stonehenge and the River Jordan, their presumed Golden Prime Meridian, deliberately sought a site just as far from the Jordan as Stonehenge is, but in the opposite direction!

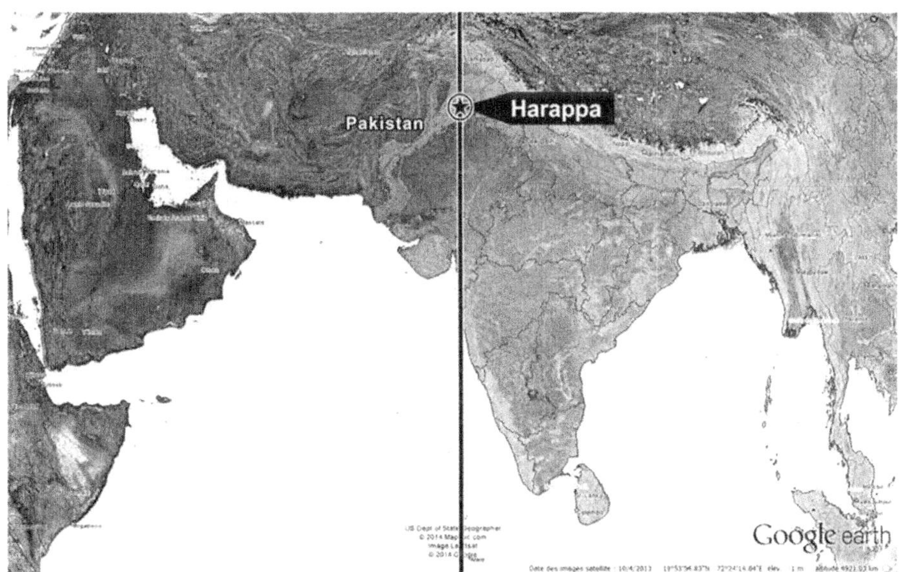

Fig. 32. The Druidic city of Harappa in the Indus Valley civilisation.

To sum things up in a single question: was the sudden emergence of Harappa somehow influenced by MPDs, perhaps accompanied by Middle Eastern or Sumerian people?

Another major Harappan site called Ganeriwala, situated in the desert halfway between Mohenjo-daro and Harappa but to this day still unexcavated, is also a Salt Line location. It is located only one arcminute south of a Druidic Parallel.

On a more conjectural note, spirituality in India (Hinduism, Buddhism, Jainism, and so on) might find its roots in the Harappan civilisation, even though it disappeared about 3,000 years ago. To archaeologist Jean-Marie Casal, the fact is undeniable:

> There are in the religions of historical India some concepts, beliefs or behaviours that can be only explained with an uninterrupted tradition going back to the Indus civilisation. Today's Hinduism, through its preceding phase, Brahmanism [Vedism] can be attached to a body of creeds and rites that found their first expression in hymns and stories long transmitted orally from one generation to the next, and which were given to India by Indo-

> Iranian populations established on its lands from the first part or the middle of the second millennium BC.[318]

Are we bold enough to suggest that Indian spirituality might be the distant echo of Druidic wisdom? Surely this would be going too far in the interpretation of facts. But let us meditate one more time what Pliny the Elder wrote about Druids in the 1st century AD. According to the Roman naturalist, Druids from Britain were magicians and doctors, and it was probably they who had taught their knowledge to Persians:

> At the present day, struck with fascination, Britannia still cultivates this [magic] art, and that, with ceremonials so august, that she might almost seem to have been the first to communicate them to the people of Persia.[319]

The Hittites and the Druidic city of Hattusa

In archaeological terms, Turkey is an exceptional country, with vestiges of some of the oldest cities on the planet. The buried mountain sanctuary of Göbekli Tepe, for example, with its superb T-shaped limestone pillars, carved with magnificent low reliefs, is thought to be approximately 10,000 years old. That makes the site twice as old as the first European megaliths, or those of Nabta Playa in southern Egypt!

In the early 2nd millennium BC another great civilisation emerged in Anatolia in eastern Turkey—that of the Hittites. They dominated an area around their capital city of Hattusa in the northern part of central Turkey for several centuries from 1600 BC.

One remarkable aspect of Hattusa is that it is megalithic in the literal sense of the word, with colossal stone constructions. The Hittites excelled at both commerce and conquest—they invaded Mesopotamia—and they contributed in transmitting Mesopotamian laws and ways of thinking in a large portion of the Mediterranean world, from Egypt to Greece.

As usual, one striking aspect of this civilisation is that its origins remain quite enigmatic to historians. Richard Hooker, a scholar who has specialised in the Hittite civilisation, underlines the 'mysterious origins'[320]

---

[318] Casal, *op. cit*, p. 207-8

[319] Pliny the Elder, *The Natural History*, XXX, 4: http://www.perseus.tufts.edu/hopper/text?doc=Perseus%3Atext%3A1999.02.0137%3Abook%3D30%3Achapter%3D4

[320] http://www.wsu.edu/~dee/MESO/HITTITES.HTM

of this people. In his opinion, '[t]he Hittites are covered in a shroud of fog and mystery' and 'we don't know where they come from'.[321]

What if the Megalithic people played some role at the beginning? Is Hattusa also connected to the 366-degree geometry we suspect MPDs to have used? In any case, old theories that made the original Hittites invaders from the Black Sea shores or from northeastern Turkey have now been abandoned because they contradict archaeological evidence, which point to less warlike origins: 'The impression is rather that of a pacific penetration, bringing by degrees a monopoly of political power'.[322]

If the Hittite civilisation proper began at the relatively late date of c. 1600 BC, it is known that the first citadel of Hattusa was established in the late 3rd millennium BC by a non-Hittite people.[323]

Hattusa is a Salt Line location. It is located only three arc minutes from a Druidic Meridian which runs exactly one degree west of the River Jordan further south.

Fig. 33. The Druidic city of Hattusa in Anatolia.

Hattusa's cyclopean ruins—that is, built from massive irregular blocks—overlook the Turkish village of Boğazkale, at the top of a fertile plateau surrounded with precipices. It has been a UNESCO World Heritage site since 1985, 'notable for its urban organisation, the types of construction that have been preserved (temples, royal residences, fortifications) the rich ornamentation of the Lions' Gate and the Royal Gate, and the ensemble of rock art at Yazilikaya.'[324]

---

[321] *Ibid.*
[322] http://ragz-international.com/hittites.htm
[323] Francis Joannès et al., *Dictionnaire de la civilisation mésopotamienne*, Paris: Robert Laffont, 2001, p. 372
[324] http://whc.unesco.org/en/list/377

The odd thing is that nothing seemed to predestine the secluded site to become the capital of an immense empire. Historians are puzzled why the Hittites chose this location: 'Within the territories of the Hittite empire, it [the capital city] was quite eccentric: it was very much to the north, which exposed it in particular to the threat of the Kaška, some mountain people in northern Anatolia.'[325] Was the site elected because of its Druidic Meridian credentials? In any case, 'at the height of its power, it [Hattusa] was a most prestigious capital.'[326]

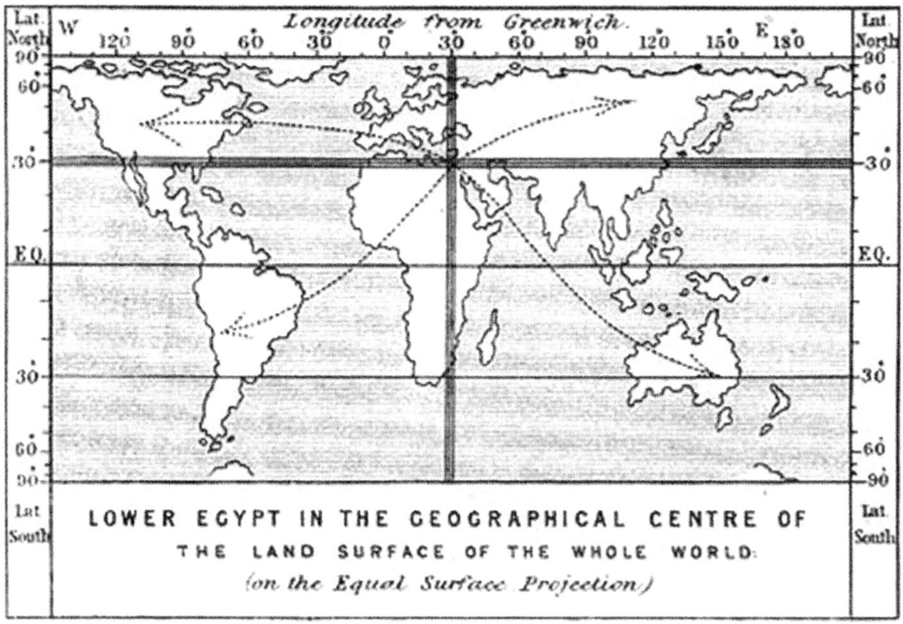

Fig. 34. Giza, the Geographical center of the Earth according to Charles Piazzi Smyth.

The geographical center of the Earth

As we have seen in the previous chapter, the Giza plateau is often cited as being the geographical center of the Earth (GCE). This was first suggested in the nineteenth century by Charles Piazzi Smyth.[327]

More recent calculations though place the GCE further north, and a bit further east. I was struck to discover that the spot now reckoned to be the GCE is situated in Turkey, and even more amazed to see that it

[325] Joannès, *op. cit.*, p. 372
[326] *Ibid.*, p. 374
[327] Charles Piazzi Smyth, *op. cit.*

was positioned right on a Druidic Meridian! To my continuing amazement, I found out that its precise geographic coordinates were not very different from those of... Hattusa! Just compare the two:

Hattusa: 40°01'N-34°37'E. GCE: 40°52'N-34°34'E

The Druidic Meridian runs at 34°34'E. Hattusa skirts the Salt Line, while the GCE is a perfect Salt Line location. The only minor difference between Hattusa and the GCE is in latitudinal terms, but the discrepancy amounts to less than a degree (51' or 51 modern arc minutes).

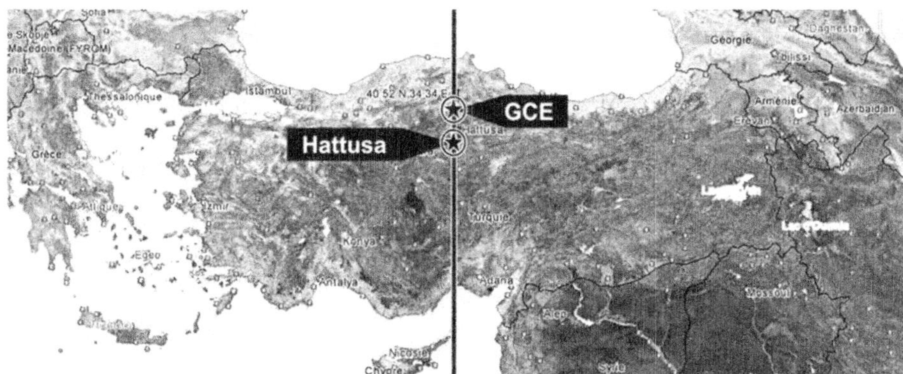

Fig. 35. The (modern) Geographical Center of the Earth and Hattusa are very close to each other, and are located along the same Druidic Meridian.

The following question might sound absurd at this juncture but please allow me to ask it anyway: Was Hattusa built in the first place because whoever decided on the location knew, or at least thought, it was the geographical center of the Earth? It remains of course a mystery as to how either the Hittites or MPDs could have determined the GCE with such accuracy.

The Minoans of Crete and Thera

The first great civilisation of continental Greece is that of the Myceneans, which owes much to the beautiful Minoan civilisation of Crete which we mentioned in Chapter Seven.

The Minoan palaces are not Salt Line locations, but Phaistos, where the Phaistos Disc was recovered, along with the Minoan administrative center of Agia Triada, were built along the Ieropotamos, the 'Sacred River', which flows into the Mediterranean right where a Druidic Meridian runs (at at 24°43'E).

It is also interesting to note that the island of Santorini, which is the volcanic caldera resulting from the major Thera eruption occurring c. 1628 BC and that destroyed the Minoan civilisation there (some say it gave rise to the myth of Atlantis), is also a perfect Salt Line location. The 37th Druidic Parallel north of the equator runs right through the central crater (incidentally the same Druidic Parallel along which Nineveh was built, see Chapter Ten). One fascinating aspect of the Minoan civilisation at Thera is that, just like the Megalithic people, they were a seafaring people. In the words of German archaeologist and historian Fritz Schachermeyr, Thera was a 'maritime republic'. [328] It is also very interesting to note that, on a huge fresco depicting life in Thera (among other things, ships and people) in the 16th century BC, you can see what looks like a sacred tree surrounded with a stone circle.[329] Is it a Megalithic stone circle?

Once more, one really strange aspect of the Minoan civilisation is that it appeared quite suddenly, with no visible transition between simple village communities and the refined Minoan palaces. According to archaeologist Henri van Effenterre, who devoted half a century studying Aegean cultures, the sudden explosion of a palatial system in ancient Crete can only be explained by an outside influence or, in his own terms, by 'a foreign fashion which might well have woken Crete up'.[330] Did MPDs play a role in this awakening? We have already stressed that the Minoan foot, just like the Megalithic yard, was a perfect subdivision of the Earth's polar circum–ference in 366-degree geometry.

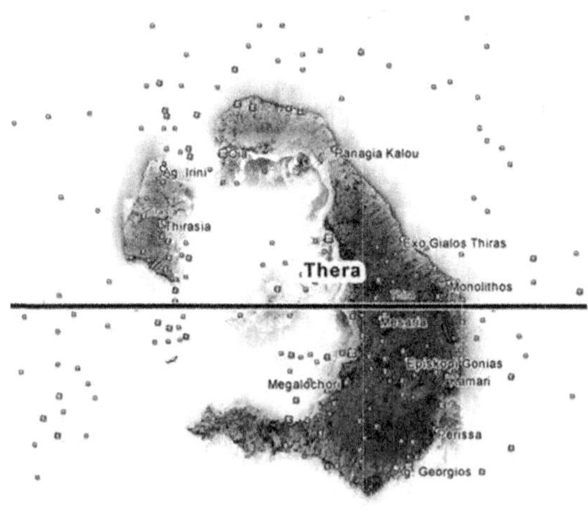

Fig. 36. The Thera volcanic caldera is located right on the 37th Druidic Parallel north of the equator.

[328] Henri Van Effenterre, *Les Egéens. Aux Origines de la Grèce, Chypre, Cyclades, Crète et Mycènes,* Paris: Armand Colin, 1986, p. 104
[329] Ibid., 100-9
[330] Effenterre, *op. cit.*, p. 133

The Pelasgians and the founding of Mycenaean Greece

Greek legends, as well as Homer and Herodotus, mention an elusive sea people who sailed to Greece well before the Hellenic people came. They are referred to as the Pelasgians or *Pelastikoi*, and myths have it that these brave seafarers were capable of wonders. It is generally thought that the Mycenaeans owe much to these people.

The Pelasgians are thought to be the Greek name of the Philistines, who gave their name to Palestine, and the people the Egyptians called the Peleset, part of the Sea Peoples who tried to invade Egypt under the rule of Ramses III. In the words of archaeologist Paul Faure, all these slightly different names refer to one and the same people, a sailing people who lived on Mediterranean islands: 'And like... the Philistines, in Hebrew Pelishtim, are the Peleset in Egyptian texts, that is, in Greek, Pelasgians, Pelasgikoi or Pelastikoi, they refer to islanders in general, and not only Cretans'.[331] It is interesting to note that the adjective *pelagic*, which derives from the Greek, means 'relating to the open sea.'

In his *Odyssey*, Homer went so far as to say that the Pelasgians were a 'noble' race living in Crete among other peoples: 'There is a fair and fruitful island in mid-ocean called Crete; it is thickly peopled and there are nine cities in it: the people speak many different languages which overlap one another, for there are Achaeans, brave Eteocretans, Dorians of three-fold race, and noble Pelasgi.'[332] Is it possible that MPDs, because of the great astronomical, geometrical and navigational knowledge they must have had, were later interpreted as 'noble' people, i.e. philosophers belonging in a high-ranking class?

Could also the taller stature of many people from northern Europe have impressed local populations? In the Bible, David, the future King of Israel, confronts the Philistine Goliath, who is probably described as a 'giant' warrior because many Mediterraneans are shorter than Northern people. According to the Bible, the Philistines came from 'Caphtor,'[333] which is generally construed as Crete. Were some of the Pelasgians Megalithic sailors who had settled in Thera and Crete? The archaeological record appears to confirm this hypothesis, as four skulls genetically belonging to the Atlantic-European group have been

---

331 Paul Faure, *La Vie quotidienne en Crète au temps de Minos*, Paris: Hachette, 1973, p. 151

332 Homer, *The Odyssey*, XIX: http://classics.mit.edu/Homer/odyssey.19.xix.html

333 Jeremiah 47:4 and Amos 9:7

excavated in Crete.[334] According to author Jürgen Spanüth, the Philistines were actually Frisians coming from the North Sea.[335]

Herodotus wrote that the Pelasgians spoke a 'Barbarian language'.[336] According to the historian, the Pelasgians lived for some time with Athenians, and many Greek cities have lost their original name but were founded by the Pelasgians. Herodotus also stated that Pelasgians even brought their language to some parts of Greece.[337] Last but not least, Herodotus asserted that the Pelasgic race never really multiplied: 'Moreover it is true, as I think, of the Pelasgian race also, that so far as it remained Barbarian it never made any great increase.'[338] Is it additional evidence that MPDs left more *memes* than genes on the local populations they met, as geneticist Cavalli-Sforza proposed? Were the Pelasgians pacific people who had something to teach rather than lust for land and domination?

In Greek mythology, the Pelasgians' ancestor was named Pelasgos. This Greek hero was a native of Arcadia and the son of Poseidon.[339] As Poseidon was the Greek God of the Sea, it leaves little doubt that the Pelasgians were truly people travelling on the sea. According to Jürgen Spanüth, the Greek God of the sea is an alteration of Fosite, a Frisian God residing in Heligoland, literally the 'sacred island' of the North Sea. If the Pelasgians came from the North Sea, they may have brought to Greece some Megalithic knowledge we should be able to trace.

Interestingly, the Philistines are known to have founded the city of Ashkelon (today situated in the Southern District of Israel) on the Mediterranean coast. The city is a perfect Druidic Meridian location, as it is located right on the 34°34'E Druidic Meridian (like Hattusa).

Mycenae, Tiryns and Argos: Druidic cities of Greece

As we said, Mycenae is generally regarded as the first great civilisation of continental Greece. Mycenaeans were powerful, wealthy, warlike people who built architectural splendours throughout Greece. According

---

[334] Faure, *op. cit.*, p. 112-3
[335] See Jürgen Spanüth, *Atlantis—The Mystery Unravelled*, London: Arco Publishers Ltd, 1956, or *Atlantis of the North*, London: Sidgwick & Jackson Ltd, 1979
[336] Herodotus, *The Histories*, I, 57
[337] *Ibid.*
[338] *Ibid.*, I, 58
[339] Guirand and Schmidt, *op. cit.*, p. 798

to Henri van Effenterre, Mycenaeans probably had a maritime origin.[340] They arrived in Greece c. 2400-2000 BC, and favoured the rapid development of the peninsula.[341] The first great Mycenaean dynasties, however, date back to c. 1700 BC. In Peter Levi's opinion, the Minoans probably initiated much of Mycenaean culture and knowledge.[342]

Just like the Minoans, the Mycenaeans proved excellent navigators: 'But mariners they were... which implies they had long been familiar with the sea, something you wouldn't expect for tribes coming down from central Europe on terrestrial ways.'[343] And because they were able to erect huge defensive structures, using stones weighing up to 100 tonnes, the Mycenaeans were considered by later Greeks as gods or demigods. Mycenaean tombs were topped by enormous *tholoi,* also styled beehive tombs, similar to those found inside the cairn of Barnenez in Brittany about 3,000 years before!

The archaeological sites of Mycenae and Tyrins in the northeastern Peloponnese, both of which were major Mycenaean cities, have been UNESCO World Heritage sites since 1999 because they 'are the imposing ruins of the two greatest cities of the Mycenaean civilization, which dominated the eastern Mediterranean world from the 15th to the 12th century B.C. and played a vital role in the development of classical Greek culture.'[344] The fortified city of Mycenae has 40-foot cyclopean walls[345] which are traditionally called 'Pelasgian walls,'[346] and is famous for its Lion Gate, the monumental sculpted main entrance to the acropolis with two lionesses flanking a central sacred column carved in high relief.

The walls of Tiryns, according to Pausanias, a Greek geographer living in the 2nd century AD, were 'no less marvellous' than the pyramids of Egypt.[347]

It will now come as no surprise for the reader that both cities of Mycenae and Tiryns are Salt Line locations. Mycenae once stood right

---

[340] Effenterre, *op. cit.*, p. 166
[341] *Ibid.*
[342] Peter Levi (1980), *Atlas du monde grec,* Paris: Fernand Nathan, 1982, p. 34
[343] Effenterre, op.cit., p. 184
[344] http://whc.unesco.org/en/list/941
[345] *Dictionnaire de la Grèce antique,* Paris: Encyclopaedia Universalis and Albin Michel, 2000, p. 869
[346] Pierre Lévêque, *La Naissance de la Grèce. Des Rois aux cités,* Paris: Gallimard, 1990, p. 26
[347] Pausanias, *Description of Greece*, 9, 36, 5

along a Druidic Meridian running 13 Megalithic degrees west of the River Jordan (25 degrees east of Stonehenge), while Tyrins is located along the very same Druidic Meridian further south.

Another major Mycenaean stronghold was Argos, which is located approximately between Mycenae and Tiryns, along the very same Druidic Meridian, but slightly more to the west. Argos is traditionally recognised as Greece's oldest city, and legend has it that it was founded by Inachus, King of the Pelasgians.[348]

Heracles is said to have been born in Tiryns, and he was particularly revered in Argos.[349] The Greek hero, who is said to have founded Alesia in Gaul, is definitely linked to 366-degree geometry.

Athens, Druidic city of Greece

Today's capital city of Greece, Athens, is also a Druidic Meridian location. Not surprised? Well, even if readers are by now used to these revelations, it shouldn't make them less impressed. On the contrary, one should keep in mind that the more Druidic cities we find, the more impressed we should be, because every new find is novel evidence of a common denominator in cities which are usually thought to have no common denominator at all! Of course, some cities might happen to be Salt Line location by pure chance, but it certainly cannot be the case for every one of them.

In Mycenaean times Athens was already an important center and the Acropolis a major fortress. The early Cyclopean walls can still be seen underneath the later constructions on the Acropolis.[350] Athens is located right on a Druidic Meridian that runs one Megalithic degree east of the meridian of Mycenae, Tyrins and Argos. The city of Athens stands precisely 12 Megalithic degrees west of the River Jordan and 26 Megalithic degrees east of Stonehenge. Today Athens is still the largest city of Greece.

Herodotus' opinion was that the first Athenians were Pelasgians,[351] in accord with Greek legends telling of Pelasgians occupying the Acropolis when Athens was founded.[352]

---

[348] Guy and M.-F. Rachet (1985), *Dictionnaire de la civilisation grecque*, Paris: Références Larousse, 1986, p. 44

[349] Guirand and Schmidt, *op. cit.*, p. 224

[350] Levi, *op. cit.* p. 116

[351] Herodotus, *The Histories*, I, 57

Dodona

One last place of interest in Mycenaean Greece is Dodona. This wild, isolated site in northwestern Greece, far from Attica and the Peloponnese, was an oracle devoted first to the Mother Goddess, and later to Zeus. The sacred oak-tree played a cardinal role in this oracle.

It is second in importance after Delphi, the Greek 'navel of the world.' It is interesting to note that the priests officiating at Dodona, who are described as 'priests-kings', might have been very similar to our hypothetical MPDs, at least in Salomon Reinach's view.[353]

Once more, we know from Homer that Dodona is linked to the Pelasgians.[354] Because the oracle of Delphi was rarely favourable to them, Athenians preferred Dodona.

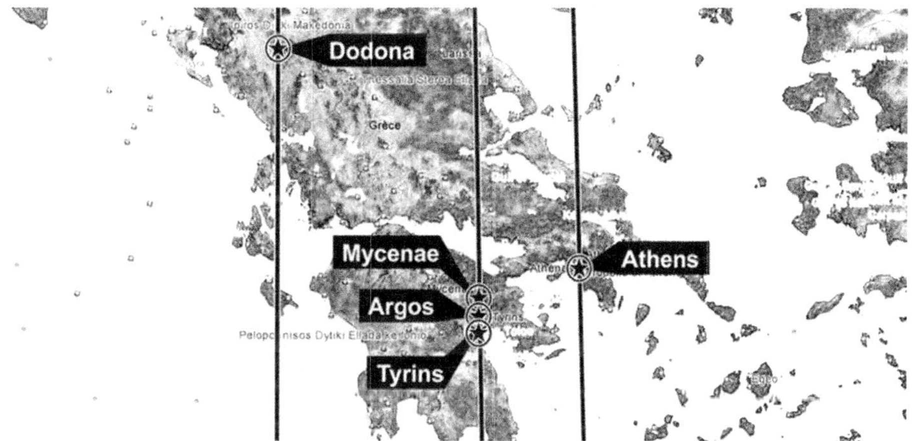

Fig. 37. Druidic cities of Greece: Athens, Mycenae, Argos, Tyrins and Dodona.

Once more, defying all odds, the site of Dodona is a perfect Druidic Line location. It is precisely located on a Druidic Meridian running 15 Megalithic degrees west of the River Jordan, or 23 Megalithic degrees east of the Druidic Line graced with Stonehenge and Avebury in Britain. If this major sacred site accidentally happens to be a Druidic Meridian location, it is yet another extraordinary coincidence defying common sense. In the light of what we now know about the origins of Mycenaean

---

[352] Rachet, *op. cit.*, p.49

[353] Salomon Reinach (1905-23), *Cultes, mythes et religions*, Paris: Robert Laffont, 1996, p. 223

[354] Homer, *The Iliad*, XVI: http://classics.mit.edu/Homer/iliad.16.xvi.html

Greece, the mainstream view that Dodona first emerged as a simple cult site for mountain shepherds[355] seems hardly plausible.

Main points

- **Harappa, in the Indus Valley civilisation, is a Druidic Meridian location**
- **Hattusa, the capital city of the Hittites, is a Druidic Meridian location**
- **Hattusa happens to be located very close to the geographical center of the Earth**
- **The volcanic caldera of Thera, where Minoans once thrived, is a Druidic Parallel location**
- **According to tradition, Mycenaean Greece was founded by 'noble' people called Pelasgians, who are known to have been sea people**
- **Major Mycenaean cities such as Mycenae, Tiryns, Argos and Athens are Druidic Meridian locations**
- **The sacred oracle of Dodona, which Athenians tended to prefer to Delphi, is a perfect Druidic Meridian location**

[355] Levi, *op. cit.*, p. 12

Chapter Thirteen: Druidic Cities of the New World

After studying the Old World my eyes naturally turned to the New World. Would I find out that the Megalithic sailors had also crossed the Atlantic? Would I discover that MPDs left traces of 366-degre geometry in the Western hemisphere? Would I find as many Druidic Line locations in the pre-Columbian Americas as I had in Megalithic Britain, Celtic Gaul, Mesopotamia, Egypt, the Indus valley, Anatolia and Greece? Were the great Andean cities of the Inca in South America, for instance, Salt Line locations as well? What about the Olmec, Maya or Aztec cities in Central America?

It was high time I checked the geographic coordinates of the major centers of the ancient great civilisations of the New World.

Caral, the Golden 'Mother City' of South America

If truth be told, I was first disappointed to see that none of the great Inca cities in South America appeared to be Druidic Line locations. But as the Inca empire came into existence relatively recently, c. 13th century AD, this was actually hardly surprising.

My initial disappointment, however, faded away when I saw that Caral, the city considered to be the oldest city of the Americas (or, as it is usually referred to, the 'Mother City of the Americas') was a Druidic Meridian location.

Although the site was initially discovered as early as 1905, nobody imagined what kind of archaeological treasure lay hidden in the desert Supe Valley, 85 miles north of Lima, and only 12 miles away from the Pacific coast. It was only in 1994 that archaeologist Ruth Shady, from the San Marcos University in Lima, noticed that what looked like natural hills in the desert were actually the vestiges of ancient pyramids. The site comprises step pyramids, a circular plaza and luxurious residences.[356] Caral even had an amphitheatre and a temple, and used an ingenious irrigation system. The society appears to have been peaceful with absolutely no trace of warfare, and its inhabitants consumed sardines and anchovies from the nearby ocean. They also made cotton clothes and fishing nets, which they probably traded for fish on the coast, and played music on flutes made of condor or pelican bones.

Radiocarbon dating gave the astonishing date of 2627 BC,[357] making the pyramids of Caral 4,000 years older than the beginning of the great Inca empire, and contemporaneous with (and even slightly older than) the conventional date of the Giza pyramids!

And now for the other major fact about Caral—the one that quite electrified me when I discovered it: the Caral pyramids are located only three arc minutes east of the Druidic Meridian running 115 Megalithic degrees west of the River Jordan (or 77 Megalithic degrees west of Stonehenge). Was the Mother City of the Americas founded there by people acquainted with 366-degree geometry? If so, the position of Caral near the *west* coast of South America, on the *Pacific* side rather than on the Atlantic, implies that the Megalithic sailors (or whoever it was) either sailed across the Pacific Ocean, or passed the Strait of Magellan four millennia before Magellan! We'll discuss this further in a moment.

Tiwanaku, the Druidic city of the Andes

More to the south, the ruins of the famous site of Tiwanaku near Lake Titicaca in Bolivia survive some 3,885 meters above sea level. The ancient Andean city was inscribed on the UNESCO World Heritage list in 2000 because it used to be the 'capital of a powerful pre-Hispanic empire that dominated a large area of the southern Andes and beyond,'[358] and because it contains 'monumental remains' which 'testify to the cultural and political significance of this civilisation'.[359]

Tiwanaku once possessed temples covered with gold and colourful textiles.[360] Although the city was considerably damaged in the 20th century—stone blocks were used to build the city of La Paz and a

---

[356] 'Ruins of a 4,600-year-old city in Peru challenge theories of civilization,' *San Franscisco Chronicle*, 27 Apr. 2001

[357] *The Lost Pyramids of Caral*, BBC 2, 31 Jan. 2002

[358] http://whc.unesco.org/en/list/567

[359] *Ibid.*

[360] http://emuseum.mnsu.edu/prehistory/latinamerica/south/sites/tiahuanaco.html

neighbouring railway—what remains of Tiwanaku is still breathtaking, with stones weighing up to 150 tonnes. Among the major architectural accomplishments of Tiwanaku are the Pyramid of Akapana, which used to rise to over 18 meters; the Kalasasaya, a large rectangular open temple which might have been an observatory; and the famous Gate of the Sun. It is a monumental slab of andesite, a volcanic rock, forming a huge doorway topped by an elaborate bas-relief frieze thought to depict God Viracocha by some, or the Sun God by others. The central figure on the lintel is surrounded by 48 squares, all looking at the deity, the ensemble being evocative of a calendar.

One strange aspect of the discoveries made in Tiwanaku is the presence of a bearded statue unearthed in 1934 in the Semi-Subterranean temple,[361] which has been interpreted as Viracocha, the pre-Inca and Inca civilising God, who is usually represented with a beard[362]—an odd fact as most Native males in the Americas were beardless. According to myth, Viracocha emerged from Lake Titicaca and 'painted and sculptured models of a race of giants,' and then 'created giants in his likeness,'[363] but because these would-be servants defied and disobeyed their creator, Viracocha turned them into stone: the megaliths we can see today at Tiwanaku. Then Viracocha created a second race of humans and proceeded to civilise the continent, before vanishing over the Pacific Ocean.[364] Is this bearded God the reminiscence of a MPD or, who knows, a Celtic Druid in relatively more recent times? Is Viracocha the distorted memory of the sages who founded Caral, or does it describe a subsequent 'visit' to South America centuries, or more probably millennia, after the first one?

Tiwanaku is believed to have been founded around 1200 BC,[365] about 1400 years after Caral. First it was a small settlement or a village, but around 300 BC it seems to have become a moral and cosmological center, the end point of a pilgrimage route,[366] before becoming a powerful empire in c. 300-400 AD. Experts agree that the Inca

---

[361] Richard W Keatinge (editor), *Peruvian Prehistory: An Overview of Pre-Inca and Inca Society*, Cambridge University Press, 1988, p. 174

[362] Félix Guirand and Joël Schmidt, *Mythes et mythologies. Histoire et dictionnaire*, Paris: Larousse-Bordas, 1996, p. 536

[363] Paul R Steele, *Handbook of Inca Mythology*, Santa Barbara: ABC-CLIO Ltd, 2004, p. 53

[364] *Ibid.*, p. 56

[365] http://whc.unesco.org/en/list/567

[366] Alan L Kolota, *The Tiwanaku: Portrait of an Andean Civilization*, Oxford: Wiley-Blackwell, 1993

civilisation is the inheritor of the Tiwanaku culture, as they share both architectural and socio-political traits.[367] Going backward in time, Tiwanaku is thought to be the inheritor of the Chavín culture, which flourished about 1,000 km to the north,[368] and Chavín may itself be the successor of the Caral civilisation.

In any case, what's really intriguing about Tiwanaku is that, just like Caral, it is a Salt Line location. More specifically, as is almost always the case in our research, Tiwanaku is a *Druidic Meridian* location, as the ancient city is located only three arc minutes away from a Druidic Meridian. This Druidic Meridian runs 106 Megalithic degrees west of the River Jordan, or 68 Megalithic degrees west of Stonehenge.

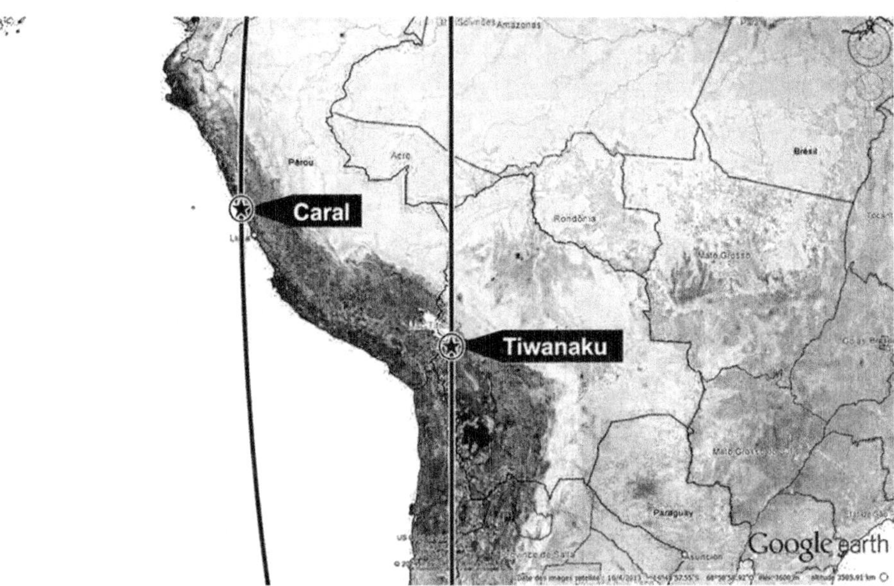

Fig. 38. Druidic cities of pre-Columbian South America: Caral and Tiwanaku.

Are Caral and Tiwanaku part of the Eldorado, i.e. the mythical 'Cities of Gold' the Spanish were looking for in South America? Were these cities made of actual gold, or was it their location on the globe that made them golden?

---

[367] http://www.wsu.edu:8080/~dee/CIVAMRCA/TIA.HTM

[368] Henri Stierlin, *Le Monde de l'Amérique précolombienne,* Paris: Princesse, 1979, p. 85

Circumnavigating the globe 4,000 years before Magellan?

If Caral and/or Tiwanaku were indeed founded by MPDs, does it entail that they managed to circumnavigate the world four millennia before Ferdinand Magellan? As Stonehenge, Mesopotamia, Egypt and the Indus Valley civilisation all seem to have suddenly developed in the late 4th and early 3rd millennium BC, are we to believe that some Megalithic sailors continued their way east, ultimately crossing the Pacific and finally reaching the coasts of what is today known as Peru around 2627 BC? This is of course highly speculative, as only two sites—Caral and Tiwanaku—appear to be linked with 366-degree geometry and, to remain as objective as we have been so far in this truth-seeking book, both sites are located three arc minutes away from the nearest Druidic Meridians, a lack of perfection which could very well be explained if the Golden credentials of these two cities are just meaningless random events.

Of course, it can be argued that the considerable distance from the presumed Golden Prime Meridian (be it the River Jordan or Stonehenge) made it incredibly difficult for the founders of Caral and Tiwanaku to determine the exact position of the local Druidic Meridians, and that the elected sites of the two cities, each being located only three arc minutes away from the closest Druidic Lines, can be regarded as major achievements indeed.

Whatever the truth, it is interesting to note that in China the initiator of the Chinese civilisation is traditionally thought to be Huangdi or the Yellow Emperor, who would have lived c. 2600 BC. He is said to have lived near Xinzheng, which is a Druidic Parallel location: with a latitude of 34°24'N, it is situated only two arc minutes south of the nearest Druidic Parallel, which runs at 34°26'N. The Chinese calendar starting point is the year 2698 BC.[369] Did the Megalithic astronomers play any role in China after they influenced the Indus Valley on their way to the Pacific? This is of course pure speculation, but as China is on the way to the Pacific from India, this simple fact opens fascinating avenues for future research.

The Olmecs and the first Druidic city of Mesoamerica

Another area where great civilisations flourished in the Americas is of course Mesoamerica, which comprises Central America and the southern

---

[369] Endymion Wilkinson, *Chinese History: A Manual*, Revised and enlarged, Cambridge (MA) and London: Harvard University Asia Center, 2000

part of North America, or modern Mexico. These grand civilisations, however, are more recent than their counterparts in South America, as they do not seem to be older than c. 1200 BC, which makes them nearly a millennium and a half more recent than the Caral Pyramids in Peru.

The first of these civilisations is that of the Olmecs, who appear to have invented a very precise form of calendar and a form of writing, which continued to be in use with the Maya and even the Aztecs at the time of the Spanish conquest. The Olmecs seem to have been peaceful people.[370] Most curiously, but in a very similar way to what transpired elsewhere in the world, as we have seen, the Olmec civilisation appears to have been highly developed *right from the beginning*: 'It is in the field of sculpture and carving that the Olmec artists prove right from the beginning to be surprisingly skilled, something that was never surpassed in any other pre-Columbian culture.'[371] According to the very serious *Encyclopaedia Universalis,* 'architecture set aside, it can be said that Olmec art attained at once the highest summits of pre-Columbian art.'[372]

In addition, the Olmecs' refined culture appeared quite suddenly c. 1200 BC, around the same time as the founding of Tiwanaku. Was the Olmec civilisation somehow influenced by people sailing from the Old World? Interestingly, 1200 BC is also the date when the Megalithic civilisation in Western Europe came to an end, and when the Sea People tried to invade Egypt. Is there a link? Did Megalithic ships, or at least Mediterranean ships in a broader sense, manage to cross the Atlantic at the time, influencing the birth of the Olmec culture, which suddenly started to use writing and an elaborate calendar?

I would like to stress immediately that, once again, the suddenness of the emergence of this civilisation and the proximity of dates of the beginning of the Olmec civilisation and the end of Megalithic Europe might just be another coincidence. However, our ambition is to study facts and the archaeological record as they are in a cool-minded manner, without any preconceived idea, and see what story best fits the data.

According to Jacques Soustelle, a French anthropologist who specialised in pre-Columbian cultures, the Olmecs must have been taught their knowledge by another, more advanced culture:

> The Olmecs who, from 1200 BCE on, sculpted stone with such self-possessed talent, who modelled the [San Lorenzo] plateau at

---

[370] Jacques Soustelle, *Les Olmèques. La plus ancienne civilisation du Mexique,* Paris: Arthaud, 1979, p. 141

[371] *Encyclopaedia Universalis 2000*

[372] *Ibid.*

> the cost of gigantic efforts and who built a system of underground ducts and artificial lakes which we still do not understand the meaning of, seem to appear suddenly as a people already possessing its technique and art. We have to admit that they came from another region, where they had been taught how to handle and sculpt stone blocks...[373]

As he sums up, 'stone art, be it monoliths weighing tens of tonnes, delicate figurines or ear ornaments which are so fine as to be nearly transparent, *appears in adulthood and in full possession of its strength from the beginning till the end*'[374] (my italics).

Another intriguing fact is that many Olmec male representations include beards and moustaches,[375] when most Native Americans did not have facial hair at all. Such is the case in the well-known Olmec basalt statuette dubbed 'the Wrestler,' which was discovered in 1933. Another bearded man, this time tall with an aquiline nose, was found in the site of La Venta, and was nicknamed 'Uncle Sam.'[376]

Similarly, the Mesoamerican divinity Quetzalcoatl, or 'Feathered Serpent' in Nahuatl, the Aztec language, was often represented as a man with a beard,[377] just like Viracocha in South America. Even more baffling, this great God was even sometimes depicted as a *white*, bearded civilising God.[378] Interestingly, Quetzalcoatl was said to have come from the East.[379] Is this white-skinned bearded deity the reminiscence of a MPD coming from the Old World (the East) after crossing the Atlantic?

Most interesting of all, according to independent researcher Graham Hancock, the Feathered Serpent is said to have 'measured the Earth'![380] Is that evidence of 366-degree geometry being exported to Mesoamerica? In any case, it might be apt to note here that the Peleset or Philistines, the Sea People who invaded Egypt at roughly the same time as the Olmecs started to use writing and a calendar, wore a headdress made of

---

[373] Jacques Soustelle, *Les Olmèques. La plus ancienne civilisation du Mexique,* Paris: Arthaud, 1979, p. 60-1

[374] *Ibid.*, p. 76-7

[375] *Ibid.*, 35-6

[376] *Ibid.*, 35

[377] *Encyclopaedia Britannica*: http://global.britannica.com/EBchecked/topic/487168/Quetzalcoatl

[378] Félix Guirand and Joël Schmidt, *Mythes et mythologies. Histoire et dictionnaire,* Paris: Larousse-Bordas, 1996, p. 529

[379] 'Les Quatre soleils,' Maya and Aztec tale in Vladimir Hulpach and Miroslav Troup, *Contes d'Amérique du Sud*, Paris: Gründ, 1976, p. 7

[380] Graham Hancock (1995), *Fingerprints of the Gods. A Quest for the Beginning and the End,* London: Arrow Books, 1998, p. 113

plumes. Was Quetzalcoatl, the Feathered Serpent, a Peleset who had just crossed the Atlantic—that is, according to our conjecture, a MPD or at least of a member of a people culturally closely related to the Megalithic civilisation?

The Druidic city of San Lorenzo Tenochtitlán

One of the very first Olmec cities seems to be La Venta, which is located only 10 miles from the Gulf of Mexico. It means that it is perfectly plausible for the native Olmecs to have been initially influenced by sailors coming from the Atlantic and landing there.

At almost the same time as La Venta, however, the city of San Lorenzo, much further inland, rapidly became the first great Olmec center as early as 1200 BC. It comprises in fact three sites which are all very close to one another—Tenochtitlán, Potrero Nuevo and San Lorenzo.

What's really amazing about San Lorenzo is that the plateau where it stands is *man-made*. It has a height of 50 meters and a length of 1.2 kilometers from north to south. It must have required the Olmecs huge efforts to create this artificial plateau more than three millennia ago. Not only did they create a plateau, they also dug deep ravines on three sides out of the four and about twenty *lagunas* or artificial lakes, as well as a very clever underground drainage system. There were also hundreds of mounds positioned so as to have squares surrounded with pyramids. In the words of J E Gullberg from the University of California in Berkeley: 'What's obvious is that an amazing amount of ingenuity and human labor was used to build from scratch this San Lorenzo site'.[381] San Lorenzo is also famous for its colossal heads made of stone—about a hundred of them have been found. Not to mention the extremely beautiful bas-reliefs and statuettes.

Why was such hard labour initiated in the middle of the rainforest at this time? Nobody really knows. Unless of course it is yet another golden thread in the 366-degree geometry world tapestry. So the key question is, Is San Lorenzo in any way connected to 366-degree geometry? As it turns out, it is. San Lorenzo is located immediately north of the 18th Druidic Parallel. As always of course, it might be purely coincidental, but that's yet another coincidence in the ever-expanding collection of

---

[381] J E Gullberg quoted by Jacques Soustelle, *Les Olmèques. La plus ancienne civilisation du Mexique,* Paris: Arthaud, 1979, p. 29

Druidic Line locations around the world, all of which are key sites or cities in the world's first great civilisations.

The Olmec expansion in central Mexico allowed for the growth of daughter civilisations, first the Cuicuilco civilization near Mexico City, then Teotihuacán in its vicinity.[382] Are these sites Salt Line locations as well?

The three Golden pyramids of Mexico City

As I scrutinised a Mexico City area map in an atlas, I noticed that there were three pyramids in the city. Curiously, they appeared to form a roughly straight line in a north-south axis. Checking the geographic coordinates of the pyramids only confirmed my hunch: all of them are located along a Druidic Meridian, one that runs 137 Megalithic degrees from the River Jordan, or 99 Megalithic degrees from Stonehenge.

One of them is quite ancient, Cuicuilco, and the other two are comparatively much more recent, Tenayuca and Santa Cecilia Acatitlan, which are Aztec pyramids. Is it just another coincidence? Maybe so, but we can reasonably raise some doubts.

Let us focus on Cuicuilco first. Just like the Caral pyramids in South America did, this result electrified me: not only did it seem to confirm that the Cuicuilco culture was the inheritor of the Olmecs, it was also, apparently, another piece of evidence of 366-degree geometry knowledge in the New World. And once more, the Cuicuilco pyramid is located on a Druidic Meridian—the lines which are the most difficult to determine for ancient people.

The Cuicuilco pyramid, which is situated in the southern part of Mexico City, is one of the oldest pyramids in Mesoamerica, just slightly more recent than the Olmec pyramids further south. According to Ana María Salazar Peralta, who works at the Instituto de Investigaciones Antropológicas at the Universidad Nacional Autónoma in Mexico: 'At the moment, Cuicuilco is considered as the oldest known civilisation of the central high plateaus in Central America, with the vestiges of an ancient ceremonial center'.[383] The pyramid was built in c. 800 BC.

---

[382] Jacques Soustelle, *Les Olmèques. La plus ancienne civilisation du Mexique,* Paris: Arthaud, 1979, p. 86

[383] www.saa.org/publications/saabulletin/16-4/SAA21.html

According to ancient manuscripts written in the Aztec language, Cuicuilco was the 'Prayer Place,' or the 'Rainbow Place'.[384] One of the most striking aspects of the Cuicuilco Pyramid is its circular shape, which is quite unusual. It is about 25 meters high and has five levels, and there used to be a temple at its top. The nearby Xitle volcano eruption c. 200 BC forced its inhabitants to leave the pyramid and the city around it, as lava covered everything until the pyramid was rediscovered in 1922. The migrating people probably founded Teotihuacán (see next section) shortly after the event.

The other two Mexico City pyramids are this time located in the northern suburbia, about 25 km north of Cuicuilco. The two pyramids are only 2 km or so away from one another, and are much more recent. They were built by the Aztecs, the great civilization that met such a tragic fate with Hernán Cortés and his men during the Spanish conquest.

The Tenayuca pyramid was at the center of a Chichimeca capital and dates back to c. 1224 AD.[385] The massive pyramid, also called the Pyramid of Serpents, was dedicated to Quetzalcoatl. It is 62 meters wide and, in all, at least six constructions have been superimposed. Two coiled snakes known as the 'Turquoise Serpents' have their crests crowned with stars and aligned with the Sun's rising position at the solstice.[386] The smaller Santa Cecilia Acatitlan pyramid is even more recent, dating back to c. 1250 AD.

This is just speculation, admittedly, but one cannot help thinking that these two pyramids might have been built on other, more antique structures dating back to Cuicuilco times. In any case, future investigations might yield more clues to this enigma: Why are the three pyramids of Mexico City roughly aligned in a north-south axis, and why is this axis, with an error of between two and three arc minutes only, also a Druidic Meridian?

So far, the Mesoamerica material was good enough but, just as in South America, it lacked full precision, and still left room for doubt. So I naturally turned my eyes to Teotihuacán, the 'Birthplace of the Gods,' to see what story the ancient city had to tell.

---

[384] F. Muller, *La cerámica de Cuicuilco B: Un rescate arqueológico*, 11 (INAH, Mexico 1990), quoted by Ana María Salazar Peralta: www.saa.org/publications/saabulletin/16-4/SAA21.html

[385] Joyce Kelly, *An Archaeological Guide to Central and Southern Mexico*, Norman: University of Oklahoma Press, 2001

[386] http://www.roughguides.com/destinations/north-america/mexico/mexico-city/north-center/tenayuca/

Teotihuacán, the Druidic 'Birthplace of the Gods'

About 40 kilometers northeast of Mexico City are the very impressive pyramids of Teotihuacán, which in Nahuatl, the Aztec language, means the 'Place Where Gods Were Born.'

Teotihuacán was listed as a World Heritage site by UNESCO in 1987 because 'it is characterized by the vast size of its monuments—in particular, the Temple of Quetzalcoatl and the pyramids of the Sun and the Moon, laid out on geometric and symbolic principles. As one of the most powerful cultural centers in Mesoamerica, Teotihuacan [*sic*] extended its cultural and artistic influence throughout the region, and even beyond.'[387] To put it in a nutshell, it is quite simply one of the great wonders of Mesoamerica, even pre-Columbian Americas as a whole: 'This prodigious cult complex probably represents the most remarkable achievement of pre-Columbian urbanism, as much for its monumental proportions as for the global organisation of space and the unflinching rigor with which the general layout was implemented.'[388]

Located on a plateau about 2,300 meters above sea level, the city is impressively vast. An estimated 200,000 people may have lived in Teotihuacán.

The bigger pyramid is the Pyramid of the Sun, with sides more than 220 meters long and a height of 63 meters. The smaller Pyramid of the Moon, at one end of the so-called Avenue of the Dead, is 42 meters high. If the pyramids date back to c. 100 AD and 200 AD respectively, the origins of Teotihuacán go back to the 5th century BC,[389] i.e. in Olmec times. The Temple of the Feathered Serpent, which is located at the southern end of the Avenue of the Dead, is another, smaller six-level step pyramid. Interestingly, this temple contained 366 sculptures.[390]

The names of the pyramids are of particular interest in our study. If these names are not very ancient, they may follow an ancient tradition—we just don't know. What's really interesting is that these names remind us of the Ring of Brodgar and the Standing Stones of Stenness in Orkney which, as the reader will probably remember, are nicknamed the 'Temple of the Sun' and the 'Temple of the Moon' respectively. Those two major

---

[387] http://whc.unesco.org/en/list/414

[388] Henri Stierlin, *Le Monde de l'Amérique précolombienne,* Paris: Princesse, 1979, p. 43-5

[389] *Ibid.*, 46

[390] Michael S Werner (ed.), *Concise Encyclopedia of Mexico*, Chicago: Fitzroy Dearborn Publishers, 2001, p. 378

Megalithic sites (arguably the most impressive Megalithic monuments of Scotland) are Druidic Parallel locations, and not just any—the 60th Druidic Parallel north of the equator.

Amazingly enough, the Pyramids of the Sun and the Moon in Teotihuacán are

1. also located along a Druidic Line
2. also located, more specifically, along a Druidic *Parallel*
3. located, more specifically, along the *20th* Druidic Parallel north of the equator

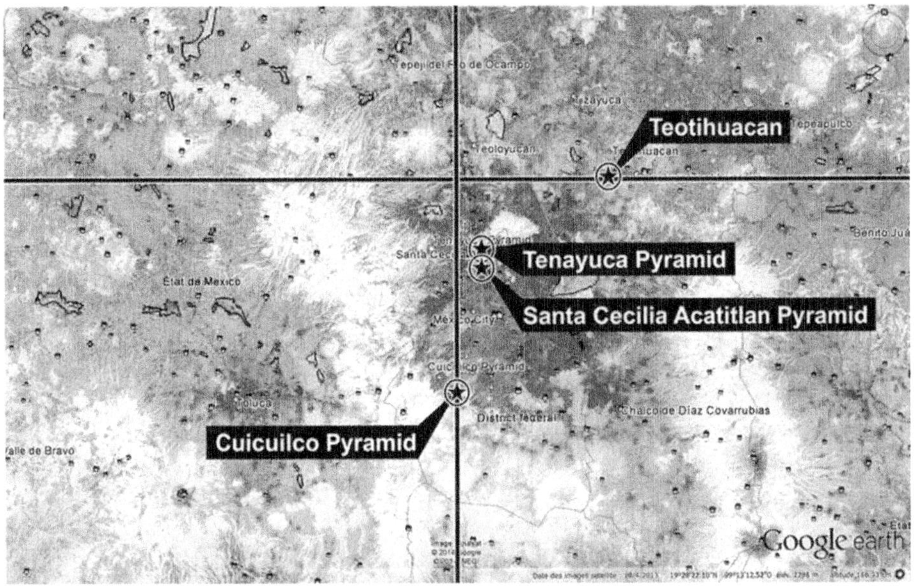

Fig. 39. Druidic cities in or near Mexico City: the Tenayuca Pyramid, The Santa Cecilia Acatitlan Pyramid, the Cuicuilco Pyramid and Teotihuacán, the 'Birthplace of the Gods.'

The error is less than two arc minutes for the Pyramid of the Moon, and one half arc minute for the Pyramid of the Sun, a considerable achievement which is no worse than the one achieved in Orkney—assuming, of course, this result is not a mere coincidence. In my humble opinion, the more plausible theory, of course, is that Teotihuacán was founded there by MPDs who knew of 366-degree geometry, or by Mesoamerican sages who had been taught it. Applying Occam's razor, this scenario seems more reasonable than repetitive luck.

The Golden Mayan sacred site of Chichén Itzá

The most visited Mayan-Toltec site in Yucatán, Mexico, is Chichén Itzá, probably because of its exceptional architecture and its privileged geographic position. It has been a World Heritage site since 1988 because, according to UNESCO, it is 'one of the greatest Mayan centers of the Yucatán peninsula' and because it is 'one of the most important examples of the Mayan-Toltec civilization in Yucatán.'[391]

The site comprises, among others, a magnificent step pyramid called El Castillo or The Castle, also named Temple of Kukulcan, the Mayan equivalent of Quetzalcoatl. There is the amazing Temple of the Warriors flanked by the 'Thousand Columns', which used to support an extensive wooden roof, and El Caracol or 'The Snail', a star observatory.

This sacred site was founded relatively recently, in 514 AD by priest Itzamna, according to tradition.[392] El Caracol dates to the early 10th century AD, not long after El Castillo, c. 9th century AD, but we know from excavations that it was built on another, older pyramid.[393] Today's pyramid is a wonderful sight with four stairways (like the number of seasons), each of them with 91 steps, which add up to 364 steps in all, plus one step at the top, making a total of 365, like the number of days in a year. El Castillo is also a Sun temple which is unique in the world. At the foot of each stairway is Kukulcan, the Feathered Serpent, with its open mouth, and twice a year, during the equinoxes, the pyramid is graced with an incredible, almost magical sunlight show. The afternoon sun's rays strike off a corner of the pyramid and casts seven triangular shadows against the balustrade, creating the optical illusion of Kukulcan, the Feathered Serpent, crawling down the Mayan edifice toward its sculpted mouth. This extremely clever light show, of course, is reminiscent of similar ingenious systems developed in the Mnajdra temple in Malta, Newgrange in Ireland, or Abu Simbel in Egypt. Such a phenomenon is possible only because those who designed it cleverly conceived the pyramid, and oriented it, so as to produce this breathtaking effect at the desired time.

One final oddity about Chichén Itzá is the Templo del Hombre Barbudo or Temple of the Bearded Man, which displays in the bas reliefs of its inner walls the carving of a man with a long beard. Once again, is

---

[391] http://whc.unesco.org/en/list/483
[392] www.tourbymexico.com/yucatan/chichen/chichen.htm
[393] Henri Stierlin, *Le Monde de l'Amérique précolombienne,* Paris: Princesse, 1979, p. 39

this the depiction of a MPD or a Celtic Druid coming from another continent?

As the reader may have guessed by now, Chichén Itzá is also a Salt Line location. Like San Lorenzo and Teotihuacán, but unlike most Druidic sites around the globe we have discussed in this book, the site has been built along a Druidic Parallel. More precisely, it is located less than two arc minutes from the 21st Druidic Parallel north of the equator. Again, it might be a coincidence... but don't too many coincidences kill coincidence? I will let the reader be the final judge.

If it is true that Mesoamerican calendars differ greatly from those of Old World civilisations, whoever designed them achieved an incredibly high degree of accuracy: they estimated that a tropical year (solar year) lasted 365.2420 days,[394] whereas the true number is 365.2422 days, which makes Mesoamerican calendars accurate to (an almost unbelievable) 99.99994 per cent!

On a more speculative note, it is interesting to see that the starting year of the Long Count Mayan calendar is 3114 BC, a year that is close to 3102 BC, the starting year of India's Kali Yuga, the last stage of the world we are now in; both dates are very close to the foundation of Stonehenge c. 3100 BC. As we have seen, the great acceleration in Olmec culture occurred only c. 1200 BC. Why would Mesoamerican people pick a date so far back in time? Are the Mayan Long count and the Kali Yuga hazy remembrances of the foundation of Stonehenge, echoing in the great canyons of time?

Main points

- **Caral and its pyramids, the 'Mother City' of the Americas, is a Druidic Meridian location**
- **Tiwanaku, the monumental Andean city near Lake Titicaca, is also a Druidic Meridian location**
- **Tiwanaku is dedicated to Viracocha, the bearded civilising God of the Andes, who is reminiscent of a Druid**
- **Caral suggests that the Megalithic Proto-Druids might have circumnavigated the globe about 4,500 years ago**
- **Quetzalcoatl, the Feathered Serpent God of the Aztecs, a white bearded civilising God who is said to have come from the**

---

[394] Emile Biémont, *Rythmes du temps. Astronomie et calendriers*, Paris: De Boeck, 2000, p 305-6

East and who had 'measured the Earth' is also reminiscent of a Druid

- The great Olmec civilisation appeared in Mesoamerica very suddenly
- The first great Olmec center of San Lorenzo Tenochtitlan is a Druidic Parallel location
- The Cuicuilco pyramid, along with two Aztec pyramids in Mexico City, are Druidic Meridian locations
- Teotihuacán, the 'Birthplace of the Gods' with its famous Pyramid of the Sun and Pyramid of the Moon, is located on the 20th Druidic Parallel
- The sacred Mayan site of Chichén Itzá, with its star observatory and 'magic' pyramid dedicated to Kukulcan, the Mayan Feathered Serpent God, is another Druidic Parallel location

PHOTO GALLERY

Stonehenge, England is located at the intersection of two Druidic Lines. Was it a 'Temple of the Heavens'?

The Great Broken Menhir at Locmariaquer in Brittany, France. The biggest standing stone ever erected in Europe.

The huge stone circle and its henge at Avebury, England is located on the same Druidic Meridian as Stonehenge. Avebury was probably a major location for the presumed Proto-Druids. Was it a 'Temple of the Sun,' and was it the Avalon of Celtic legends?

The Crucuno Rectangle in Brittany is made of two Pythagorean 3-4-5 triangles joined together and appears to use the Megalithic yard as its basic unit.

Silbury Hill near Avebury, England. It is located on the same Druidic Meridian as Avebury and Stonehenge. Was it a 'Temple of the Moon'?

The author standing in front of a dolmen in the village of Crucuno in Brittany, France.

The Ring of Brodgar in Orkney, Scotland. There used to be 60 standing stones set inside a circular henge, and it is located on the 60th Druidic Parallel.

The (probably Masonic) Falicon Pyramid near Nice, France, which is located on the French Pyramids Line.

The (Masonic) Monceau Pyramid in Parc Monceau, Paris, which is located on the French Pyramids Line.

The unfinished pyramid on the one-dollar banknote, which was probably inspired by the Masonic Monceau Pyramid in Paris, with the help of Benjamin Franklin.

The Couhard Pyramid near Autun, France, is part of the French Pyramids Line. Its origins are most probably Druidic, and it is located at the Golden Section of the other two pyramids. It is also located at one end of the *Axe majeur* (the 'Major Axis'), the city of Cergy being at the other end.

The Peace Pyramid in Astana, Kazakhstan. Just like Newgrange in Ireland, it is located at a very significant distance from the Great Pyramid of Giza, alluding both to the precise polar circumference of the Earth and to 366-degree geometry.

The Louvre Pyramid in Paris, France, which was commissioned by former French President François Mitterrand. It is located on the eastern end of the Historical Axis of Paris.

The Giza pyramids in Egypt. The Great Pyramid (right) is what might be termed a temple of Druidic geometry, and uses the Megalithic yard at its base. The Djedefre Pyramid is located 10,000 Megalithic yards away from the Great Pyramid, and points to Alesia, which is 366 times further away.

Newgrange, Ireland. The distance between the Great Pyramid and Newgrange is exactly one-tenth of the Earth's equatorial circumference.

The two sides of the Phaistos Disc, which is believed by Alan Butler to have been a 366-day calendar. This Minoan artefact appears to be directly related to 366-degree geometry.

Two Druids on an 18th-century engraving, reproducing a bas-relief found at Autun, France

A sea urchin shell. Probably what Druids called a 'serpent's egg.'

The author with Alan Butler in Avebury

Glastonbury Tor, traditionally 'the holiest earthe in England,' is a hill on the 52nd Druidic parallel, like Stonehenge. It is linked in legend with the Isle of Avalon.

The Pyramid of the Sun (here depicted) and the Pyramid of the Moon at Teotihuacán ('The Place Where Gods Were Born') in Mexico stand on the 20th Druidic Parallel.

The Reims Cathedral in France stands on the same Druidic Meridian as Alesia. Most French kings were crowned in Reims, almost never in Paris.

The Astronomical Island on the *Axe majeur* in Cergy, France, which leads straight to the Couhard Pyramid. This 'Major Axis' is also connected to Stonehenge, Alesia and the Rock of Solutré, which is 366 km away.

The four-apex Cité de l'Or (i.e. the City of Gold) in Saint-Amand-Montrond, in the very heart of France. Does it symbolise the central G in the Square and Compasses symbol?

The Capitol Building in Washington, DC. According to Alan Butler the building is located at one tip of a 'Masonic triangle' which uses units of 366 Megalithic yards. The city is located 366 km away from New York City by road according to Google Maps.

A central detector in the CERN near Geneva, Switzerland. The CERN is located at the intersection of two 'Sion' Druidic Lines. The Large Hadron Collider can arguably be called a 'superhenge' to study the universe itself.

Photo Credits

1. © Sylvain Tristan 2016
2. © Llann Wé[2] 2014 https://commons.wikimedia.org/wiki/File:W1530-Locmariaquer_GrandMenhirBrise_0003N8.JPG
3. © JimChampion 2008 https://commons.wikimedia.org/wiki/File: Avebury_stones_north_west_quadrant.jpg
4. © Sylvain Tristan 2015
5. Public domain
6. © Sylvain Tristan 2015
7. Public domain
8. © Jpchevreau 2015 https://commons.wikimedia.org/wiki/File:La_pyramide_de_Falicon_et_le_mont_Chauve_en_arri%C3%A8re-plan.JPG
9. ©Guillaume Jacquet 2006 https://commons.wikimedia.org/wiki/File: Parc_Monceau_20060812_03.jpg
10. Public domain
11. ©Nguyenld 2006 https://commons.wikimedia.org/wiki/File:Autun_Pyramide_de_Couhard.jpg
12. © ShadowNinja1080 2016 https://upload.wikimedia.org/wikipedia/commons/2/24/Palace_of_Peace_and_Reconciliation.jpg
13. ©Martin Falbisoner 2012 https://commons.wikimedia.org/wiki/File:Louvre_at_dusk.JPG
14. © Filip Maljković 2008 https://commons.wikimedia.org/wiki/File: The_Great_Giza_Pyramids_(2714816217).jpg
15. Public domain
16. Public domain
17. Public domain
18. ©Sea Urchin Shell Series 2010, https://commons.wikimedia.org/wiki/File: Sea_Urchin_Shell_Series_(4254567390).jpg
19. © Kate Butler 2015
20. © Sylvain Tristan 2016
21. © Ralf Roletschek / fahrradmonteur.de 2015 https://commons.wikimedia.org/wiki/File:15-07-13_Teotihuacan_la_Avenida_de_los_Muertos_y_la_Pir%C3%A1mide_del_Sol-RalfR-WMA_0251.jpg
22. © Eric Pouhier 2006 https://commons.wikimedia.org/wiki/File: Cathedrale_de_Reims_1.jpg
23. © Pline 2011. https://commons.wikimedia.org/wiki/File: Axe_majeur_de_Cergy_P1090788.JPG
24. © Patrick Merle 2013
25. © Sylvain Tristan 2013
26. © Mark Williamson 2007 https://commons.wikimedia.org/wiki/File: UA1_detector_chamber.jpg

PART III

FAST FORWARD: DRUIDIC KNOWLEDGE LIVES ON

(100 AD – TODAY)

Chapter Fourteen:
The French Pyramids Line

Let us now refocus geographically on Western Europe and chronologically at the time when Celtic Druidism started to begin its downfall due to the Roman invasion of Gaul.

The Druidic continuum

We saw in Part I that it was highly unlikely that the Druidic knowledge was altogether erased with the Romans' repressions of Druids in the 1st century AD. As Nora Chadwick maintained, their knowledge had lived on, at least for a few centuries: 'it is unlikely that they [the Druids] would completely disappear quickly.'[395] She wrote that 'we cannot doubt that... the druids had ample scope in Gaul for underground activities' and that 'they continued to exert their influence on the Gallic youths.'[396] Her firm belief was that the repression had never been effective enough: 'What, after all, does our evidence for the actual "suppression" amount to? Very little indeed!'[397]

The contention that Druidism did not die off is reinforced by the fact that (as seen in Part II) Druidism had probably existed for several millennia *before* it was described by the Roman and Greek authors, with a seemingly unbroken chain of knowledge we can trace back to Megalithic times and which appears to reveal itself in most great civilisations of antiquity. So, after following the golden thread through the tapestry of time in periods preceding the Celtic Druids, let's now see if this golden thread has continued to run in the warps and wefts of the last two thousand years, after the Druids were slaughtered on the island of Mona in the 1st century AD.

What evidence do we have that Druidic knowledge continued to be transmitted through underground channels in the Roman era and

---

395 Nora K. Chadwick, op.cit., p. 74

396 Ibid., p. 76

397 Ibid.

beyond? It so appears that the evidence for such a 'Druidic continuum' is massive.

A 36-degree slanted line

We saw that there was every reason to believe that around 1300 BC Alesia replaced Stonehenge as the main Druidic sacred center. But with the fall of Alesia in 52 BC the Druids must have needed to find another place or *places*, this time more discreet, to preserve their knowledge in Roman times.

As we have seen, the Alesia Druidic Meridian runs exactly 6°M (6 Megalithic degrees) east of the Stonehenge-Avebury-Silbury Druidic Meridian. One 'logical' thing for the Druids to do would have been to use the Druidic Meridian that ran midway between the two lines, i.e. 3°M east of the Stonehenge Druidic Meridian and 3°M west of the Alesia Druidic Meridian (let's call this line the Midway Druidic Meridian or MDM[398]).

But there was an evident problem: as the Romans had a refined civilisation and possessed their own mathematicians, Druids couldn't afford to be too obvious. Compelling evidence exists that Druids—most probably the Aedui Druids who were the allies of the Romans—helped the Romans choose locations for the construction of brand new cities. In appearance, the locations of these cities looked pretty random, but in reality these locations held a secret significance in Druidic terms—they were directly connected to the MDM, as we shall soon see.

The MDM runs at 01°07' east of Greenwich. It crosses the coastline of northern France a few miles east of Dieppe in Normandy—we'll call this place 'the X Spot'. But no site of interest is located on this particular Druidic Meridian. The Druids most probably needed to be more discreet than they had ever been, as they soon found out that being a Druid would make you a dead man under Roman law. It seems that, instead of following this line due south across Gaul, they decided to 'draw' a *slanted* line from this point. As Druids love geometry, another 'logical' thing to do was to slant this line with an angle of 36° (or, in Megalithic terms, 36.6°M)—which is one-tenth of a full circle of course, a very significant number to geometers. Such a segment, starting close to Dieppe on the

---

[398] This Midway Druidic Meridian is very similar to what authors Guy-Claude Mouny and Guy Gruais termed *le Méridien lumineux*, ' the Luminous Meridian,' which in their opinion ran at 01°10'E. See Guy-Claude Mouny and Guy Gruais, *Guizeh, au-delà des grandes secrets*, Paris: Editions du Rocher, 1997, p. 90

French coast of Normandy, and extending not southward but south-eastward with a 36-degree angle, finishes its course on the Mediterranean coast, very close to the city of Nice (founded by the Greeks of Massalia a few centuries earlier, c. 350 BC).

The idea that such a slanted axis does exist would of course be pure speculation if it was not clearly borne out by undeniable, observable facts, as we are about to see.

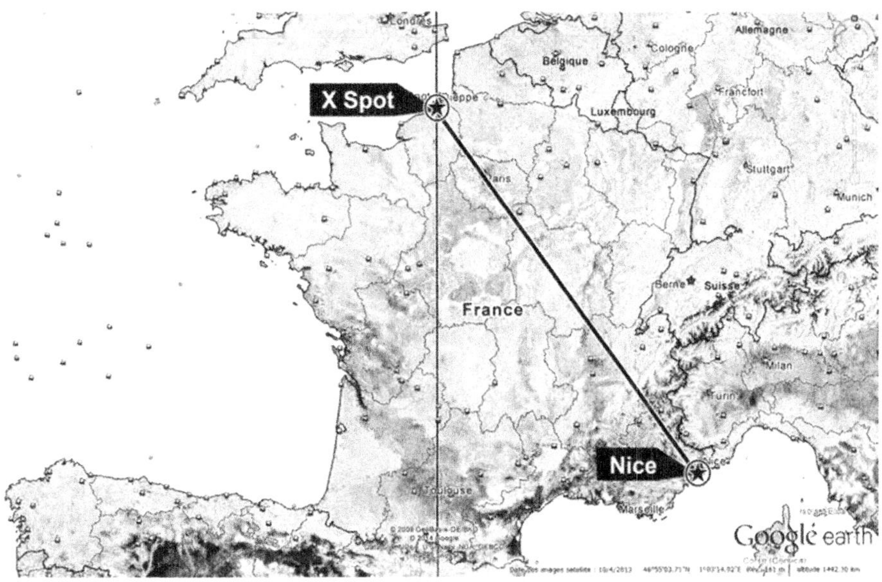

Fig. 40. The Slanted Line starting at the 'X Spot' on the Midway Druidic Meridian (i.e. the Druidic Meridian running halfway between the Stonehenge Druidic Meridian and the Alesia Druidic Meridian).

Augustodunum or New Bibracte

As we have seen in Part I, the former capital of the Aedui, Bibracte, was replaced by Augustodunum (now called Autun) around c. 15 BC, now called Autun. One can still admire the Roman gates, theatre and the so-called temple of Janus in this city in Burgundy.

Bibracte was a Druidic Meridian location, as it was situated on Mont Beuvray, a natural hill located along the Druidic Meridian graced with the three Alesias. In the very last decades BC, Bibracte was abandoned and a new Roman city was created from scratch about 15 miles to the east—Augustodunum or 'Fort of Augustus', which was to become the *soror et aemula Romae,* the 'sister and emulator of Rome', no less! With Lugdunum

(Lyon) and Rotomagus (Rouen), it soon became one of Gaul's top three cities in prestige and importance. As related earlier, by 12 BC Augustodunum already possessed a prestigious Roman university. It is clear that the Romans, by building this new city, wished to eclipse, and possibly stifle, the power of Druids in the region.

There is no doubt, however, that local Druids played a key role in the choice of the geographic site of the new city, as Bibracte was not only a 'Sister to Rome' but also the new capital of the Aedui, who were the allies of Rome. Did the Aedui choose this alliance as a tactic to preserve Druidism in total secrecy? After all, the Romans were extremely powerful and often merciless, and rather than being killed, wasn't cooperation with the enemy the wisest strategy? Druids could keep their own knowledge more secret than ever, especially if they stopped calling themselves Druids. Wouldn't this strategy be the best for the clever Diviciacus and his followers? To be sure, this policy looks like a sort of 'quiet vengeance' against the Roman conquerors of Gaul. Interestingly, the very name *Diviciacus* seems to derive from the Latin word *divincere* (a form of the verb *devinco*, 'defeat, conquer, subdue'), and his name would more or less translate as 'the Avenger.'[399] Was Diviciacus a true friend to the Romans, or did he secretly devote his life to taking revenge on them, setting a new path for future Druidism?

In any case, coincidence or not, if you trace a 36-degree (or 36.6-Meg. degree) line starting from the X Spot in Normandy and pursue it all across Gaul, you will precisely end up in Augustodunum! The suspicion that this is no accident but the result of deliberate choice by the Druids is high. In other words, the former Aedui capital, a Druidic Meridian location, was transferred to a new, Druidic *Slanted* Line location nearby. Of course, as always, except for the Druids, nobody could have the slightest idea of the geographical significance of Augustodunum, even the Romans, who, as far as is recorded, were never aware of 366-degree geometry.

---

[399] Xavier Delamarre, *Dictionnaire de la langue gauloise. Une approche linguistique du vieux-celtique continental*, Arles: Errance, 2008, p. 145

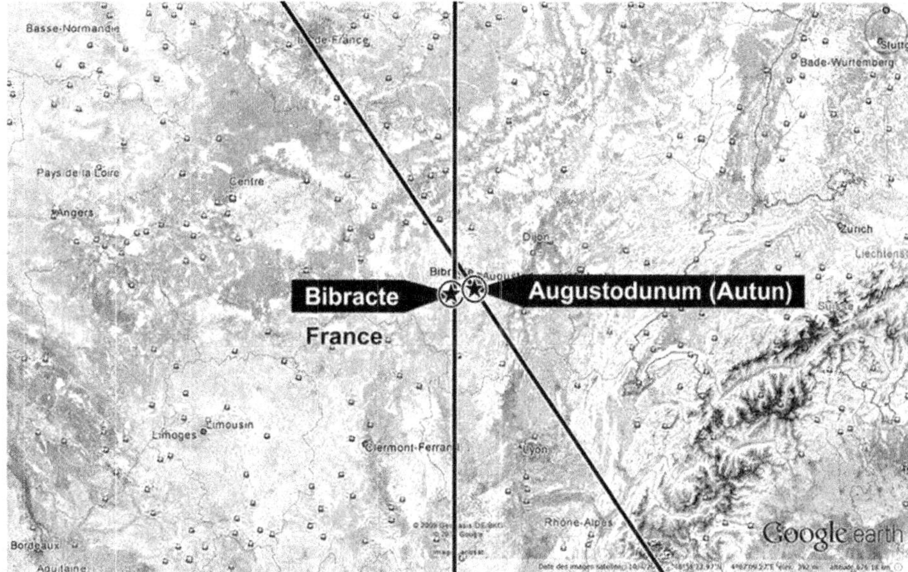

Fig. 41. Close-up on Bibracte (located along the Alesia Druidic Meridian) and Augustodunum (located on the Druidic Slanted Line).

The Couhard Pyramid

One of the most mysterious constructions of Augustodunum is certainly the massive Couhard Pyramid which overlooks the city from the southeast.

This pyramid, made of stone and mortar, dates back to the 1st century AD and used to be 33 meters high. The monument seems to be either a tomb (but it doesn't appear to contain any funerary chamber) or a cenotaph (a monument commemorating an important figure). From a gold medal allegedly found in the 17th century which had the phrase *Gloria Ædorum druidumque* inscribed on it, the pyramid has long been said to be dedicated to Diviciacus, the Druid who helped Romans to settle in the area.

Today the pyramid is partly destroyed but it is well preserved. It was classified as a historical monument in 1840. I personally love the place, as it is a little known, apparently 2,000-year-old French pyramid—which is quite unique—dominating the city of Autun, and of course because it is closely connected to Druidism. One of the best aspects of it, of course, is that it is *precisely* located on the Druidic Slanted Line.

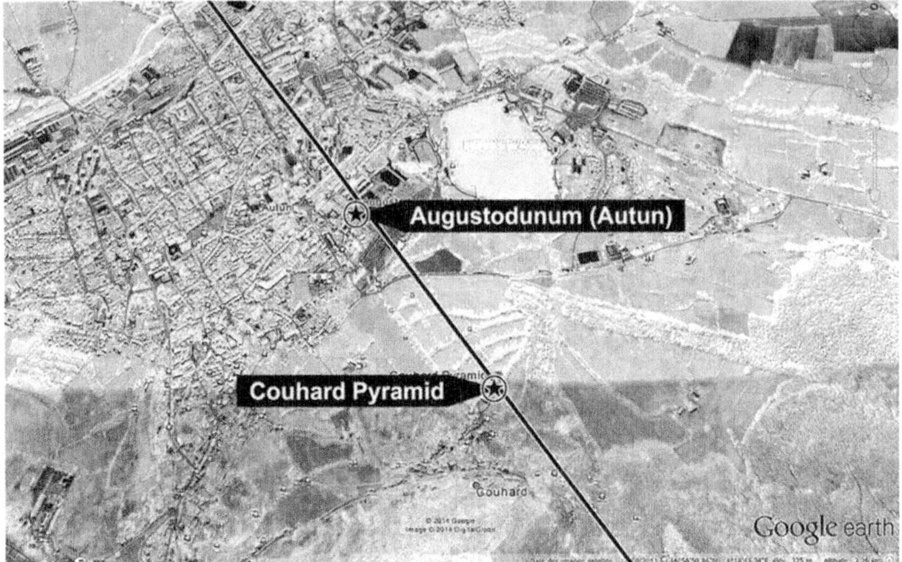

Fig. 42. Close-up on Augustodunum. The Druidic Slanted Line passes right through the city, and also right through the Couhard Pyramid.

The origins of Paris

Let us now come to one of the most fascinating aspects of this hypothetical Druidic Slanted Line originating near Dieppe at the X Spot. This slanted axis happens to pass over a major location which is *not* a Druidic Line location: Paris. The modern capital city of France, just like Augustodunum (Autun) and the Couhard Pyramid, is actually a Druidic Slanted Line location!

Archaeologists disagree on the precise location of the Gallic city of Lutetia, home of a Gallic tribe called the Parisii. It might have been either on the Ile de la Cité (where the Notre Dame Cathedral today stands), the Ile Saint Louis just next to it, or even more likely in Nanterre, about ten kilometers west of the center of Paris.

In any case, just as the Roman Augustodunum replaced Bibracte, a Roman Lutetia replaced the Gallic one. Although at first this new Roman city was of minor importance, it progressively became greater and greater, before being renamed Paris and becoming the capital of France centuries later. The center of the Roman Lutetia is thought to be located at the top of the Sainte-Geneviève hill in the Rue Saint-Jacques, which was its *cardo maximus*, or principal north-south street. What's truly extraordinary is that this new city was built right on the course of the Druidic Slanted Line! If this is not a mere coincidence, the implications of this are phenomenal: it means that the city that was to become Paris has been built there because of its position along a slanted line derived from 366-degree geometry. The heart of the Roman Lutetia lies at the intersection of the Druidic Slanted Line and the Seine, immediately south of the Ile de la Cité. What are the odds that the Druidic Slanted Line that we have just been describing, starting at the X Spot, a Druidic Line location, and running right through both Augustodunum and the nearby Couhard Pyramid down in Burgundy, also runs accidentally right through the heart of Roman Lutetia, or, in modern terms, the heart of the Latin Quarter in Paris? Very small for sure—and yet, this is exactly what happens!

One reasonable explanation to this mystery is that, once again, the place was carefully selected by Druids, who secretly knew about the characteristics of the location in 366-degree geometry terms.

The truly amazing thing about the Sainte-Geneviève hill is that it is also the place where some of the most prestigious schools of France were later constructed, such as the world-famous Sorbonne, the Collège de France, the former Ecole Polytechnique, the Ecole Normale Supérieure, the Curie Institute and the former Law Faculty. It is also home of the esteemed Lycée Henri IV, a high school which is partly the remains of the Sainte-Geneviève abbey, which was founded by Clovis in 502 AD.

In addition, almost at the top of the hill, *right where the Druidic Slanted Line runs*, is the Panthéon, a neoclassical monument in the mid-18th century. Originally built to be a church dedicated to Sainte Geneviève, it was converted during the French Revolution to a mausoleum, where distinguished French citizens are interred. Amongst them are Mirabeau, a leader of the French Revolution; Voltaire, the Enlightenment writer, philosopher and historian; philosopher Jean-Jacques Rousseau; the explorer Bougainville; the writers Victor Hugo, Emile Zola and Alexandre Dumas; Louis Braille, the inventor of the writing system for the blind; Jean Moulin, the hero of the French Résistance during World War II; and Pierre and Marie Curie, the famous physicists. Interestingly, the Panthéon is 83 meters high, which converts into a neat 100 MY.

Last but not least, the Druidic Slanted Line, on the right bank of the Seine, cuts in almost two equal parts the Tuileries Garden near the Louvre, as if the rectangle of the garden had been deliberately designed on either sides of the virtual line. The garden was created by Catherine de' Medici in the 16th century.

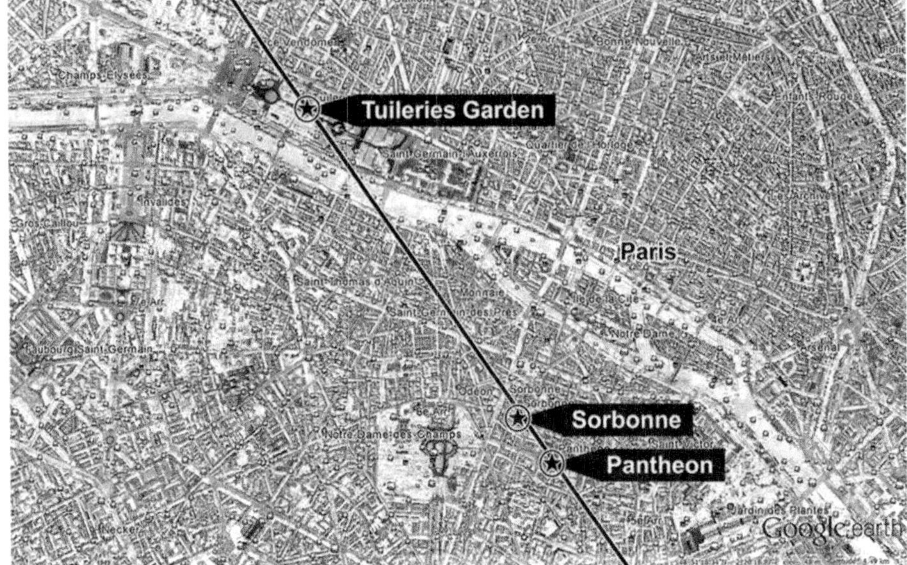

Fig. 43. Close-up on Paris. The Druidic Slanted Line passes right through the heart of Lutetia (modern Paris), neatly cutting in two the Tuileries Garden, and right through the domes of the Sorbonne and the Pantheon.

Are these just other extraordinary coincidences, or does it mean that 366-degree geometry and the Druidic Slanted Line were still secretly known, and used, by a select few as late as the 18th century?

The Falicon Pyramid

If you pursue the Druidic Slanted Line southeast to the Mediterranean coast, you'll see that it finishes up its course just east of Nice on the French Riviera. The interesting thing is that, in the mountains overlooking the city at the north are the remains of an old pyramid, near the village of Falicon. Once again, the Druidic Slanted Line *perfectly* intersects the pyramid on its course, making it extremely difficult to be a mere happenstance.

Unlike the Couhard Pyramid, the Falicon Pyramid is a relatively small stone monument. Today unfortunately the pyramid is half crumbled, but it was classified as a French historical monument in 2007. It was discovered in 1803 by Domenico Rossetti, an Italian lawyer holidaying there. Nobody knows exactly when or why the pyramid was built, but it was most likely constructed in the late 18th century.

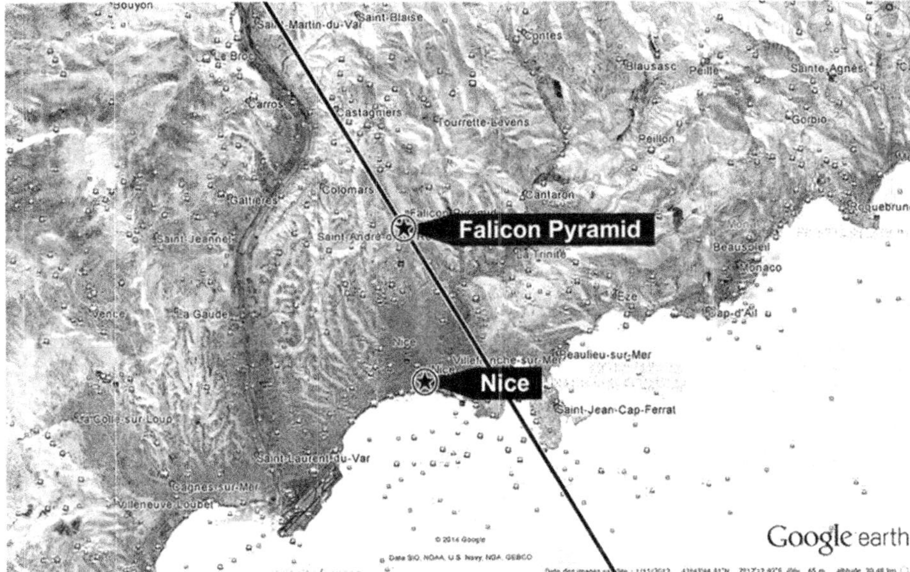

Fig. 44. Close-up on the southern part of the Druidic Slanted Line. It passes right through the Falicon Pyramid, and finishes its course alongside the city of Nice.

Different authors, without presenting any definite evidence, have contended that the pyramid was probably a Masonic monument. The pyramid marks an entrance to the Ratapignata Cave, or 'Cave of Bats', where Freemasons allegedly met for secret gatherings in the late 18th century. Unfortunately, we just do not know for sure; very little is known about this mysterious pyramid.

Its remarkable attribute, of course, is that it is located on the Druidic Slanted Line and that, just like the Pantheon in Paris, it is a relatively recent monument that was built approximately 16 centuries after the Couhard Pyramid. The implications of this are quite astounding, as it seems to mean that Druidic knowledge—366-degree geometry and the Druidic Slanted Line—has survived until modern times, being secretly passed down from the Roman era to the Romantic era, not dying off during the alleged Dark Ages nor the Middle Ages nor the Renaissance. Who kept this knowledge? How is it they were never spotted by anyone during recent history? More intriguing still, it seems to imply that this Druidic knowledge has been carried along in Freemasonic circles.

I fully appreciate that at this juncture the whole thing is starting to sound like *The DaVinci Code*, or any similar fictitious or incredible story. What other evidence do we have?

The Parc Monceau Pyramid

Let us now come back to Paris. In the northwestern section of the French capital, just a few hundred yards north of the Avenue of the Champs Elysées, is another small pyramid standing under the trees of Parc Monceau, a small island of greenery in Paris' poshest neighbourhoods.

The pyramid was built for Louis Philippe d'Orléans, Duke of Chartres, not long after he was named Grand Master of the Grand Orient de France in 1773. This time then, the connection of this pyramid to Freemasonry is undeniable. At the time, the city of Paris was much smaller than today and didn't extend to what is now Parc Monceau. In 1769 the Duke had acquired a plot of land there and then had a central, two-floor octagonal pavilion built in the middle of it. In 1773 he asked Louis Carrogis Carmontelle to design a garden in his property. The result came five years later as the *Folie de Chartres*, a landscape garden including a series of follies such as a fort with a tower and a portcullis, a watermill, a Dutch windmill, temples, an obelisk, Turkish tents, and many other exotic items. One of them was an 'Egyptian' pyramid which survives today, while most other follies no longer do.

The pyramid does not look like a usual pyramid, as its angle is pretty high. In fact, it looks just like the pyramid depicted on the American one-dollar banknote (see next section).

Louis Philippe d'Orléans had created his own Masonic lodge, and in his octagonal pavilion he had a reception room and also an underground room for Masonic gatherings and initiations, apparently with a statue of the Egyptian Goddess Isis.

Remarkably, the Druidic Slanted Line runs *right through* this pyramid as well, making it once again extremely difficult for this state of affairs to be a mere happenstance. What we have here is truly stunning, as there are very few pyramids in France; and here we have a 36-degree-angled line starting right at the X Spot, the northernmost French point of the Midway Druidic Meridian or MDM running halfway between the Stonehenge Druidic Meridian and the Alesia Druidic Meridian, which intersects not one nor two but *three* pyramids—two Masonic pyramids of the late 18th century, and between them a 1st-century Roman pyramid probably dedicated to a Druid.

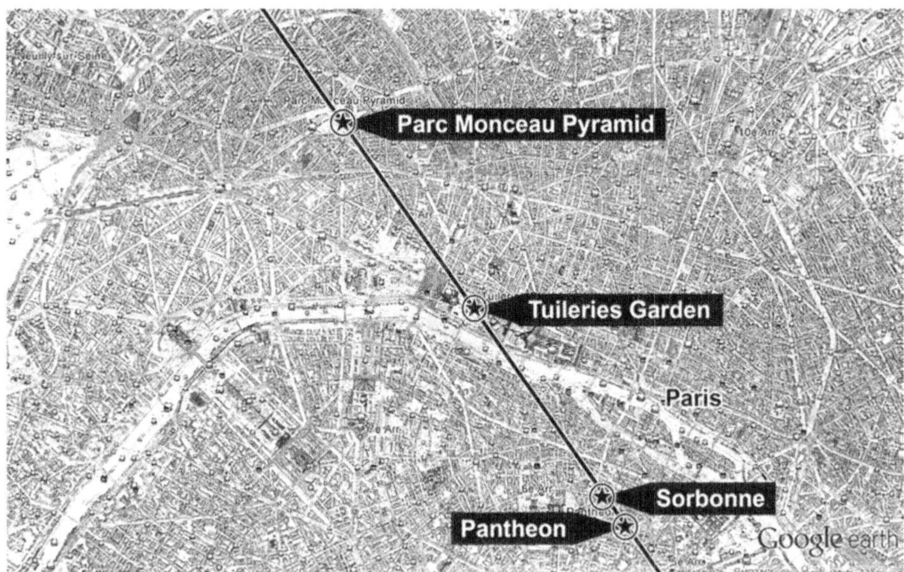

Fig. 45. The Druidic Slanted Line also passes right through the Parc Monceau Pyramid in Paris. This line can aptly be renamed the 'French Pyramids Line.'

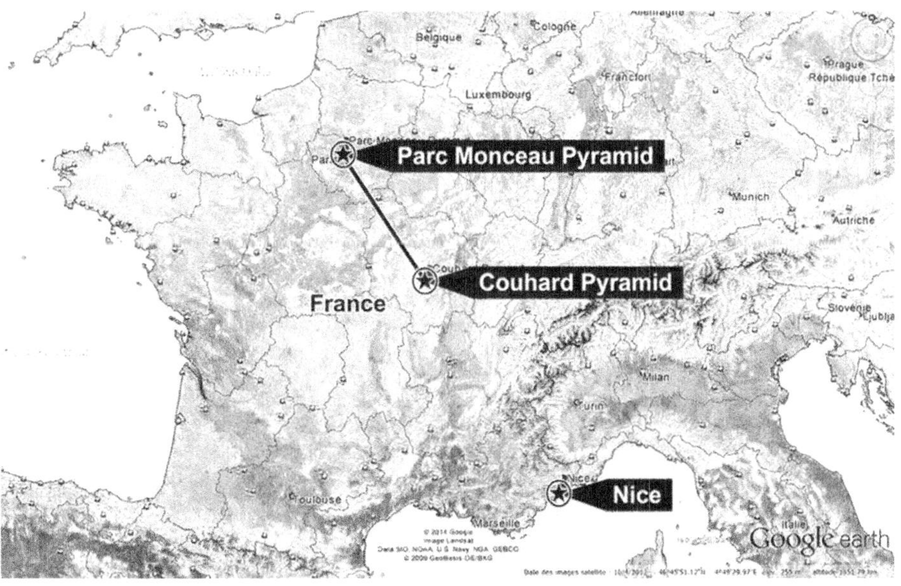

Fig. 46. The distance between the Parc Monceau Pyramid and the Couhard Pyramid is 262.2 km or 162.9 mi. Both numbers are strangely reminiscent of Phi, the Golden Section.

Phi and the French Pyramids Line

Once again, the relative distances of the pyramids will help us gain rock-solid confidence that the Falicon Pyramid and the Parc Monceau Pyramid have been deliberately positioned on this line as well. The distance between the Parc Monceau Pyramid and the Couhard Pyramid is 262.2 km[400] (162.9 mi.), both numbers being strangely reminiscent of Phi, the golden section (Phi = 1.618... and Phi^2 = 2.618...).

But that is far from being all. The distance between the Monceau Pyramid and the Falicon Pyramid is 685.56 km[401] (426.1 mi.), and that between Couhard and Falicon is 423.34 km[402] (263.1 mi.). What it means is that the Couhard Pyramid stands at the golden section between the Falicon Pyramid and the Parc Monceau Pyramid (423.34/685.56 = 0.6175), to an astounding accuracy of 99.92 per cent! It seems then clear that the two later pyramids were carefully positioned, not only on the course of the Druidic Slanted Line, but also at relative distances to the Couhard Pyramid so as to encapsulate Phi, the Divine Proportion, into the equation.

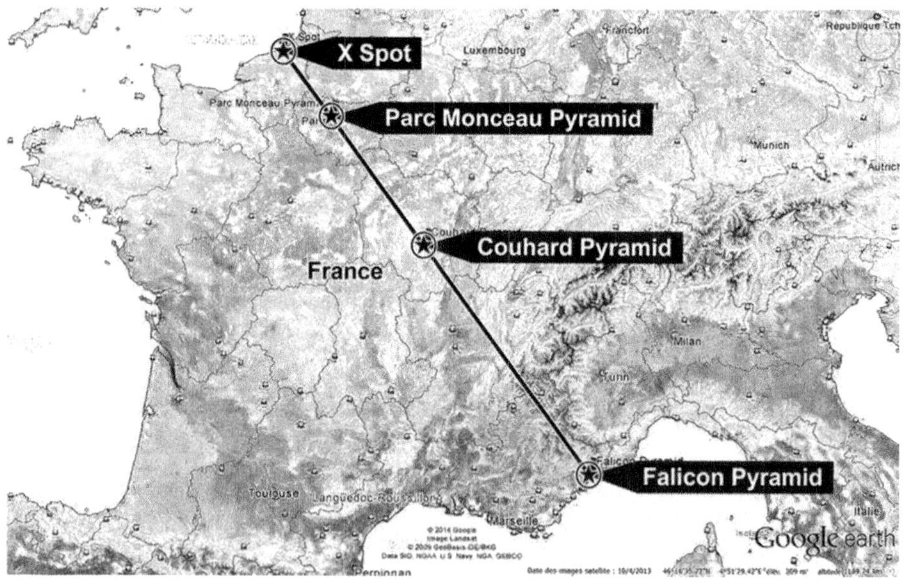

Fig. 47. The French Pyramids Line. The Couhard Pyramid stands at the Golden Section of the other two pyramids.

[400] Google Earth data
[401] Google Earth data
[402] Google Earth data

The reader will note that the same thing has been apparently done on the Alesia Druidic Meridian, with the city of Troyes standing at the golden section of the Aalst-Alès distance (see Chapter Three). You will also remember from Chapter Nine that there were 162 postholes in the Sanctuary at Avebury, and 163 (162 plus one in the middle) postholes in Woodhenge. Was Phi already known to the Megalithic people?

The implications are now obvious and almost inescapable:

1. The Druidic Slanted Line exists and it was designed by Druids in Roman times

2. Augustodunum (the future Autun), the Roman Lutetia (the future Paris), and the Couhard Pyramid were built on this line

3. Some 18th-century Freemasons knew about this line and built two more pyramids on its course, meaning they inherited from the Celtic Druids' knowledge

To me, all this simply cannot be a coincidence, but of course, you are free to weigh the data and decide for yourself. In any case, I shall from now on refer to the Druidic Slanted Line as the *French Pyramids Line.*

The first researchers to notice this astonishing axis are Guy-Claude Mouny and Guy Gruais,[403] but the authors used the Louvre Pyramid instead of the Parc Monceau Pyramid in their diagram. It is true that the Louvre Pyramid (completed in 1989) stands very close to the French Pyramids Line, but it isn't quite on its course (it is about 340 meters away from it). To stress it one more time, all the pyramids discussed in the present book, as well as the Panthéon, are *perfectly* positioned on the course of the line. As for the Louvre Pyramid, is it evidence that Druidic knowledge has survived to this very day? We will come back to this key question in due time.

The proof by the Lac des Settons

Need a final proof that the French Pyramids Line is not a figment of our imagination?

As discussed earlier, the main Druidic Line in Gaul (and future France, as we shall see) is the Alesia Druidic Meridian, with Bibracte, the three Alesias, Rheims and Troyes materialising it on the ground. And as we have just seen, the French Pyramids Line also appears to have been a very crucial line as well since the Roman period.

---

403 Guy-Claude Mouny and Guy Gruais, *Guizeh, au-delà des grandes secrets*, Paris: Editions du Rocher, 1997, p. 84

I was curious to see if the place where these two incredibly important lines intersect was in any way special. It certainly ought to be, so I traced these two lines with the Google Earth ruler and checked what lay at the crossing point. The answer was... water—more specifically, lake water!

The Lac des Settons in Burgundy is an artificial lake which was created in the 19th century from 1854 to 1861, following the construction of a dam. Well, in appearance, nothing really unusual here... or is there? It turns out that the lake is 3.66 sq. km, or 366 hectares[404] (904.02 acres). Unless of course it is just another coincidence of some sort, in the metric system such a result is certainly very meaningful! Was this lake designed by people 'in the know' so that its area would be a Megalithic number?

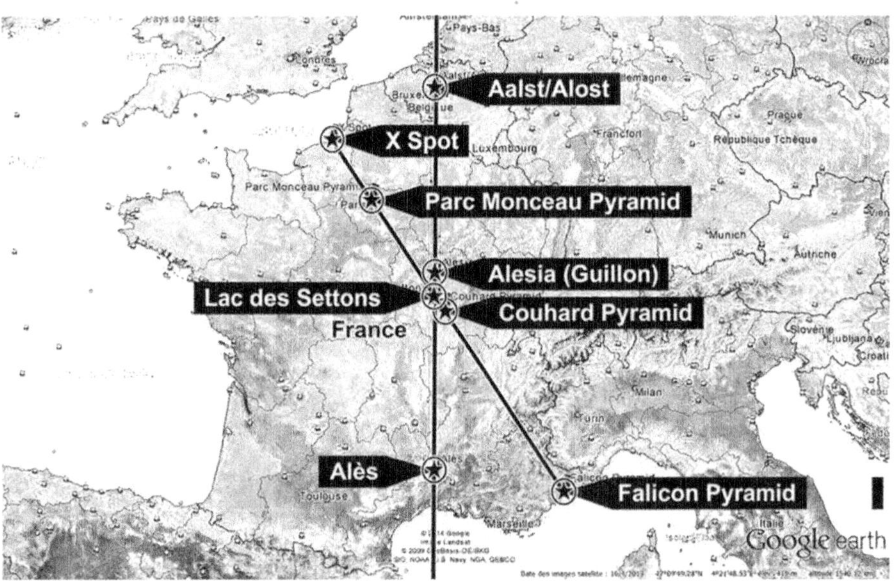

Fig. 48. The Alesia Druidic Meridian and the French Pyramids Line. The artificial Lac des Settons lies at their intersection.

The suggestion would sound utterly ludicrous were it not for the mounds of corroborating evidence amassed in this chapter, and throughout this book. Is it possible that, in the mid-19th century, there were in France influential people, perhaps Freemasons, who amused themselves to perpetuate age-old Druidic mathematical knowledge, in this case in the guise of an artificial lake? We have followed the golden thread for about five millennia, and the 19th century is 'yesterday' compared to Megalithic times or even Celtic times. Does it mean these

[404] or 367 hectares depending on the source

people still exist today? Are some Freemasons heirs to the legacy of Druidic knowledge? How is that even possible? Why keep this information a secret, and what for? What are their ambitions? Is it just a game? How is it possible nobody ever unmasked them?

Fig. 49. The Lac des Settons, a 19th-century artificial lake which lies at the intersection of the Alesia Druidic Line and the French Pyramids Line, has an area of 3.66 sq km or 366 hectares.

I must admit that, being a sceptic myself, I had difficulty believing I was not dreaming. But more and more evidence was about to pile up, as you will see. Still today, after years of research, I still have the greatest difficulty to accept the story the collected evidence tells us, as it certainly looks much more like fiction than reality. And yet, one should go where the evidence leads, don't you think?

The creation of the Lac des Settons was the idea of a local deputy named André Dupin, who was also a lawyer, a prosecutor, a politician and a member of the French Academy. He was also a close friend of Louis Philippe I, the very last French King in 1830, and the son of Louis Philippe d'Orléans, the man who supported the French Revolution and who had the Parc Monceau Pyramid built. André Dupin was also a Freemason and, according to a 19th-century book about Freemasonry and a biography of its French members, 'more than once the happiest improvisations were heard from him [in Freemasonic circles].'[405]

The Paris Meridian or Green Meridian

If Paris is *not* a Druidic Meridian location, it ultimately became a Prime Meridian. The Paris Prime Meridian was designed in 1667 when the Paris Observatory was built. In modern terms, it runs at a longitude of 02°20'E (the Greenwich Prime Meridian was defined two centuries later and adopted in 1884, see Chapter Seventeen). In a very symbolic way, the meridian flies over the Louvre Palace where French kings used to reside, a few yards away from the Louvre Pyramid, built in 1989.

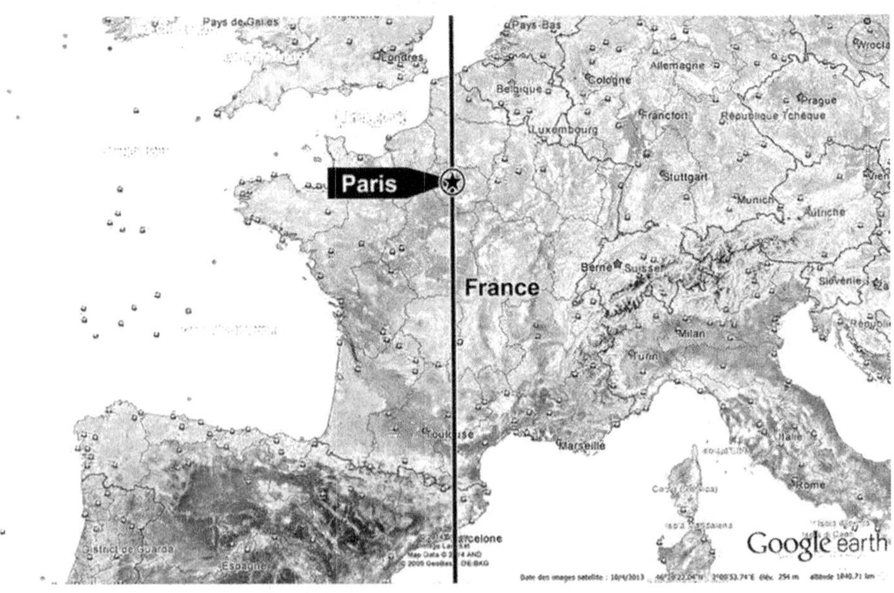

Fig. 50. The Paris Meridian, which runs at a longitude of 02°20' east of Greenwich.

What's interesting in our study is that in the year 2000 the French architect Paul Chemetov created the Green Meridian Project, which consisted in planting trees all along the Paris Meridian from the north to

[405] Jean-Claude Besuchet, *Précis historique de l'ordre de la Franc-maçonnerie, depuis son introduction en France jusqu'en 1829, suivi d'une biographie des membres de l'ordre, les plus célèbres par leurs travaux, leurs écrits, ou par leur rang dans le monde, depuis son origine jusqu'à nos jours; et d'un choix de discours et de poésies*, Tome 2, Paris: Rapilly, 1829, p. 102

the south of France. Although most of the trees soon died, the Paris Meridian is still often referred to as the Green Meridian, and the towns and villages which stand along it have signs indicating the presence of the *Méridienne verte*. It crosses 337 *communes* (French administrative divisions), meaning either villages or towns or cities, 20 *départements* (French subdivisions of regions), 8 regions, and of course one country (France). Now for the prestige of the magic trick:

337+20+8+1=366

An odd coincidence, isn't it? Or was it all actually planned across the centuries so that the count falls right? Reason tells us that it must be a coincidence, for who would care for such meaningless additions?

And yet, take time to ponder this: there are about 36,600 *communes*[406] in France. That's between 4 to 5 times more than the average number in other Europeans countries for an equivalent portion of territory, as well as 4 to 5 times more than the average number in other European countries relative to their total number of inhabitants! In other words, it looks just like the French, unlike any other nationality in the rest of the world, decided to create a disproportionately high number of towns and villages in their country, so that the number finally reaches 36,600. Just a coincidence, or is it yet another hidden message from DIs?

The Parc Monceau Pyramid on the Great Seal of the United States?

Let us conclude this chapter with the topic of the creation of the Great Seal of the United States of America which, oddly enough, seems to be intimately linked to the French Pyramids Line, or more specifically to the Parc Monceau Pyramid. It all started when I noticed the resemblance between the pyramid depicted on the one-dollar banknote and Carmontelle's pyramid in Paris. So I decided to investigate the matter.

Among the people who designed the Great Seal was Benjamin Franklin, who is known to have been a Freemason from 1731 until his death in 1790. Benjamin Franklin was also ambassador to France for nine years, from 1776 to 1785. The Monceau Pyramid, as we have seen, was built between 1773 and 1778, so Franklin would have seen a brand new pyramid at the time. But did he actually see it?

---

[406] 36,552 in continental France, 36,681with the overseas territories, according to the official count, INSEE, 01 Jan. 2014: http://www.insee.fr/fr/methodes/nomenclatures/cog/documentation.asp

The only apparent problem is that Franklin had made his propositions for the Great Seal *before* living in France. But there were actually three committees named by Continental Congress to design the Great Seal. Franklin was part of the first one, along with Thomas Jefferson and John Adams. This committee was formed right after independence in 1776. Franklin's proposals were not retained, and the same year he was sent to France.

Only a few of the initial propositions of the three men were retained, among which the Eye of Providence set in a radiant triangle. But this triangle was *not* a pyramid, and the slopes of the sides were much less slanted. As Franklin was living in France as an ambassador, a second committee was set up in 1780, in which it was decided to include the number thirteen, the number of the American colonies at the time, on the Great Seal. But this committee also failed to persuade Congress, and a third committee was set up in 1782. This third committee didn't manage to reach its goals right away either, and they had to seek help from a young Philadelphia lawyer named William Barton, known for his artistic skills. Barton is the man who actually drew up the thirteen-step unfinished pyramid on the reverse of the Great Seal. The thirteen brick levels represented the first thirteen colonies who had freed themselves from Britain, while the unfinished state of the pyramid symbolised work in progress, strength and duration of the newly-created country.

Above the pyramid Barton set the Eye of Providence that had initially been proposed by the first committee. Again the propositions of the third committee were not all retained, but as it happened the Secretary of Congress, Charles Thomson, chose to include this pyramid in the final design. The key point is that the pyramid did *not* spring out of Barton's imagination. Barton had merely copied it from a pyramid designed for one of the Continental currency's banknotes, the fifty-dollar note, which had been created in 1778. The man who had drawn it up was Francis Hopkinson, the man who designed the first flag of the United States.

The interesting thing is that Benjamin Franklin was a good friend of Francis Hopkinson's father. They had known each other at university. Although Francis Hopkinson was much younger than Benjamin Franklin, it is known the two men exchanged letters. It is also well known that Hopkinson first wrote to Franklin when the latter was in Britain years before the Monceau pyramid was erected. The two men shared the same interest in designing paper money and coinage.

Franklin was also a Freemason in France; he was even made Grand Master of a French Masonic Lodge for two years. It seems that Franklin must have seen the Parc Monceau Pyramid, and that he participated in

Masonic rites in the underground room of Louis Philippe d'Orléans's octagonal pavilion. Because he's known to have kept a correspondence with Hopkinson, it seems quite possible, even likely, that he described the pyramid to Francis Hopkinson in one of his letters. This would have occurred between 1776 and 1778.

We can easily guess what happened next: Hopkinson drew the pyramid on the 50-dollar banknote as it had been described by Franklin, and this pyramid ultimately ended up on the design of the Great Seal, and thus on today's one-dollar banknote. At any rate, the dates, circumstances and events make such a scenario a very plausible one.

Main points

- **Druidic knowledge seems to have survived in secret circles until very recent times**
- **Druids appear to have created a Druidic Slanted Line with an angle of 36° from the Midway Druidic Meridian running halfway from the longitudes of Stonehenge and Alesia**
- **Augustodunum, Rome's sister city, was built right on this line**
- **The Couhard Pyramid, probably dedicated to a Druid, stands right on this line too**
- **The Roman Lutetia (future Paris) was created on this line as well**
- **The Panthéon, an 18th-century building where illustrious French figures are entombed, stands right on this line too**
- **The (probably) Masonic Falicon Pyramid near Nice stands right on this line as well**
- **The Masonic Parc Monceau Pyramid in Paris stands right on this line too**
- **These three pyramids are positioned so that the Couhard Pyramid stands at the golden section of the other two**
- **The Lac des Settons, a 19th-century artificial lake which stands at the intersection of the French Pyramids Line and the Alesia Druidic Meridian, has a surface area of 366 hectares**
- **There are 36,600 *communes* (French administrative divisions) in France**
- **Many of the people who appear to have inherited Druidic knowledge are Freemasons**
- **The pyramid depicted on the Great Seal of the US seems to have been inspired by the Parc Monceau Pyramid**

Chapter Fifteen: The Stonehenge-Alesia Sacred Line

If both Stonehenge in Britain (from c. 3100 BC to c. 1300 BC) and Alesia in Gaul (from c. 1300 BC to 52 BC) were successively held as the most sacred Druidic places of all, then what happened after the Roman conquest? Did Druids adopt a new sacred place, possibly a more discreet one, to gather together and hold Druidic meetings?

We saw that Augustodunum replaced Bibracte as the new Aedui capital in Burgundy, and that the Roman Lutetia replaced the capital of the Parisii (wherever it might have been located precisely). But what city, if any, replaced Alesia?

Rotomagus, the new sacred (and secret) place of the Druids?

It occurred to me that a clever, neat way to found a new sacred place for Druids might have been halfway between Stonehenge (which was probably remembered by oral transmission despite the fact that it had lost its status for more than a millennium by then) and Alesia (which had just fallen down with Vercingetorix). Interestingly, as Stonehenge (and Avebury) and Alesia (the three Alesias, in fact) are 6 Megalithic degrees apart in terms of longitude, it meant that taking the midpoint of the Stonehenge-Alesia line meant that the new location was also a Salt Line location, as it had to be located on the Druidic Meridian running 3 Meg. degrees east of Stonehenge, and 3 Meg. degrees west of Alesia. In other words, the MDM intersecting the French coast at the X Spot in Normandy, which is the starting point of the French Pyramids Line.

I traced the Stonehenge-Alesia line on Google Earth and took a look midway. It so happens that the Stonehenge-Alesia line also intersects the MDM in Normandy, but more to the south. The exact spot lies immediately to the northeast of the modern city of Rouen (Rotomagus in Roman times), which is today the capital of the region of Haute Normandie. Is it just a coincidence? It seems it is not.

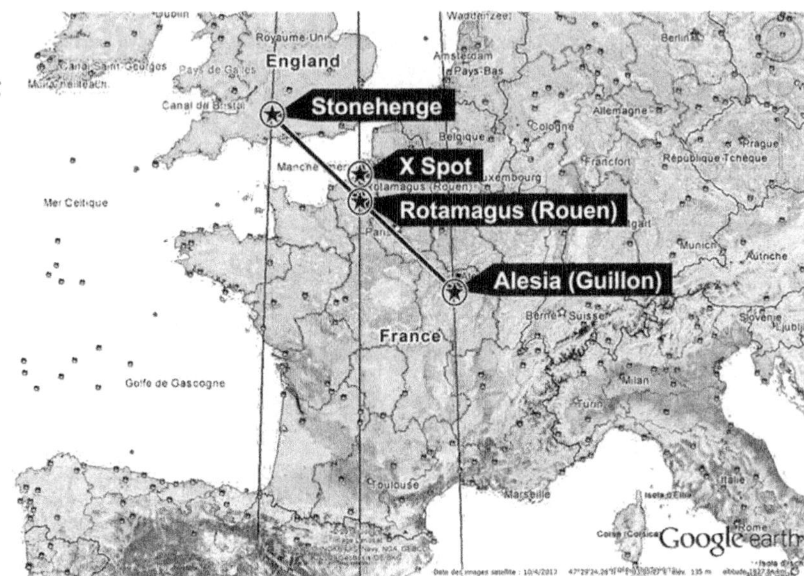

Fig. 51. The Roman city of Rotamagus was built halfway between Stonehenge and Alesia, along the Midway Druidic Meridian.

At the time of its foundation, Rotomagus was the capital of a Gallic tribe named the Veliocasses. Rotomagus (probably meaning the 'Round Plain' or the 'Round Market') was established at the time of Roman emperor Augustus (late 1st century BC) on the right bank of the Seine, outside the bend of the river, along the MDM, and exactly *in between the Stonehenge-Alesia Line and the Seine.* It had then the triple 'advantage' of being at the same time a Druidic Meridian location, of standing halfway between the most sacred Druidic sites ever (for all we know), and of having a port on the Seine, not very far away from the English Channel (downriver) and Lutetia (upriver).

It is known that Rotomagus soon became the second biggest city of Gallia Lugdunensis (i.e. the name of a Roman province corresponding to the northern part of Gaul) after Lugdunum, probably even bigger than Augustodunum, which would have been number three. About three centuries later, it even became the chief city of the new, divided province of Gallia Lugdunensis II. Rotomagus had its own Roman amphitheatre and thermae. Are we to believe this is just another extraordinary coincidence, or was again the location of Rotomagus carefully selected by Druids who were the only ones to know about its geographical attributes in terms of 366-degree geometry, and because it also had a particular symbolic significance for them, historically speaking?

Was Rotomagus the place where, after the fall of Alesia, Druids from all over Gaul continued to hold secret meetings, not calling themselves

Druids any more after a while of course? Were Druids in Roman times only driven 'to the backwoods,' as Nora Chadwick puts it, or did they progressively understand that perhaps the best hiding place of all was in plain sight, i.e. in one of the biggest cities of Gaul? Was Rotomagus the place where this new form of Druidism started to flourish, with Druids in 'civil' clothes who stopped labelling themselves as Druids and met there incognito? If so, how long did Rotomagus (or Rouen) keep this privilege? Until very recent times, maybe? Until today?

The origin of the English mile

Because I had used the kilometer as the default unit, I didn't see it at first. But when I did, my heart skipped a beat. The Stonehenge-Alesia distance, when converted into miles, is exactly 366 units! Was it just another happenstance?

We saw in Chapter Seven that the Megalithic yard was a perfect subdivision of the Earth's circumference (as well as the Minoan foot), and in Chapter Three that such was also the case of the Gallic league (and the Roman mile).

Today, of course, two modern units are also perfect subdivisions of the Earth's circumference: the kilometer is by definition very close to 1/40,000th of it, while the nautical mile (1,852 m) is by definition one modern arcminute along the meridian, or 1/60th of a modern degree. Interestingly, the Roman stadium (185.25 m) was almost exactly one-tenth of a modern nautical mile, while the Roman digitus (1.8525 cm) was almost exactly 1/100,000th of a nautical mile, meaning both ancient units were also perfect subdivisions of the Earth's circumference (see Appendix 2).

One thing that had long bothered me in my research was that the English mile did *not* appear to be any straightforward subdivision of the Earth's circumference. Interestingly, one mile is very close to being one kilometer multiplied by Phi, but not quite: it is 1.609 km, not 1.618 km.

But suddenly it struck me: the English mile must be a Druidic unit. It had been secretly defined as *1/366th of the distance between the Druids' most sacred locations, Stonehenge and Alesia.* Is it a far-fetched interpretation? Not necessarily. The mile used today (1.609344 km) is called the international mile and has been in use since 1959. It replaced the statute mile, which was defined in 1592 under the rule of Queen Elizabeth I and had a length of 1.699 km. It was officially derived from the length of 1760 English yards at the time. But is this the whole story? An alternate possibility for the definition of the mile is that some influential English people at the time, who had inherited from Druidic knowledge, arranged for this to happen. In other words, people who wanted to impose this unit of 1/366th of the Stonehenge-Alesia distance, concocted a pseudo-definition of the statute mile: 'The statute mile will be 8 furlongs of 40 poles of 16½ feet, hence 5,280 feet or 1,760 yards', while the real meaning was kept secret by Initiates only. From now on I will use the term *DIs* or *Druidic Initiates* to define the members of the presumed brotherhood of people who appear to have inherited Druidic knowledge since the downfall of the Celtic Druids.

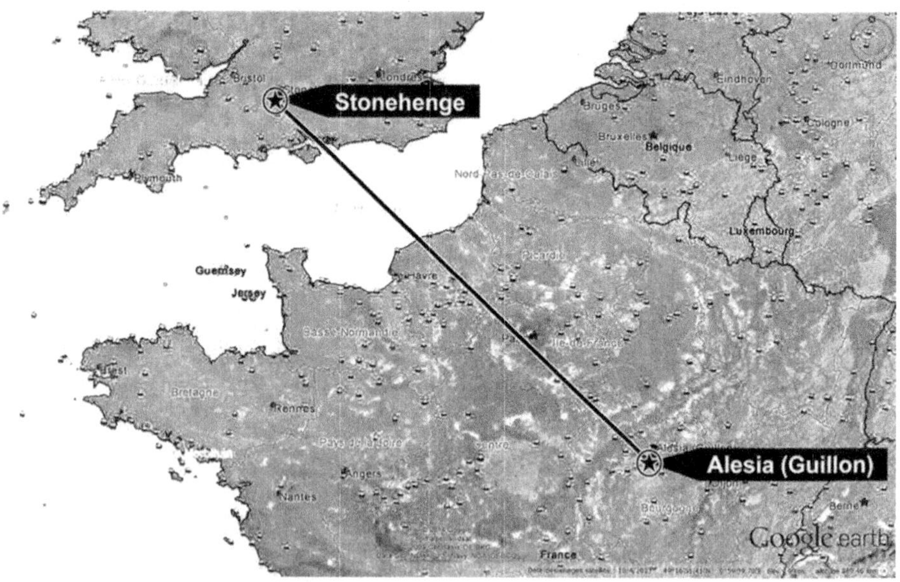

Fig. 52. The distance between Stonehenge and Alesia is a precise 366 miles.

The implication is that at some juncture the DIs crossed the Channel and 'came back' to Britain (the why and when will be discussed later). Now, if this conjecture proves true, it also has some logic in it: if indeed there had been a time when Druids were centered in Stonehenge in Britain, then later in Alesia in Gaul, then later in Rotomagus in Gaul (now Rouen), and if indeed at some point some of these DIs sailed to Britain, wasn't it particularly appropriate for them to honour their long history and the generations of Druids before them by creating a unit of measurement that was a perfect subdivision of this Stonehenge-Rotomagus-Alesia Sacred Line? Wasn't 366 (their most sacred number) the best number to employ to come up with their novel unit which echoed their past? And because they were now 'back' to Britain, wasn't using the distance between Stonehenge and Alesia the most apt way to come full circle? When you think of it, it all just makes perfect sense.

There are more curious correspondences between English and metric units via the number 366. Twelve feet or four yards is almost exactly 366 centimeters—365.76 cm to be precise, or 99.93% of 366. Inversely, 366 cm is almost exactly four yards: 4.0026 yards, or 12.008 feet. Four yards or 12 feet is 144 inches, and for what it's worth, 144 plus 222 equals 366. The number 222 also comes up in the Gallic league, which is 2222.5 meters. Likewise, one foot or 12 inches is 0.3048 m, and 3.66 divided by 12 is 3.05.

366 km also equals 227.4 miles, which is only one half of one percent greater than 366 / Phi or 226.2.

The Megalithic yard had 40 inches, and the meter itself is fairly close to 40 inches, measuring exactly 39.37 inches. Of course, the metric system was introduced in the French Revolution.

Maurice Leblanc's Golden Triangle

If some DIs did cross the Channel, some of them apparently never did, or crossed it back, perhaps generations later. Maurice Leblanc (1864-1941), the French novelist and famous author of the gentleman thief and detective Arsène Lupin, appears to have been a DI in recent times.

It should be stressed right away that I am in no way the first to claim that Leblanc is a DI of some kind. French author Patrick Ferté has written a whole book about it in 1992.[407] The 550-page book lists hundreds of examples from the numerous books written by Leblanc which seem to allude to some obscure secret, even if Ferté fails to clearly explain what exactly the secret might be. It is not known whether Leblanc was a Freemason (many of them choose to remain discreet about it), but could Leblanc have been a DI, i.e. an inheritor of Druidic knowledge?

First of all, Leblanc was born in Rouen. Secondly, in his book *The Hollow Needle*, published in 1908, Leblanc clearly alludes to a geographical triangle made up of three vertices—the cities of Rouen, Le Havre and Dieppe, all of them in Normandy. This triangle is referred to as *le triangle cauchois* ('The Triangle of the Caux area'), defining the region where Leblanc's antihero, Arsène Lupin, resides. This geometric figure is

[407] Patrick Ferté, *Arsène Lupin, Supérieur inconnu: La Clé de l'oeuvre codée de Maurice Leblanc*, Paris: Editions de la Maisnie, 1992

sometimes called the Golden Triangle, in reference to the title of another Arsène Lupin story published ten years later.[408] If this triangle seems to serve purely fictional purposes only, it is actually strong evidence that Leblanc was a DI if you carefully look at its numerous characteristics, as we will see.

The first clue that there is much more in Leblanc's Golden Triangle than first meets the eye is the very curious fact that the three cities are all Druidic Line locations; more telling even, all three cities are Druidic Meridian locations, which the reader will recall has been a recurrent feature since Megalithic times. We have already seen that Rouen stands at the midpoint of the Stonehenge-Alesia Line; the interesting thing is that Le Havre, which stands west of Rouen, and Dieppe, which stands north of Rouen, form with Rouen a nearly right-angled triangle, with the right angle set on Rouen and the hypotenuse roughly corresponding to the coast. Finally, the hypotenuse of the triangle intersects the golden section of the Stonehenge-Alesia Sacred Line, making this triangle golden indeed![409]

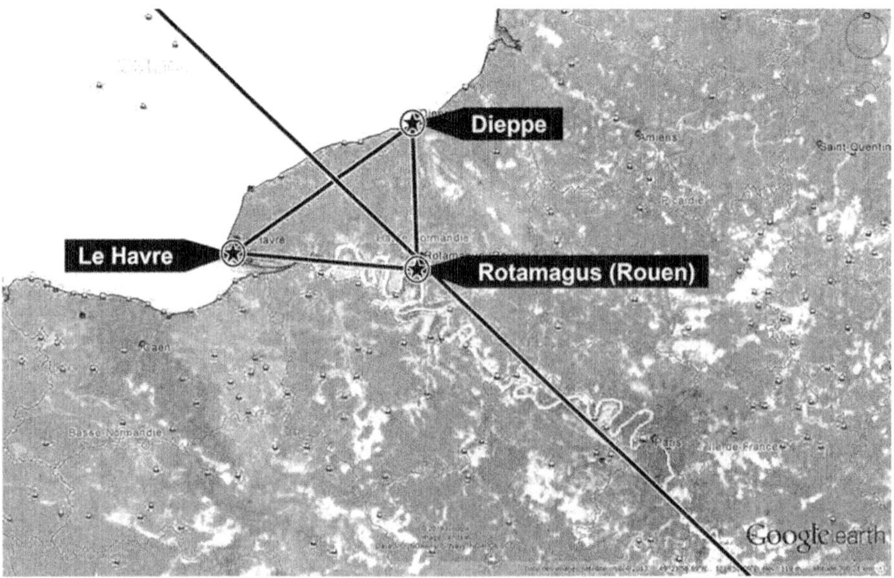

Fig. 53. Maurice Leblanc's 'Golden Triangle' formed by Rouen, Le Havre and Dieppe. Its hypotenuse is located at the Golden Section of the Stonehenge-Alesia Druidic Line.

---

[408] Muriel Rosemberg, *Le Roman policier: Lieux et itinéraires*, Revue Géographie et cultures5 No67, CNRS, Paris: L'Harmattan, 2007, p. 15

[409] The precise Golden section point of the line is in the hamlet of Vinchigny, which stands about 1½ km away from the coast.

Is this just another extraordinary coincidence, or was Leblanc a DI who was fully aware of Druidic secrets of yore? If so, it would mean that Druidic knowledge has been secretly passed down until as late as the early twentieth century. Does it mean that some people today (hiding in Freemasonry or other secret societies) still learn and pass down Druidic knowledge? We'll soon be able to answer this fascinating and intriguing question.

Nicolas Flamel and the Pontoise confirmation

An incredible piece of evidence which backs up the validity of the Stonehenge-Alesia axis is the double city of Cergy-Pontoise, which joins the very ancient city of Pontoise, hometown of the well-known 'alchemist' Nicolas Flamel, and Cergy, a *ville nouvelle*, i.e. a 'new town' created from scratch in the second half of the 20th century.

If it is now thought that Nicolas Flamel (c. 1330-1418) never really was an alchemist but a successful businessman who also happened to marry a wealthy widow, the myth of the alchemist seeking and ultimately making the Philosopher's Stone to transmute base metals into gold endures in most people's psyches. He and his spouse Perenelle are also said to have achieved eternal life. If the story is a myth, what is not is that Pontoise is a perfect Salt Line location, as the city stands right on the Druidic Meridian running at 02°06'E, about 28 km to the northwest of Paris along the River Oise. Incidentally, it is also located ¾ miles away from the French Pyramids Line. The city of Pontoise has existed since at least Roman times, and was a major city during the so-called Middle Ages (one of the biggest cities of the French kingdom at the time, with nearly 10,000 inhabitants living there).

In the mid-1960s, it was decided to create from scratch a whole series of new towns in France, mainly around Paris. A plan for these future towns was designed by Paul Delouvrier, a high-ranking functionary and politician, who also happened to be a Freemason.[410] Amongst these new cities are Cergy, originally a very small village abutting Pontoise, which after 1968 grew to a big town. Although Pontoise is the capital of the Val-d'Oise *département*, the official building is located in Cergy, a unique

---

[410] Ghislaine Otteinheimer and Renaud Lecadre, 'Des connexions invisibles,' extracts from *La Vérité sur les francs-maçons*, *L'Express*, 19 Apr. 2001: http://www.lexpress.fr/informations/des-connexions-invisibles_642090.html

case in France, which reinforces the strong tie between the two joined towns. But what is so special about Cergy-Pontoise, you may ask?

Pontoise happens to be a city where a very beautiful mathematical fact is possible: the Stonehenge-Pontoise distance is very close to the golden section of 366 miles (366/Phi mi), while the Alesia-Pontoise distance is very close to be the golden section of 366 km (366/Phi km)! As a consequence, to the DIs' eyes the city of Pontoise was three times golden, as it was at the same time a perfect Druidic Meridian location, and stood at the golden sections of two 'sacred distances,' i.e. 366 miles and 366 km from their two most sacred locations, Stonehenge and Alesia respectively. Did the legend of Nicolas Flamel discovering the secret of the Philosopher's Stone and its ability to turn lead into gold develop as a hidden, coded way (cunningly spread by DIs) to sacralise Pontoise as a 'golden' city?

The only little problem with Pontoise was that its center (say, the Saint-Maclou Cathedral) is off the ideal point by about 2 km. For good measure, DIs *had* to specify a more exact location, which would be *exactly* at the right distances from both Stonehenge and Alesia. That's how the new town of Cergy came up as a necessary creation.

Cergy or the golden proof

At the center of the new town of Cergy is a gigantic new neighbourhood aptly named the *Axe majeur*, *t*he 'Major Axis.' The *Axe majeur* was designed by Israeli artist Dani Karavan from 1980, and is still not completely finished at the time of writing. It is a huge garden overlooking Paris, and the skyscrapers of La Défense which can be seen not far off. It includes a series of impressive artistic monuments—a big rectangular plaza, a monument with twelve columns, a stage and an amphitheatre, an artificial lake with a bridge leading to a circular island called the Astronomical Island, all of which run in a straight line, clearly giving the direction of an axis. The only monument which is *not* standing on the axis proper but slightly more to the east of it is a pyramid emerging from the waters of the lake. We'll call this last monument the Water Pyramid.

The starting point of the axis is a huge semi-circular plaza conceived in 1985 by Spanish architect Ricardo Bofill with a tower called the Tour Belvédère. The dimensions of the tower beautifully exemplify circle geometry: its height is 36 meters (or maybe 36.6 meters?) and its width 3.6 meters (or is it 3.66 m?); in addition, the tower has a 3-degree tilt in the direction of the axis.[411] Around the Tour Belvédère and inside the huge semi-circular plaza is a smaller circle illustrating the 360 degrees of a circle. From the top of the tower is a panoramic viewpoint from which a laser beam illuminates the whole neighbourhood, the vanishing point of the beam being the so-called Ham road intersection, marked by an H-shaped sculpture standing three kilometers away from the tower.

The first obvious thing to check, of course, is to see what this Major Axis points at. Using Google Earth, it is easy to see that, strangely enough, the axis doesn't point to Paris but slightly west of it. You might wonder why it doesn't. Wouldn't it be a natural thing to do for the artists and architects who designed it to direct the axis to, say, the Eiffel Tower or the Tour Montparnasse (see below)? It doesn't. But the *Axe majeur* does point to something else. To my amazement, I quickly saw that the *Axe majeur* (starting right at the Tour Belvédère and following the axis through the round-shaped Astronomical Island) perfectly indicates the direction of the Couhard Pyramid, which stands 289.2 km (179.8 mi) to the southeast!

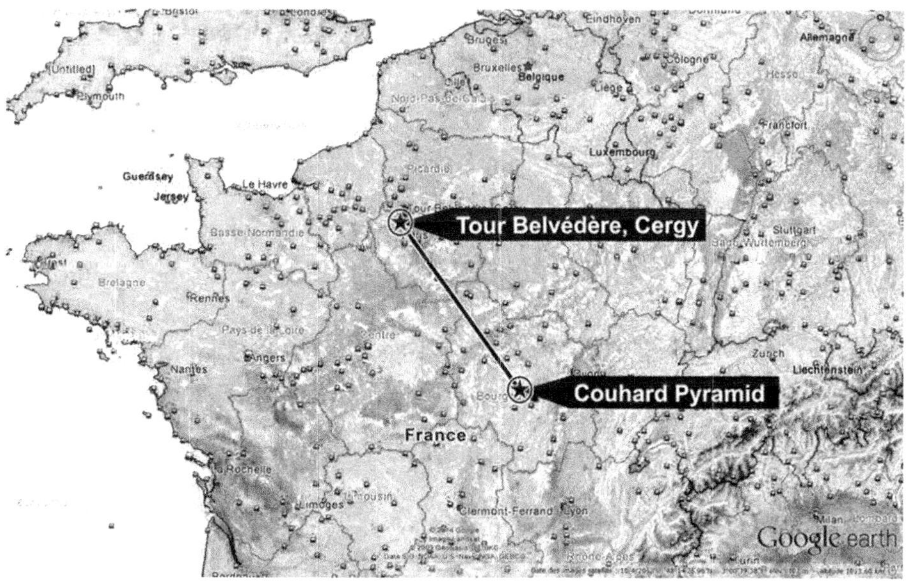

Fig. 54. The Axe Majeur (Major Axis) in Cergy leads right to the Couhard Pyramid.

[411] Data given by the official website of the Axe majeur: http://www.axe-majeur.net/

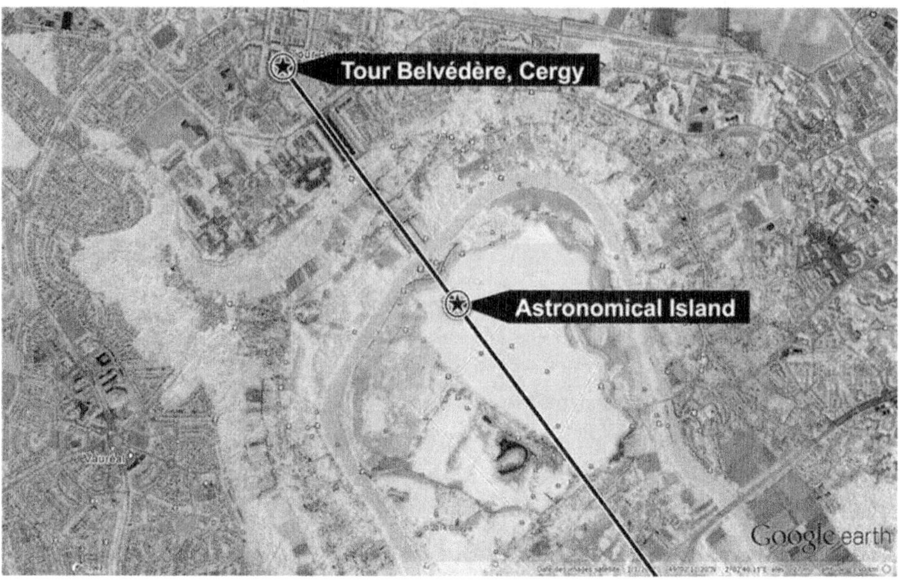

Fig. 55. Close-up on the Major Axis in Cergy. The axis neatly cuts the small Astronomical Island in two.

But that's far from being all. Tracing another line, still originating at the Tour Belvédère, but this time in the direction of the Water Pyramid, will lead you to Alesia! By now the reader may not be surprised, but in addition, the distance from the Tour Belvédère to the highest point of the Montagne de Verre (308 m) in Alesia is the *exact* golden section of 366 km (or 366/Phi km = 226.2 km). Most interestingly, this Minor Axis, as I have styled it, flies over Paris and, by an extremely curious coincidence, happens to perfectly intersect, to a staggering accuracy of 100 per cent, the highest building of Paris, the Tour Montparnasse—in fact, the only skyscraper in Paris proper! (The skyscrapers of La Défense mentioned above technically stand in different municipalities—Puteaux, Courbevoie and Nanterre.)

Starting the same line at the Water Pyramid instead of the Tour Belvédère) and ending it at exactly 366/Phi km again will lead you to *the highest point of the Montfault* (325 m), the other height in Alesia-Guillon. This is all absolutely true to an accuracy of 100 per cent once again, and I invite readers to check for themselves these astounding results on Google Earth.

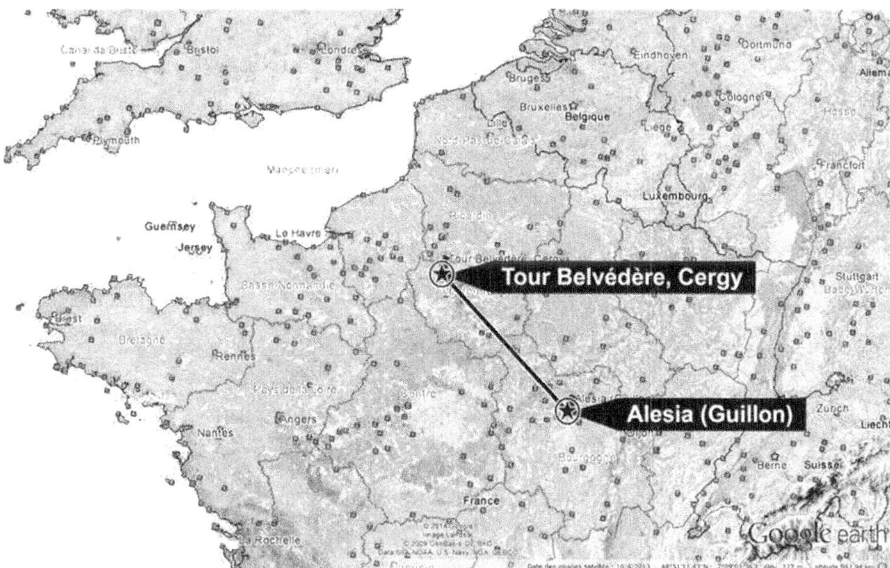

Fig. 56. The Minor Axis, also starting in Cergy but following the direction of the Water Pyramid in the Cergy lake, leads right to Alesia. Its length is the Golden Section of 366 km.

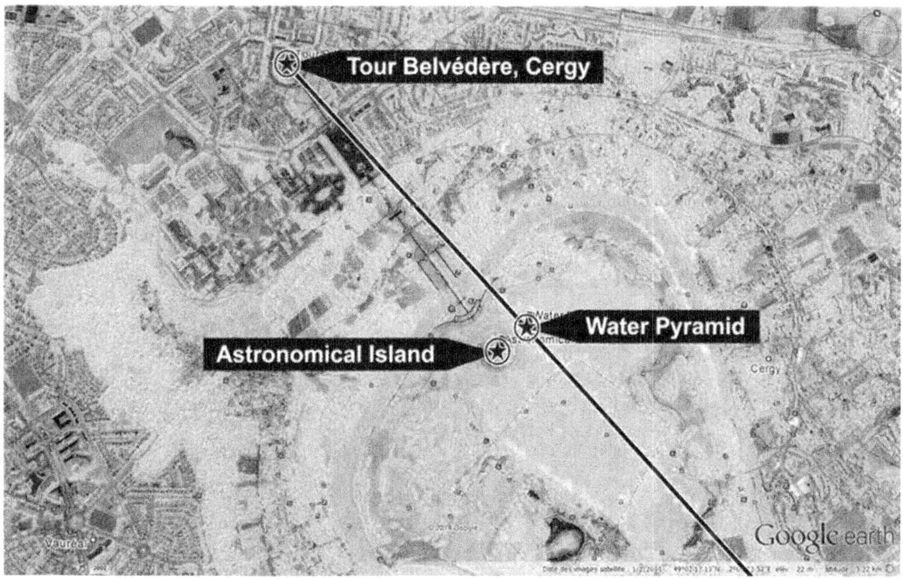

Fig. 57. Close-up on the Minor Axis in Cergy. The axis flies right over the Water Pyramid emerging next to the Astronomical Island.

Tracing a line from the Tour Belvédère and pursuing it to the northwest in the direction of Britain and ending it in Stonehenge (we can call this line the Upper Axis) yields a distance of 226.13 miles, which is the golden section of 366 miles to an accuracy of 99.98 per cent! The very slight 'error' might even be voluntary as a similar line starting in Stonehenge but ending on the circular Astronomical Island (a curious analogy to Stonehenge, by the way) yields a distance of 365.25 km, obviously the number of days in a year, a very astronomical number indeed!

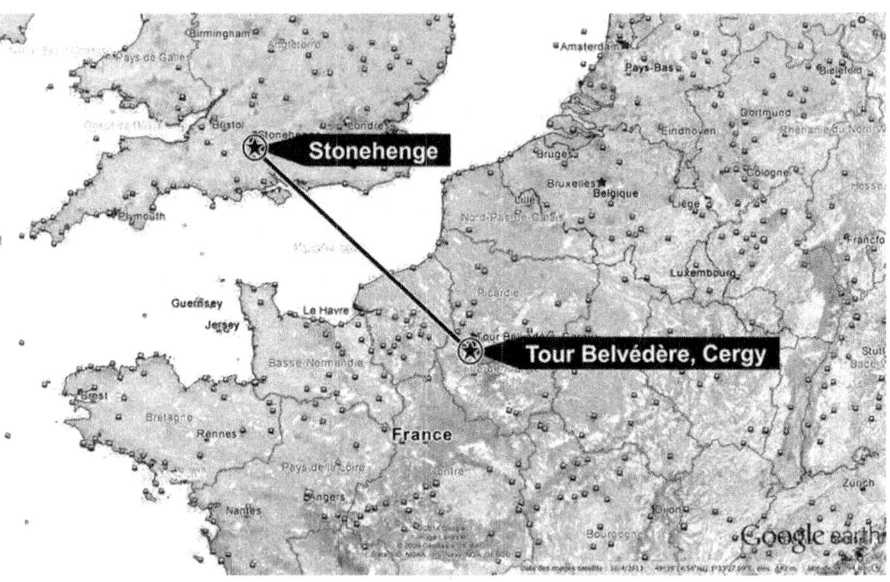

Fig. 58. The Upper Axis between Cergy and Stonehenge. Its length is the Golden Section of 366 miles.

The odds that all this is coincidental are exceedingly low already. It clearly implies that Druidism, as it seems to have endured for millennia, still exists today, with DIs perpetuating an age-old secret tradition to this very day, something real but that had never been spotted before in history. Again, I perfectly realize this might sound crazy, but here are the facts, easy to check and defying common sense. Yet that's still not all.

Cergy—an inverted Y

Here's one of my favourite confirmations that Cergy and its *Axe majeur* have been carefully designed by DIs as a verifier of the Stonehenge-Alesia line. Were such a corroboration to be found in a novel or a film, many people would complain the scenario verges on the grotesque, as it really looks like something unlikely to occur in the real world. Well, it is all real, as you will soon find out.

We have drawn three lines starting in Cergy. The first one (the Minor Axis) points to Alesia, and its length is 366/Phi kilometers. The second one (the Upper Axis) points to Stonehenge, and is 366/Phi miles long. The third one (the main one or Major Axis) points to the Couhard Pyramid, a highly symbolic Druidic monument, arguably the most symbolic Druidic monument in France. These three lines, when drawn on a map, form a roughly inverted Y.

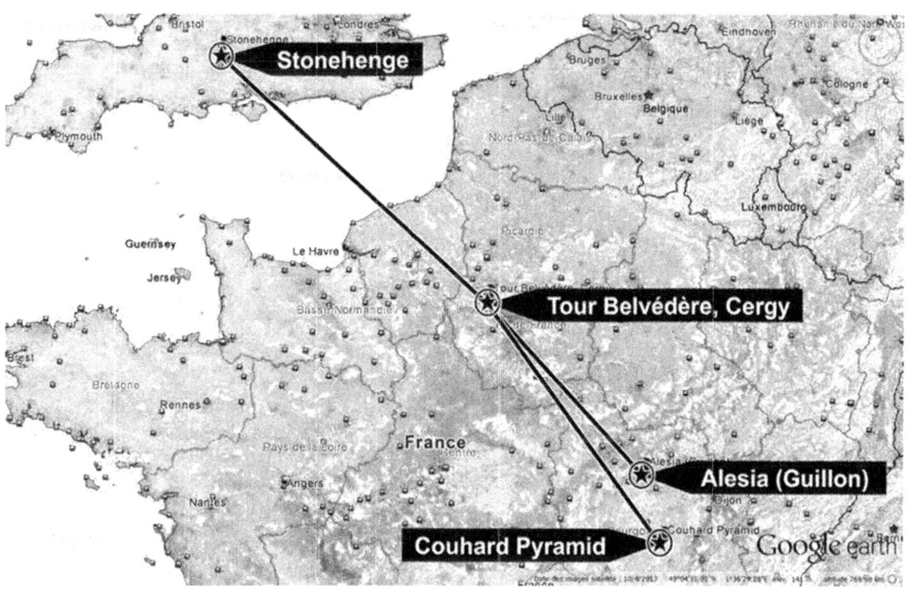

Fig. 59. The combination of the Major Axis, Minor Axis and Upper Axis form a reversed Y, echoing the fact that the word Cergy spelt backwards reads Ygrec, meaning 'Y' in French.

Now reverse the letters of the name *Cergy*. What you end up with is *Ygrec*, which in French means Y (the letter wye, also the twenty-fifth letter of the alphabet in French). What it means is clear: the town name *Cergy* is a reversed Y too! Of course, it all appears like a coincidence, as it is said that the name derives from an old hamlet named Sergy on ancient maps. Which of these two facts is untrue?

Here's the clincher. On the coat of arms of the city is a white tower-like building which is also a bridge with two pillars. What it really looks like, in fact, is a reversed Y! Quite unbelievable, but true. Please make your own conclusions. Additionally, the design at the bottom of the coat of arms looks like an inverted step pyramid.

Fig. 60. The Cergy coat of arms clearly depicts a tower which is an inverted Y.

The François Mitterrand connection

As if to hammer in their point, the ones who conceived Cergy included two more beautiful pieces to their magnum opus. Let us now introduce former French president François Mitterrand.

Mitterrand was the French president for two seven-year terms, or fourteen years (1981-95), and he's one of the most enigmatic political figures of recent French history. His name is associated to many secrets and he was thus nicknamed 'The Sphinx.' Amongst these secrets, Mitterrand was diagnosed with cancer in the very first months of his first term, and yet he managed to conceal the disease to his citizens for an impressive 11 years, until 11 September, 1992, when he had to be operated on. The married man also had a mistress, Anne Pingeot, who gave him a daughter, Mazarine Pingeot, facts that broke the news as late as 1994. Mitterrand is also infamous for a telephone tapping scandal which lasted several years in the 1980s, where famous people or notables (politicians, lawyers, as well as a journalist and a writer) were being spied on by the president.

Here is a series of additional strange facts about Mitterrand's life. To begin with, Mitterrand had an official office in Paris at the address of 9, Rue Frédéric Le Play in Paris, a few steps away from the Eiffel Tower. In the very same building but at a different floor, his mistress and his secret daughter had a flat, into which Mitterrand could, and would, easily sneak up. The building, just like the Tour Montparnasse, is located exactly on the course of the *Axe mineur*, to an astounding accuracy of 100 per cent, as anyone can easily check on Google Earth. Who is playing with whom?

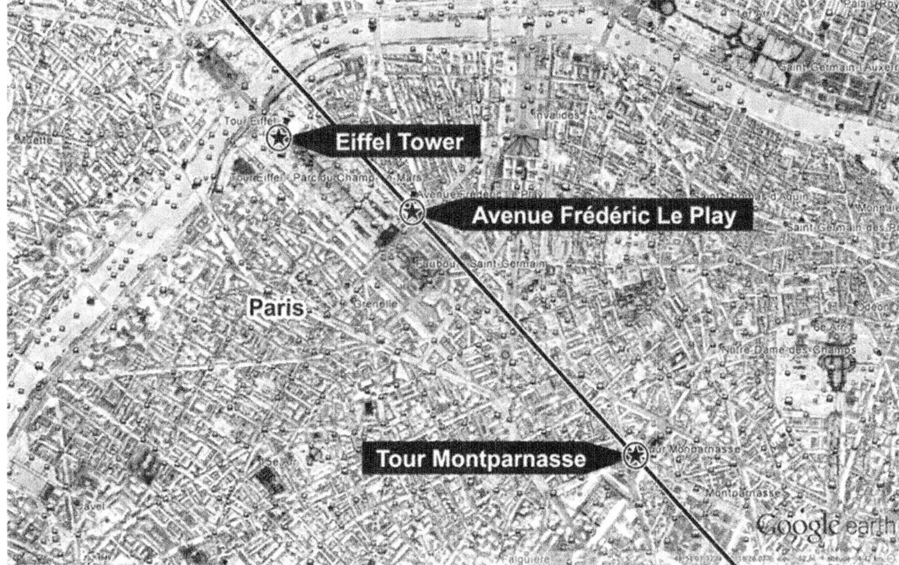

Fig. 61. The Minor Axis skirts the Eiffel Tower, and flies right over François Mitterrand's secret flat in Paris, and right over the famous Tour Montparnasse.

On a lighter note, it is also interesting to see that Mitterrand's daughter is named Mazarine, a not-so-common name which is also the name of the oldest public library in France, and which is also located right on the Paris Meridian, immediately south of the Seine. There is thus a very Druidic symbol through her name, as this library is both a potent symbol of knowledge, while its location, be it by accident or not, alludes to geometry.

Well, if you're smiling right now, I perfectly understand you. After all, these examples might just look like meaningless coincidences. But please bear with me.

The *Axe majeur* neighbourhood in Cergy was built from the 1980s onward, during Mitterrand's presidency. If you study the tangential lines of the astronomical island (as always, starting at the Tour Belvédère), two additional places, both of them closely linked to Mitterrand, are highlighted. The first tangent (the one more to the east), drawn in between the *Axe majeur* and *Axe mineur*, which we will call Eastern Tangent, if prolonged, ends up right into the Grande Arche de la Défense just outside Paris, a great hypercube which houses government offices. The Grande Arche was inaugurated in 1989 to commemorate the bicentennial of the French Revolution, but the project had been launched back in 1982 by Mitterrand *lui-même*. The clincher is that it is located exactly 22.62 km away from the Tour Belvédère, which of course is 36.6/Phi km.[412]

Interestingly, the Grande Arche is supposed to complete the *Axe historique* (the 'Historical Axis,' see Chapter Sixteen) of Paris, which starts at the Louvre's modern glass pyramid, another project of Mitterrand, which was also inaugurated in 1989, amidst considerable controversy. The line continues through the Tuileries Garden and the Egyptian obelisk, then to the Champs Elysées and the Arc de Triomphe. The only problem is that the Grande Arche is not exactly in line with the rest: it is turned at an angle of 6.33° with regard to the axis. Are the technical reasons invoked (nearby motorway and train) real, or is the truth slightly different? In other words, was the precise location of the Grande Arche chosen so as to discreetly remind DIs that it was also located on another axis—the secret Eastern Tangent?

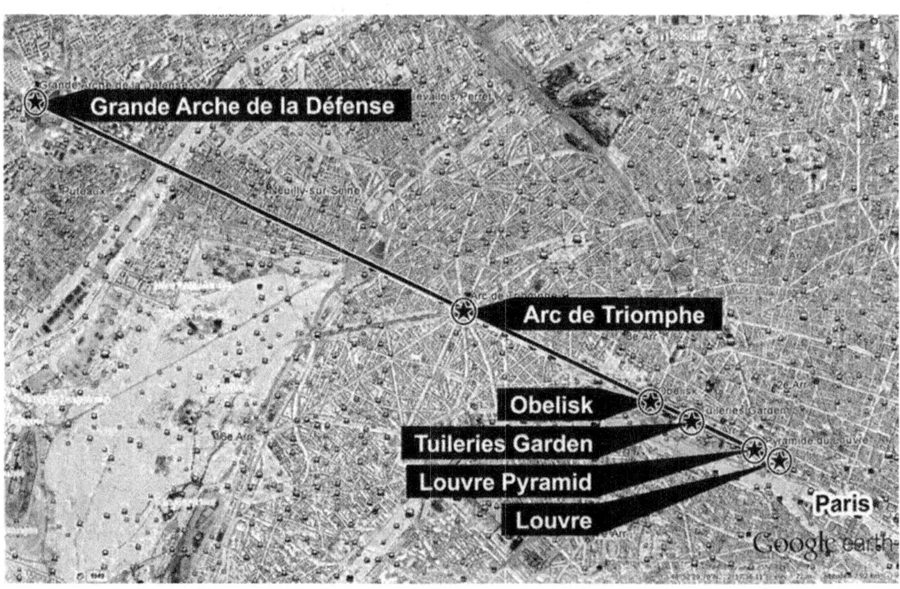

Fig. 62. The Historical Axis in Paris. From west to east, one finds the Grande Arche de la Défense, the Arc de Triomphe, the Champs Elysées, the Egyptian obelisk, the Tuileries Gardens, the Louvre Pyramid and the Louvre.

Continue tracing the Eastern Tangent and you arrive at the church of Notre-Dame-de-l'Arche-d'Alliance (*Arche d'Alliance* is French for 'Ark of the Covenant'), a modern church which is cube-shaped. Interestingly, the steeple is 37 meters high (36.6 meters?), while each side of the cube is 18

---

[412] My heartfelt thanks to Quentin Leplat, one of my readers, for this discovery

meters (18.3 meters?). According to the official website of the church, the cubic shape of the church symbolises the 'Heavenly Jerusalem' mentioned in the Book of Revelation.[413] And guess what, the church was commissioned by Mitterrand himself back in 1983. In a 1988 article about the church that was about to be built, a French major newspaper wrote that no other church had been built in Paris for twenty years.[414] The church was finally consecrated in 1998, and the last stained-glass windows were placed in 2001. As anyone can easily check on Google Earth, the Tour Belvédère, the Grande Arche de la Défense and Notre-Dame-de-l'Arche-d'Alliance are perfectly aligned.

Interestingly, the name of the Grande Arche itself seems to hint at the church further on the same axis, as the word *arche* both means 'arch' and 'Ark' in French. In addition, the structures have a similar cubic or hypercubic shape. Is the Ark of the Covenant hidden under the church?

Fig. 63. The Eastern Tangent leads right to the Grande Arche de la Défense, and to the small modern church Notre-Dame-de-l'Arche-d'Alliance (Our Lady of the Ark of the Covenant).

---

413 http://www.ndarche.org/cadre2.html

414 http://www.ndarche.org/Historique/histo_88.html

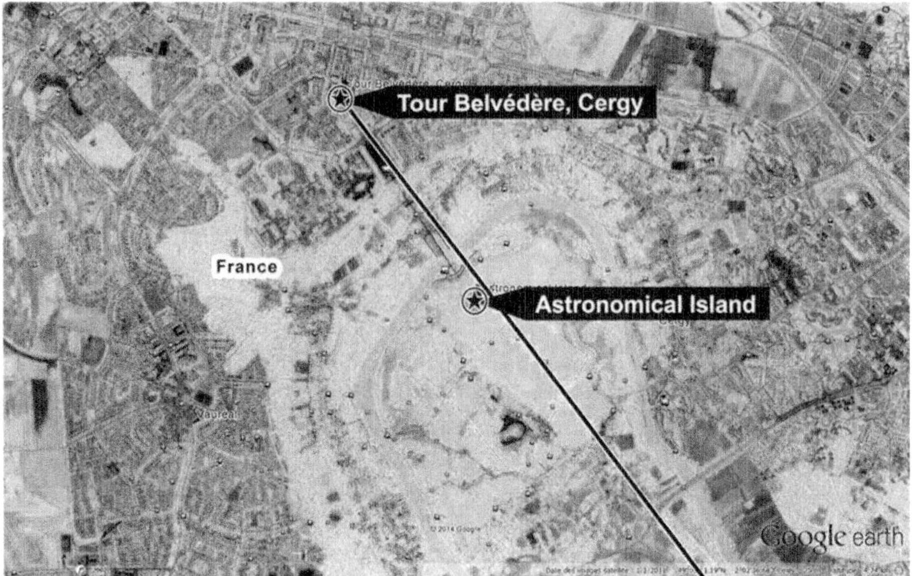

Fig. 64. Close-up on the Eastern Tangent in Cergy. The axis is tangent to the Astronomical Island on its eastern side.

The second tangent to the astronomical island in Cergy (still starting its course at the Tour Belvédère), oriented more to the south than the *Axe majeur* and which we will call the Western Tangent, is doubly interesting. First, it flies right above the Mont Valérien, a 162-meter-high hill west of Paris with a fortress overlooking the Bois de Boulogne—or perhaps is it a 161.8-meter-high hill—100 x Phi in meters? Second, the fortress is said to house the telephone tapping agency of the French army. Of course, the government won't confirm this, but according to Claude Angeli, one of the journalists whose phone conversations were listened to under Mitterrand in the 1980s, the fact is real.

But the best is yet to come. If you prolong the Western Tangent, after 366 km you will arrive on the Rock of Solutré, a 493-meter-high, somewhat Sphinx-like limestone escarpment in Burgundy, which Mitterrand ritually ascended every year on Whitsunday. The event started to be highly mediatised from 1981 on. Mitterrand's conventional explanation was that he had traditionally made the ascent since World War II with his friends from the French Resistance (underground fighters against the Nazi German occupation of France). Or is it just a myth? After all, nothing at all proves that Mitterrand had really been climbing the Burgundian hill before 1981. Did the event serve the purpose of 'sacralising' a Sphinx-like hill that was also 366 km away from the Tour Belvédère in Cergy? As there was already a 366-mile line, a

366/Phi-mile line, and a 366/Phi-km line, the only missing one to attain full harmony was a 366-km line.

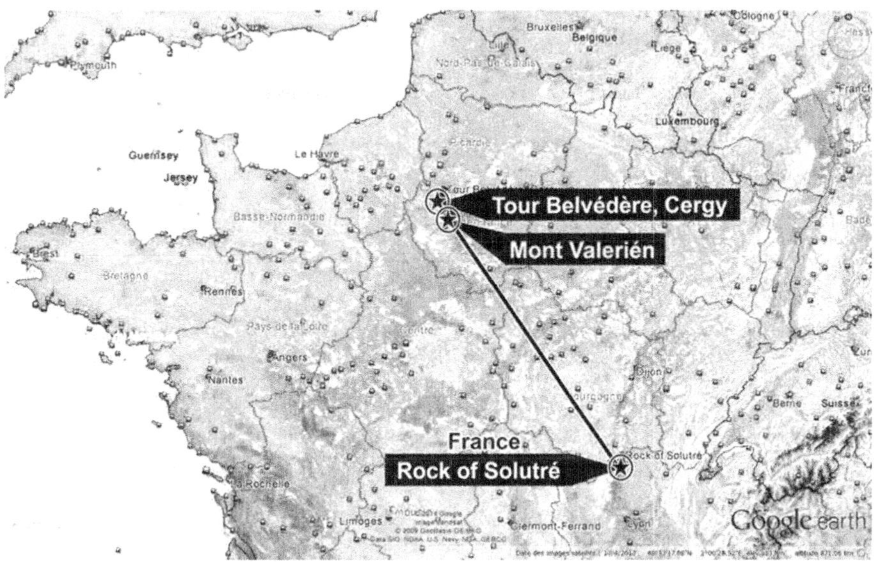

Fig. 65. The Western Tangent. It flies right above the Mont Valérien near Paris and ends up in the Rock of Solutré, which stands 366 km away from the Tour Belvédère in Cergy.

Fig. 66. Close-up on the Western Tangent in Cergy. The axis is tangent to the Astronomical Island on its western side.

Main points

- Rotomagus (now Rouen) is a Druidic Meridian city which also stands halfway between Stonehenge and Alesia
- There are strong reasons to believe Druidism continued to thrive secretly in Rotomagus/Rouen centuries after the fall of Druidism
- The English mile appears to have been defined by English Druidic Initiates (legatees of Druidic lore) as 1/366th of the Stonehenge-Alesia distance
- French novelist Maurice Leblanc seems to have been a recent Rouen Druidic Initiate who was perfectly aware of the Stonehenge-Alesia Sacred Line
- 'Alchemist' Nicolas Flamel's city of Pontoise is a Druidic Meridian location, and stands almost exactly 366/Phi miles *and* kilometers away from Stonehenge and Alesia respectively
- The exact spot was specified in the late 20th century as the Tour Belvédère in the new town of Cergy next to Pontoise
- The *Axe majeur* neighbourhood in Cergy appears to be a huge verifier of the Stonehenge-Alesia line, using 366 and Phi as basic numbers
- The *Axe majeur* points at the Couhard Pyramid
- Cergy stands at the junction of a huge reversed Y, while its very name is a reversed Y too (the French name for the letter Y is *y grec*)
- French president François Mitterrand appears to have been a Druidic Initiate whose life was in many ways directly linked to Druidic knowledge
- Mitterrand left much evidence (both abstract and solid) that he was perfectly aware of 366-degree geometry

Chapter Sixteen: Druidic Initiates amongst the Knights Templar

We have seen in the two previous chapters that, right after the fall of Alesia, two Druidic lines rose to importance in Gaul: the Pyramids Line, whose origin lies at Spot X right where the MDM intersects the coastline in Normandy; and the Stonehenge-Alesia line, which links the Druids' two most sacred locations of the past.

But this does not mean that the Alesia Druidic Meridian—the Aalst-Alesia-Alès Meridian—was forgotten. As we have seen in Chapter Three, two major French cities also lie along the course of this line, Reims and Troyes.

The Druidic city of Troyes in Champagne

As we saw in Chapter Three, Troyes in Champagne lies at the golden section of the Aalst-Alès line segment. What it seems to imply is clear: Druids probably knew about Phi (the golden ratio), and decided to found a city which would be both a Druidic Meridian location (in terms of longitude) and the golden section of the Aalst-Alès segment (in terms of latitude).

Much like Augustodunum (Autun) and Lutetia (Paris), Augustobona Tricassium (Troyes) was founded in the 1st century BC at the beginning of the Roman era. The name derives from the name of the Gallic tribe inhabiting the area, the Tricasses.

Is it possible that Druidism continued to secretly exist in Troyes in the ensuing centuries, much like what we think happened in Rouen and Paris? As we are going to see, much evidence shows that such was probably the case.

The rise of the Knights Templar

In 1099 Jerusalem was recaptured by Christians, and two decades later (in 1120) the French knight Hugues de Payens suggested creating a monastic order to keep the highways free for the Pilgrims travelling to the Holy Land. King Baldwin II of Jerusalem granted the first nine Frenchmen a headquarters on Temple Mount (from the alleged remains of the Temple of Solomon) in the Al-Aqsa mosque, hence their name of Poor Fellow-Soldiers of Christ and of the Temple of Solomon, which was later simplified into Knights Templar.

In 1129 the Order was officialised at the Council of Troyes with the help of Saint Bernard of Clairvaux, founder of the Cistercian order and also a nephew of André de Montbard, one of the nine founding knights. Interestingly, Clairvaux Abbey (created by Saint Bernard) is a Druidic Parallel location, as it was built along the 49th Megalithic Parallel north of the equator. The Knights Templar took vows of poverty, chastity and obedience, but also received money, land and businesses. As a consequence, they soon became a major power not only in the Holy Land but also all across Western Europe, and from 1139 on, the Order was exempted from obedience to local laws, meaning only the Pope stood above them, until the Order was suppressed by Pope Clement V a bit less than two centuries later.

Many clues tell us that the Order counted in its members DIs who had inherited Druidic knowledge. First of all, the fact that Saint Bernard, who played a key role in the founding of the Order, built the famous Clairvaux Abbey on a Salt Line location, is a curious coincidence, as is of course the fact that the Order was officialised in Troyes, certainly a very meaningful Salt Line location in the eyes of our presumed DIs.

Similarities between the Knights Templar and Druids

Were the Knights Templar DIs who somehow revived Druidism in their own time? There are many common points between the Knights Templar and Celtic Druids.

They both dressed in white robes;

Druids never wrote anything down, while Knights Templar were not allowed to possess any books;[415]

---

[415] John J Robinson (1989), *Born In Blood: The Lost Secrets of Freemasonry*, Lanham, Maryland: M. Evans, 2009, p. 94-5

Templar initiations, just like their chapter meetings, were conducted in absolute secrecy, and of course they had no right to divulge anything about these to anyone, including Knights Templar of lower ranks, all of which appears to be very similar to the proceedings of Druidism;

most of the Templar churches were circular in shape, which reminds us both of the circular structures of Megalithic people (stone circles, henges, mounds such as Newgrange, artificial hills such as Silbury), and the circular pits of the Celtic Druids' sacred precincts (the *temene* mentioned in Chapter Two), as well as circle geometry itself, which lies at the heart of Druidic knowledge, as we have seen all along this book.

So, once again, were some high-ranking members of the Order—presumably the highest-ranking members—DIs?

The origins of the English pound

Troyes and the surrounding region are also famous for the Champagne fairs which were held annually (twice a year in the case of Troyes) in the 12th and 13th centuries, in which people from all across Europe would buy textiles, leather, fur and spices. Interestingly, the avoirdupois pound of Britain, just like the Troy pound for precious materials, are thought to have been devised in the city of Troyes (see further). The key points here are that these fairs are closely associated (both geographically and chronologically) to the Knights Templar, and that the avoirdupois pound might be directly derived from 366-degree geometry.

Let me immediately stress that the results that follow might be purely coincidental for, just like the facts observed in the Great Pyramid, they are utterly astonishing, even world-shattering. So maybe it is just a huge coincidence... or maybe it is not.

Today the mass of the Earth is generally quoted as being 5.9736×10^{24} kg. The international avoirdupois pound is defined as exactly 453.59237 g. Imagine the world is an orange with many segments. As Alan Butler noticed,[416] if you take a one-Megalithic-second segment of the Earth (by our definition, one 360th of one 366th of our planet) and weigh it, you will notice that it is almost exactly 10^{20} avoirdupois pounds, to an accuracy of 99.95 per cent!

$$5.9736 \times 10^{24} / (366 \times 360) = .4533697632 \times 10^{20}$$

[416] Alan Butler and Christopher Knight, *Civilization One*, London: Watkins, 2004, p. 124

In other words, when weighed in pounds, a one-Megalithic-second segment of the Earth is an almost perfectly round number (a 1 with 20 zeros). So, to sum things up (as we saw in Chapter Seven) the apparent distance covered by the Earth's equator relative to the Sun in one Megalithic second of time is a beautiful 366 Megalithic yards, while the corresponding segment of the Earth (measuring one Megalithic arcsecond at the equator) theoretically weighs a neat 10^{20} avoirdupois pounds. Just splendid and harmonious, as always!

Fig. 67. A one-Megalithic-second segment of the Earth weighs almost exactly 10^{20} avoirdupois pounds.

Once again, the implications of this result are quite phenomenal. Unless it is just a happy coincidence, it means that the mass of the Earth was known back in c. 1300 AD, for that's the date when the avoirdupois pound came into general use in Britain. It also implies that the pound was devised (with Megalithic numbers) using that incredible knowledge. How is that possible in the High Middle Ages?

Nobody seems to know exactly where the avoirdupois pound comes from. The troy pound, however, which was used by apothecaries and jewellers in England to measure precious metals (gold, silver, platinum and gems), is known to owe its name to the French city of Troyes, visited by English merchants during the Champagne fairs.[417] As the name *avoirdupois* is French, there is little doubt that the standard pound also hails from Troyes. And because Megalithic numbers are used, the avoirdupois pound must be directly linked to the Knights Templar, i.e. DIs.

All this of course raises many questions. Did DIs know the mass of the Earth? Did the Celtic Druids, and MPDs, know the mass of the Earth already in their own times? If so, how is that possible? Did they manage to calculate it , or were they given this information? Or did the Knights Templar find this knowledge in Jerusalem?

Druidic Gothic cathedrals

The rise of Gothic cathedrals, first in France and then in its neighbouring countries in Western Europe, also coincides with the time of the Knights Templar. Gothic architecture represents a major innovation at the time and the term *major* is almost a euphemism when you see the sheer grandeur of Gothic churches suddenly raising toward heaven in a period of alleged relative social backwardness. Is it just a coincidence, or did the Order play a role in the emergence of this major architectural development?

The time of cathedrals is often referred to as the Renaissance of the 12th century, which preceded the Italian Renaissance by about three centuries, as major scientific and philosophical improvements were made at the time, radically transforming life in this period traditionally known as the High Middle Ages. Did the Knights Templar find ancient architectural documents in Jerusalem that allowed these developments? Did they decide to use their own geometric and astronomical knowledge as well, if they were indeed DIs as we hypothesise?

We saw in Chapter Eight that many cities of northern France were Druidic Line locations. In most of these big cities very impressive Gothic cathedrals were built at this period, generally at Druidic Line locations. The very first Gothic cathedral ever built is the Saint-Etienne Cathedral in Sens, northern Burgundy. Construction work began in 1135, only six years after the Order of the Knights Templar was officialised in Troyes. Besides, Sens is only 60 km (37 mi.) away from Troyes.

---

[417] Ronald Edward Zupko, *Dictionary of Weights and Measures for the British Isles: The Middle Ages to the 20th Century*, Darby, Pennsylvania: Diana Publishing Co, 1985

To sum things up, in alphabetical order, the cathedrals of Beauvais, Besançon, Dijon, Evreux, Reims, Rouen and Troyes are Druidic Meridian locations, while the Lisieux and Sens cathedrals are Druidic Parallel locations. These were all built at the time of the Knights Templar. Later Gothic cathedrals built after their time, such as those in Lilles, Nantes and Vannes, are also on Druidic Lines.

Gothic cathedrals were not built on Druidic Lines only in France. In England, Canterbury Cathedral, one of the oldest. most splendid and most important cathedrals of England, is a Druidic Meridian location, standing only two arc minutes west of the Druidic Meridian running at 01°07'E—the MDM itself. Salisbury Cathedral stands at nearly the same longitude as Stonehenge, which makes it a Druidic Meridian location as well. It is located only two arc minutes east of the 01°50'W Druidic Meridian.

Quite remarkably, the largest Gothic church in northern Europe, the Cologne cathedral in Germany, is also a Druidic Meridian location, as it stands only about three arc minutes west of the 07°01'E Druidic Meridian.[418]

Last but not least, Ulm Münster, a Roman Catholic church which later became a Lutheran church, built from 1377 to 1890, is also a Druidic Meridian location, as it stands only one arcminute away from the 09°58'E Druidic Meridian.[419] Interestingly, its huge, recently built steeple is 161.5 meters high, a very close approximation of 100 x Phi, the golden ratio, 1.618... in meters.

The Druidic city of Reims in Champagne

One additional proof that Druidism persevered underground after the fall of Celtic Druids is that the city of Reims, which is situated north of Troyes on the very same Druidic Meridian as the three Alesias and Bibracte, proved to be a major site for French monarchs in the alleged last millennium and a half.

First of all, Reims is famous for its superb Gothic cathedral named Notre-Dame-de-Reims. Built in the 13th century, it has been a World Heritage site since 1991. According to the UNESCO website, the cathedral is 'one of the masterpieces of Gothic art' showing '[t]he

[418] 3 arcminutes in its easternmost part, 4 arcminutes in its westernmost part, according to our habit of rounding off results to the nearest arcminute

[419] 1 arcminute in its westernmost part, 2 arcminutes in its easternmost part, according to our habit of rounding off results to the nearest arcminute

outstanding handling of new architectural techniques in the 13th century, and the harmonious marriage of sculptural decoration with architecture.'[420] In its nave, attributed to the 9th-century, lie the remains of Archbishop St Rémi (440 AD-533 AD), who instituted the Holy Anointing of the French kings by baptising Clovis in 496 AD. With only a few exceptions such as Henry IV, nearly all French Kings were legitimated by a coronation ceremony performed in the Reims cathedral, from the year 816 AD with King Louis I the Pious down to King Charles X in 1825.

Reims is also famous for its Saint Remi Basilica, located about a mile away from the cathedral. It dates back to the 11th century.

Like Troyes, Reims is located in Champagne. Is it possible that Champagne has remained a hotbed of DIs in the last 2,000 years? Is it possible that the coronation ceremony of French monarchs was not performed in Paris, the French capital, but in Reims, precisely because it was located on the most sacred Salt Line of all in Druidic history, i.e. the Alesia Druidic Meridian? In other words, could influential people, who also happened to be DIs, have perpetuated this sacred tradition for most of recent French history? As the tradition can be traced back to Clovis in the late 5th century AD, are we to believe that Clovis himself was a DI, or was influenced by them?

The *Axe historique* connection to Troyes

As we briefly saw in the previous chapter, one of the most famous features of Paris is a five-mile-long axis usually referred to as the *Axe historique* (The 'Historical Axis') or the *Voie triomphale* ('The Triumphal Way').

Although the *Axe historique* is supposed to be an old way to get from the Louvre Palace in Paris to the countryside royal palace of Saint-Germain-en-Laye (a Druidic Meridian location, see Chapter Eighteen), about 20 km west of Paris, anyone equipped with Google Earth can easily see the directions are quite different. So why was the axis designed in the first place?

The origins of the *Axe historique* can be traced back to the early 17th century when Catherine de' Medici decided to extend the central axis of the royal Tuileries Gardens at the Louvre to the west, which as we saw earlier is also split in two sideways by the Pyramids Line. The swamps were drained, creating what was to become the famous Champs Elysées.

---

[420] http://whc.unesco.org/en/list/601

In the 19th century, the Arc de Triomphe was erected at its western end. More recently, as we saw, François Mitterrand had the Grande Arche in La Défense and the Louvre Pyramid built on either end of this long axis which intersects the French capital. It is also interesting and telling to note that the Paris City Hall also lies right on the axis, slightly to the east of the Louvre.

The key question, of course, is, 'Is the Historical Axis in any way connected to Druidism?' The simple answer is, 'Yes, it is.' Prolong the axis to the east, and it ends up in Troyes! Although the fact is absolutely not known (nobody ever seems to have noticed it), I was stunned to see that the *Axe historique* precisely gives the direction of the Troyes Cathedral. What it seems to mean is clear (unless of course it is only an umpteenth coincidence): the *Axe historique* was designed by DIs, or people influenced by DIs, who wished to secretly indicate a key Druidic Meridian city of theirs, Troyes, where the Order of the Knights Templar and the Champagne fairs once flourished many centuries ago.

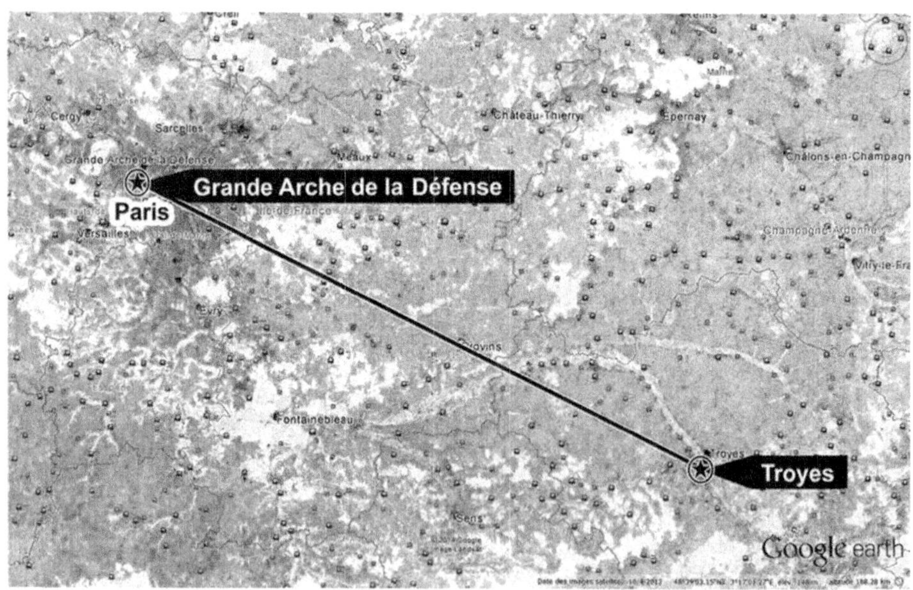

Fig. 68. The Axe historique, or Historical Axis of Paris, if prolonged, leads straight to the Troyes Cathedral.

The fall of the Knights Templar

Even if the time and circumstances are quite different, the fall of the Knights Templar in 1307 is somewhat reminiscent of the fall of Druidism more than an alleged millennium before them. The reasons why King Phillip the Fair issued secret orders to have them all arrested on 13 October 1307, and the details of the arrests, are outside the scope of this book. Officially, the Knights Templar were guilty of a list of shameful charges including sodomy, desecration of the crucifix and witchcraft, but most scholars today agree that the charges were fictional rather than real. It is clear that the king couldn't bear the fact that Templars were extremely powerful. In 1314, the Grand Master of the Order at the time, Jacques de Molay, who had first confessed the charges under torture and then retracted, was burned at the stake in Paris.

What seems to be clear is that, contrary to the Pope and King Phillip's opinions, the Knights Templar were innocent of the charges against them: indeed such were the opinions of the bishops of Aragon, the archbishop of Compostela in Castile, the king of Portugal, the Templar preceptor Hugo of Gumbach in Germany, and Prince Amalric in Cyprus.[421] Before dying, Jacques de Molay addressed the crowd and said, 'I must declare, that the Order is innocent.'[422]

An interesting point is that, according to legend, a Templar fleet of eighteen ships mysteriously disappeared on the night before the arrests, and was never heard from again. The truth of the legend is open to debate, but many authors think that some Templars (presumably some high-ranking members) managed to escape to Britain, more specifically to Scotland.[423] We'll see in the following chapter if we can find some evidence supporting that claim.

Rather ironically, Pope Clement V passed away in April 1314, just over a month after Jacques de Molay's execution, while King Phillip died in November of that year from an unexplained disease that had struck him a few weeks before during a hunt. Some people at the time claimed Phillip might have been poisoned.[424] Were they assassinated by DIs avenging themselves?

---

[421] John J Robinson (1989), *Born In Blood: The Lost Secrets of Freemasonry*, Lanham, Maryland: M. Evans, 2009, p. 137

[422] *Ibid.*, p. 142

[423] See for example John J Robinson (1989), *Born In Blood: The Lost Secrets of Freemasonry*, Lanham, Maryland: M. Evans, 2009, p. 151

[424] Paulin Pâris, *Les Grandes Chroniques de France*, tome 5, Paris: Techener, 1836-8, p. 221

Main points

- The Order of the Knights Templar was officialised in Troyes, a Druidic Meridian city standing at the golden section of the Aalst-Alesia-Alès line
- The Knights Templar share many common traits with the Celtic Druids, making them probable Druidic Initiates
- The English pound probably comes from Troyes, and is a perfect subdivision of the Earth's mass in 366-degree geometry
- Most Gothic cathedrals were built in Salt Line locations at the time of the Knights Templar, as though the Templars had found architectural secrets in Jerusalem
- The coronation ceremony of nearly all French kings was performed in the Druidic Meridian city of Reims
- The famous Historical Axis of Paris is oriented on the Troyes cathedral

Chapter Seventeen: Druidic Initiates as Freemasons in Britain and America

Did some high-ranking Knights Templar manage to escape from France and perpetuate their secret tradition somewhere else? It is often said that eighteen Templar ships vanished from the port of La Rochelle on the night before the arrest of the Knights Templar in 1307, and were never seen again. Were the highest-ranking Knights Templar, possibly DIs, warned just in time to flee to Scotland?

Knights Templar were also arrested in England, but a few months later, as it took longer for the papal bull to reach London, and this left time for William de la More (the English Grand Master at the time) and his men to escape as well. The papal bull was never published at all in Scotland, making that country a legal haven for fugitive Knights Templar (both from France and England).[425]

Is Freemasonry derived from Templar fugitives in Scotland?

Freemasonry officially and publicly began in London in 1717, more than four centuries after the fall of the Order of the Knights Templar. In his book *Born in Blood: The Lost Secrets of Freemasonry*,[426] American author John J Robinson makes the very convincing case that Freemasonry developed as a secret organisation in Scotland from Knights Templar fugitives who couldn't admit to being Templars any more in the early 14th century, for obvious reasons. If high-ranking Knights Templar were indeed DIs, and if the first high-ranking Freemasons were indeed escaped Knights Templar, it follows that high-ranking Freemasons were, and probably still are, DIs. We have seen in the preceding chapters that such a conjecture held water.

---

425 John J Robinson (1989), *Born In Blood: The Lost Secrets of Freemasonry*, Lanham, Maryland: M. Evans, 2009, p.151

426 John J Robinson (1989), *Born In Blood: The Lost Secrets of Freemasonry*, Lanham, Maryland: M. Evans, 2009

It is undeniable that the Knights Templar and Freemasons share many common traits. Just like the Order, Freemasonry is a secret organisation. The Old Charge of Freemasonry requires that Masons tell no secret of any member of the brotherhood that might cause him (until very recently Freemasonry was exclusively masculine) to lose his life and property,[427] a rule that seems more than logical for any fugitive Templar. When a new Mason is initiated, the candidate is told that the degree he is about to reach will make him 'a brother to pirates and corsairs,'[428] a phrase that really makes sense if Freemasons are indeed the inheritors of the Knights Templar, who fled by sea.

Freemasons must assert their belief in a Supreme Being,[429] whoever this Supreme Being might be, which could be an innovation from the Knights Templar's belief in the Christian God. The reason why it is so may derive from the need to trust newcomers, and one way to do that was by making them swear before God they will not break their oath of secrecy. More importantly, Freemasonry bases many of its rituals on the (alleged) Temple of Solomon in Jerusalem, which of course closely echoes both the origins and the very name of the Order of the Knights Templar.

The Masonic apron received by the Entered Apprentice at his initiation used to be a white lambskin tied around his waist as a symbol of innocence and purity, which is highly reminiscent of the sheepskin girdle the Knights Templar wore around their waists as a reminder of their vow of chastity.[430]

One of Robinson's most convincing pieces of evidence that Freemasons are fugitive Templars from France is to be found in Masonic language, which uses terms that are unique to Freemasonry. French Knights Templar spoke French, so did the English upper-classes at the time, who had been Norman-French for two centuries since William the Conqueror in 1066. And as law made English the official language in trials only in 1362, it makes it all the more likely that such Masonic terms as *tyler*, *Peter Gower* and *Freemason* find their origin in the French language spoken by Templars in the early 14th century. According to Robinson, the tyler (which is the name of the office of outer guard of a Masonic lodge) probably derives from the French word *tailleur* (the 'cutter'), the

---

[427] Ibid., p. 166

[428] Ibid., p. 165-6

[429] Except in France, where Freemasons have also been free to be either agnostics or even atheists since the late 19th century.

[430] John J Robinson (1989), *Born In Blood: The Lost Secrets of Freemasonry*, Lanham, Maryland: M. Evans, 2009, p. 238-9

man who stood outside the door with a drawn sword in hand;[431] in Masonic verbal communication Pythagoras is called 'Peter Gower' because it probably comes from the French *Pythagore*;[432] and the very name Freemason may well derive from the French *Frère Maçon*, which means 'Brother Mason,' the first term of which perfectly applies to the Knights Templar, as Templars of all classes called each other *Frère* ('Brother').[433]

Finally, one additional 'coincidence' is the strange similarity between the six-sided star, a symbol also known as the Star of David (sometimes referred to as the Seal of Solomon), and the Square and Compasses (the symbol of Freemasonry). What the Square and Compasses symbol really looks like is that it was created as a veiled simplification of the Star of David, as if Freemasons secretly paid tribute to the (alleged) Temple of Solomon or the Holy Land (and the Knights Templar?).

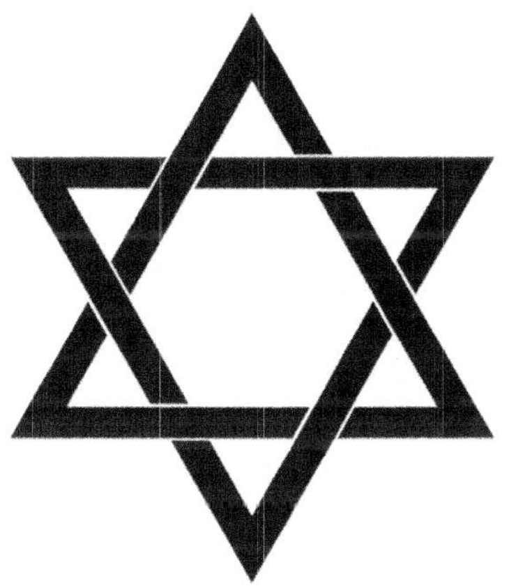

Fig. 69. A six-sided star, a symbol also known as the 'Star of David' or 'Seal of Solomon.'

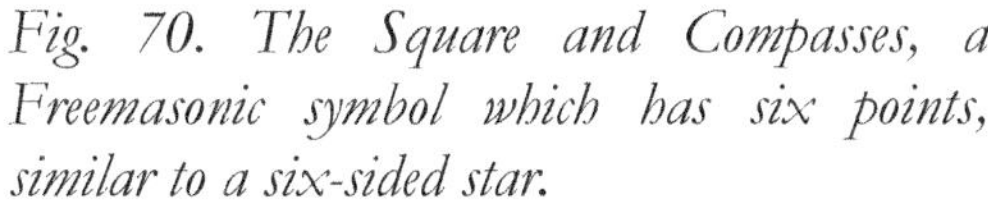

Fig. 70. The Square and Compasses, a Freemasonic symbol which has six points, similar to a six-sided star.

[431] John J Robinson (1989), *Born In Blood: The Lost Secrets of Freemasonry*, Lanham, Maryland: M. Evans, 2009, p. 225

[432] Ibid., p. 230-1

[433] Ibid., p. 230-1

Similarities between Freemasons and Celtic Druids

Apart from the obvious common point of secrecy, more specific similarities between Masons and Celtic Druids include the belief in the immortality of the soul, and an interest in the seven liberal arts and sciences—grammar, rhetoric, logic, arithmetic, music, and of course astronomy and geometry—which the future Mason is encouraged to study in-depth.

Masonic initiates wear a white robe, while Knights Templar were dressed in a white mantle, both garbs being of course reminiscent of the white robes worn by Druids and Pythagoreans.

During his initiation, the newly made Fellow Craft Mason is directed to a symbolic (sometimes real) Middle Chamber of the Temple of Solomon, which is reached by passing between Jachin and Boaz, two columns that are said to have flanked the outer porch of the temple. The intriguing aspect of these columns is that they support globes. The first one represents a map of the world and the second one a map of heaven. These globes are meant 'to motivate all Masons to study astronomy, geography and navigation.'[434] We have seen that these disciplines were absolutely central in the Celtic Druids' knowledge: as we saw in Chapter Two, Druids 'profess to know the magnitude and form of the earth and the world, the motions of the heaven and the stars,' and of course MPDs must have been first-rate sailors and masters of 366-degree geometry already. Is this just a coincidence if these disciplines are also central in Freemasonry?

The future Mason is also told that 'the original columns were hollow and used to protect the secret documents of Masonry from flood and fire.'[435] We have seen in Chapter One that, according to Strabo, water and fire were the most dreadful elements of all: 'However, not only the Druids, but others as well, say that men's souls, and also the universe, are indestructible, although both fire and water will at some time or other prevail over them.' Is it just a coincidence, or are we to believe that at some point of history, these two columns did exist in Jerusalem, and that Druids had concealed their secrets inside them? Are these secrets those recovered by the Knights Templar in the early 12th century?

In English-speaking countries the symbol of Freemasonry, the Square and Compasses, are often depicted with a capital G in the center.

---

[434] Ibid., p. 213
[435] Ibid., p. 213

Interpretations of this letter G vary from 'God,' the 'Great Architect of the Universe' and 'Geometry,' which according to Freemasons is the 'noblest of sciences,' and 'the basis upon which the superstructure of Freemasonry is erected.'[436] Indeed, during their initiation future Masons are told that geometry is a science which is fundamental both to architecture and to understand the ins and outs of the universe. Even more interesting perhaps, the word *geometry* is sometimes used as a synonym for Freemasonry.[437] As we have come to learn that geometry (essentially 366-degree geometry) was most probably the key discipline of MPDs, Celtic Druids and DIs, the fact that it is also the 'noblest of sciences' of Freemasons and their very 'basis' is either an extraordinary coincidence again, or clear evidence that DIs have hidden themselves in Freemasonry in the last centuries.

The official birth of Freemasonry in London in 1717

According to John J Robinson, when Freemasonry officially came out in London in 1717, it had already existed underground for four centuries, first in Scotland, then in England. Can we find independent confirmation of Robinson's bold claim? And can we find definite proof that Freemasonry is indeed the inheritor of Druidism?

Many authors claim that Rosslyn Chapel, a very strange Catholic church built in 1456 in Scotland, is connected either to the Knights Templar or Freemasonry. According to Alan Butler and Christopher Knight, there is a secret chamber underneath, and a tunnel going to the nearby Roslin Castle. The tunnel covers a distance of exactly 366 MY, which is also one Megalithic arcsecond at the equator.[438] Is it a mere coincidence, or can we see here the DIs' signature?

Here is Alan Butler's latest opinion about the Scottish chapel:

> Rosslyn Chapel is without doubt one of the most remarkable and yet strangest structures to be found anywhere in Western Europe. There can be no doubt... that a multitude of ancient beliefs and observations went into its construction—many of which owe nothing to Christianity but everything to pre-Christian conventions. Included amongst these is the use of the Megalithic

---

[436] Malcolm C Duncan, *Duncan's Masonic Ritual and Monitor*, 1866, p. 77: http://sacred-texts.com/mas/dun/dun03.htm

[437] John J Robinson (1989), *Born In Blood: The Lost Secrets of Freemasonry*, Lanham, Maryland: M. Evans, 2009, p. 242

[438] Alan Butler and Christopher Knight, *Before the Pyramids: Cracking Archaeology's Greatest Mystery*, London: Watkins, 2009, p. 206

> yard. The Megalithic yard is most probably present within the dimensions of the chapel itself but this is hard to prove specifically because of the small size of the building. What is not in doubt is that the distance between Rosslyn Chapel and Rosslyn [Roslin] Castle, where the builders of the chapel lived, is a very definite 366 Megalithic yards – which of course also represents one second of arc of the polar circumference of the Earth when expressed in Megalithic geometry. This is particularly noteworthy since Rosslyn Chapel was also clearly built as a naked eye astronomical observatory, from which observations of the planet Venus especially would have been easy to undertake. Since the Megalithic yard is irrevocably tied to the observed movements of Venus, the orientation of the Chapel and its unparalleled view of an unobstructed sky from North, through East to South is especially appropriate. It has been suggested, though never proved, that Rosslyn Chapel was built upon the site of a much earlier structure, most probably a henge.[439]

Two centuries later, there is some evidence of DIs leaving Scotland and going south, penetrating London society. Before Freemasonry came public in London, its members may have met in what is termed the Invisible College, a precursor group to the Royal Society, which formed in the 17th century. According to Robinson,

> there was a new source of recruits for the Freemasons in Britain, men who had reason to meet to share their ideas and findings in secret, away from the eyes and ears of the church. Men of science in London, Oxford and Cambridge met in secret in what has been termed an 'invisible college,' which now appears to have existed in secret Masonic lodges in those areas. Their first known meeting was held in 1645... The man destined to become their most famous member, Sir Christopher Wren, was just thirteen at the time.[440]

Sir Christopher Wren (1632-1723), who later founded the Royal College, was a Freemason, just like every other founder of the society. Interestingly, he was an astronomer and a geometrician, and of course an architect who supervised the rebuilding of more than fifty churches in London after the Great 1666 Fire. Wren definitely looks like a DI.

Wren's greatest achievement is the rebuilding of St Paul's Cathedral. It is officially 111.3 meters high,[441] which converts into 365.15 feet... or is it

---

[439] From a personal communication

[440] Ibid., 243-4

[441] http://www.stpauls.co.uk/Cathedral-History/Explore-the-Cathedral/Climb-the-Dome

actually 366 feet? In addition, the distance between the center of St Paul's and the center of Temple Church, a 12th-century church which was the Knights Templar's headquarters, is a neat 1,000 MY (this distance, of course, if intentional, cannot be attributed to Wren). Now, of course, one could easily dismiss these results, claiming that the units used (feet and MY) are different. Fair enough. And London is not a Druidic Line location either. To be convinced we are not dreaming things up, we need an even more coherent pattern.

Oddly enough, we found that English DIs developed a parallel line system of their own, based on 360 degrees.

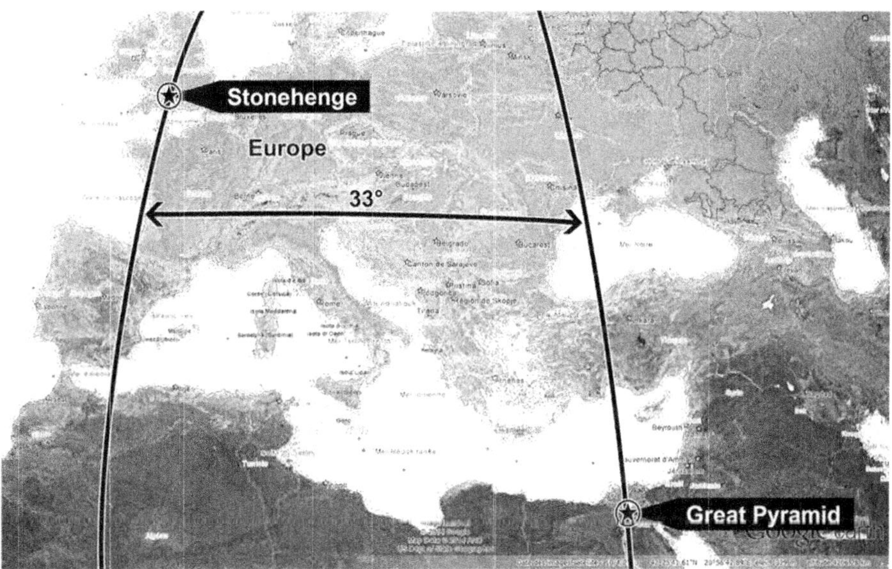

Fig. 71. There are almost exactly 33 modern arcdegrees between the Great Pyramid and Stonehenge.

The Amber Lines

Perhaps because (as we saw in Chapter Eleven) the Great Pyramid of Giza appears to play a cardinal role in the origin of Druidic knowledge, and because Stonehenge and Avebury are obviously the most important Megalithic sites of Britain, it seems that the English DIs developed a parallel world grid of their own, not with 366 degrees but with 360 modern degrees. First of all, they seem to have noticed that Stonehenge and the Great Pyramid are almost exactly 33 modern degrees apart in terms of longitude. (Was it a deliberate choice at the start? Had DIs known that all along?) Keeping in mind that 33 is a central number in

Freemasonry (there are 33 degrees in the Scottish Rite of Freemasonry), it seems likely that this particular number of degrees in the Scottish Rite was chosen by DIs *because it represented the longitudinal distance, in modern degrees, between two key places—Stonehenge and the Great Pyramid.* Granted, this is pure guesswork, but it really does make sense when you look at the whole picture and think about it in a rational way.In any case, when the British empire spread all around the world, British DIs seemingly decided to build their capital cities, or use existing cities, so that they would also be at round distances from Stonehenge (or the Great Pyramid) in 360-degree geometry.

Let us posit that Stonehenge, which stands on a 366-degree geometry Druidic Meridian at 01°50'W, also stands on a 360-degree geometry Amber Meridian. The Great Pyramid, which stands at 31°08' East of Greenwich, is only two arc minutes away from the nearest theoretical Amber Meridian (running at 31°10'E), which according to the definition we have been using all along this book, makes it an Amber Meridian location as well.

The expression *Amber Lines* derives from a discussion I had with a fellow researcher from Toulouse, Patrick Merle, who was the first one to spot this 360-degree world grid. Because I was using the expression *Golden Lines* (rather than Druidic Lines) for the 366-degree world grid at the time, he suggested using the expression *Amber Lines* (Amber Meridians and Amber Parallels) for this theoretical, similar system of lines crisscrossing the globe.

Interestingly, the MDM or Midway Druidic Meridian, which runs halfway between Stonehenge and Alesia at 01°07'E, is also by our definition an Amber Meridian location, as it runs only 3 arc minutes west of the 01°10'E Amber Meridian. Oddly, this last line is also what Mouny and Gruais called *le Méridien lumineux* (the Luminous Meridian or LM).[442] These two authors thought this line was of prime importance, as it is, according to them, the starting point of the Pyramids Line, and because its longitude is exactly 30° west of Giza. But Mouny and Gruais appear to have made a slight mistake, as the starting point of the Pyramids Line (on the coast) is actually (according to my own assessment) at the longitude 01°07'E (i.e. at the Druidic Meridian longitude), not 01°10'E (i.e. at the Amber Meridian longitude). What's more, Mouny and Gruais failed to see why this line was so important: as we are going to see, capitals of the British empire appear to have been chosen at round

---

[442] Guy-Claude Mouny and Guy Gruais, *Guizeh, au-delà des grandes secrets*, Paris: Editions du Rocher, 1997, p. 90

distances from this Amber Meridian they called LM, Luminous, rather than from Stonehenge, although that was also used at times, as we shall see.

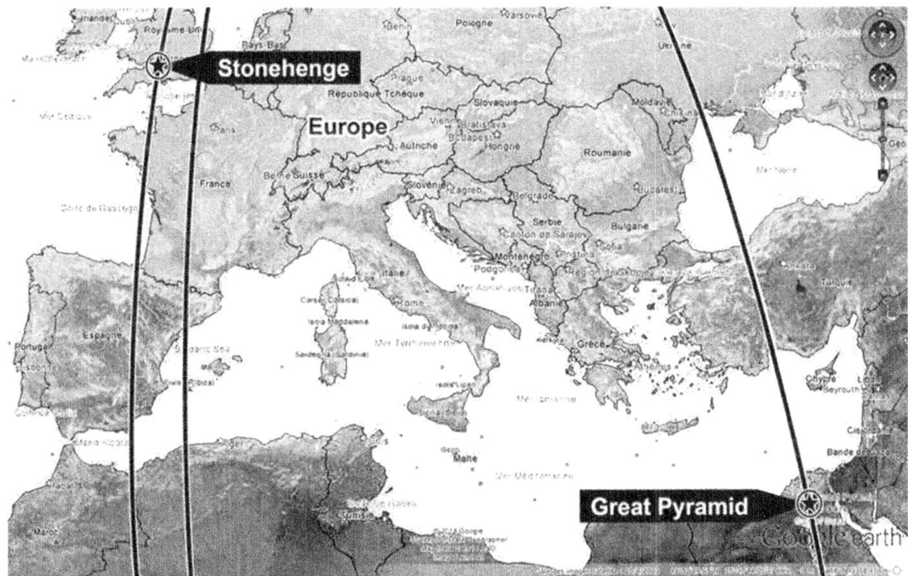

Fig. 72. Three Amber Meridians: The Stonehenge Meridian (which is also a Druidic Meridian), the 'Luminous' Meridian, and the Giza Meridian.

Quite incredibly, Australia's capital city, Canberra (long. 149°09'E), lies almost exactly 148° east of the LM, while the main city of the land down under, Sydney (long. 151°11'E), lies almost exactly 150° east of the LM, a round number—within one arc minute. This of course might look like a coincidence, but as it is known that the army units sent to Australia to guard the first British convicts exported Freemasonry there in their travelling military lodges, these results come as no surprise at all.

The likeliness of a mere coincidence significantly recedes when you study the British colonies in China. Hong Kong, a British colony until 1997 (long. 114°11'E) is located almost exactly 113° east of the LM. Shanghai is *not* an Amber Meridian location, but it is located very close to the Amber Meridian (long. 121°10'E) running at exactly 120° east of the LM, another round number, which also happens to represent exactly one-third of the Earth's circumference. The Amber Line actually flies over the suburbs of Shanghai, and as this city predates the arrival of the British, one wonders if the British who settled there in 1845 weren't DIs who were perfectly aware that this city stood almost exactly 120° from the LM.

Belmopan (long. 88°46'W), the capital city of Belize in Central America (earlier British Honduras), misses its status of Amber Meridian location by only one degree, standing only 4 arc minutes away from the Amber Meridian running at 88°50'W. Interestingly, this meridian runs at exactly 90° west of the LM, another round number which also happens to represent one-fourth of the Earth's circumference. Can all this be a series of meaningless coincidences, or were there among the British settlers DIs who influenced the course of history, selecting key locations in their secret 360-degree world grid?

If Georgetown, the capital city of British Guiana, is *not* an Amber Meridian location, the country is centered around the 58°50'W Amber Meridian, which also happens to be the meridian running at exactly 60° west of the LM, which of course represents exactly one-sixth of the Earth's circumference. As British Guiana is the only British colony in continental South America, it is really hard to conceive that this result is accidental. There must have been a willingness from the English DIs to settle places in these key points all around the globe.

Mbabane (long. 31°08'E), the administrative capital and the largest city of Swaziland, which became a British protectorate in 1903, is located only two arc minutes away from the nearest Amber Meridian, which also happens to run at exactly 30 degrees east of the LM, another round number which also represents exactly one-twelfth of the Earth's circumference. The same is true for Lobamba (long. 31°10'E), the traditional, spiritual and legislative capital city of Swaziland, which stands right on the same Amber Meridian. This meridian is also the one that flies over the Great Pyramid, and that skirts Cairo, which also became a British protectorate in the early 20th century. The landlocked country of Lesotho inside the Republic of South Africa, which became a British protectorate in 1868, is intersected by the 30°00'S Amber Parallel (while the Great Pyramid stands right along the 30°00'N Amber Parallel). Are these mere coincidences? Once again, it just defies common sense.

Kingston (long. 76°48'W), the capital of Jamaica, stands only two arc minutes away from the 76°50'W Amber Meridian. It was established in 1692 in the British colony of Jamaica, a quarter of a century before Freemasonry came public in London. It is located 78° west of the LM, or a neat 75° west of Stonehenge.

Port Stanley (long. 57°51'W), the capital city of the Falkland Islands, a British Overseas Territory, is only one arcminute away from the nearest Amber Meridian running at 57°50'W. It is located 59° west of the LM.

The port of Port Moresby (long. 147°09'E), the capital and largest city of Papua New Guinea, stands almost exactly on the nearest Amber

Meridian running at 147°10'E, 146° east of the LM. Port Moresby was established in 1873 by the English captain John Moresby, who named the settlement after his father.

Hamilton (long. 64°47'W), the capital city of the British Overseas Territory of Bermuda, is located only three arc minutes away from the 64°50'W Amber Meridian, itself running exactly 66° west of the LM.

Yangon (also known as Rangoon, long. 96°09'E), former capital of Burma and taken by the British in 1852, stands almost exactly on the 96°10'E Amber Meridian, running exactly 95° east of the LM.

Strill having doubts? New Delhi (long. 77°13'E), the capital of India, the greatest ex-British colony of all, stands only three arc minutes away from the nearest Amber Meridian running at 77°10'E, exactly 76° east of the LM.

Last but not least, Pretoria (long. 28°11'E), the administrative and de facto capital city of South Africa (Cape Town being the legislative capital), stands almost exactly on the 28°10'E Amber Meridian, itself running 27° east of the LM, or a neat 30° from Stonehenge (making the longitudinal distance an exact one-twelfth of the Earth's circumference). Needless to say that South Africa became a British colony in the early 19th century.

Are these astounding results accidental, or were most, if not all, of these cities founded or selected for their Amber Lines credentials? Just as was the case with Druidic Lines locations (most of them Druidic Meridian locations), apart from Lesotho all of these examples are Amber *Meridian* locations. Isn't there a recurrent pattern here? In my humble opinion, it certainly looks like the history of British Empire capitals was greatly influenced, even bent, by DIs who have long proved their irrepressible taste for geometry. As always though, the reader is left free to make their own conclusions.

The Greenwich Prime Meridian and a fearful symmetry

The Greenwich Prime Meridian was defined in 1851 and universally adopted during the 1884 International Meridian Conference held in Washington, DC. The French abstained from the vote, though, and continued to use their own meridian (the Paris Meridian, see Chapter Fourteen) in the ensuing decades, before following suit with the rest of the world. As most English people know, the Greenwich Prime Meridian passes through the Royal Observatory in Greenwich, London.

First of all, it must be noted that the Greenwich Prime Meridian is *not* an Amber Meridian, as those (as we have just seen) have their geographic coordinates ending in either -50'W or -10'E (based on Greenwich!).

What is funny about the Greenwich Prime Meridian (00°00'W/E) is that it is located as far west of the LM (01°10°'E) as the Paris Meridian (02°20'E) is located east of it: Were we to use the LM as the Prime Meridian of the world (00°00'W/E), the longitude of the Paris Meridian would be 01°10'E, while the longitude of Greenwich would be 01°10'W! So, coincidence or not, there is a perfect symmetry between the Paris Meridian and the (London) Greenwich Meridian, and the axis of symmetry is the LM!

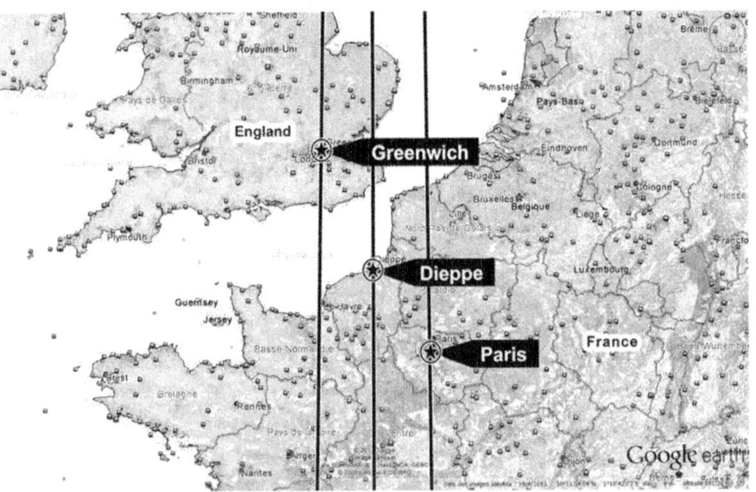

Fig. 73. The Greenwich Prime Meridian, the Paris Meridian, and the Luminous Meridian, which runs exactly halfway between the other two.

The reader will recall that the MDM also plays a similar role, as it is located halfway from the Stonehenge Druidic Meridian and the Alesia Druidic Meridian. And, as we saw in the previous section, the MDM (01°07'E) and LM (01°10'E) virtually represent the same line, with a difference of only three arc minutes.

So, to sum things up, it seems that MPDs first used the Stonehenge Druidic Meridian (which might have been their original Prime Meridian[443]); then the Celtic Druids used the Alesia Druidic Meridian, 6 Megalithic degrees east of Stonehenge; and then, in Roman times, Druids

[443] The River Jordan was either the Golden Prime Meridian, or merely the basis on which to create the Stonehenge Prime Meridian, running exactly 38 Megalithic degrees west of it.

(or DIs) might have used the MDM in between, arranging to have Rouen built right along it. Centuries later, the Paris Meridian was designed, and two centuries later the Greenwich Meridian was created. Most curiously, these last two meridians are almost equidistant to the MDM, and perfectly equidistant to the LM, these last two meridians being virtually one and the same thing.

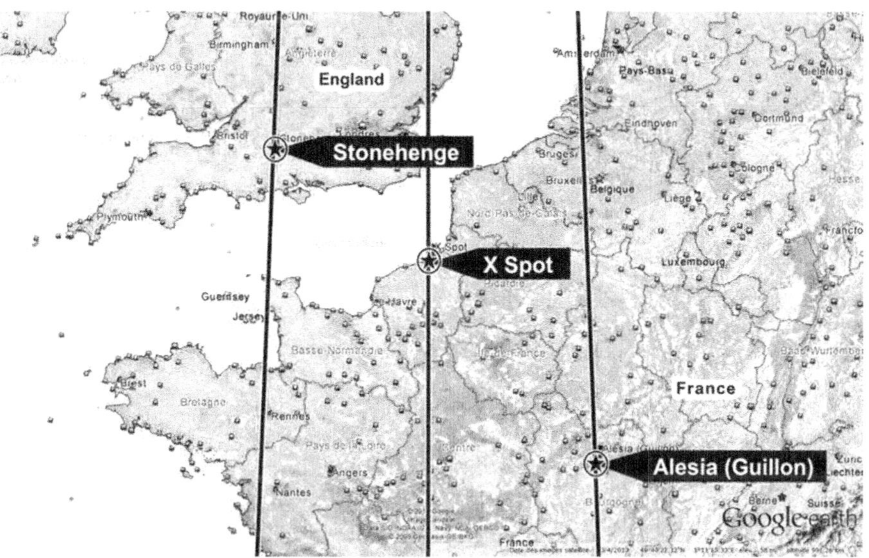

Fig. 74. The Stonehenge Druidic Meridian, the Alesia Druidic Meridian, and the Midway Druidic Meridian which runs exactly halfway between the other two.

Are we to believe that these 'fearful' symmetries are accidental, or are they yet another proof that behind the stages are people who 'know' and pull the strings of history—DIs in Paris and London who secretly allude to their own history, perpetuating this knowledge across millennia, perhaps once battling for primacy at the Washington, DC International Meridian Conference in 1884?

Interestingly, since the year 2000 the Paris Meridian has been referred to as the Green Meridian, as we saw in Chapter Fourteen, while Greenwich has green in its name, and ever since 16 December 1999 (half a month before the year 2000) a laser at the Greenwich Observatory has been shining a green light north across the London evening sky. Were these wishes to make these two meridians 'green' at the turn of the millennium, both in London and Paris, mere accidents of history, or do they show on the contrary that modern DIs in these two capitals still weigh over the course of history?

DIs in Washington DC Freemasonry

Did DIs cross the Atlantic and thrive in America? The quick answer is yes, they most probably did.

To make a long story short, it is quite known that the United States of America was founded by Freemasons. Although this is often disputed by 'rationalist' debunkers, and those who take an interest in this are sometimes labelled conspiracy theorists, there is no denying that George Washington, Thomas Jefferson and Benjamin Franklin were Freemasons. The last two signed the Declaration of Independence, along with 13 other Freemasons, while the first one became of course the first president of the United States. In all, nearly 27 per cent of the people who signed the Declaration of Independence were Masons,[444] which is quite considerable. In addition, Washington and Franklin both signed the Constitution. How many of the Founding Fathers were DIs is of course open to speculation.

Is there any evidence that these people were DIs? We have already seen that Benjamin Franklin was probably one of them, and that he certainly met other DIs during his time in France.

The most obvious pieces of evidence are to be found in Washington, DC, the capital city of the US. Here are the results from a field trip I undertook in the US capital in the summer of 2013. Fellow researcher Alan Butler wrote several books about Washington, DC,[445] showing beyond any reasonable doubt (see below) that the layout of the city revolves around units of distance that are multiples of 366 MY (i.e. 1 Megalithic arcsecond in terms of distance). Yes, incredible as it may sound, when the city was designed in the late 18th century, multiples of 366 MY were used, which can mean only one thing: these people knew about the 366-degree geometry that was used millennia before them by MPDs and Celtic Druids.

The layout of Washington, DC is known to have been designed by the French-born American architect Pierre Charles L'Enfant, who was a Freemason. He had been initiated in New York City in 1789. And there is little doubt he was amongst these high-ranking Freemasons who were also DIs.

---

[444] http://www.rapidnet.com/~jbeard/bdm/Psychology/mashist.htm

[445] See Alan Butler and Christopher Knight, *Before the Pyramids: Cracking Archaeology's Greatest Mystery*, London: Watkins, 2009, and Alan Butler, *City of the Goddess*, London: Watkins, 2011

Units of 366 Megalithic yards in Washington, DC

Let us briefly sum up Alan Butler and Christopher Knight's theory. Their investigation led them to believe that the Washington Ellipse (also called President's Park South, a public park located south of the White House), hides an underground chamber perhaps containing ancient secrets kept by high-ranking Freemasons. Very near its center is the Meridian Stone, which commemorates Jefferson's idea of a Prime Meridian running across Washington, DC. Butler and Knight carefully measured the length of the Ellipse from the center of the path on the west side of the Ellipse to its counterpart on the east side and found that the length was an exact 366 MY, *not* 1,000 feet as it is generally claimed. Although they measured it directly on the ground, this fact is also easy to check with the ruler instrument of Google Earth.

Incredible though it may sound, they then found out that distances between the Meridian Stone in the Ellipse to the centers of major Washington monuments were all multiples of 366 MY. For example, the distance between the Meridian Stone and the center of the Capitol building is almost exactly 8 x 366 MY (or 8 Megalithic arcseconds). In my reckoning, this is true to an accuracy of 99.79 per cent.[446] Is it just a coincidence?

Washington, DC is a very symmetrical city with an elaborate grid of crisscrossing streets and parks. The distance between the Meridian Stone to the centers of McPherson Square and Farragut Square, which are located northeast and northwest of the White House respectively, is 3 x 366 MY for each. I personally found this to be true to an accuracy of 98.6 and 99 per cent respectively.[447] Not completely convincing yet perhaps, but please bear with me.

Butler and Knight claim that the distance between the Meridian Stone and the centers of Logan Circle Park and Dupont Circle, still further to the north, are 6 x 366 MY. I found this to be untrue, but by my own reckoning, the distance is an exact 1 nautical mile, to an accuracy of 99.86 and 99.98 per cent respectively![448] It might be a haphazard result of course, but it does seem to indicate that major Washington features were located according to the center of the Ellipse. The nautical mile is a perfect subdivision of the Earth's circumference (it represents one modern arcminute along the meridian, or 1/60th of a modern degree).

---

[446] Google Earth data
[447] Ibid.
[448] Ibid.

Let us continue. Butler and Knight then claim that the distance between the Meridian Stone and the centers of Mount Vernon Square and Washington Circle Park, which are more to the south, is 5 x 366 MY. I found this to be true to an accuracy of 99.8 and 99.83 per cent respectively![449] How can all these results be accidental? They *could* be, of course, but it also means that we are incredibly lucky!

The District of Columbia itself, the federal district commonly referred to as 'DC,' was created in 1790, with each neighbouring state (Maryland and Virginia) giving land for its creation. DC was initially a perfect square in shape, but positioned like a diamond on the map, with each side being 10 miles long (in 1846 the territory of Alexandria in the southwest of the district was ceded to Virginia). By a curious coincidence, a distance of 10 miles is also almost exactly 53 x 366 MY: by using Thom's value of the Megalithic yard in England (2.722 feet, which precisely converts into 82.96656 cm), 53 x 366 MY = 16,093.85 m, which is 10 miles to an accuracy of 99.997 per cent! Is it an accidental result, or was the fact known by the founders of DC? Were it an isolated fact, the question wouldn't even be asked, but in the light of the aforementioned data, it certainly looks like an intentional choice.

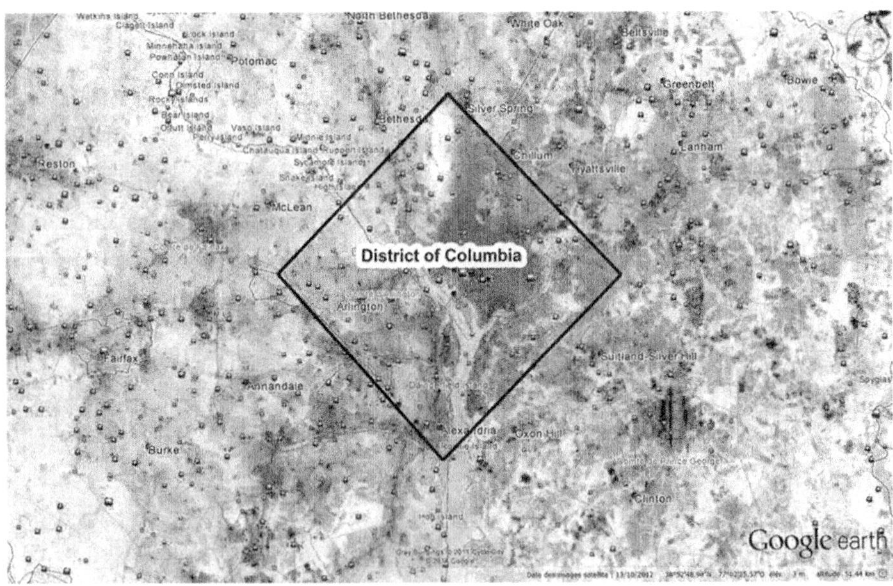

Fig. 75. Each side of the original square of the District of Columbia is exactly 53 x 366 MY long.

449 Ibid.

There are many other examples (see below). But let us pause for a minute. Butler and Knight think these lines, if drawn on a Washington map, draw a gigantic arrow pointing to the very center of the Ellipse, under which a presumed secret chamber was created in the 19th century. They think that Freemasons brought some secret documents there from the presumed chamber underneath Rosslyn Chapel in Scotland. I perfectly understand this statement might at first sight look like the synopsis of a Dan Brown novel—and yet it all seems to be true. Although the details of this story are outside the scope of the present book, it must be noted that their theory is highly convincing, not only because of the distances just mentioned (all of which express themselves in units of 366 MY), but also because the Ellipse belongs to the federal government of the US and will remain out of construction in the future. The Ellipse just looks like a dream place for a brotherhood of influential people wishing to keep there something concealed for the centuries to come.

More examples. The US Naval Observatory in northwest Washington, DC, which was built in the 1830s and 40s, is a perfect circle which has a diameter of nearly exactly 2 x 366 MY. According to the US Navy's official website, the Naval Observatory's mission is, *inter alia*, to '[d]etermine the positions and motions of celestial bodies, motions of the Earth, and precise time' and to '[p]rovide astronomical and timing data required by the Navy and other components of the Department of Defense for navigation, precise positioning, and command, control, and communications.' [450] According to Butler and Knight, the Naval Observatory is nothing else than a modern henge.[451] Incidentally, the Vice President of the United States has had its official residence on the grounds (called Number One Observatory Circle) since 1974.

This unit of 366 MY is the Megalithic arcsecond we think was used by MPDs in Britain several millennia ago. How on earth is it that it ends up in the most significant distances in the layout of the capital city of the United States? The most plausible explanation that comes to mind is that L'Enfant, and probably other Freemasons around him, were also DIs who were perfectly aware of 366-degree geometry. Improbable as it may sound, this sacred geometry must have been passed down for countless generations of Druids and DIs across the millennia, even crossing the

---

[450] http://www.usno.navy.mil/USNO/about-us/the-usno-mission

[451] Alan Butler and Christopher Knight, *Before the Pyramids: Cracking Archaeology's Greatest Mystery*, London: Watkins, 2009, p. 162

Atlantic in recent times. And apart from DIs, nobody ever suspected it even existed.

Fig. 76. The US Naval Observatory in Washington DC is a perfect circle with a diameter of almost exactly 2 x 366 MY.

A Masonic-Druidic Triangle in Washington, DC

Still not convinced? Just look at what follows.

Although Butler and Knight don't mention it, I found that the center of the circular pool in the Women in Military Service for America Memorial, located at the western end of Memorial Drive at the entrance to Arlington National Cemetery, was almost exactly 10 x 366 MY away from the Meridian Stone in the Ellipse, to an accuracy of 99.57 per cent.[452] The memorial was built in 1932, which of course implies that DIs continued to use units of 366 MY well after L'Enfant's time.

Let's now give a few more striking examples from Butler and Knight. We have seen in the previous section that the distance between the Meridian Stone in the Ellipse and the center of the Capitol building was 8 x 366 MY. The distance between the Meridian Stone and the Pentagon, the headquarters of the US Department of Defence, is a beautiful 10 x 366 MY. My own estimation of the distance yields an accuracy of 99.7

[452] Ibid.

per cent.[453] The distance between the center of the Capitol to the center of the Pentagon is a neat 15 x 366 MY. In my estimation, the result is true to an accuracy of 99.67 per cent.[454] These three places (the Meridian Stone in the Ellipse, the Capitol and the Pentagon) form a giant Megalithic triangle with sides of 8, 10 and 15 x 366 MY. These results are astounding, but true.

But let's not forget the grand finale:

$$8 + 10 + 15 = 33$$

We have already stressed the importance of 33 in the Freemasonic Scottish Rite, which has 33 degrees, as there are 33 modern degrees between Stonehenge and the Great Pyramid in terms of longitude.

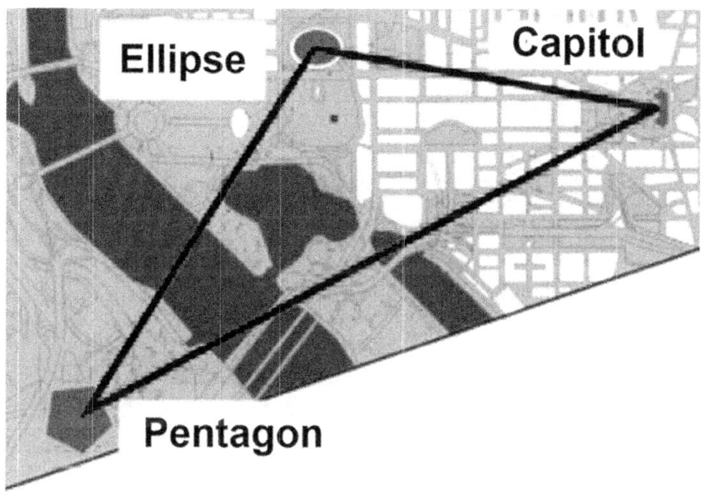

Fig. 77. Alan Butler and Christopher Knight's Washington DC Masonic Triangle, which has a perimeter of exactly 33 x 366 MY.

Ground was broken for the future Pentagon on 11 September 1941, which, by an extraordinary twist of fate, was 60 (a very Megalithic number) years to the day before it was struck by the 9/11 attacks. If the project was the brainchild of the then Secretary of War Henry L Stimson, President Franklin Delano Roosevelt personally involved himself in the design and even the precise location of the building, which at the last minute was shifted south from the previous location chosen to a slum then called Hell's Bottom.[455] An important detail to note is that President

---

[453] Ibid.
[454] Ibid.
[455] Alan Butler and Christopher Knight, *Before the Pyramids*, p. 191

Roosevelt is known to have been a 33rd-degree Freemason. He must have been a DI as well, because if the Pentagon weren't standing at the exact location it stands today, the Megalithic triangle described above simply wouldn't exist.

It is even to be wondered whether there are other degrees, even more secret than the official 33, above the 33rd, amongst which DIs hide from view, including that of most Freemasons. Although it is pure speculation, we can easily imagine that DIs are comfortably hidden at the very top of Freemasonry, say, at completely secret 34th, 35th and 36th degrees (wouldn't number 36 be quite appropriate for DIs?) that have never been made public. Those who are accepted at these levels would be (in the eyes of these DIs) the most deserving ones, the most trustworthy ones, those whom they deem are the best acquainted with Druidic knowledge and who will fully respect Druidic values.

Speaking of Entered Apprentices in Freemasonry, John J Robinson writes:

> New members of secret societies are confined to a small group of new and low-level members until their trustworthiness is beyond doubt, so that they can betray only a minimum number of their own low entry level, whether maliciously or by accident. To bolster that security, entry-level initiates are led to believe that they are full-fledged members fully acquainted with the leaders of the society. Ideally, they don't even suspect that there are higher levels and much more important members and superiors totally unknown to them.[456]

Such a concept can easily apply to the case of high-ranking Freemasons who, according to our hypothesis, are also DIs. To continue with the example of the Scottish Rite, we can imagine there are more strata than those that have ever been made public, say, 36 instead of 33, and only exceptionally deserving, exceptionally trustworthy 33rd-degree members are ever aware that there are higher levels—the DIs' levels.

The Pentagon

One additional stunning fact about the Pentagon, discovered by Butler and Knight, is that a circle around the five-sided building has a circumference of 5 x 366 MY, so the arcs of each of its sides have a length of 366 MY!

---

[456] John J Robinson (1989), *Born In Blood: The Lost Secrets of Freemasonry*, Lanham, Maryland: M. Evans, 2009, p. 228

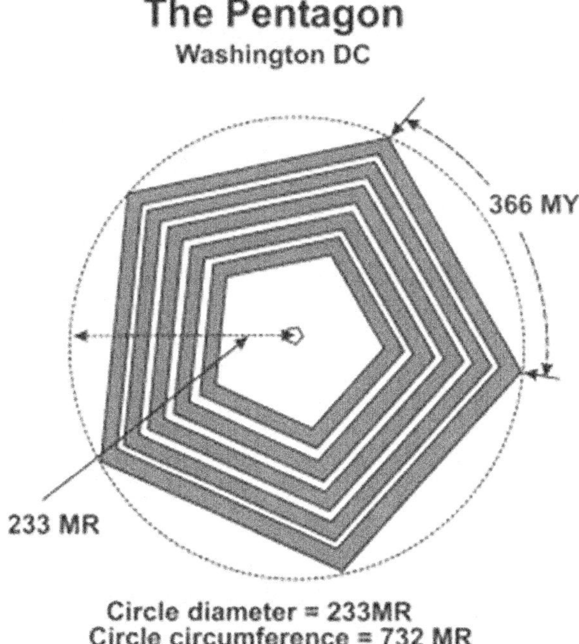

Fig. 78. Each of the five arcs of the Pentagon in Washington DC has a length closely approximating 366 MY.

According to Butler and Knight, this is true to an accuracy of 'over 99.9 per cent.'[457] Using the official length of the outer walls, 921.6 feet[458], however, yields arcs of only 361.9 MY, which implies that Butler and Knight's statement is true to an accuracy of 98.9 per cent only. But is the information given by the American government correct? After all, the Pentagon is the Headquarters of the US Department of Defense, and you do expect a certain amount of secrecy, discretion and possibly disinformation in such sensitive places, whatever the precise reasons might be. So, are the lengths that have been made public the exact ones? My first personal estimation of the radius length made a few years ago was 241.5 meters,[459] which implies arcs of 365.78 MY, which is 366 MY to an accuracy of 99.94 per cent. More recent estimations, however, yielded a radius of 239.9 meters, implying arcs of 363.36 MY,[460] which is not as close a result, but is still accurate to 99.3 per cent. Because the angles of the Google Earth satellite photos create slight deformations of objects on the ground, the ruler instrument cannot be 100 per cent accurate, so we have to work with a small margin of error which prevents us from knowing the exact truth.

---

[457] Alan Butler and Christopher Knight, *Before the Pyramids: Cracking Archaeology's Greatest Mystery*, London: Watkins, 2009, p. 189
[458] http://www.globalsecurity.org/military/facility/pentagon.htm
[459] Google Earth data
[460] Ibid.

Whatever the exact length of these arcs, one has to admit they are very close to being 366 MY long. In fact, in the light of what has been described in the previous sections, there are strong suspicions to think they *are* 366 MY long, and that the radius length was chosen by Roosevelt who, as we already mentioned, also personally selected the exact location of the future building—the only possible location for the 33 x 366 MY triangle to exist.

The New York City-Washington, DC distance

Let us end this chapter with a short statement: if you measure the driving distance between New York City and Washington, DC (for example with Google Map), you will find a curious result—366 km. That the most famous city in the world and the site chosen for the capital city of the United States are precisely 366 km distant by road might be just a coincidence... or not.

Main points

- **There are good reasons to believe that many Knights Templar escaped to Scotland and founded Freemasonry there**
- **There are many common points between Freemasons and Knights Templar, and between Freemasons and Celtic Druids, suggesting that high-ranking Freemasons today are still Druidic Initiates**
- **Stonehenge and the Great Pyramid are almost exactly 33 modern degrees apart, which could have led Scottish Rite Freemasonry to have 33 degrees**
- **Rosslyn Chapel and Roslin Castle are 366 MY apart**
- **An outstanding number of capital cities of the former British empire are located on Amber Lines, a 360-degree world grid whose Prime Meridian might be either the Luminous Meridian or Stonehenge**
- **Just like the Midway Druidic Meridian is an axis of symmetry to the Stonehenge Druidic Meridian and the Alesia Druidic Meridian, the Luminous Meridian (virtually the same line as the MDM) is an axis of symmetry to the modern Greenwich and Paris meridians**
- **Key founders of the United States and its capital, Washington, DC, were Freemasons who must have been Druidic Initiates as well**

- Key distances in Washington, DC, in particular relative to the Ellipse (the visible part of an underground chamber?) are units of 366 MY
- The Ellipse, the Capitol and the Pentagon form a triangle with a perimeter of 33 x 366 MY
- The Pentagon, which owes much to President Franklin D Roosevelt (a 33rd-degree Freemason) inscribes in a circle whose perimeter is nearly 5 x 366 MY
- The driving distance between New York City and Washington, DC is 366 km

Chapter Eighteen: France or the Druidic Country

There is strong evidence that DIs coming from Scotland didn't only settle in England in the 17th century, but also settled more to the south in France—the country where, a few centuries before, the Knights Templar (presumably their spiritual ancestors) had been hunted down. On the other hand, there is also some evidence that many DIs of Templar times never left France at all, passing down their knowledge across generations of DIs in total secret, yet still influencing the highest spheres of power. How else can be explained the fact that the coronation ceremony of French kings was performed in the Druidic Meridian city of Reims for so long?

The Golden château of Saint-Germain-en-Laye

Evidence of 366-degree geometry knowledge is not only palpable in France through the location of cathedrals in general, or because French kings were crowned in the Reims Cathedral in particular. The fact that two major French châteaux or palaces are also Druidic Meridian locations shows that kings themselves, or more probably people who could directly influence them without the monarchs suspecting it, were DIs.

The first striking example is the Château of Saint-Germain-en-Laye, located some 20 km west of Paris. In the first half of the 16th century the château soon became King Francis I's favourite. In 1539 the king completely transformed the former castle into the château that still exists today. If the earliest castle dates back to 1124, Francis I had many places to choose from to reconstruct an older castle into a Renaissance-style château. Why did he pick a location that was a Druidic Meridian location? True, it is situated a short distance from Paris. But it is also located just a few dozen yards away from the longitude of 02°06'E, which is the exact running of a Druidic Meridian. Was the king, who had been crowned in Reims in 1515, a DI who knew about the importance of that particular location? Alternatively, was he strongly influenced by DIs around him? How could this be yet another haphazard result?

The Golden palace of Versailles

In the second half of the following century, Louis XIV was also spending much of his time at the château of Saint-Germain-en-Laye, where he was born. In 1660 he suddenly decided to improve the marshy hunting grounds of his father Louis XIII to build the Palace of Versailles, one of the greatest palaces ever built in France, or even in Europe.

The Palace of Versailles was inscribed on the UNESCO World Heritage list as early as 1979 because it is, quite simply, one of the most famous châteaux in Europe, and because it 'provided Europe with a model of the ideal royal residence for over a century.'[461]

Like the Château of Saint-Germain-en-Laye, the Palace of Versailles is a Druidic Line location. It is located only one arcminute away from the Druidic Meridian of Saint-Germain-en-Laye, but further to the south.

Was the Sun King, who had been crowned in Reims, a DI as well? Or were there DIs smart and influential enough around him that weighed over his decision? One possible candidate was Nicolas Fouquet, Louis XIV's Superintendent of Finances from 1653 to 1661, and builder of the well-known Château of Vaux-le-Vicomte.

The Vaux le Vicomte-Marseillan Axis

In 1641, Nicolas Fouquet, a young man of only twenty-six years, inherited a fortune from his late wife, and then purchased grounds about 40 km southeast of Paris. Oddly enough, these grounds are located on the Minor Axis (see Chapter Fifteen). The Château of Vaux-le-Vicomte was built years later, from 1658 to 1661, exactly the time frame when Louis XIV decided to build his own palace in Versailles. Did Fouquet have anything to do with the King's decision to build his new palace there? Is it possible Nicolas Fouquet was a DI?

On 17 August 1661 Fouquet organised a dazzling fête in his brand-new luxurious château in honour of the king, with a copious banquet, a ballet comedy play in the gardens, and stupendous fireworks. Unfortunately for him, Louis XIV, only 22 at the time, felt humiliated by Fouquet's lavish party and his splendid château. Thinking the money of

---

[461] http://whc.unesco.org/en/list/83

the country had been ill-used by his superintendent, Louis had Fouquet arrested on 5 September, the very day of the king's birthday. Fouquet was later sentenced to life imprisonment.

What is so special about the Château of Vaux-le-Vicomte? First of all, Louis XIV was certainly right about the beauty of the small palace. The château and its surrounding gardens are absolutely splendid—in fact, it's my personal favourite French château. What's more, although it is *not* a Druidic Line location, the estate clearly follows an axis which is not exactly oriented north-south, but slightly deviating to the southeast. Stranger still, the village situated immediately to the north of the château is named St-Germain-Laxis. The last word is both reminiscent of the French word *l'axe* ('the axis') and the Latin word *axis*, as if we were urged to pay attention to an axis there.

If the ideas expressed in the previous paragraph sound far-fetched, this one might just look more surreal. In the summer of 2009, as I was holidaying in Calabria in southern Italy, I was approached by a very strange waiter in a restaurant. As he saw we were a French party, he accosted us and started to talk, saying he had spent much time in Paris. He said his name was Rocco and his age was quite advanced, whilst his eyes shone an odd twinkle and his lips always stood between seriousness and jocundity. He quickly added that he had spent time in southern France as well, in a small town called Marseillan on the Mediterranean coast. After less than five minutes of conversation, he said something completely unexpected: the Marseillan harbour was 'a very important place, with seven gates that mimic the Hebrew seven-branched menorah.' He looked at us very strangely, as if he meant to convey something else, or as if to check if I understood what he *didn't* say. Of course I didn't know what he was talking about, and why he was broaching such out-of-the-way subjects in such a disconnected context.

Later checking what he had said, I never found anything about a seven-gated port in Marseillan. A few years later though, I was stunned to see that prolonging the Vaux-le-Vicomte axis, starting from the village of Saint-Germain-Laxis, led straight to Marseillan. More baffling still, the length of this axis is... 366 miles! So, by starting the line in the middle of the Rue Grande, which is the main street of Saint-Germain-Laxis, and finishing it at the tip of the pier of the Marseillan-Plage port, you do not only perfectly overlap the axis of the Vaux-le-Vicomte gardens from north to south, you also draw a line segment whose length is an exact 366 miles[462] (to an accuracy of 100 per cent!).

---

[462] Google Earth data

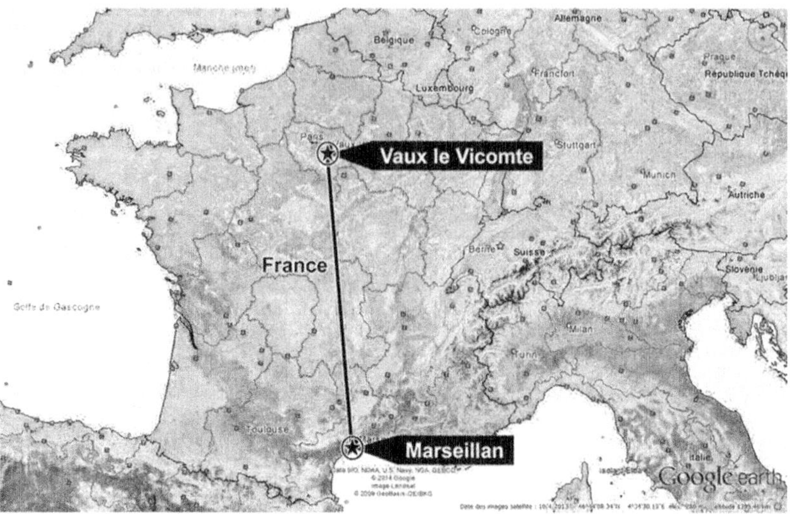

Fig. 79. The axis given by the gardens of the Château of Vaux-le-Vicomte, starting in the village immediately north of it (i.e. St.-Germain-Laxis) and ending at Marseillan on the Mediterranean coast, is exactly 366 miles long.

Fig. 80. Close-up on the gardens of the Château of Vaux-le-Vicomte. The axis of the gardens gives the direction of the 366-mile-long line ending at the Mediterranean, which aptly starts at the village of St.-Germain-Laxis (i.e. 'The Axis').

Does it mean that Rocco knew something about it? Was he a DI? Is Marseillan connected to the Holy Land? Was it the port used by the Knights Templar when they came back to France after they supposedly found something in Jerusalem? Did Nicolas Fouquet know that as well when he designed the gardens of his château? It certainly looks as if he did! Did Louis XIV suspect anything, and was the subsequent arrest of his superintendent somehow linked to this knowledge? Your guesses are just as good as mine.

Rather ironically, Fouquet spent the rest of his life behind the bars of the Pignerol prison (modern Pinerolo, Italy), which is located right on the Minor Axis too, if prolonged from Alesia. Fouquet's valet in jail was named Eustache Dauger, who might have been the mysterious Man in the Iron Mask according to the Encyclopaedia Britannica.[463] But this is another story. Let's not get too speculative and stick to the facts directly relating to Fouquet, which are mysterious enough.

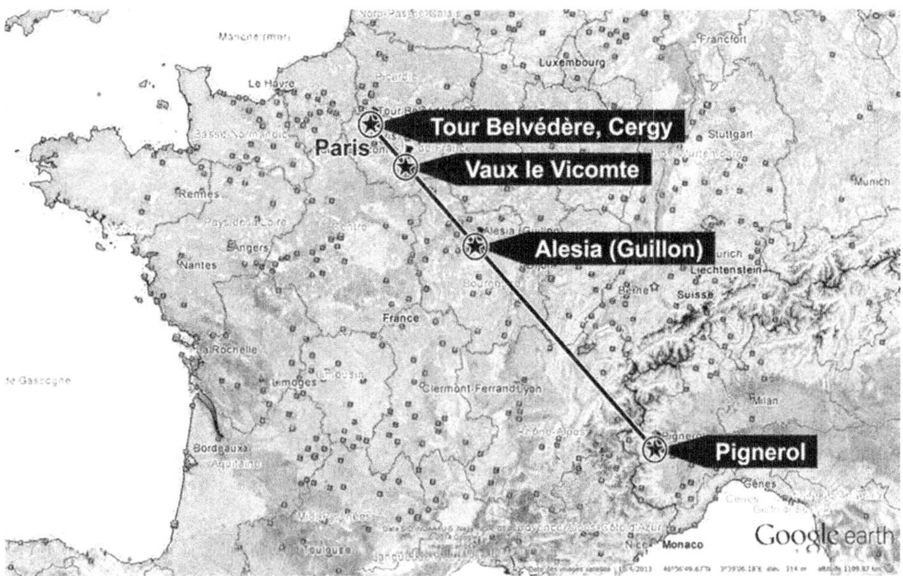

Fig. 81. The Minor Axis, if prolonged, flies right over Pinerolo, Italy (Pignerol in French), the place where Nicolas Fouquet was imprisoned until his death.

A very mysterious letter

Facts, though, are sometimes stranger than fiction.

Let us get back to April of 1656, five years before Fouquet's arrest. That year, the abbot Louis Fouquet—Nicolas Fouquet's brother—paid a visit to the French painter Nicolas Poussin (1594-1665), who spent most of his career in Rome. There, Louis Fouquet wrote a very unusual letter to his brother, by then promoted Superintendent of Finances to King Louis XIV. The letter is well-attested and most historians simply cannot

---

463 http://global.britannica.com/EBchecked/topic/294481/the-man-in-the-iron-mask

explain it rationally, for it doesn't seem to make sense. Talking about Poussin, Louis Fouquet wrote:

> He and I planned certain things of which I shall be able to inform you in detail in a short while, that will give you, through Monsieur Poussin, advantages (if you're not to scorn them) which kings would have great trouble to draw from him, and which after him perhaps no one in the world will ever rediscover in the centuries to come; and what is more this will be without great expenses and could even be turned to profit, and these are things so difficult to seek that nothing now on this Earth can have greater value nor be their equal.[464]

What these 'advantages' or 'things so difficult to seek that nothing on this Earth can have greater value nor be their equal' might be, is open to debate.

It is known that back in 1612 Poussin, then 18 years of age, had met King Louis XIII's personal mathematician. Did Poussin learn anything from him? In 1623 Poussin moved to Rome, but in 1640 Poussin had to come back to Paris at the request of King Louis XIII. Although reluctant at first, Poussin finally complied and travelled back to Paris, leaving his wife in Rome, to become the King's official painter. Poussin doesn't seem to have much enjoyed his life in the Louvre Palace, preferring travel to painting. In 1642 he finally left for Rome again (on the pretext he was going to persuade his wife to come to live in Paris) and never came back to France.

Was Poussin a DI? Was Poussin persuaded into becoming a DI at some juncture? Did he turn down the offer, which could explain why he finally exiled himself in Rome? Interestingly, Poussin was born in the town of Les Andelys, Normandy, very close to the Alesia-Stonehenge Sacred Line and the Druidic city of Rouen. Had he been initiated there very early in his life?

Nicolas Fouquet's rise to power

Whatever Poussin knew, it seems like Nicolas Fouquet learned about them through his brother Louis visiting Poussin in Rome. Nicolas Fouquet was a very ambitious man, and luck certainly served him well. Coincidentally or otherwise, Fouquet had bought the grounds for the future Château of Vaux-le-Vicomte during the two-year interlude when Poussin was back in France.

Why was Fouquet lucky? First of all, Fouquet married his first wife, Louise Fourché, dame de Quéhillac, in January of 1640. This was a good

---

[464] My translation

match because she brought in a significant dowry of 160,000 pounds. Then the next month Nicolas's father died at age fifty-three, and two months later Fouquet's wealth considerably inflated, as his father left him a huge inheritance estimated at 815,914 pounds—a real fortune in France at the time. On 22 December, 1640, five days after the recorded arrival of Nicolas Poussin in Paris, the Superintendent of Finances Claude de Bullion died. This was the position which Fouquet got a few years later. Fouquet then bought the domain at Vaux-le-Vicomte in February of 1641. Sadly, Fouquet's wife, Louise Fourché, died in August of that year, at the premature age of twenty-one. Upon her death, of course, Fouquet was again bequeathed a significant sum of money. Coincidentally, Fouquet's grandfather, on his mother's side, had also died in the first months of 1641, which made Fouquet head of the clan. To be sure, Fouquet found himself rolling in money. This newly-found wealth enabled him to gradually purchase more and more land at Vaux-le-Vicomte, making his domain vaster and vaster.

In July of 1642, Marie de' Medici—King Louis XIII's mother who had always fought for power—died in Cologne. In December of that same year, Cardinal Richelieu, the King's chief minister, also died at age fifty-seven. He passed away shortly after Poussin's departure. Finally, in May of 1643, King Louis XIII, aged only forty-two, breathed his last breath as well.

All these deaths—that makes seven of them—occurred within a time-span of just three years, and they greatly helped Fouquet's rise to power. Incidentally, this time interval roughly corresponds to Poussin's time in France. I'm not suggesting Poussin killed all these people, but that Fouquet might have been involved in *some* of these deaths remains a potential possibility. His wealth and connections certainly allowed him to have some of them poisoned, for example.

Louis XIII's demise, in particular, is quite mysterious. For six weeks the king experienced terrible diarrhoea and vomiting. His illness is today identified as Crohn's disease, an inflammatory bowel infection, but many historians believe that his personal doctor, Bouvard, gave him the *coup de grace*. Coincidentally, the king started to be sick shortly after Poussin arrived in France. Ironically, Louis XIII died on the same day of the year as his father Henry IV, who was stabbed to death on 14 May, 1610, exactly 33 years before the death of Louis XIII. Yes, *thirty-three* years—a very Masonic number, three quarters of a century before Freemasonry came public in London!

Did Fouquet arrange to have the king poisoned? Was Louis XIII given a bigger shot of poison on 14 May, 1643? Was the king's doctor,

Bouvard, one of Fouquet's accomplices? Had Bouvard been generously bribed by Fouquet to poison the king?

Well, we shall probably never know, of course. Maybe all these deaths were just happy twists of fate for Fouquet. Or maybe did Fouquet lead a conspiracy against the all-powerful French monarchy of the time, which also helped his own rise to power? When Louis XIII died, his son Louis XIV was only a five-year-old child. The death of all these most prominent figures of French royalty of the time allowed Fouquet to have elbow room in a country which had lost its heads. In the ensuing years Fouquet did everything to serve his ambitions, and it finally paid off—ten years later, he succeeded into becoming the king's Superintendent of Finances and right-hand man.

Is Fouquet a DI who turned sour? Or were there among the DIs of the time people who wanted to get rid of French monarchy, which they viewed as tyrannical? Or did Fouquet simply ill-use Druidic knowledge given him by Poussin?

Fouquet's family symbol was a squirrel with the motto, *Quo non ascendet?*, a Latin phrase meaning 'What heights will he not scale?' Well, he seems to have scaled them all... that is, until his own downfall, of course.

A bit more than a century later the Americans and the French had their revolutions, with many actors in them Freemasons. Although there were Freemasons among both the French pro-and anti-revolutionaries, major pro-revolutionary figures include Freemasons such as Danton, the Duke of Orléans, Hébert, Marquis de Lafayette, Marquis de Condorcet, Mirabeau and Voltaire. Were they DIs? Did they finish the job Nicolas Fouquet was not able to complete a century earlier? Whatever the truth, the motto of the GODF (Grand Orient de France, the largest French Masonic lodge, and also the oldest one on the continent) is *Liberty, Egalité, Fraternité* ('Liberty, Equality, Brotherhood'), which remains the motto of the French Republic today, going back to the French Revolution. According to the GODF's official website, Masons were 'in both camps' people debating the necessity of a revolution in France, and 'the Masonic sociability and the functioning of lodges have certainly greatly contributed, perhaps unconsciously in many cases, to the spreading of novel ideas.'[465] Just unconsciously? Or were they perfectly aware of what they were doing?

---

[465] http://www.godf.org/index.php/pages/details/slug/histoire-de-la-franc-maconnerie

Number 36

We saw in Chapter Fourteen that there were 36,600 *communes* in France, as if this outstandingly high number had been planned and ultimately achieved by DIs as part of their secret agenda, although the reasons for doing this remain unclear. Is it just symbolical? A signature? Is it a way to signify the importance of number 366 and base 10 to future generations? Or is it just a meaningless coincidence?

Just for the sake of it, here is a short speculative parenthesis.

Is it a coincidence if the headquarters of the Parisian criminal division of police are often referred to as *36, quai des Orfèvres* (literally, '36 Goldsmiths Wharf') from the address of the building on the Ile de la Cité, near Notre Dame Cathedral? Haven't DIs proved that they were the goldsmiths of history and that 36 was one of their favourite numbers? Isn't it funny that their close British equivalent, Scotland Yard, named so because a street named Great Scotland Yard is also the rear entrance of the original headquarters of the Metropolitan Police Service of London, might also discreetly allude to the Megalithic yard, perhaps first designed by MPDs very long ago in Scotland? To be true, I do not personally believe there is anything more than mere coincidences in these two cases, yet, in the light of what we have uncovered about Druidism and the remarkable influence of Druids throughout history (MPDs in the remote past, Celtic Druids 2,000 years ago, DIs in more recent times), I can't help wondering if these examples might not be deliberate, tongue-in-cheek hints of their existence, knowledge and secret influence over society.

Is it also just a coincidence if French children have only 36 weeks of school in a year? Is it just a happenstance if *trente-six* (French for '36') is often used as a placeholder number usually meaning 'a lot' in the French language? France is by no means the only country where number 36 holds an importance. An English yard, for example, divides itself into 36 inches, and in the United Kingdom, a standard beer barrel is 36 gallons.

More generally speaking, is it just an accident of history if the Book of Numbers in the Bible has 36 chapters? If what is referred to in the Bible as the Number of the Beast (666) is the sum of the first 36 integers? And if the chemical element whose atomic number is 36 is krypton, which comes from the Greek *kryptos*, meaning 'the hidden one'?

And by the way, in a regular pentagram (i.e. a five-pointed star) the four fundamental lengths are in golden ratio (Phi) to one another, whilst each angle of the points is exactly 36 degrees, which is also, of course, 36.6 Megalithic degrees. Strange.

Fig. 82. In a regular pentagram the four fundamental lengths are in Golden Ratio (Phi) to one another, whilst each angle of the points is exactly 36 modern degrees (or 36.6 Meg. degrees)

The shape of France or the Druidic ideal

What about the shape of the country itself? In French media and literature, France is often metonymically referred to as 'The Hexagon,' due to its shape, which is roughly six-sided. Of course it hasn't always been so. Now, you may ask, why would have some very influential French people endeavoured to make France a six-sided country?

Fig. 83. The Square and Compasses symbol of Freemasonry perfectly fits into the French territory, with each tip of the tools pointing at the six points of the hexagonal country.

The question is more easily answered with a diagram than with extended sentences: because it is a perfect symbolical expression of a six-sided star or, better still, of the Square and Compasses, which in my humble opinion is as much a Druidic symbol as it is a Freemasonic emblem. Of course it might just be a coincidence, but I can't think of any other country on Earth (and I have a world map before my eyes at this very moment) with such a geometrical, symmetrical shape. That this country is also the one where Druids of yesterday lived, and one amongst the modern countries (along with the US and Britain) where DIs still seem more active than ever, is either another extraordinary coincidence, or else more evidence of the DIs' efforts to load the landscape (and indeed political borders) around them with heavy-duty symbology.

The *Cité de l'or* or City of Gold

What about the letter G in the middle of the Square and Compasses symbol, you may ask? First of all, it should be pointed out that French Freemasons, in their symbology, do not use the capital G in the middle of the Square and Compasses as the English-speaking Freemasons do.

Now what do we have at the center of the hexagon-shaped country? Do we strike Gold? (Yes, in English, Gold starts with a G—just like Geometry, God and the Great Architect of the Universe!) The simple answer is, yes, we do.

The center of France is supposed to be located at the Tour Malakoff,[466] a tower named after the victorious troops of Napoleon III in the battle of Malakoff during the Crimea campaign of 1855. The tower is in the middle of nowhere, in a field just outside a hamlet appropriately named La Tour ('The Tower'). The nearest city is Saint-Amand-Montrond, whose subprefecture building is about[467] (please don't ask me why) 3.66 km from the tower. Should anyone criticise the choice of the subprefecture building as the center point of the city, it must be stressed at once that this very building is the reference point of the city on both Google Earth and the French IGN maps provided by the website Geoportail,[468] an online web mapping service provided by the French government.

In the suburbs of the city is the *Cité de l'or* (the 'City of Gold'), a 34-meter-high blue glass pyramid with four apices which was opened in the year 2000 to celebrate the city's long history of goldsmiths and jewellers. It is located exactly 2.26 km (which is also 3.66/Phi km!) away from the tower.

Is the Cité de l'or celebrating the figurative Goldsmiths of History and Geography (i.e. DIs) as well as the literal goldsmiths of the city? Is the Cité de l'or the central G (the G-spot?) of the Freemasonic symbol, right in the heart of six-sided France, which itself is a symbolic representation of the Square and Compasses?

---

466 *Quid 2000,* Paris: Robert Laffont, 1999

467 Depending where you place the arrival point on the building

468 http://www.geoportail.gouv.fr/

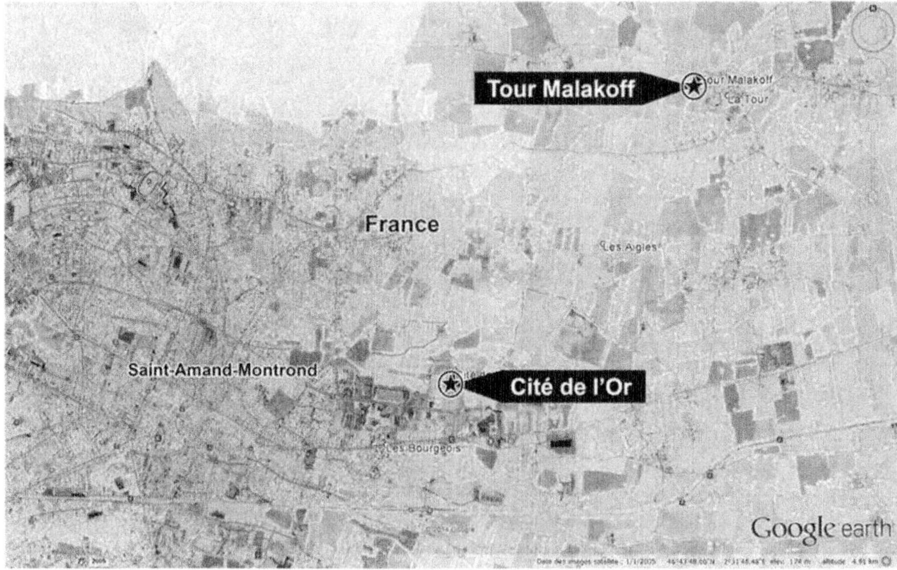

Fig. 84. The Tour Malakoff, which is supposed to stand at the very center of France, is 3.66 km from the subprefecture building of Saint-Amand-Montrond, while the Cité de l'Or (the 'City of Gold' Pyramid) stands exactly 3.66/Phi km away from the tower.

The Modulor

In the 1940s the Swiss-born French architect Le Corbusier developed a scale of proportions based on the human body. His wish was to create a harmonious scale reconciling the metric and imperial systems, whilst at the same time using the golden ratio, as the navel is positioned almost exactly at the golden proportion of the human body (navel at 1.619 vs. Phi = 1.618). He christened this scale the Modulor, a portmanteau word blending the words *module* and *or*, the second one meaning 'gold,' in reference to the golden ratio.

Claiming that a height of 6 feet (1.829 meters) was the 'ideal' height for a man because 'in English detective novels, the good-looking men, such as policemen, are always six feet tall,' Le Corbusier decided that the Modulor Man's height should be 1.83 meters, whilst his raised arm would reach the height of 2.26 meters. At least, so the conventional story goes. Is there any chance that Le Corbusier's explanation is a mere 'cover story'?

Isn't it quite astonishing that the famous architect used a height of 1.83 meters, which is exactly half of 3.66 meters, rather than any other height? To be fair, Le Corbusier had initially settled for a height of 1.75

m, which better corresponds to an average Frenchman's height, but he later modified it to the height of the 'English detective.' And isn't it quite astonishing that the extended arm of his Modulor Man, according to his definition, reached 2.26 meters, which is nothing else than 366/Phi meters, *again*?

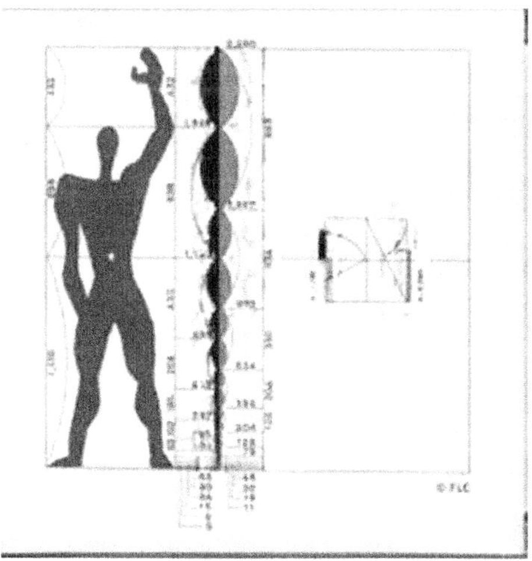

Fig. 85. Le Corbusier's Modulor Man has a height of 183 cm (which is exactly half of 366 cm), whilst his raised arm reaches the height of 226 cm (or 366/Phi cm).

Le Corbusier definitely looks like a DI who tried to push forward a system quite obviously derived from 366-degree geometry, to which he must have been initiated.

Two Golden Zions

Mount Zion, transliterated *Sion* in French, is the name of a sacred mount in Jerusalem, on which is a place known as the City of David. Although it is distinct from the Temple Mount, Zion is often used as a metonym meaning either the Temple Mount, or even Jerusalem itself.

Several places are called Sion in France and Switzerland. Two are especially interesting to us, as they are both situated on mounts and because they are both Druidic Line locations as well.

The first one is Sion, which is located in Valais, a French-speaking canton of Switzerland. The city is dominated by the Valère basilica (also called Valère castle) which stands on a rocky mount. This site is a perfect Druidic Parallel location, as it is precisely located on the 47th Druidic Parallel north of the equator. Although the name Sion derives from the Latin name *Sedunum*, the fact that it has been called Sion for several centuries makes it symbolically interesting, as this holy place echoes

Mount Zion in Jerusalem, both in name and situation. Interestingly, the basilica was founded at the time of the Knights Templar.

The second Sion which interests us is a mount called *Colline de Sion-Vaudémont*, the hill of Sion-Vaudémont, in northeastern France. This mount was already a sacred place in Celtic times. On the hill stands the Notre Dame de Sion basilica, whose oldest parts go back to the 15th century. A novel written by French writer Maurice Barrès in 1913, *La Colline inspirée* (translated as *The Sacred Hill)*, tells the story of three monks who decide to turn the mount into a place of worship. The book, which is considered as one of the best French novels of the first half of the 20th century, starts with the famous sentence, 'There are places where the spirit breathes.' A monument dedicated to Maurice Barrès was built in 1928 on the highest point of the mount.

The Sion-Vaudémont hill is a Druidic Meridian location. It is located about one or two arc minutes east of the 06°02'E Druidic Meridian, depending which side of the mount is taken as a reference point, as it is quite wide. Did Maurice Barrès know about Druidic Lines? Was he a DI? Of course, we can't know for sure, but again, there is strong suspicion he did.

But the strangest aspect of these two Sion hills is to come.

The Internet and CERN

The first odd thing about these two mounts called Sion is that the distance between them is almost exactly 161.8 miles, or 100 x Phi miles, depending of course on the starting and ending points you use. The distance between the center of the Valère basilica in Sion, Valais, to the Maurice Barrès monument in Sion-Vaudémont is 162.07 miles, which is 100 x Phi to an accuracy of 99.84 per cent.

The oddest thing of all about these two Sions is what lies at the intersection of the two Druidic Lines on which they are located—the CERN headquarters!

The CERN or European Organization for Nuclear Research, which lies at the Franco-Swiss border in the Geneva suburbs, houses the Large Hadron Collider, which is the world's largest and most powerful particle collider. The huge particle accelerator lies in a vast circular tunnel which is 27 km in circumference. As most people know, the aim of the giant collider is to address, and try to solve, some of the most fundamental questions of physics, such as understanding the deep structure of space and time, studying the possibility that other dimensions exist in the universe, or investigating the nature of dark matter.

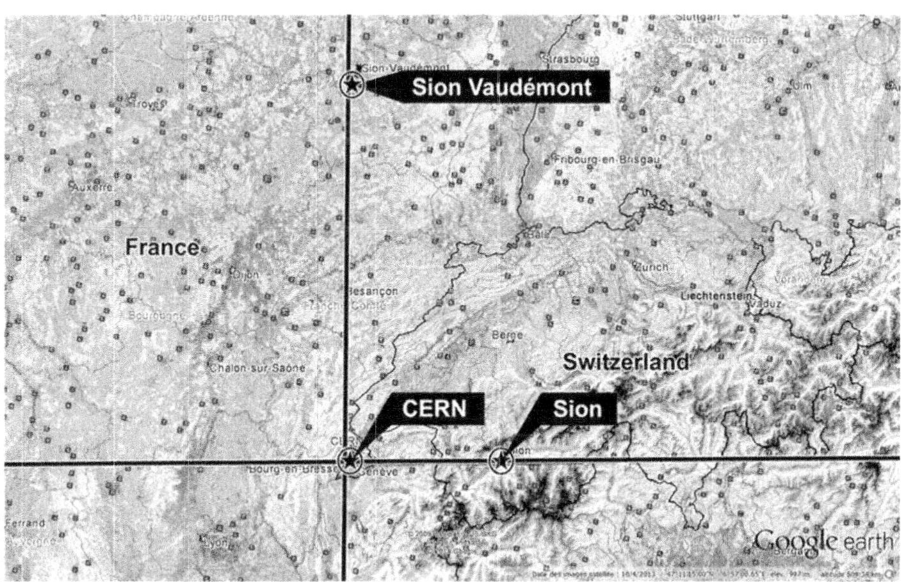

Fig. 86. Sion-Vaudémont, France and Sion, Switzerland are both located on Druidic Lines which intersect at the CERN in Geneva. In addition, the distance between the two Sions is almost exactly 161.8 miles (Phi x 100 in miles).

Just as interesting, the World Wide Web that most of us now use on a daily basis when browsing the Internet, was invented by British computer scientist Tim Berners-Lee and Belgian computer scientist Robert Cailliau in 1990 at the CERN.

Incredible though it may seem, the location chosen for the CERN is the intersection of two Druidic Lines, but not just *any* Druidic Lines—those with a *Mont Sion* on them. What are the odds for this to be coincidental?

The CERN library, which is circular, has a diameter of almost exactly 183 meters, which of course is half of 366.

Want more? There is another Sion in the neighbourhood—a small village called Sion, renamed Val-de-Fier recently, which is situated in the French *département* of Haute-Savoie more to the southwest. Using the largest building of the CERN headquarters as a starting point, the Château de Sion is located at a distance of exactly 36.6 km from the CERN (to an accuracy of 100 per cent). On our way there, in a beeline, the line intersects another château, the Château des Roches, which stands at a distance of 22.6 km (36.6/Phi km)!

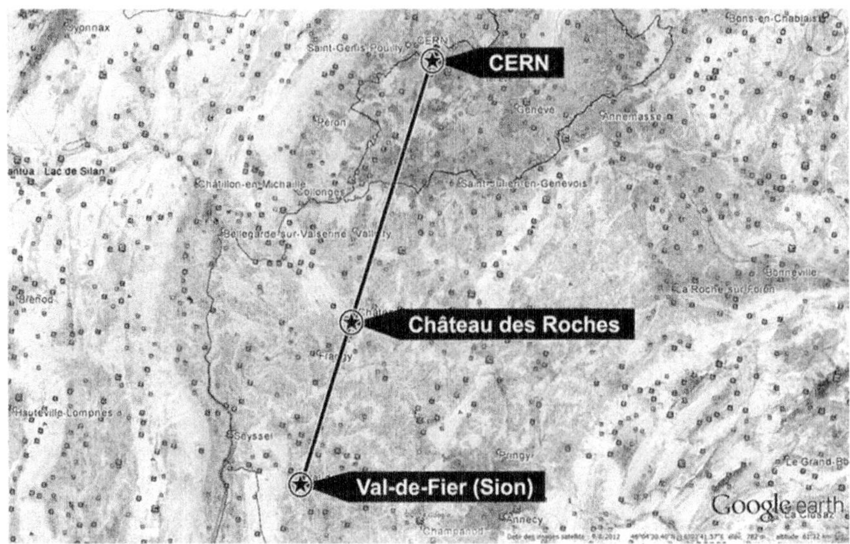

Fig. 87. The distance between the largest building of the CERN headquarters and the Château of Sion (the village of Sion is now called Val-de-Fier) is exactly 36.6 km, whilst the distance between the CERN and the Château des Roches, which stands on the way, is 36.6/Phi km.

The Sion connections to the CERN are simply mind-boggling, especially when one realizes that the CERN is a cutting-edge scientific location on Earth, that the World Wide Web is absolutely central in 21st-century everyday life, and that the Large Hadron Collider is basically the modern avatar of a henge—we might call it a *superhenge* that is here to study not the stars and the cosmos, but the microcosmos, the very structure of the matter the universe is made of.

Now, if these connections are not accidental, we have yet to explain them. Why would influential DIs make their best efforts to have the CERN built at the intersection of two 'Sion' Druidic Lines? Maybe because in the eyes of DIs, who might count in their spiritual forefathers the Knights Templar, Mount Zion in Jerusalem is the sacred place *par excellence*, and the CERN's scientific ambitions are nearly divine. In a way, what scientists working at the CERN are trying to do is to explore the deepest secrets of the Great Architect of the Universe. In DIs' minds, the CERN may be the ultimate Zion, the Zion of all Zions or, more aptly, the Sion of all Sions.

Main points

- The Château of Saint-Germain-en-Laye, King Francis I's favourite residence, is a Druidic Meridian location
- The Palace of Versailles, built for Louis XIV, the Sun King, is a Druidic Meridian location too
- Nicolas Fouquet's Château of Vaux-le-Vicomte indicates a 366-mile-long axis that ends up in the Mediterranean port of Marseillan
- There is some evidence that Fouquet heard about Druidic knowledge from French painter Nicolas Poussin, who may have been a DI
- There is some evidence that DIs tried, and eventually succeeded in, overthrowing the French monarchy
- France is a six-sided country which looks like the Square and Compasses Freemasonic symbol
- The 'City of Gold,' right in the center of France, is a four-apex pyramid associated with number 366 and Phi
- The Modulor, created by architect Le Corbusier, is a scale of proportions apparently based on number 366 and Phi
- Two major Sion ('Zion') hills in France and Switzerland are also Druidic Line locations
- The CERN (which houses the world's largest particle accelerator and the place where the World Wide Web was invented) lies at the intersection of the two Sion Druidic Lines
- The CERN, which is a sort of superhenge aiming at understanding the deepest secrets of the universe, is also closely associated to number 366 and Phi

Chapter Nineteen: Astana and the Giza Connection

As incredible as it might look to laypeople, there is hardly any doubt left that Druids are still among us, two full millenniaafter Caesar. Although they don't call themselves Druids any more, these DIs still leave evidence that they are the masters of a 366-degree geometry that was already in use amongst presumed MPDs five millennia before us. This evidence is to be found in France, in the very Gallic lands where Caesar once found them; in Britain, where the Megalithic people once erected Stonehenge and the Ring of Brodgar; and even in America, where their astronomical and geometrical knowledge was most apparently exported with Freemasonry more recently.

In fact, in our increasingly globalised world, the footprint of DIs can be found in the remotest lands including, for example, the Republic of Kazakhstan in Asia. But why Kazakhstan?

The Druidic city of Astana

Astana, which means 'capital' in Kazakh, has been the capital city of the ex-Soviet republic of Kazakhstan since 1997. The city was founded in 1830, and in 1991, when the country became independent, it was named *Akmola*, meaning 'White Temple.' One year after becoming the new capital of the country (in 1998) it was renamed *Astana.*

Why did Almaty, the former capital and largest city of Kazakhstan, lose its status of capital? Why was Akmola, which became Astana, granted this favour? True, Almaty stood in a seismic zone and was not in a central position. On the other hand, Astana lies in an isolated area in the Kazakh steppe with extremely long, freezing cold, windy winters (with temperatures easily going down to -35°C in January) and very hot summers (rising to +35°C in July), making the choice highly controversial in Kazakhstan.

Is there another reason, unbeknownst to most people and known only to a select few, for electing Astana as the new capital? First and foremost,

Astana is a Salt Line location, as it is located right on the 52nd Druidic Parallel north of the equator. Yes, this is the same Druidic Parallel where Stonehenge was erected thousands of years before Astana. Incidentally, Glastonbury (traditionally said to be 'the holiest earthe [sic] of England') also stands right on this Druidic Parallel. Glastonbury Tor, believed by some to be the legendary island of Avalon (although in the author's view Avebury is a much more likely candidate) because it once was an island, may owe its 'holiness' to the fact that it is a Druidic Line location, and not just any Druidic Line location—a place located on the *Stonehenge* Druidic Parallel.

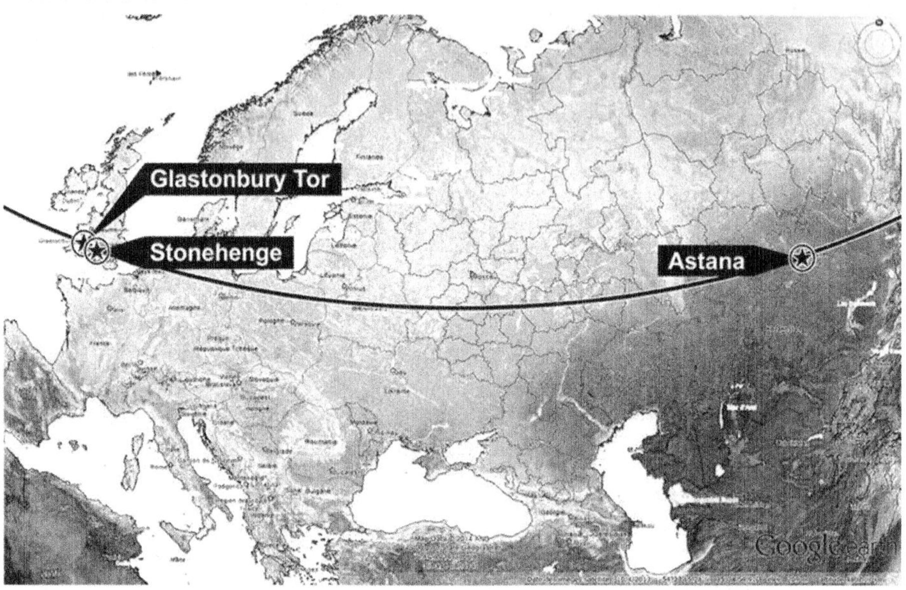

Fig. 88. The Glastonbury Tor, Stonehenge, and Astana (Kazakhstan) all stand along the same (52nd) Druidic Parallel.

Is it just a coincidence if Astana is also on this Stonehenge Druidic Parallel? Well, of course, it might be. However, Astana is much more than a simple Druidic Line location.

First of all, the main modern monuments of Astana follow an axis. The huge Ak Orda Presidential Palace, built south of the city, stands on a three-mile axis extending from the Khan Shatyr Entertainment Center, a giant transparent marquee, to the Palace of Peace and Reconciliation, a glass pyramid whose goal is to unite the world's different faiths, which we shall call the *Peace Pyramid.* Also on this axis stands the Bayterek observation tower. Interestingly, the distance between the Presidential Palace and the Peace Pyramid is an exact 4 x 366 MY (as far as I can assess it, to an accuracy of 100 per cent). Is Astana a futuristic, Washington DC-like, Druidic city?

Right in between the Presidential Palace and the Peace Pyramid, a gigantic dove-shaped pool has been constructed on the ground. Interestingly, the tip of the dove's beak lies at the golden section (Phi = 1.61803...) of the distance between the centers of the Presidential Palace and the Peace Pyramid. The pyramid itself is 203 feet high, which is also 61.88 meters, which is highly reminiscent of the golden section (1/Phi = .61803...). Finally, the height of the Presidential Palace is 80 meters or 262 feet, which is also highly reminiscent of Phi, as $Phi^2 = 2.61803...$.

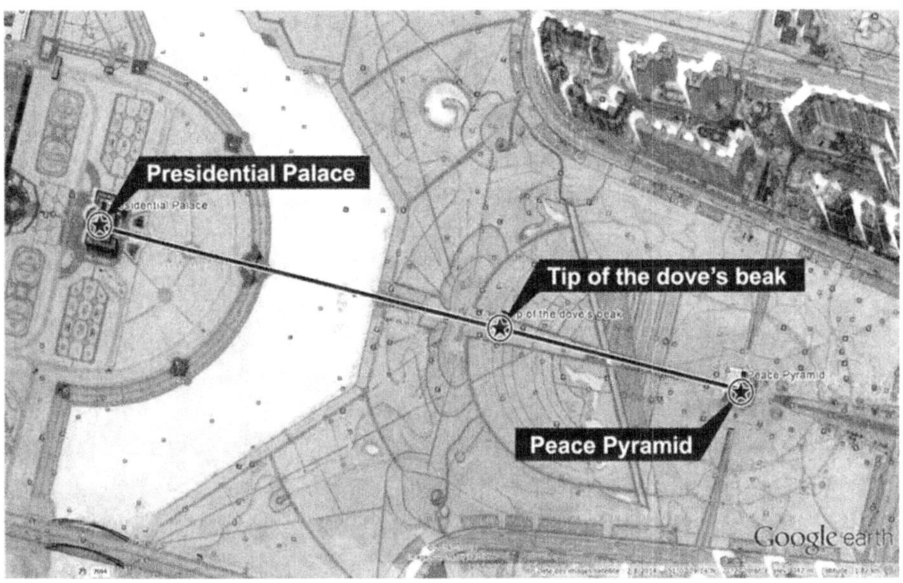

Fig. 89. The distance between the Presidential Palace and the Peace Pyramid in Astana is exactly 4 x 366 MY, whilst the tip of the symbolic dove's beak on the ground lies at the Golden Section.

Both the Khan Shatyr Entertainment Center and the Peace Pyramid were completed in 2006, and both were designed and built by Fosters and Partners, an architectural firm based in London.

Astana thus seems linked to Stonehenge and London, and to 366-degree geometry. It is also, in quite obvious a way, a hymn to Phi, the Divine Proportion. Is it just a fanciful interpretation, or have we spotted yet another proof that Druidism is still alive and kicking thousands of miles from home, thousands of years after it was probably born?

The Great Pyramid-Astana Peace Pyramid Arc

Here comes what might be the final proof.

Remember the Great Pyramid-Newgrange Arc described in Chapter Eleven? The distance between the Great Pyramid of Giza and the Megalithic circular mound of Newgrange in Ireland is an exact one-tenth of the Earth's equatorial circumference. Ironically enough, Newgrange is as much a 'White Temple' as Astana, which was also dubbed 'White Temple' not so long ago.

The distance between the Great Pyramid and Astana's Peace Pyramid is 4067.79 km. True, this number is not that close to a one-tenth section of the Earth's polar or equatorial circumference. But please bear with me for a few more seconds, and remember another aspect of the Great Pyramid-Newgrange Arc. We saw in Chapter Eleven that this arc nicely followed the western part of the Nile Delta, intersecting the Mediterranean coastline precisely 180 km away from Giza. As 180 is exactly half of 360, it is a clear allusion to 360-degree geometry.

The astounding thing is that the Great Pyramid-Astana Peace Pyramid Arc also nicely follows the Nile Delta but on its eastern side, and intersects the Mediterranean coastline precisely 183 km away from the Great Pyramid! As 183 is exactly half of 366, what better (yet discreet) hint could there be that the geometry used to measure this arc is the sacred (but secret) 366-degree geometry used by Druids for thousands of years? Is there a 'secret code' there?

Let us break the code by 'converting' 4067.79 km from Megalithic to modern by dividing it into 366 degrees, and then multiplying it by 360:

$$4067.79 \times (360/366) = 4001.10$$

The Earth's polar circumference is 40,007.86 km. A distance of 4001.10 km is 1/10th of the Earth's circumference to an amazing accuracy of over 99.992 per cent! That's almost the astounding level of accuracy we have found for the Great Pyramid-Newgrange Arc.

Need 100 per cent accuracy? Were we to position our end point not in the Peace Pyramid center but a few yards to the east, right in front of the stylised dove's beak, perfect accuracy of 100 per cent is attained. Is this spot a present (or future) location for an underground chamber housing some of the DIs' most secret documents? Is the modern architectural complex we see in Astana only the tip of the iceberg?

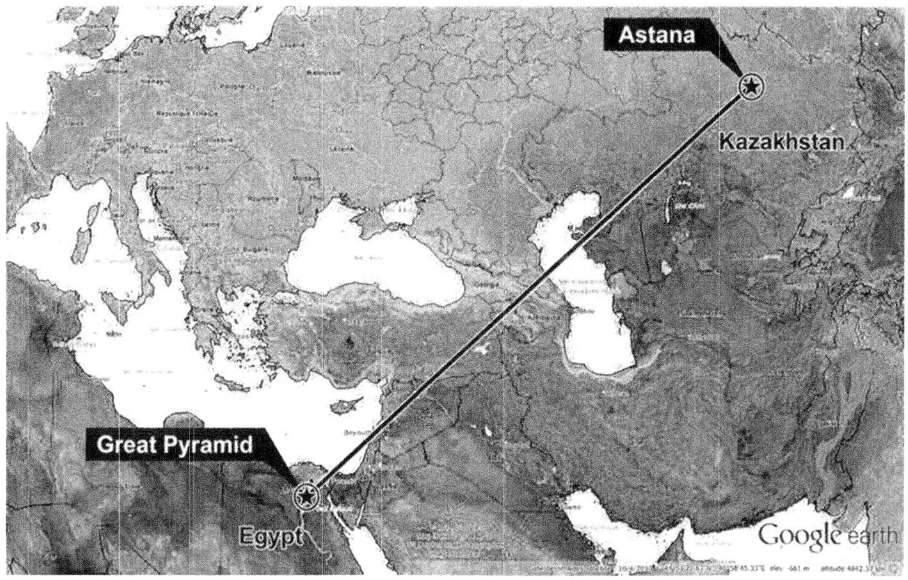

Fig. 90. The Great Pyramid-Astana Arc, which secretly gives the 1/10th polar circumference of the Earth in 366-degree geometry.

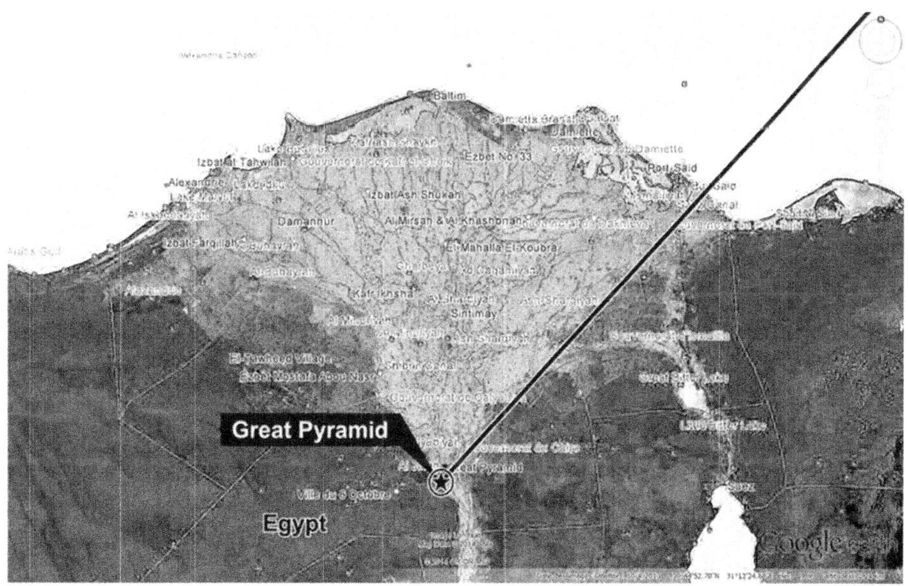

Fig. 91. The Great Pyramid-Astana Arc crosses the coastline a precise 183 km away from the Great Pyramid.

Giant Square, Compasses and G

Let's sum things up. Thousands of years ago, the circular mound of Newgrange in Ireland and the Great Pyramid of Giza were built at a distance of exactly one-tenth of the Earth's equatorial circumference. Millennia later, in 2006, the Peace Pyramid was consecrated in Astana, Kazakhstan, at a distance which is one-tenth of the Earth's *polar* circumference, when the distance is converted from 366- to 360-degree geometry (a direct echo of the Megalithic yard, which is a perfect subdivision of the Earth's *polar* circumference in 366-degree geometry). The two arcs meet in Giza, virtually forming a right angle.

In an almost inexplicable way, each arc intersects the coastline at a very appropriate distance from the Great Pyramid if expressed in kilometers: 180 km for the arc using 360-degree geometry (let's call this spot 'A'), and 183 km for the arc using 366-degree geometry (let's call it spot 'B'), each number of km being half of the number of degrees in each geometry. If referring to the kilometer might at first sight look like an aberration, one should keep in mind that the meter (as seen in Chapter Eleven), appears to be one of the basic units of the Great Pyramid. So the French, in the 18th century, merely rediscovered a unit that was already in use millennia earlier in Egypt.

Tracing the two axes on Google Earth, what you end up with is a gigantic stylised square such as the steel squares used by carpenters and that also appears of the Freemasonic symbol of the Square and Compasses. Although the angle is closer to 82° rather than 90°, it visually looks like a square angle. What's more, it is also very odd to note that the coastline between spots A and B, the northern edge of the Nile Delta, forms an arc of circle. Isn't nature beautiful? It looks like it was once made by a giant pair of compasses, with the spike positioned at Giza. And of course the nearly-right angle is located at Giza as well, which starts with the letter G.

So what we have here is the combination of a gigantic square and a quasi-circular arc made by an imaginary pair of giant compasses, with the right angle meeting the imaginary compass spike at the Great Pyramid of Giza. In other words, a huge stylised version of the Freemasonic symbol of the Square and Compasses, with the G meaning either God, Geometry or... *Giza*!

Once again, we are drawn back to Giza, as though this site lay at the very origins of Druidic knowledge. Alternatively, Giza was built as a repository of Druidic knowledge.

Stunning.

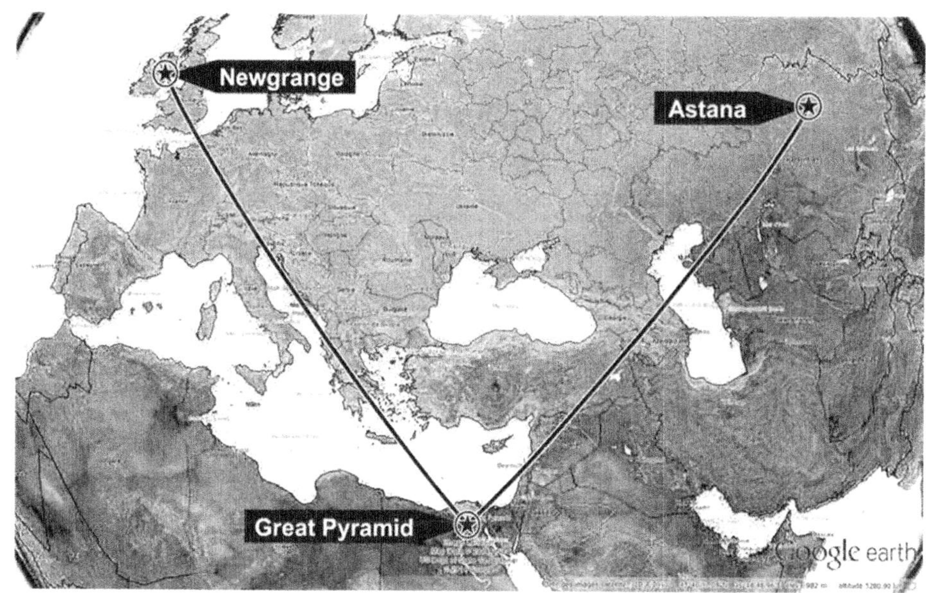

Fig. 92. The Great Pyramid-Newgrange Arc and the Great Pyramid-Astana Arc form a giant carpenter's square on the globe.

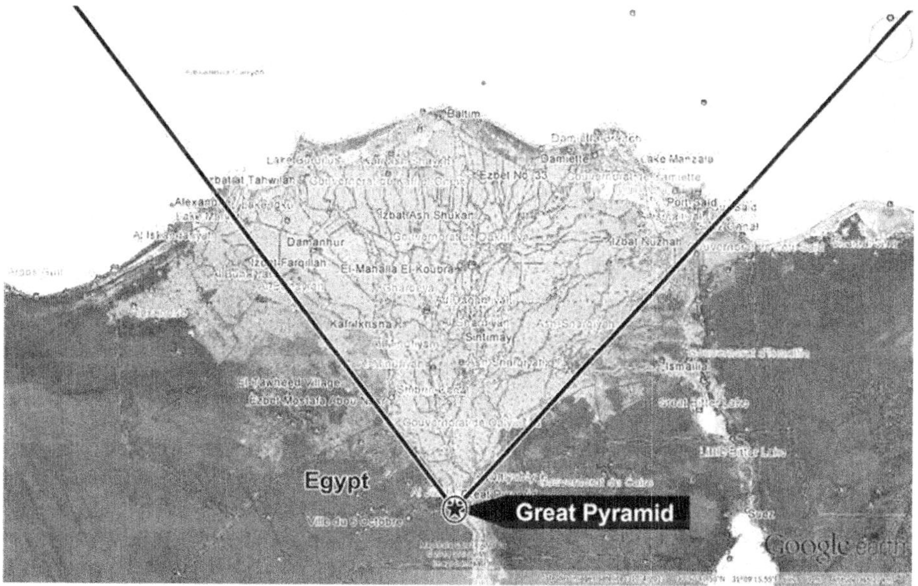

Fig. 93. Close-up on the Great Pyramid-Newgrange Arc and the Great Pyramid-Astana Arc in the Nile Delta area. The coastline forms an arc, as if drawn with a giant pair of compasses with its spike positioned at Giza.

Main points

- Astana, the new capital of Kazakhstan, is a Druidic Line location
- Like Stonehenge and Glastonbury, it is located on the 52nd Druidic Parallel north of the equator
- Astana appears to make use of units of 366 MY and Phi, the golden section
- The distance between the Great Pyramid and the Peace Pyramid in Astana, when 'converted' from 366- to 360-degree geometry, is a near-perfect one-tenth segment of the Earth's polar circumference
- The exact endpoint of the arc lies in front of a giant stylised dove, which is a perfect place for an underground chamber
- The Great Pyramid-Newgrange Arc and the Great Pyramid-Astana Arc look like a giant stylised square on a world map
- The coastline north of the Nile Delta is a near-circular arc, as if made by a giant compass with its spike positioned at Giza
- It looks like Druidic geometry has its origins at Giza or, alternatively, Giza was conceived as a repository of Druidic knowledge

PART IV

NUMBERS OF THE GODS

Chapter Twenty: Three Divine Numbers

366-degree geometry, and the numbers that are used in it, most notably 366, 40 and base 10, is not only a geometry that has probably been secretly used for millennia by MPDs, Celtic Druids and modern DIs. Incredibly, these numbers are also fundamental in the physics of our world, and the biology of our species. Is there a Great Architect of the Universe who fine-tuned our world with these particular numbers?

I personally like to refer to these three numbers as the 'Divine Triad.' Let us see why.

Earth's number

We saw in Chapter Seven that in a year the Earth makes almost exactly 366 ¼ spins on itself, which is also 366 10/40 of course (to an amazing accuracy of 99.998 per cent!).[469] This very basic astronomical feature of our planet encapsulates what can arguably be considered the three most fundamental numbers of Megalithic geometry. 366 is the very basic number of earth rotations in a year, the number of degrees in the Megalithic circle, and also the number of Megalithic yards in a Megalithic second. 40 is the number of years after which a 366-day calendar gets exactly one month late, and the number of Megalithic inches in a Megalithic yard, and 10 is our most basic number, our base today as we have 10 fingers.

It then seems quite logical that the system was first devised with the three numbers of the Divine Triad because the physics of our planet 'tell' us so. The question, 'How did ancient people manage to devise such a clever system in the first place?' is baffling enough, but now we come to another question: 'How come these three numbers also come up in basic physical characteristics of our world?'

---

[469] 366 10/40 = 366.25. In reality, during one orbit around the Sun the Earth rotates about its own axis 366.256363004 times.

The Earth-Moon coincidences

The following discoveries were made by Alan Butler and Christopher Knight in 2005.[470] It should be stressed though that I disagree with their conclusions (they explain the results with time travel), and that I slightly changed the way they present the data. I prefer to expound the facts as unexplainable *dual coincidences.*

As we have just seen the Earth rotates on its axis a little more than 366 times in a year, or in one rotation around the Sun. The Moon spins much more slowly, as it takes almost a month for our natural satellite to accomplish just one spin on itself and also make a full trip round the Earth.

Now for the first oddity. The Moon's orbital period (the exact number of days it takes the Moon to make a full revolution round the Earth), and sidereal period (the times it takes the Moon to rotate round its axis relative to the stars), is also almost exactly 10,000 divided by 366, or about 27.32 days, to an astounding accuracy of 99.997 per cent![471]

Stranger still, the circumference of the Earth is also 366 per cent that of the Moon, and the Moon's circumference is 10,000/366 or 27.32 per cent that of the Earth, and this to an accuracy of 99.76 per cent.[472]

What a coincidence that the physics of the Earth-Moon duet should use two of the three members of the Divine Triad, 366 and base 10, in such a crystal-clear way! And of course the coincidence is double as it happens not in one but in *two* (not to say three) distinct aspects of the duet's physics—rotation and revolution periods, and circumferences!

I have submitted the facts to Konstantin Grigoriev, a famous astronomer in Moscow,[473] who confirmed that there is absolutely no reason why this should be so, for there is no known link between concepts as different as planet revolution, rotation speed and circumference. Consequently as a scientist, Grigoriev attributes these results to chance—and of course he must be right: we are being extremely lucky here. And yet, the Earth and the Moon orbiting around it *appear* to share a privileged link, an extremely mysterious physical bond which expresses itself twice with number 366 and base 10. The consequence of these coincidences, incidentally, is that the linear rotation

---

[470] Alan Butler, Christopher Knight, *Who Built the Moon?*, London: Watkins, 2005

[471] 10,000/366 = 27.3224. The sidereal rotation period of the Moon is 27.3216 days.

[472] The Earth's mean circumference is 40,041.4385 km, whereas the Moon's mean circumference is 10,914.5212 km.

[473] Personal correspondence with Konstantin Grigoriev, 2005

speed of the Moon at its equator is a near-exact *one hundredth* of the linear rotation speed of the Earth at its equator.

What are the odds? It is both very strange and unusual.

The Moon-Sun coincidences

The circumference of our star, the Sun, is much greater than that of our natural satellite, the Moon. Strangely, the Sun's circumference is almost exactly 400 times bigger than that of the Moon, again to an accuracy of 99.76 per cent.[474] Of course, 400 is also 40 x 10, two members of the Divine Triad.

Fortunately, the Sun is also a great deal further from the Earth than the Moon. Although this distance varies, our star is also about 400 times further away than the Moon, strangely enough.[475]

There is absolutely no reason why this should be so, as the size of these bodies is not directly connected to their distance from Earth. This was also confirmed by the astronomer Konstantin Grigoriev. And once again, the coincidence is dual, as it uses two Megalithic numbers in two different physical aspects (circumference and distance).

This apparent special relationship between the Sun and the Moon has an important consequence for Earth-dwellers: it makes the Moon appear to have the exact same size as the Sun most of the time. Otherwise, we wouldn't have these superb total solar eclipses. A total solar eclipse is one of the most beautiful natural events on Earth, something almost magical.

Again, what are the odds?

The Earth-Sun coincidences

The circumference of the Sun is more than a hundred times greater than that of our planet. Strangely, the Sun's circumference is almost exactly 40,000/366 (or about 109.3) times bigger than that of the Earth, to an

---

[474] The Sun's equatorial circumference is 4,379,000 km, whereas the Moon's equatorial circumference is 10,921 km, meaning the Sun's equatorial circumference is 400.97 times bigger than the Moon's.

[475] As the distance between the Earth and the Sun, and that between the Earth and the Moon, vary, the result is not always perfectly accurate (but of course sometimes it is 100 per cent accurate).

incredible accuracy of 99.98 per cent.[476] Whereby 40 and 366 are of course two members of the Divine Triad.

Stranger still, the maximal distance between the Earth and the Sun is also about 40,000/366 Sun diameters (or about 109.3 Sun diameters).[477]

As Konstantin Grigoriev also confirmed, there is absolutely no reason why this should be so, as the Sun diameter is not directly connected to the Earth diameter, or to the distance between the Sun and the Earth. As Grigoriev wrote, these results are meaningless coincidences, or happy twists of fate, even though the coincidence, once again, is double: it uses two members of the Divine Triad, 366 and 40 (or even the three of them as base 10 is factorised here) in two different physical aspects of the Earth-Sun duet.

What it means is that the Earth and the Sun also appear to have a privileged bond, for one consequence of this dual coincidence is that you can fit as many Earths in the Sun's diameter as you can fit Suns between the Sun and the Earth! Again, what are the odds? It just leaves me speechless. It is mind-blowing.

The Lunar and Solar arcseconds

One amusing consequence of all these coincidences is that you can neatly divide the Sun and the Moon using 366-degree geometry, as you can do with the Earth.

As we have already seen, in one Megalithic arcsecond on Earth, there are 366 MY. On the Moon, one Lunar Megalithic arcsecond is almost exactly 100 MY (to an accuracy of 99.91 per cent),[478] whereas on the Sun one Solar Megalithic arcsecond is almost exactly 40,000 MY (to an accuracy of 99.85 per cent)![479] Absolutely beautiful, and again almost magical. And possible only with the use of 366-degree geometry.

---

[476] The Sun's equatorial circumference is 4,379,000 km, whereas the Earth's equatorial circumference is 40,075.017 km, meaning the Sun's equatorial circumference is 109.27 times bigger than the Earth's.

[477] As the distance between the Earth and the Sun varies, the result is not always perfectly accurate (but of course sometimes it is 100 per cent accurate).

[478] Using the Moon's equatorial circumference of 10,921 km: 10,921/(366 x 360 x 0.0008296) = 99.91 MY per Lunar arcsecond. Using the Earth's equatorial MY (.8310 m) instead of the Earth's polar MY, the result obtained for the Moon is 99.74 MY per Lunar arcsecond.

[479] Using the Sun's equatorial circumference of 4.379×10^{6}km: 4.379×10^{6}/(366 x 360 x 0.0008296) = 40,061,076.54 MY per Solar arcsecond. Using the Earth's equatorial

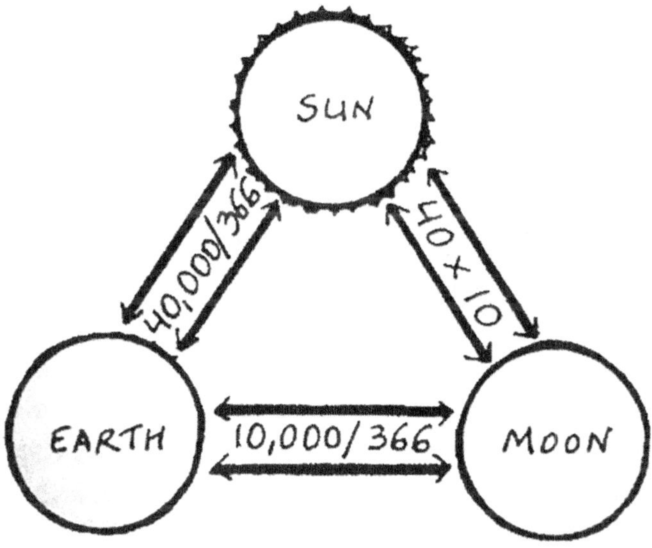

Fig. 94. The physical characteristics of the Earth-Moon-Sun triad, which are directly associated with numbers 366, 40 and 10.

The Sun's synodic period

The Sun's synodic rotational period (the time it takes the Sun to rotate round its axis as seen from Earth) is 27.27 days. It is incredibly close to the Moon's orbital and sidereal period of 27.32 days.

What it means is that the Sun's synodic period is 10,000/366 days, to an accuracy of 99.8 per cent.

Wow again.

Temperatures and water

As I was teaching English in the French school of Moscow in 2005, I noticed a recurrent sign in the streets—a blue sphere with the number 36.6 in white font standing out in the middle of it. Russians soon informed me that 36.6 was, according to Russian medicine, the human body average temperature in Celsius as measured under the armpits. The sign I kept seeing was the name of a famous Russian pharmacy chain.[480]

MY, the result obtained is 39,993.58 MY per Solar arcsecond, which is 40,000 MY to an accuracy of 99.98 per cent!

[480] http://www.366.ru/

The Celsius scale is one of the most 'logical' scales of temperatures ever made on Earth, as it is based on water's freezing and boiling points at standard pressure on our planet, both of which are easily noticeable features. Water, of course, is fundamental on our Earth, which is also referred to as the Blue Planet, because it is mostly covered in water.

When the scale was devised in the mid-18th century, it was decided that 0°C would be water's freezing point, and 100°C would mark water's boiling point. Using base 10, of course, it could just as well have been decided to make the boiling point 10, or 1,000. As everyone can agree, it is only a matter of *definition.*

Now imagine an alternate Celsius scale (°A) which would define the boiling point of water as 1,000°A rather than 100°C. In this new scale the human body temperature, as measured under the armpits, becomes... 366°A, to an accuracy of 100 per cent! Isn't it amazing? Please also keep in mind that human bodies are mainly made up of water. What an odd coincidence again!

But that is not all. If water is so vital to our life, or to life in general on the planet, it is because it has a very unusual property: contrary to most known pure substances, which become denser as they cool, water has a maximum density which occurs at the temperature of about 4°C, which in our alternate scale is exactly 40°A, to an accuracy of over 99.5 per cent![481] Above *and* below this temperature water is less dense.

Thanks to this unusual property, ice doesn't sink. One can easily imagine what would happen if ice did sink in liquid water: it would freeze rivers or lakes from the bottom up during cold spells, causing underwater life (such as fish, molluscs and crustaceans) to die. But because water has a maximum density, this does not occur, as water at the bottom of frozen lakes or rivers remains at the temperature of 4°C (40°A). Apart from the fact that nature has been provident enough to make water special, allowing underwater life to thrive on during the most severe winters, it is remarkable to see that, once again, the three members of the Divine Triad come up at most fundamental levels: base 10 is used to devise the water-based scale, 366°A corresponds to the average human body temperature, and 40°A is water's maximum density temperature. To sum things up:

---

[481] 3.98°C precisely, but only because water's boiling point is now defined as 99.9839°C (because the Celsius scale is defined by the triple point of Vienna Standard Mean Ocean Water, which is very slightly warmer than absolute zero) rather than 100°C. If water's boiling point were 100°C, its maximum density temperature would indeed be 4°C or an extremely close approximation of it.

0°A = freezing point of water (= 0°C)

40°A = maximum density of water (= 4°C)

366°A = average human body temperature (= 36.6°C)

1,000°A = boiling point of water (= 100°C)

Simply mind-boggling again.

Well, that is still not all. You have probably heard of absolute zero. It is the lower limit of the thermodynamic temperature scale or, in more simple words, the lowest temperature possible in the universe. Absolute zero is 0°K (Kelvin), which corresponds to -273.15°C. Does this number remind you of anything? Well, it is very similar to the sequence of digits appearing in the physics of the Earth-Moon duet (27.32). Is it just a coincidence?

Let's define a third scale of temperatures (°B). In this third scale absolute zero is defined not as -273.15°C but as -1,000°B. Let's say that in this third scale the freezing point of water is 0°B (which is also 0°C in the Celsius regular scale.) Incredibly enough, in this third scale, the boiling point of water is... 366°B, to an incredible accuracy of 99.97 per cent!

This is a direct consequence, of course, of the fact that the number 273.15 is almost exactly 100,000/366 (just as 27.32 is almost exactly 10,000/366). To sum things up:

-1,000°B = absolute zero (= -273.15°C)

0°B = freezing point of water (= 0°C)

366°B = boiling point of water (= 100°C)

Again, what are the odds? There is no reason this should be so, but it is! To reuse a word that has by now become quite trite, it is mind-boggling.

As an additional curious note, in this third scale the temperature of 40°B corresponds to 14.6°C, which is *exactly* the average surface temperature on Earth in both 2012[482] and 2013.[483] To be fair, these years recorded higher temperatures than in the twentieth century (where the average temperature was only about 14°C). Unless of course 14.6°C is the *normal* average surface temperature on Earth over much longer periods?

---

[482] http://www.dw.de/hot-temperatures-in-2012-part-of-a-growing-trend/a-16523841

[483] http://climatestate.com/2014/01/23/2013-is-the-fourth-hottest-year-on-record/

The human body and mind

It is interesting to note that childbirth occurs about 38 weeks after conception, which is also 40 weeks from the start of the last normal menstrual period (or 280 days, as we saw in Chapter Eleven). It means that a human child will be born, on average, 40 weeks after a woman's last menstrual period.

As everyone knows, if it takes approximately 40 weeks to create a living human body, it takes much more to make a human mind, as a human baby is unable to speak and reason. Interestingly, according to the canon law of the Catholic Church used in France, a very Druidic country, the age of reason and moral responsibility is seven years. In common law used in English-speaking countries, seven years also used to be the age of reason, and children under this age were considered 'incapable of committing a crime because they did not possess the reasoning ability to understand that their conduct violated the standards of acceptable community behaviour.'[484] Seven years is also very close to 366 weeks!

To sum things up, it takes about 40 weeks to make a living human body, and 366 weeks more to make a reasonable, responsible human mind. Very odd.

Of course one can argue that the seven-day week is an arbitrary human concept, not a natural law, or that it is based on the phases of the moon. And yet, in the light of the astonishing facts revealed in the previous sections, it looks like another striking example of members of the Divine Triad cropping up in our world, this time in the very biology of our species.

Squaring the circle

I have kept the best part for the end.

Draw a square. Then draw a circle that perfectly fits in it. Obviously, the square's area is bigger than the circle's. Hold your breath, for the square will *always* be 27.32 per cent bigger than the circle—and 27.32 = 10,000/366, to an astounding accuracy of 99.994 per cent!

---

[484] http://legal-dictionary.thefreedictionary.com/Age+of+Reason

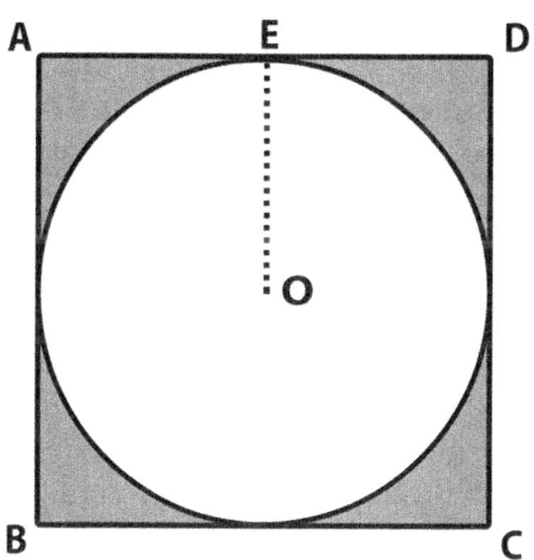

Fig. 95. A square will always be 10,000/366 per cent bigger than the circle that just fits inside it.

Here's a variation of the problem. Draw a circle over a square. For the square to have the exact same perimeter as that of the circle, the circle's diameter must be bigger than the side of the square. It must be 27.32 per cent bigger, meaning that if the square has a side of 1 unit, the diameter of the circle must be 1.2732 units long, or 1 + (10,000/366) units, again to an accuracy of 99.994 per cent.

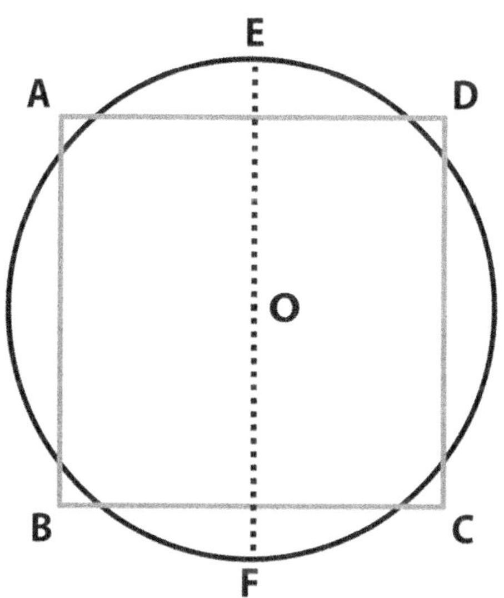

Fig. 96. For a circle to have the same perimeter as that of a square, the diameter of the circle must be 10,000/366 per cent bigger than the side of the square.

The implications of this are just phenomenal. It means that base 10 and number 366 are not only encrypted in potentially unstable physical phenomena such as those we have seen in the previous sections, but also in a mathematical constant defining the connection between a square and a circle! No word or sentence can convey the sheer magnitude of such a result.

In fact, it looks exactly as if the physics and biology of our world had been somehow 'fine-tuned' so as to echo this mathematical constant defining the difference between these two basic geometrical figures that are the square and the circle.

One can now easily understand why Freemasons are so attached to the symbol of Square and Compasses, the two tools that are necessary to draw a square and a circle! And one can now just as easily understand the full symbolical meaning of the giant square and compasses originating in Giza. I'm letting the reader find their own adjective to describe what has just been explained, for the author is running out of vocabulary.

Conclusion

If this doesn't blow your mind, please read the whole chapter once or twice again. Take your time. But I am pretty sure that most of you by now have probably understood why I call numbers 366, 40 and 10 the Divine Triad. I know of nothing in this world that has stronger philosophical implications than their omnipresence in some of the most fundamental aspects of our world—the physics of the Earth, the Moon, the Sun, temperature and water, and the biology of our species—and of course the mathematics of the most basic geometrical figures, the square and the circle. To use Louis Fouquet's words in his letter to his brother, 'nothing now on this Earth can have greater value nor be their equal,' for numbers 366, 40 and 10 are truly the Numbers of the Gods.

It all looks like there is a Great Architect somewhere out there. You might call Him/Her God if you're a monotheist. Or you might call them Gods if you're a polytheist. Call It either Chance or Lady Luck if you're an agnostic or an atheist. This God, or Gods, or Lady Luck, is/are expressing themselves with these numbers. As I prefer to call it, there is a Grand Universal Mystery that no one on this planet can begin to explain or even fathom. Or has our world been made by a superadvanced alien civilisation mastering space and energy? Are we living in a Matrix, a simulated reality or a fabulously realistic computer programme?

There is a well-known fact which has been widely reported on the web for years now. In the Bible, God says 'Fear Not' 366 times. Perhaps 'someone' is sending us a message here: 'Don't be afraid, just admire the beauty.'

Can you now hear the music of our world, the celestial hum, the melody of the heavens? Can you now see what Pythagoras termed the Harmony of the Spheres? Can you now perceive this magical harmonious ensemble that MPDs, Celtic Druids and DIs appear to have identified, at least partly so, in the last millennia?

Main points

- In our world three numbers appear to be absolutely fundamental: 366, 40 and base 10, which I have christened the Divine Triad
- The Earth rotates almost exactly 366 and 10/40 times in a year
- The Moon's orbital and sidereal periods are almost exactly 27.32 or 10,000/366 days, and the Moon's circumference is almost exactly 10,000/366 per cent that of the Earth
- Because of the above, the linear rotation speed of the Moon at its equator is almost exactly 100 times slower than the Earth
- The Moon's circumference is almost exactly 40 x 10 times smaller than the Sun's, but it is also 40 x 10 times closer
- Because of the above, the discs of the Moon and the Sun appear to be the same, which lends the possibility of occasional, magnificent, total solar eclipses
- The Sun's circumference is almost exactly 40,000/366 times bigger that the Earth's, and the maximal distance between the Earth and the Sun is also 40,000/366 Sun diameters
- Because of the above, you can fit as many Earths in the Sun diameter as you can fit Suns between the Sun and the Earth
- Also because of the above, there are almost exactly 366 MY (Megalithic yards) to the Megalithic arcsecond on Earth, 100 MY on the Lunar Megalithic arcsecond, and 40,000 MY to the Solar Megalithic arcsecond
- The Sun's synodic rotational period is also almost exactly 10,000/366 days
- On a scale where water freezes at 0° and boils at 1,000°, water has a maximum density at 40° and the average human body temperature is 366°; the human body is also composed mostly of water.
- On a scale where absolute zero is defined as -1,000° and water freezes at 0°, water boils at 366°
- It takes about 40 weeks to make a new living human body, and about 366 weeks more to make a responsible human mind
- A square is almost exactly 10,000/366 percent (27.32%) bigger than the circle that fits inside it

Epilogue:
A New Paradigm

That's almost the end of our journey across land and through time. But there are still a few more riddles.

Perhaps the most baffling question of all is this: How could the ancient Druids make such incredible discoveries in the distant past? Did they discover everything by themselves or were they helped in any way—and if so, by whom?

How can we explain that this geometry also seems to be encapsulated in our universe?

Last but not least, how did the Druids and their successors manage to keep their secrets for so long, without anyone else ever noticing anything until today?

Appendix 1: The Phaistos Disc

Because the Phaistos Disc is unique and uses a completely unknown form of writing, it is difficult to know for sure what it was exactly. Many clues, though, point to a calendar, as the reader will see.

A 366-day calendar?

When he first came to know about it while staying in Crete, Alan Butler stood fascinated by the clay artefact and its mysterious symbols stamped on it inside two spirals.

Alan's first intuition was that it could be a calendar. There are 123 symbols on one side of the disc, which are distributed in 31 spaces, and on the other there are 119 symbols in 30 spaces. Indeed, if the numbers 123 and 119 do not seem to suggest anything obvious at first glance, 31 and 30 spaces immediately suggest a calendar with alternating months of 31 and 30 days, very much like the one we use today. Applying Occam's razor or principle of parsimony, this straightforward explanation seemed promising to Alan. Now, the interesting thing with a calendar that would alternate 31-day and 30-day months is that it adds up to a total of 366 days. It was mere speculation at the time, of course, but Alan thought the Minoans might have used a calendar with a 366-day year, rather than a 365-day year.

The Earth rotates on its axis about 366¼ times in a year, meaning there are 366¼ sidereal days, not 365¼. The reason why a year is only 365 'tropical' or 'solar' days is because of the Earth orbit around the Sun. The Earth rotates counter-clockwise both around its axis and around the Sun. A day is defined as a return to the same position towards the Sun. To do this, each day it must rotate around itself plus one degree, to keep up with its new position in its solar orbit. In this way, it loses a sidereal day in a solar year—it needs to rotate on its axis 366 times to make 365 sunrises.

Each tropical or solar day is the time it takes for the Earth to align again to the Sun, and each solar day is longer than a sidereal day (or sidereal night, as measured by the apparent rotation of the stars) by about four minutes.

It is easy to grasp why this discrepancy exists by making your own experiment with, say, a plum and a grapefruit, the plum representing the Earth and the grapefruit in lieu of the Sun. Simulate the rotations of the plum on itself while it gradually revolves around the grapefruit, and you'll soon see how part of each rotation of the plum goes toward the rotation around the larger fruit.

In any case, the sidereal day is not particularly relevant to Earth-dwellers. What's relevant to us is the solar year, which lasts about 365 days, not 366. So why would a people have chosen to use a 366-day year? One possible answer is that if you consider that a day begins at sunrise, then there are 366 sunrises in a solar year, the 366th one being for a quarter of a day. Another reason could be that they were avid starwatchers.

Now, of course, if Minoans truly did consider a year to be 366 days long, this would have been about three fourths of a day too much, which would have created some problems, as the calendar would have been one month late exactly after 40 years, or 14,640 days (366 days x 40 years = 14,640). Just like our own modern 365-day calendar has to be adjusted every four years (by adding a leap year or 366-day year), it seems reasonable to think the Minoans had devised a way to adjust their calendar too.

One obvious way to do that could have been to suppress one month every 40 years, which would have brought the calendar back on track, but letting the calendar lag so far behind the astronomical reality seems very unlikely. The Minoans would have found themselves way out of season for very long periods, and nobody can really afford to allow such a discrepancy between the calendar and the astronomical and meteorological reality of the seasons.

Interestingly, Alan noticed that the product of the numbers of symbols on both sides of the disc yielded a familiar number:

$$123 \times 119 = 14{,}637$$

The number obtained was only three days off the number of days in 40 years of 366 days! What if Alan's intuition was true? Was the Phaistos Disc a calendar? Was it a *366*-day calendar?

The idea was that the spaces on each side represented *days*. Starting with one side of the disc, there are 31 spaces in the first spiral, hence you could count off 31 days. Then you would flip the disc over and begin counting days off the second spiral, representing a new month. This second spiral has only 30 spaces, meaning the following month had 30 days only. Then you would flip the disc over again and begin another 31-day month, and so forth till day 366 at the end of the twelfth month.

The trouble with such a calendar is that it gets one day late every one and a third years. Four months into the second year, one day should be taken off, or 'leapt over,' to readjust to the true course of the Earth round the Sun.

In his book, Alan Butler suggested that this could be done every 492 days, or four periods of 123 days (as there are 123 symbols on side A of the disc). The details of his analysis can be found in his book.[485]

After reading the book in 2001, I contacted Alan Butler and we exchanged many emails discussing this question amongst others. A few years later, in 2008, I suggested the corrections could be made every 487 days, which in my view yielded even better results: 487 is the sum of 3 x 123 and 119, minus 1. So the Minoans could have followed the 123-symbol sequence on side A three times, and then the 119-symbol sequence on side B once. At the end of the 119-symbol sequence, they would have skipped or leaped over the last day, meaning the fourth period would have actually lasted 118 days. This would be very much like skipping the last day of our modern April in the second year.

After this 'day-leaping,' a new sequence could begin. They would follow again three 123-symbol sequences and one 119-symbol sequence the following year, skipping the very last day, like skipping the last day of August in the third year. Then in the fourth year they would skip the very last day of the year, like our 31 December. Then the process could start over again from the beginning.

This method would keep the calendar accurate for more than a century. We can even imagine that Minoans celebrated such times when one day was skipped. Maybe (this is just a suggestion) the traditional bull-leaping of Minoan Crete was linked to those times when days were leapt over in the calendar.

A 365-day calendar?

It recently occurred to me that the Phaistos Disc could also be a 365-day calendar, quite similar to the one we use today.

---

[485] Alan Butler, *The Stone Age Computer Disc*, Cippenham, Slough, Berkshire: Quantum (1999)

I noticed that 123 + 119 + 123 = 365, which could mean that the Minoans first followed a 123-day period (or three 31-day months and one 30-day month), then a 119-day period (or three 30-day months and one 29-day month), and finally another 123-day period of three 31-day months and one 30-day month. This process was repeated in the second and third years, and on the fourth year, just like us, they would have had a leap year of 366 days, thus *adding* one extra day (say, for example, in the second period of the year, which would have become a *120*-day period of four 30-day months.)

We can even imagine that the symbols could be read and formed a mnemonic device to remember how to work the calendar, as was first suggested by Alan. For example, side A of the disc could read, 'At the beginning and at the end of the year, count three thirty-one-day months on this side of the disc, and one thirty-day month on the other side,' and side B might read, 'In the middle of the year, count three thirty-day-months on this side of the disc, and one twenty-nine-day month, which will become thirty every fourth year.' In this example, I used 31 words for my first mnemonic sentence, and 30 for the second, which fits with the number of divisions on each side of the disc. I stress that these sentences are not meant to be taken as literal decipherments of the disc, merely as examples of what it *could* have read.

Of course all this is highly speculative. I have personally worked out other ways to operate the disc, but there is simply no easy way to prove which one is the right one, let alone demonstrate there is one way at all. Maybe the symbols on the disc were just a form of writing that has yet to be deciphered, but I doubt it. A few scholars even think it might be a hoax. The problem is that so far only one such disc has ever been found, and every sort of conjecture can be made about it. For a full understanding of how the calendar worked, if it was indeed a calendar, would require the finding of others, for a start. Without any such discoveries, there is little hope the Phaistos Disc will ever be fully understood or convincingly decrypted. At least Alan Butler's proposed decryption, along with my additional suggestions, perfectly fits the number of symbols and spaces on each side of the disc.

Appendix 2:
Units of Distance that appear to be subdivisions of the Earth's polar circumference

Polar circumference = 40,007,860 m

- Megalithic yard (MY): 40,007,860 m/(366 degrees x 60' x 6" x 366)=.8296 m
- Minoan foot: 40,007,860 m/(366 degrees x 60' x 6" x 1,000)=.3036 m
- Gallic league: 40,007,860 m/(360 degrees x 50)=2,222.6 m (conventional length given: 2,222.5 m)
- Roman mile: 40,007,860 m/(360 degrees x 75)=1,481.8 m (conventional length given: 1,482 m)
- Roman stadium: 40,007,860 m/(360 degrees x 60' x 10)=185.2 m (conventional length given: 185.25 m)
- Roman perch=Roman mile/500=2.9636 m (conventional length given: 2.964 m)
- Roman step=Roman mile/2,000=.7409 m (conventional length given: .741 m)
- Roman foot=Roman mile/5,000=.2964 m (conventional length given: .2964 m)
- Roman palm=Roman mile/20,000=.0741 m (conventional length given: .0741 m)
- Roman finger=Roman stadium/10,000=.01852 m (conventional length given: .0185 m)

Note: the Roman stadium and the Roman finger are extremely reminiscent of the modern nautical mile, which (contrary to the other units listed above) is by definition the length of an arcminute along an Earth meridian: 40,007,860 m/(360 degrees x 60')=1,852 m

Appendix 3:
The World’s Druidic Lines
(also called Salt Lines)

1- Geographic coordinates of the 366 longitudinal Druidic Lines (Druidic Meridians) on the globe (rounded off to the nearest minute)

Example: 10°W) 25° 42’ E:

the 10th longitudinal Druidic Line west of the (presumed) River Jordan Prime Meridian runs at 25° 42’ east of Greenwich Prime Meridian (modern 360-degree geometry).

183°W/E) 144° 27’ W
182°E) 145° 26’ W
181°E) 146° 25’ W
180°E) 147° 24’ W
179°E) 148° 23’ W
178°E) 149° 22’ W
177°E) 150° 22’ W
176°E) 151° 21’ W
175°E) 152° 20’ W
174°E) 153° 19’ W
173°E) 154° 18’ W
172°E) 155° 17’ W
171°E) 156° 16’ W
170°E) 157° 15’ W
169°E) 158° 14’ W
168°E) 159° 13’ W
167°E) 160° 12’ W
166°E) 161° 11’ W
165°E) 162° 10’ W
164°E) 163° 09’ W
163°E) 164° 08’ W
162°E) 165° 07’ W
161°E) 166° 06’ W
160°E) 167° 05’ W
159°E) 168° 04’ W
158°E) 169° 03’ W
157°E) 170° 02’ W
156°E) 171° 01’ W
155°E) 172° 00’ W
154°E) 172° 59’ W
153°E) 173° 58’ W
152°E) 174° 57’ W
151°E) 175° 56’ W
150°E) 176° 55’ W
149°E) 177° 54’ W
148°E) 178° 53’ W
147°E) 179° 52’ W
146°E) 179° 09’ E
145°E) 178° 10’ E
144°E) 177° 11’ E
143°E) 176° 12’ E
142°E) 175° 13’ E
141°E) 174° 14’ E
140°E) 173° 15’ E
139°E) 172° 16’ E
138°E) 171° 17’ E
137°E) 170° 18’ E
136°E) 169° 19’ E
135°E) 168° 20’ E
134°E) 167° 21’ E
133°E) 166° 22’ E
132°E) 165° 23’ E
131°E) 164° 24’ E
130°E) 163° 25’ E
129°E) 162° 26’ E
128°E) 161° 27’ E
127°E) 160° 28’ E
126°E) 159° 29’ E
125°E) 158° 30’ E
124°E) 157° 31’ E
123°E) 156° 32’ E
122°E) 155° 33’ E
121°E) 154° 34’ E
120°E) 153° 35’ E
119°E) 152° 36’ E
118°E) 151° 37’ E
117°E) 150° 38’ E
116°E) 149° 38’ E
115°E) 148° 39’ E
114°E) 147° 40’ E
113°E) 146° 41’ E
112°E) 145° 42’ E
111°E) 144° 43’ E
110°E) 143° 44’ E
109°E) 142° 45’ E
108°E) 141° 46’ E
107°E) 140° 47’ E
106°E) 139° 48’ E
105°E) 138° 49’ E
104°E) 137° 50’ E
103°E) 136° 51’ E

102°E) 135° 52' E
101°E) 134° 53' E
100°E) 133° 54' E
99°E) 132° 55' E
98°E) 131° 56' E
97°E) 130° 57' E
96°E) 129° 58' E
95°E) 128° 59' E
94°E) 128° 00' E
93°E) 127° 01' E
92°E) 126° 02' E
91°E) 125° 03' E
90°E) 124° 04' E
89°E) 123° 05' E
88°E) 122° 06' E
87°E) 121° 07' E
86°E) 120° 08' E
85°E) 119° 09' E
84°E) 118° 10' E
83°E) 117° 11' E
82°E) 116° 12' E
81°E) 115° 13' E
80°E) 114° 14' E
79°E) 113° 15' E
78°E) 112° 16' E
77°E) 111° 17' E
76°E) 110° 18' E
75°E) 109° 19' E
74°E) 108° 20' E
73°E) 107° 21' E
72°E) 106° 22' E
71°E) 105° 23' E
70°E) 104° 24' E
69°E) 103° 25' E
68°E) 102° 26' E
67°E) 101° 27' E
66°E) 100° 28' E
65°E) 99° 29' E
64°E) 98° 30' E
63°E) 97° 31' E
62°E) 96° 32' E
61°E) 95° 33' E
60°E) 94° 34' E
59°E) 93° 35' E
58°E) 92° 36' E
57°E) 91° 37' E
56°E) 90° 38' E
55°E) 89° 38' E
54°E) 88° 39' E
53°E) 87° 40' E
52°E) 86° 41' E
51°E) 85° 42' E
50°E) 84° 43' E
49°E) 83° 44' E
48°E) 82° 45' E
47°E) 81° 46' E
46°E) 80° 47' E
45°E) 79° 48' E
44°E) 78° 49' E
43°E) 77° 50' E
42°E) 76° 51' E
41°E) 75° 52' E
40°E) 74° 53' E
39°E) 73° 54' E
38°E) 72° 55' E
37°E) 71° 56' E
36°E) 70° 57' E
35°E) 69° 58' E
34°E) 68° 59' E
33°E) 68° 00' E
32°E) 67° 01' E
31°E) 66° 02' E
30°E) 65° 03' E
29°E) 64° 04' E
28°E) 63° 05' E
27°E) 62° 06' E
26°E) 61° 07' E
25°E) 60° 08' E
24°E) 59° 09' E
23°E) 58° 10' E
22°E) 57° 11' E
21°E) 56° 12' E
20°E) 55° 13' E
19°E) 54° 14' E
18°E) 53° 15' E
17°E) 52° 16' E
16°E) 51° 17' E
15°E) 50° 18' E
14°E) 49° 19' E
13°E) 48° 20' E
12°E) 47° 21' E
11°E) 46° 22' E
10°E) 45° 23' E
9°E) 44° 24' E
8°E) 43° 25' E
7°E) 42° 26' E
6°E) 41° 27' E
5°E) 40° 28' E
4°E) 39° 29' E
3°E) 38° 30' E
2°E) 37° 31' E
1°E) 36° 32' E
0°) 35° 33' E
1°W) 34° 34' E
2°W) 33° 35' E
3°W) 32° 36' E
4°W) 31° 37' E
5°W) 30° 38' E
6°W) 29° 38' E
7°W) 28° 39' E
8°W) 27° 40' E
9°W) 26° 41' E
10°W) 25° 42' E
11°W) 24° 43' E
12°W) 23° 44' E
13°W) 22° 45' E
14°W) 21° 46' E
15°W) 20° 47' E
16°W) 19° 48' E
17°W) 18° 49' E
18°W) 17° 50' E
19°W) 16° 51' E
20°W) 15° 52' E

21°W) 14° 53’ E
22°W) 13° 54’ E
23°W) 12° 55’ E
24°W) 11° 56’ E
25°W) 10° 57’ E
26°W) 09° 58’ E
27°W) 08° 59’ E
28°W) 08° 00’ E
29°W) 07° 01’ E
30°W) 06° 02’ E
31°W) 05° 03’ E
32°W) 04° 04’ E
33°W) 03° 05’ E
34°W) 02° 06’ E
35°W) 01° 07’ E
36°W) 00° 08’ E
37°W) 00° 51’ W
38°W) 01° 50’ W
39°W) 02° 49’ W
40°W) 03° 48’ W
41°W) 04° 47’ W
42°W) 05° 46’ W
43°W) 06° 45’ W
44°W) 07° 44’ W
45°W) 08° 43’ W
46°W) 09° 42’ W
47°W) 10° 41’ W
48°W) 11° 40’ W
49°W) 12° 39’ W
50°W) 13° 38’ W
51°W) 14° 37’ W
52°W) 15° 36’ W
53°W) 16° 35’ W
54°W) 17° 34’ W
55°W) 18° 33’ W
56°W) 19° 32’ W
57°W) 20° 31’ W
58°W) 21° 30’ W
59°W) 22° 29’ W
60°W) 23° 28’ W
61°W) 24° 27’ W
62°W) 25° 26’ W
63°W) 26° 25’ W
64°W) 27° 24’ W
65°W) 28° 23’ W
66°W) 29° 22’ W
67°W) 30° 22’ W
68°W) 31° 21’ W
69°W) 32° 20’ W
70°W) 33° 19’ W
71°W) 34° 18’ W
72°W) 35° 17’ W
73°W) 36° 16’ W
74°W) 37° 15’ W
75°W) 38° 14’ W
76°W) 39° 13’ W
77°W) 40° 12’ W
78°W) 41° 11’ W
79°W) 42° 10’ W
80°W) 43° 09’ W
81°W) 44° 08’ W
82°W) 45° 07’ W
83°W) 46° 06’ W
84°W) 47° 05’ W
85°W) 48° 04’ W
86°W) 49° 03’ W
87°W) 50° 02’ W
88°W) 51° 01’ W
89°W) 52° 00’ W
90°W) 52° 59’ W
91°W) 53° 58’ W
92°W) 54° 57’ W
93°W) 55° 56’ W
94°W) 56° 55’ W
95°W) 57° 54’ W
96°W) 58° 53’ W
97°W) 59° 52’ W
98°W) 60° 51’ W
99°W) 61° 50’ W
100°W) 62° 49’ W
101°W) 63° 48’ W
102°W) 64° 47’ W
103°W) 65° 46’ W
104°W) 66° 45’ W
105°W) 67° 44’ W
106°W) 68° 43’ W
107°W) 69° 42’ W
108°W) 70° 41’ W
109°W) 71° 40’ W
110°W) 72° 39’ W
111°W) 73° 38’ W
112°W) 74° 37’ W
113°W) 75° 36’ W
114°W) 76° 35’ W
115°W) 77° 34’ W
116°W) 78° 33’ W
117°W) 79° 32’ W
118°W) 80° 31’ W
119°W) 81° 30’ W
120°W) 82° 29’ W
121°W) 83° 28’ W
122°W) 84° 27’ W
123°W) 85° 26’ W
124°W) 86° 25’ W
125°W) 87° 24’ W
126°W) 88° 23’ W
127°W) 89° 22’ W
128°W) 90° 22’ W
129°W) 91° 21’ W
130°W) 92° 20’ W
131°W) 93° 19’ W
132°W) 94° 18’ W
133°W) 95° 17’ W
134°W) 96° 16’ W
135°W) 97° 15’ W
136°W) 98° 14’ W
137°W) 99° 13’ W
138°W) 100° 12’ W
139°W) 101° 11’ W
140°W) 102° 10’ W
141°W) 103° 09’ W
142°W) 104° 08’ W
143°W) 105° 07’ W

144°W) 106° 06’ W
145°W) 107° 05’ W
146°W) 108° 04’ W
147°W) 109° 03’ W
148°W) 110° 02’ W
149°W) 111° 01’ W
150°W) 112° 00’ W
151°W) 112° 59’ W
152°W) 113° 58’ W
153°W) 114° 57’ W
154°W) 115° 56’ W
155°W) 116° 55’ W
156°W) 117° 54’ W
157°W) 118° 53’ W
158°W) 119° 52’ W
159°W) 120° 51’ W
160°W) 121° 50’ W
161°W) 122° 49’ W
162°W) 123° 48’ W
163°W) 124° 47’ W
164°W) 125° 46’ W
165°W) 126° 45’ W
166°W) 127° 44’ W
167°W) 128° 43’ W
168°W) 129° 42’ W
169°W) 130° 41’ W
170°W) 131° 40’ W
171°W) 132° 39’ W
172°W) 133° 38’ W
173°W) 134° 37’ W
174°W) 135° 36’ W
175°W) 136° 35’ W
176°W) 137° 34’ W
177°W) 138° 33’ W
178°W) 139° 32’ W
179°W) 140° 31’ W
180°W) 141° 30’ W
181°W) 142° 29’ W
182°W) 143° 28’ W

2- Geographic coordinates of the 183 latitudinal Druidic Lines (Druidic Parallels) on the globe (rounded to the nearest minute)

Example: 36°S) 35° 25’ S:

The 36th latitudinal Druidic Line south of the equator runs at 35° 25’ south of the equator (modern 360-degree geometry).

91°S) 89° 30’ S
90°S) 88° 31’ S
89°S) 87° 32’ S
88°S) 86° 33’ S
87°S) 85° 34’ S
86°S) 84° 35’ S
85°S) 83° 36’ S
84°S) 82° 37’ S
83°S) 81° 38’ S
82°S) 80° 39’ S
81°S) 79° 40’ S
80°S) 78° 41’ S
79°S) 77° 42’ S
78°S) 76° 43’ S
77°S) 75° 44’ S
76°S) 74° 45’ S
75°S) 73° 46’ S
74°S) 72° 47’ S
73°S) 71° 48’ S
72°S) 70° 49’ S
71°S) 69° 50’ S
70°S) 68° 51’ S
69°S) 67° 52’ S
68°S) 66° 53’ S
67°S) 65° 54’ S
66°S) 64° 55’ S
65°S) 63° 56’ S
64°S) 62° 57’ S
63°S) 61° 58’ S
62°S) 60° 59’ S
61°S) 60° 00’ S
60°S) 59° 01’ S
59°S) 58° 02’ S
58°S) 57° 03’ S
57°S) 56° 04’ S
56°S) 55° 05’ S
55°S) 54° 06’ S
54°S) 53° 07’ S
53°S) 52° 08’ S
52°S) 51° 09’ S
51°S) 50° 10’ S
50°S) 49° 11’ S
49°S) 48° 12’ S
48°S) 47° 13’ S
47°S) 46° 14’ S
46°S) 45° 15’ S
45°S) 44° 16’ S
44°S) 43° 17’ S
43°S) 42° 18’ S
42°S) 41° 19’ S
41°S) 40° 20’ S
40°S) 39° 21’ S
39°S) 38° 22’ S
38°S) 37° 23’ S
37°S) 36° 24’ S
36°S) 35° 25’ S
35°S) 34° 26’ S
34°S) 33° 27’ S
33°S) 32° 28’ S
32°S) 31° 29’ S
31°S) 30° 29’ S
30°S) 29° 30’ S
29°S) 28° 31’ S
28°S) 27° 32’ S
27°S) 26° 33’ S
26°S) 25° 34’ S

25°S) 24° 35' S
24°S) 23° 36' S
23°S) 22° 37' S
22°S) 21° 38' S
21°S) 20° 39' S
20°S) 19° 40' S
19°S) 18° 41' S
18°S) 17° 42' S
17°S) 16° 43' S
16°S) 15° 44' S
15°S) 14° 45' S
14°S) 13° 46' S
13°S) 12° 47' S
12°S) 11° 48' S
11°S) 10° 49' S
10°S) 09° 50' S
9°S) 08° 51' S
8°S) 07° 52' S
7°S) 06° 53' S
6°S) 05° 54' S
5°S) 04° 55' S
4°S) 03° 56' S
3°S) 02° 57' S
2°S) 01° 58' S
1°S) 00° 59' S
0°N/S) 00° 00' N/S
1°N) 00° 59' N
2°N) 01° 58' N
3°N) 02° 57' N
4°N) 03° 56' N
5 N) 04° 55' N
6 N) 05° 54' N
7 N) 06° 53' N
8 N) 07° 52' N
9°N) 08° 51' N
10°N) 09° 50' N
11°N) 10° 49' N
12°N) 11° 48' N
13°N) 12° 47' N
14°N) 13° 46' N
15°N) 14° 45' N
16°N) 15° 44' N
17°N) 16° 43' N
18°N) 17° 42' N
19°N) 18° 41' N
20°N) 19° 40' N
21°N) 20° 39' N
22°N) 21° 38' N
23°N) 22° 37' N
22°N) 23° 36' N
25°N) 24° 35' N
26°N) 25° 34' N
27°N) 26° 33' N
28°N) 27° 32' N
29°N) 28° 31' N
30°N) 29° 30' N
31°N) 30° 29' N
32°N) 31° 29' N
33°N) 32° 28' N
34°N) 33° 27' N
35°N) 34° 26' N
36°N) 35° 25' N
37°N) 36° 24' N
38°N) 37° 23' N
39°N) 38° 22' N
40°N) 39° 21' N
41°N) 40° 20' N
42°N) 41° 19' N
43°N) 42° 18' N
44°N) 43° 17' N
45°N) 44° 16' N
46°N) 45° 15' N
47°N) 46° 14' N
48°N) 47° 13' N
49°N) 48° 12' N
50°N) 49° 11' N
51°N) 50° 10' N
52°N) 51° 09' N
53°N) 52° 08' N
54°N) 53° 07' N
55°N) 54° 06' N
56°N) 55° 05' N
57°N) 56° 04' N
58°N) 57° 03' N
59°N) 58° 02' N
60°N) 59° 01' N
61°N) 60° 00' N
62°N) 60° 59' N
63°N) 61° 58' N
64°N) 62° 57' N
65°N) 63° 56' N
66°N) 64° 55' N
67°N) 65° 54' N
68°N) 66° 53' N
69°N) 67° 52' N
70°N) 68° 51' N
71°N) 69° 50' N
72°N) 70° 49' N
73°N) 71° 48' N
74°N) 72° 47' N
75°N) 73° 46' N
76°N) 74° 45' N
77°N) 75° 44' N
78°N) 76° 43' N
79°N) 77° 42' N
80°N) 78° 41' N
81°N) 79° 40' N
82°N) 80° 39' N
83°N) 81° 38' N
84°N) 82° 37' N
85°N) 83° 36' N
86°N) 84° 35' N
87°N) 85° 34' N
88°N) 86° 33' N
89°N) 87° 32' N
90°N) 88° 31' N
91°N) 89° 30' N

Glossary

Aalst (in French **Alost**): a Belgian city located at 50°56'N-04°03'E, directly along the Druidic Meridian running at 04°04'E.

Absolute zero: the coldest temperature theoretically possible, or -273.15°C. On a scale where absolute zero is -1,000° and the freezing point of water remains 0°, water boils at the temperature of almost exactly 366°. The reason is that on a regular Celsius scale, absolute zero is nearly equivalent to -100,000/366 degrees.

Abu Simbel: an Egyptian Sun temple built by Ramses II, located at 22°20'N-31°38'E, directly along the Druidic Meridian running at 31°37'E.

Accuracy: the exact position of Druidic Meridians is difficult to pinpoint. For the sake of practicality, the Druidic Lines coordinates have been rounded off to the nearest minute in modern Greenwich-based 360-degree geometry, but a string of clues suggest that their exact positions are close to 25 arcseconds more to the east, which is a better approximation of the River Jordan and of Stonehenge.

Alès: a French city with a Celtic oppidum located at 44°07'N-04°04'E, right on the Druidic Meridian running at 04°04'E.

Alesia (Alise-Sainte-Reine): the official location of Alesia, the city where Gallic leader Vercingetorix was defeated by Caesar in 52 BC. The site is however debated by archaeologists themselves, many features of Alise not corresponding to Caesar's description. According to Diodorus Siculus, the classical Greek historian, Alesia had been founded by Heracles and was "the hearth and mother-city of all Celtica."

Alesia (Guillon): the Celtic oppidum on the Montfault and the Montagne de Verre (the 'Glass Mountain') at Guillon, Burgundy is located at 47°32'N-04°05'E, directly along the Druidic Meridian running at 04°04'E. The site was discovered by Bernard Fèvre in 1982. Alesia stood halfway between the cities of Aalst and Alès, each located exactly 170 Gallic leagues from Alesia.

Alesia Druidic Meridian: a Druidic Meridian running exactly 6 Megalithic degrees east of Stonehenge, which might have been the

Celtic Druids' Prime Meridian. On it one can find Bibracte, Aalst, Alesia (Guillon), Alès, Reims and Troyes.

Amber Lines: a theoretical 360-degree world grid (with **Amber Meridians** and **Amber Parallels**) whose presumed Prime Meridian is Stonehenge at a longitude of 01°50'W. The Great Pyramid of Giza stands along another Amber Meridian 33° east of Stonehenge (which might explain why there are 33 degrees in the Scottish Rite of Freemasonry), while most capital or major cities of ex-British colonies also stand along other Amber Meridians.

Argos: a Mycenaean city located at 37°38'N-22°44'E, directly along the Druidic Meridian running at 22°45'E.

Assur: an Assyrian city in Mesopotamia located at 35°27'N-43°16'E, directly along the Druidic Parallel running at 35°25'N. It is thus located very close to the 36th Druidic Parallel north of the equator. Assur and Nineveh frame the Megalithic latitude 36.6°N.

Astronomical Island: a perfectly circular island in the artificial lake in Cergy, France. The *Axe majeur* flies right above it, while the Eastern Tangent and the Western tangent are tangent to it.

Athens: a Mycenaean city located at 37°58'N-23°44'E, right on the Druidic Meridian running at 23°44'E.

Augustodunum (modern name: **Autun**)**:** a Gallic city founded shortly after the Romans invaded Gaul. It is supposed to be the 'sister and emulator of Rome.' Replacing Bibracte as the capital of the Aedui, it is located on the French Pyramids Line.

Avallon: a French town 10 miles west of Alesia (Guillon).

Avebury: a village in Wiltshire situated in the world's greatest stone circle, located at 51°26'N-01°51'W, directly along the Druidic Meridian running at 01°50'W. There is some evidence that it could have been the mythical island of **Avalon**.

Axe historique: see **Historical Axis**

Axe majeur: see **Major Axis**

Axe mineur: see **Minor Axis**

Aylesbury: an English city located at 51°49'N-00°49'W, very close to the Druidic Meridian running at 00°51'W.

Babylon: ('Gateway of the God'): an ancient Mesopotamian city located at 32°33'N-44°25'E, directly along the Druidic Meridian running at 44°24'E.

Baghdad: the capital of Iraq, founded along the river Tigris in the 8th century, located at 33°20'N-44°24'E, right on the Druidic Meridian running at 44°24'E.

Beat: one-way swing of a pendulum, equal to one-half of a period.

Bibracte: a Gallic oppidum on Mont Beuvray in Burgundy, France. Used to be the capital of the Aedui, a Gallic tribe. It is located on the Alesia Druidic Meridian.

Body and mind: it takes about 40 weeks for a full human body to form in its mother's womb (40 weeks of amenorrhea on average), and another 366 weeks for a full human mind to form (the age of reason is traditionally recognised to be seven years old).

Body temperature: according to Russian medicine, the body temperature taken under the armpits precisely equals 36.6°C. On a scale where water boils at 1,000° and the freezing point of water remains 0°, the average human body temperature is thus 366°.

Brodgar, Ring of: a Megalithic stone circle in Orkney originally composed of 60 stones, located at 59°00'N-03°14'W, directly along the Druidic Parallel running at 59°01'N, which is also the 60th Megalithic parallel north of the equator). Traditionally called **Temple of the Sun**.

Cairn: a mound of rough stones, usually erected on a hilltop.

Caral: a pre-Columbian city with pyramids in Peru, considered as the 'Mother City' of South America, located at 10°54'S-77°31'W, close to the Druidic Meridian running at 77°34'W.

Celtic Druids: Druids in Roman times and in the centuries preceding the Roman invasion of Gaul and Britain, as described by a few classical authors.

CERN, French acronym for **European Organisation for Nuclear Research**: the world's largest particle physics laboratory near Geneva, Switzerland, which contains the largest circular particle accelerator on Earth. The World Wide Web was also invented there by Sir Tim Berners-Lee and Robert Caillau in 1989-1990. CERN is located at 46°14'N - 06°03'E, i.e. nearly at the intersection of two Druidic Lines running respectively at 46°14'N and 06°02'E, which also are the Druidic Lines on which Sion-Vaudémont, France and Sion, Switzerland, are located.

Chich'en Itzá: a pre-Columbian city in Central America with an astronomical observatory and a pyramid located at 20°41'N-88°34'W, very close to the Druidic Parallel running at 20°39'N.

Clairvaux: a Cistercian abbey built by Saint Bernard in 1115 AD located at 48°09'N-04°47'E, very close to the Druidic Parallel running at 48°11'N.

Cuicuilco pyramid: a circular pyramid in the southern part of Mexico City located at 19°18'N-99°11'W, very close to the Druidic Meridian running at 99°13'W.

DIs: see **Druidic Initiates**

Divine Triad: The numbers 366, 40 and base 10 are recurrent in the physics of the Earth and the biology of the human body, as if they were the signature of some 'Great Architect.'

Dodona: a sacred Mycenaean city said to have been founded by the Pelasgians or Sea People, and most ancient oracle devoted to Zeus, located at 39°33'N-20°47'E, right on the Druidic Meridian running at 20°47'E.

Druidic Initiates (or DIs): people in modern times including high-ranking Knights Templar and Freemasons, who appear to have inherited from Druidic knowledge.

Druidic Lines (**Druidic Meridians** and **Druidic Parallels**): the presumed ancient network system of longitudinal and latitudinal lines stemming from 366-degree geometry. These lines were rediscovered first by Xavier Guichard, who called them **Salt Lines**, at the beginning of the 20th century; he had noticed that France is strewn with towns and villages with place names seemingly derived from 'Alesia.' Alan Butler, in 1999, was the first to understand the system probably worked with a 366-degree circle.

Durrington Walls: A huge henge enclosure located at 51°12'N-01°47'W, close to the Druidic Parallel running at 51°09'N and the Druidic Meridian running at 01°50'W.

Earth annual rotations: the Earth rotates on its axis almost exactly 366 10/40 times in a year.

Eastern tangent: an axis linking the Tour Belvédère in Cergy to the modern church of Notre-Dame-de-l'Arche-d'Alliance in Paris. It also flies right over the Grande Arche de la Défense, the business hub of Paris. The axis is tangent to the Astronomical Island in Cergy.

Elysian Fields: in Greek mythology, mythical place of the Blessed, where heroes led an eternal life of bliss.

French Pyramids Line, also called **Druidic Slanted Line:** a 36-degree slanted line starting at the X Spot near Dieppe on the northern coast of France, and finishing its course near Nice on the Mediterranean coast. On this line can be found the Parc Monceau Pyramid, the Couhard Pyramid and the Falicon Pyramid.

Ganeriwala: a Harappan city not yet excavated, located at 28°30'N-71°04'E, directly along the Druidic Parallel running at 28°31'N.

Gallic league: a unit of measurement of the Gauls, whose value was 2222.5 m long. Curiously, there are nearly exactly 18,000 Gallic leagues in the polar circumference of the Earth, or 50 leagues to the modern degree (1/360th of the Earth's polar circumference).

GCE: see **Geographical Center of the Earth**

Geographical Center of the Earth (GCE): According to Charles Piazzi Smyth, the Great Pyramid of Giza. It is now thought to be located in Turkey, at 40°52'N-34°34'E, right on a Druidic Meridian.

Giza Megalithic Yard (GMY): The Megalithic yard derived from a Megalithic pendulum at the latitude of Giza. Its length is 82.558 cm. Each side of the Great Pyramid is 280 GMY.

Glastonbury Tor: a natural prominent hill in Somerset located at 51°09'N-02°42'W, right on the Druidic Parallel running at 51°09'N that also runs along Stonehenge. Glastonbury is said to be the 'holiest earthe in England.' Joseph of Arimathea is said to have travelled there with Jesus when he was a boy, to have brought there the Holy Grail and founded the first Christian church of Britain. On the tor are the remains of Saint Michael's church.

GMY: see **Giza Megalithic Yard**

Golden Triangle: a triangle formed by the cities of Rouen, Le Havre and Dieppe in Normandy, France, imagined by novelist Maurice Leblanc in the early 20th century. The three cities are Druidic Meridian locations. Rouen stands halfway on the Stonehenge-Alesia Sacred Line. The hypotenuse of the triangle stands at the Golden section of this line.

Great Pyramid-Newgrange Arc: this line is exactly one-tenth of the Earth's equatorial circumference

Great Pyramid-Astana Peace Pyramid Arc: this line is exactly one-tenth of the Earth's polar circumference, provided you multiply the actual distance by 360/366

Greenwich Meridian: Today's Prime Meridian, running by definition at a longitude of 00°00' W/E, based at the Royal Observatory of Greenwich, London. As of 16 December, 1999, it has been illuminated by a green laser beam.

Harappa: a city of the Indus Valley civilisation located at 30°38'N-72°52'E, close to the Druidic Meridian running at 72°55'E.

Hattusa: the capital city of the Hittites, located at 40°01'N-34°37'E, close to the Druidic Meridian running at 34°34'E.

Historical Axis (or ***Axe historique***): an axis in Paris on which one can find the Grande Arche de la Défense, the Arc de Triomphe, the Champs Elysées, an Egyptian obelisk, the Tuileries Garden, the Louvre Pyramid, the Louvre, and the Paris city hall. It leads right to the Troyes Cathedral.

Jordan, River: The river closely follows a Druidic Meridian running at 35°33'E. It could have been either the Golden Prime Meridian, or the basis on which the Stonehenge Prime Meridian was designed.

LM: see **Luminous Meridian**

Luminous Meridian (or LM): a meridian defined by Guy-Claude Mouny and Guy Gruais running at 01°10'E, which is also an Amber Meridian, perhaps the Prime Amber Meridian, from which many former British Empire capital city locations seem to derive. It is a perfect axis of symmetry to the Greenwich Meridian and the Paris Meridian. Compare the **Midway Druidic Meridian**.

Maeshowe: a large Megalithic-era mound with a stone-built chamber inside, located at 59°00'N-03°11'W, directly along the Druidic Parallel running at 59°01'N, which is also the 60th Druidic Parallel north of the equator.

Major Axis (or ***Axe majeur***): the name of a neighbourhood of Cergy, France, designed by Dani Karavan, with an obvious axis which, if prolonged, leads to the Couhard Pyramid.

Mass of the Earth: there are almost exactly 10^{20} avoirdupois pounds in a one-Megalithic-second segment of the Earth

Megalithic degree: 60 Megalithic arc minutes, or 1/366th of the polar circumference of the Earth.

Megalithic inch (or MI): a supposed unit of measurement of the Megalithic people discovered by Scottish professor Alexander Thom, equivalent to 1/40th of a Megalithic yard.

Megalithic minute: 6 Megalithic arcseconds, or 1/60th of a Megalithic degree.

Megalithic pendulum: a pendulum beating 366 times (or producing 183 periods) when the Earth turns one Megalithic degree (i.e. in one 366th of a day). The length of the string depends on the gravitational pull, which is greater at the poles than at the equator. Its length tends toward ½ a Megalithic yard at the poles.

Megalithic Proto-Druids (or MPDs): Hypothetical sages in Megalithic times from whom Celtic Druids appear to have inherited much of their knowledge.

Megalithic second: 366 Megalithic yards, or 1/6th of a Megalithic arcminute.

Megalithic yard (or MY): a supposed unit of measurement used by MPDs discovered by Scottish professor Alexander Thom, equal to 2.72 feet or 0.8296 m. It is also exactly 1/366th of a Megalithic second of arc.

MDM: see **Midway Druidic Meridian**

MI: see **Megalithic inch**

Midway Druidic Meridian (or MDM): a Druidic Meridian that runs halfway between the Stonehenge Druidic Meridian and the Alesia Druidic Meridian, at 01°07'E. It is thus a perfect axis of symmetry to the Stonehenge Druidic Meridian and the Alesia Druidic Meridian. Compare **Luminous Meridian**.

Mile: the English mile is exactly one 366th of the distance between the center of Stonehenge and the center of the Glass Mountain at Alesia (Guillon), i.e. 1,609 m.

Minoan foot: a unit of measurement of the Minoans used in all their palaces, discovered by Canadian architect J. Walter Graham, equal to 30.36 cm. It is also almost exactly 1/1,000th of a Megalithic arcsecond.

Minor Axis or ***Axe mineur*:** a secondary axis in the *Axe majeur* neighbourhood, using the Water Pyramid as a direction. The Minor Axis, if prolonged, perfectly intersects the Montparnasse Tower, and hits Alesia (Guillon) at a distance of 226.2 km (366/Phi km).

MPDs: see **Megalithic Proto-Druids**

MY: see **Megalithic yard**

Mycenae: a Mycenaean city located at 37°44'N-22°46'E, directly along the Druidic Meridian running at 22°45'E.

Nineveh: an Assyrian city in Mesopotamia located at 36°22'N-43°07'E, very close to the Druidic Parallel running at 36°24'N. It is thus located directly along the 37th Druidic Parallel north of the equator. Assur and Nineveh frame the Megalithic latitude 36.6°N.

Paris Meridian (also known since 2000 as the **Green Meridian**): a former Prime Meridian used in France, running at a longitude of 02°20'E.

Pentagram: a regular five-pointed star; each angle of the points is exactly 36 degrees, or 36.6 Megalithic degrees; the four fundamental lengths of the Pentagram are in golden ratio to one another.

Phi: the golden section or golden ratio, where the ratio a/b = b/(a+b). Also dubbed the Divine Proportion. An irrational number whose value is 1.618...

Reims: a French city in Champagne located at 49°15'N-04°02'E, very close to the Druidic Meridian running at 04°04'E. Clovis, the first French king, was baptised there. Later, the coronation ceremony of most French kings occurred there. Reims is located almost halfway between the cities of Aalst and Alesia (Guillon).

Saint-Germain-en-Laye (Château of): a Renaissance château reconstructed on an older medieval castle by French King Francis I. It is located at 48°53'N-02°06'E, right on the Druidic Meridian running at 02°06'E.

Salt Lines: see **Druidic Lines**

San Lorenzo Tenochtitlán: the capital city of the Olmecs in Mexico, located at 17°45'N-94°48'W, close to the Druidic Parallel running at 17°42'N.

Santa Cecilia Acatitlan: an Aztec pyramid in the northern part of Mexico City located at 19°33'N-99°10'W, close to the Druidic Meridian running at 99°13'W.

Silbury Hill: a British Megalithic pyramid-like mound located at 51°25'N-01°51'W, directly along the Druidic Meridian running at 01°50'W.

Sion: a city in Switzerland, the capital of Valais, located at 46°14'N-07°22'E, right on the Druidic Parallel running at 46°14'N.

Sion-Vaudémont: a hill in eastern France dubbed the "Inspired Hill." Vaudémont is located at 48°25'N-06°03'E, directly along the Druidic Meridian running at 06°02'E. Sion-Vaudémont is the last stopping place of a very ancient pilgrimage.

Skara Brae: A well-preserved stone-built Megalithic settlement in Orkney, Scotland, located at 59°03'N-03°20'W, very close to the Druidic Parallel running at 59°01'N, which is also the 60th Druidic Parallel north of the equator.

Standing Stones of Stenness: a Megalithic stone circle in Orkney originally composed of 12 stones, located at 59°00'N-03°12'W, directly along the Druidic Parallel running at 59°01'N, which is also the 60th Druidic Parallel north of the equator. Traditionally called **Temple of the Moon.**

Stonehenge: a British Megalithic temple in Wiltshire located at 51°11'N-01°50'W, right on the Druidic Meridian running at 01°50'W, and very close to the Druidic Parallel running at 51°09'N. Originally, the henge had a circumference of 366 Megalithic yards.

Stonehenge-Alesia Sacred Line: a 366-mile long line that must have been sacred to Druids and their inheritors. The city of Rotomagus (modern Rouen) stands halfway between these two sites, right along the course of the line.

Stonehenge Druidic Meridian: a Druidic Meridian running at 01°50'W, which might have been the MPDs' Prime Meridian. It runs exactly 38 Megalithic degrees west of the River Jordan, which might have been the original Golden Prime Meridian, unless the Stonehenge Druidic Meridian itself served this function. On it one can find, *inter alia*, Stonehenge, Avebury and Silbury Hill.

Tenayuca pyramid: an Aztec pyramid in the northern part of Mexico City located at 19°32'N-99°10'W, close to the Druidic Meridian running at 99°13'W.

Teotihuacán ('Place Where Gods Were Born'): a pre-Columbian city in modern Mexico located at 19°42'N-98°51'W, very close to the Druidic Parallel running at 19°40'N (the 20th Megalithic Parallel north of the equator). The two great pyramids are traditionally called **Temple of the Sun** and **Temple of the Moon**. There were exactly 366 sculptures in the **Temple of Quetzalcoatl**.

Tiwanaku: a pre-Columbian city in South America located at 16°33'S-68°40'W, close to the Druidic Meridian running at 68°43'W.

Tintagel: a ruined Cornish stronghold located at 50°40'N-04°46'W, directly along the Druidic Meridian running at 04°47'W. According to legend, Tintagel is King Arthur's place of conception.

Tiryns: a Mycenaean city located at 37°36'N-22°48'E, close to the Druidic Meridian running at 22°45'E. Heracles is said to have ruled over the city.

Troyes: a French city, former capital of Champagne, located in 48°18'N-04°05'E, built directly along the Druidic Meridian running at 04°04'E. The Council of Troyes of 1129 officially recognised the Order of the Knights Templar. The English troy pound, and most probably the avoirdupois pound, originated in Troyes during the Templar period. Troyes is located at the Golden section of the line Aalst-Alès.

Upper Axis: an axis linking the Tour Belvédère in Cergy, France, to Stonehenge. Its length is the golden section of 366 miles.

Valley of the Kings (West Thebes): the place in ancient Egypt where pharaohs were buried, located at 25°44'N-32°36'E, right on the Druidic Meridian running at 32°36'E.

Vaux-le-Vicomte-Marseillan Axis: A 366-mile long axis starting in the village of St-Germain-Laxis, immediately to the north of the Château de Vaux-le-Vicomte, continuing right above the château, following the axis of its gardens, and ending up in Marseillan-Plage, on the Mediterranean coast.

Versailles (Palace of): a 17th-century palace built for French King Louis XIV located at 48°48'N-02°07'E, right on the Druidic Meridian running at 02°07'E.

Water (maximum density of): the temperature at which water is most dense is almost exactly 4.0°C. By defining a scale where water boils at the temperature of 1,000° and the freezing point of water is 0°, this temperature becomes 40°.

Water Pyramid: a small pyramid emerging in the Cergy lake. It gives the direction of the Axe mineur.

Western Tangent: an axis linking the Tour Belvédère in Cergy to the Rock of Solutré in Burgundy. Its length is 366 km. The axis is tangent to the Astronomical Island in Cergy.

West Kennet Long Barrow: one of Britain's largest Megalithic chambered tombs. It is located at 51°25'N-01°51'W, directly along the Druidic Meridian running at 01°50'W.

Woodhenge: a Megalithic henge and timber circle located at 51°11'N-01°47'W, close to the Druidic Meridian running at 01°50'W.

Xinzheng: Huangdi, the 'Yellow Emperor' and the initiator of the Chinese civilisation is traditionally thought to have lived c. 2600 BC near Xinzheng, which is located at 34°24'N-113°44'E, very close to the Druidic Parallel running at 34°26'N.

X Spot: the intersection of the Midway Druidic Meridian running at 01°07'E and the northern coastline of Gaul/France. This location is also the northern origin of the French Pyramids Line.

Yard: An English unit of measurement equal to 36 inches.

Index

Printed in Dunstable, United Kingdom